WITHDRAWN

ALSO BY ALAN WOLFE

Religion and Democracy in the United States: Danger or Opportunity?
(with Ira Katznelson)

The Future of Liberalism

Does American Democracy Still Work?

Is There a Culture War? A Dialogue on Values and American Public Life
(with James Davison Hunter)

Return to Greatness:
How America Lost Its Sense of Purpose and What It
Needs to Do to Recover It

The Transformation of American Religion: How We Actually Live Our Faith

An Intellectual in Public

School Choice: The Moral Debate (editor)

Moral Freedom: The Search for Virtue in a World of Choice

One Nation, After All: What Middle-Class Americans Really Think About God,
Country, Family, Racism, Welfare, Immigration, Homosexuality, Work,
the Right, the Left, and Each Other

Marginalized in the Middle

The Human Difference: Animals, Computers, and the Necessity of Social Science

America at Century's End (editor)

Whose Keeper? Social Science and Moral Obligation

America's Impasse: The Rise and Fall of the Politics of Growth

The Rise and Fall of the "Soviet Threat":
Domestic Sources of the Cold War Consensus

The Limits of Legitimacy: Political Contradictions of Contemporary Capitalism

The Politics and Society Reader (with Ira Katznelson et al.)

The Seamy Side of Democracy: Repression in America

Political Analysis: An Unorthodox Approach (with Charles A. McCoy)

An End to Political Science: The Caucus Papers (coeditor with Marvin Surkin)

Political Evil

Political Evil

WHAT IT IS AND HOW
TO COMBAT IT

Alan Wolfe

ALFRED A. KNOPF · NEW YORK
2011

THIS IS A BORZOI BOOK
PUBLISHED BY ALFRED A. KNOPF

Library of Congress Cataloging-in-Publication Data
Wolfe, Alan, [date]
Political evil : what it is and how to combat it / Alan Wolfe.—1st ed.
p.   cm.
Includes bibliographical references (p.   ) and index.
ISBN 978-0-307-27185-3 (alk. paper)
1. Good and evil—Political aspects.   2. Political science—Philosophy.
3. Terrorism.   4. Genocide.   5. Political violence.   I. Title.
JA79.W65 2011
320.01—dc22   2011003409

Jacket illustration by Shasti O'Leary Soudant
Jacket design by Barbara de Wilde

Manufactured in the United States of America
First Edition

Must we not warn victorious nations that they are wrong in regarding their victory as a proof of their virtue, lest they engulf the world in a new chain of evil by their vindictiveness, which is nothing else than the fury of their self-righteousness?

—Reinhold Niebuhr (1948)

There seems to be a curious American tendency to search, at all times, for a single external center of evil to which all our troubles can be attributed, rather than to recognize that there might be multiple sources of resistance to our purposes and undertakings, and that these sources might be relatively independent of each other.

—George F. Kennan (1985)

A maxim for the twenty-first century might well be to start not by fighting evil in the name of good, but by attacking the certainties of people who claim always to know where good and evil are to be found.

—Tzvetan Todorov (2000)

CONTENTS

Political Evil

The Fundamental Question of the Twenty-first Century

PUTTING POLITICS FIRST

WHEN THE PHILOSOPHER Hannah Arendt wrote in 1945 that "the problem of evil will be the fundamental question of postwar intellectual life in Europe," she could easily have broadened her geographic scope. There is no more important problem facing the entire world today than the existence of evil, and there is no subject more characterized by muddled thinking and self-defeating responses. Evil threatens us in ways that make hurricanes, global warming, flu pandemics, and financial panics, as awful as they are, seem small by comparison. Present all around us, evil demands our best efforts to understand it if it is to be contained. In this book I offer a way of thinking designed to do that.

The problem of evil is one of our oldest intellectual conundrums. Volumes have been written attempting to define evil, to catalog its horrors, to account for its persistence, to explain its appeal, to confront its consequences. The subject has attracted philosophers, poets, artists, theologians, psychologists, novelists, composers, and physicians. Every major language has a term for evil, and every major religion—pantheistic, dualistic, or monotheistic—shows a preoccupation with it. Human beings may want to be good, but they have long recognized that they have to familiarize themselves with the bad. Because it touches so closely the mystery of human existence, evil is a subject best approached with considerable trepidation. Fortunately, this has not stopped some of the finest thinkers the world has ever known from addressing it.

The moment we begin to ask questions about the nature of evil, however, we begin to understand how difficult it will be to answer them. In the West alone, two of the greatest theologians in the Christian tradition—Saint Augustine and Thomas Aquinas—spent countless pages exploring whether evil exists and what forms it takes, work that in many ways was shaped by earlier, pre-Christian philosophers such as Plato and Aristotle. Every student asked to read *Macbeth* or *Othello* is introduced to the complexity of evil, as are those who ponder *Paradise Lost* or Goethe's *Faust*. A fascination with the problem of evil, argues the philosopher Susan Neiman, dominated the writings of such Enlightenment thinkers as Rousseau, Kant, and Voltaire and found particularly poignant expression in the post-Enlightenment philosophy of Friedrich Nietzsche. Similar concerns shaped America's writers and leaders, appearing in the sermons of Jonathan Edwards, the debates over the Constitution, the work of Herman Melville, and the speeches of Abraham Lincoln. Dostoyevsky and Conrad were only two of the great European novelists who wrote about evil in strikingly contemporary ways. As late as the 1950s, explorations of evil lay at the heart of such widely regarded scholars as Arendt, the theologian Reinhold Niebuhr, and those Jewish philosophers such as Emil Fackenheim moved by the Holocaust to reflect on just what future God had in mind for his chosen people. We know evil is there, yet we are not sure what makes people evil or whether their evil can ever be overcome.

One way to start the discussion is to narrow the focus. Evil is all too often analyzed at too high a level of abstraction. If theologians tell us that evil is what human beings do in the absence of God, they face the difficult tasks of defining God's essence, interpreting his words, and deciding which of many available deities is the authoritative one. Philosophers who conceptualize evil as a disturbance in the natural order of the universe must wrestle with the nature of the universe, not to mention the meaning of order. Contemporary neuroscientists who view evil as a product of faulty hard-wiring in our brains do not always know what is taking place in our minds. There are times and places when discussions of the theology or the metaphysics of evil are appropriate. But there are also times when they can get in the way of knowing what to do when we are confronted with terrorists who fly planes into buildings or enforcers of ethnic solidarity who rape and kill those whose land they covet.

The most important thing we need to do to come to terms with the horrors confronting us is to stop talking about evil in general and focus instead on political evil in particular. *Political evil refers to the willful, malevolent, and gratuitous death, destruction, and suffering inflicted upon innocent people by the leaders of movements and states in their strategic efforts to achieve realizable objectives.* Later on I will revisit this definition with more care; distinguish between political, everyday, and radical evil; examine the specific forms that political evil can take; and discuss the best ways to respond to each of them. But for now I want to insist that while political evil causes massive amounts of harm and directly assaults our fundamental moral sense, we need not feel hopeless in the face of it. We are unlikely ever to wipe evil per se off the face of the earth. But if we think more clearly and act more strategically, we can significantly reduce the amount of *political* evil threatening us.

Bringing the problem of evil down from the heavens into the world of politics and policy offers advantages that can help make the atrocities we face in the world today more intelligible. One is that it changes the kinds of questions we ask. Politics is not philosophy, and neither is it theology or neuroscience. Those who plan and carry out political evil no doubt have malevolence in their hearts or malfunctions in their brains. But it is not their insides that ought to concern us; it is their acts. Whether they are twisted by hatred and envy, exemplars of a depraved human nature, stunted in their development because they were abused as children, psychotic or sociopathic, unwilling to allow a savior into their lives, suffering from delusions of grandeur, obsessive-compulsive in their personality disorders, the product of a poor genetic heritage, or seriously dependent on their meds to get through the day is a matter of scant interest to us. Let them talk to their therapists, make pacts with Mephistopheles, send out videotapes explaining their acts, or seek redemption for the horrors they unleash; we have little at stake in their struggles with their demons. We can recognize their depravity, but it is their cunning that ought to concern us. We need not reform them, stigmatize them, or show them the path to salvation. We need to stop them, and in order to do that we have to focus on the political causes that attract them and their followers. Acts are easier to change than people.

A focus on political evil, in addition, reminds us of how evil and politics make for an especially toxic mix. Organized into a movement or state and motivated by a cause that gives them passion and purpose, practitioners of political evil are capable of carrying out violence on levels that far surpass those realizable by any lone individual. Evil individuals without a state or movement behind them can shed only so much blood. Those who gain command over the state's sources of revenue and monopoly of violence are capable of making that blood flow in amounts too copious to measure. One reason political evil is so omnipresent is that states are so common. Even dictators ruling over poor or not very strategically important states—Pol Pot's Cambodia, Omar al-Bashir's Sudan—can cause unimaginable suffering. Because of the growth of modern states, political evil has in a sense been democratized—and in the most frightening of ways. As the potency of means of destruction has increased, so has the number of leaders with access to them.

Paradoxically, however, the same control over a movement or a state that maximizes the power at the disposal of these leaders also tempers their extremism. For better or worse, those who commit acts of political evil have been tested; they have risen through the ranks of an organization to assume a position of control within it. Almost never elected to office, and inclined to suspend elections even when they have been, they can be as ruthless toward their followers as they are toward their enemies. Yet while they are radical in their choice of means, politically evil leaders are often conservative in how they apply them. Having spent years building a movement or assuming a position of power, they are reluctant to become too reckless for fear of destroying what they have patiently constructed. Evil leaders kill others, and they even, in the form of suicide terrorism, encourage some of their followers to kill themselves. But as *political* leaders, they are anything but suicidal. They serve a cause, and the furtherance of that cause, as well as the organization embodying it, trump everything else. Organizational weapons are therefore inevitably used cautiously. Al-Qaeda spent five years planning its bombings against U.S. embassies in Africa, two developing its attack on the USS *Cole,* and as many as seven preparing for September 11. While it is quite possible that the successful effort by the Obama administration to kill Osama bin Laden in 2011 has crippled al-Qaeda's capacity, any further attacks the group or its offshoots may be planning, based on its earlier record, will not be precipitately chosen. One does not become engaged in politics unless one's cause has a future. Once a group's vision becomes future oriented, its conduct in the present becomes constrained. If the politics in political evil makes us shudder, it also gives us hope.

When confronted with political evil, we are better off responding to the "political" rather than to the "evil." Politics does not ask that we eradicate evil from the dark hearts of men and women. It does demand that when faced with tactics that threaten our way of life in the pursuit of political goals, we at least make an effort to understand why those goals were chosen in the first place. Fighting evil with evil contaminates, but fighting politics with politics does not. We confuse the two at great risk to ourselves. There will be situations when we will be tempted to conclude that the methods used against us are so evil that there is nothing to discuss with those who employ them. But precisely because those methods are so evil, we might also decide that we ought to do everything in our power to bring them to an end, even if doing so means engaging politically with people we rightly despise. Political evil gives us choices. We are foolish, and not nearly as moral as we may congratulate ourselves for being, if we refuse to make them.

Because my focus is on political evil and not evil in general, this book, despite its subject matter, will not be a pessimistic one. It is true that we live in an era when the means of political evil are available to so many. But it does not follow that we must accustom ourselves to the status of potential victims who might at any moment be subject to the worst horrors in history. The fact that some employ terror does not mean that everyone should be terrorized. For every practitioner of genocide, there exist activists, lawyers, judges, and humanitarians with real-world experience in bringing genocide to an end. Even the most hate-spewing heads of state with access to weapons of mass destruction do not necessarily want to risk destroying their own people by actually using them. We are only aware of the ubiquity of political evil because we have learned that there are other and better ways for states to manage their affairs than by oppressing their own people or seeking to swallow up their neighbors. We should never doubt the ugliness of political evil. But nor should we doubt our intelligence, both the kind that enables us to think clearly about what we face as well as the kind that helps governments adopt the best national security strategies for responding to the attacks against them.

Political evil, in short, while a problem of utmost seriousness, is not a bottomless quandary. When a new example of political evil breaks out in the world, the last thing we should do is throw up our hands in theological, philosophical, or literary despair. Helplessness only furthers hate. The problem of political evil should concentrate our minds rather than cloud our judgment. Politics always takes place in this world, and it is in this world that we are obligated to remain if we are to combat political evil with any success. It is certainly important to turn to the great classic texts of the Western tradition to understand human malevolence at its worst. But we also need to think politically about the choices confronting us if we are to bring into being a world with just a little less evil than the one we see around us. Doing so will not produce a perfect world, but it would be a notable achievement nonetheless.

A THOROUGHLY HUMAN PRODUCT

THE UBIQUITY OF political evil cannot be doubted. We all know by now how gargantuan were the mortality levels associated with the most evil regimes of the twentieth century. As the very last survivors of the Nazi *lagers* and Stalinist gulags pass away, and as the definitive histories of that era and those regimes are written, the enormity of what took place still shocks. Of course we have the testimonies of such writers as Elie Wiesel, Aleksandr Solzhenitsyn, and Primo Levi, all of whom experienced the full brunt of those horrors and managed to tell their tales. But this only means that when political evil strikes again today—whether in Africa, the Middle East, Asia, or once again in Europe—the killing may not be as bad but the stain on our conscience is worse. It is one thing for carmakers to copy last year's models. It is another for malevolent leaders to replicate yesterday's horrors.

Death is not the only way in which political evil manifests itself. Political evil exists when terrorists spread fear among those who survive their attacks; troops motivated by ethnic hatred order the forced removal of people from their homes or even their country; torture is used to coerce information or induce confession; leaders of autocratic regimes hire thugs to intimidate potential opponents; women are raped and children taken from their parents; camps are built to confine the innocent; and organized crime rings silence those who oppose or investigate them. Not a day goes by without the mass media spreading stories of cruelties that would be unimaginable were they not so widespread.

The immediate victims of political evil are those singled out for direct attack: women stoned to death for their presumed adultery; villagers living in the path of wild-eyed militia organized to kill them because they belong to the wrong tribe; young men systematically executed and buried in mass graves before they reach the age when they can defend their homeland from attack; demonstrators protesting in the streets killed for merely asserting their rights; families out for a visit to the seashore who come under terrorist lines of fire; innocent bystanders caught up in a zealous search for potential suspects who are then forced to undergo torture or extradition. Portraits of the political evil around us today have so far failed to achieve the status of the literary classics that emerged from the Holocaust and the gulag. But this time we have cell phones and Facebook, Twitter, and other forms of social media to bring the plight of those directly under the gun to the attention of the world. The pleas of political evil's victims reach us all. Although we cannot imagine the pain they suffer, we cannot fail to be cognizant that they are suffering pain.

At the same time, political evil targets everyone, not just those chosen for immediate harm. I mean this in the most literal sense possible: nuclear weapons are currently possessed by states either unable to contain sectarian furies within or engaged in holy wars without. As chilling as the confrontations of the cold war were, the leaders of both the United States and the Soviet Union managed to avoid dropping their nuclear arsenals on each other. The era of mutually assured destruction, in retrospect, appears surprisingly stable. Regimes with the power to kill in the millions had leaders who, for whatever reason, opted not to use that power.

No such confidence is warranted today. Pakistan, one of the most unstable political systems in the world, not only possesses nuclear weapons but has allowed its Directorate for Inter-Services Intelligence to maintain links with the Taliban, all to protect itself against its rival India, a state with nuclear weapons of its own. The potential link between political evil and nuclear weapons, moreover, is hardly confined to South Asia. In the summer of 2009, Iran, a country well on its way to acquiring nuclear capacity, reelected a Holocaust-denying president committed to the destruction of Israel and did so in a blatantly illegal manner requiring the suppression of dissenting voices in its own streets and universities. Moving to another part of the globe, the impenetrable North Korean regime, totally indifferent to the threat of sanctions from the United Nations, engages in nuclear testing as if to remind the world that it just might, whenever it chooses to do so, seek the dominance over the Korea Peninsula it failed to win half a century ago by more conventional means. It took years for the death camps of the twentieth century to be constructed in ways that enabled them to carry out their mission. Evil regimes in possession of nuclear weapons could achieve vast levels of death and destruction in an instant.

Political evil harms us figuratively as well. When ice caps melt at the poles or when drought causes massive starvation in the world's poorest regions, we feel that we should have taken steps to avoid the resulting catastrophes, but the causal links are complicated and still being explored, and the promised results far off. To be sure, there are things we can do, such as buying hybrid cars, turning down thermostats, and volunteering to do good deeds abroad, and these will no doubt help modify the severity of the harms. But we also recognize that while we have some control over nature, nature has a way of making up its own mind. When it does, our responsibility ends. This is not to deny the scope of realities such as climate change, drought, AIDS, malnutrition, and inadequate sanitation, all of which are among the most serious problems the world needs to solve and require massive human intervention to rectify. They are, however, best addressed by calling upon the powers of invention and technology rather than by raising the fundamental questions that have puzzled theologians and moral philosophers over the centuries.

The question of political evil is entirely different. A thoroughly human product, political evil shatters every practice and institution we put in place to protect all of us against the ugliest things of which some of us are capable. When political evil appears in the world, we know, even if we do not always acknowledge the fact, that something has gone fundamentally awry in the human situation. We might have persuaded ourselves that peace is possible in our time, but when ethnic groups seek to wipe each other out, the conviction that people can find ways of peaceably resolving their differences is put to the severest test. Gratified by the ability of adherents of different religions in the West to find ways to live together, we are forced to rethink everything we once thought we knew about God and his ways when we see terror carried out in his name. We want life to be as normal as possible, but when other states deny our own state's right to exist, and then take actions to destroy it, we have little choice but to accept the inevitability of abnormality. A hurricane devastates a city, and people rush to help. Terrorists carry out their dirty work, and we are, at least at first, paralyzed. It is much easier to understand nature than to forgive our fellow human beings.

Political evil attacks the body while killing the soul. Brutality destroys faith in humanity just as bloodlust undermines belief in reason. The mere existence of political evil means that we are not living up to the promise we hold out for ourselves. Political evil wreaks its havoc on its immediate victims by taking their lives or destroying their dignity. But it targets its more remote victims—that is, the rest of us—by threatening our sense that there exist agreed-upon moral principles that can be taken for granted across national and cultural boundaries. Political evil is never on automatic pilot. No matter what form it takes, the question of who is responsible for it can never be left unaddressed. The existence of political evil forces us to think about who we are and what our legacy to future generations will be.

As crucial as it is to deal more effectively with political evil, however, we all too often do it in ways that are confused if not contradictory. Overwhelmed by the horrors once associated with totalitarianism, we apply too many inappropriate comparisons with the Nazi and Stalinist period to the events of our own day. We either exaggerate the human capacity for evil by finding it lurking in everyone or make it more difficult to control evil by ascribing to evildoers an almost supernatural ability to get their way in the world. We try to solve political problems by relying on humanitarian instincts—and vice versa. We find ourselves calling for the impossible goal of ending evil instead of the achievable one of containing it. We seek solace or explanation by turning to a God who, if he does exist and is all-powerful, must have willed the evil to occur in the first place. We blame a malevolent human nature when there are just as many people trying to stop evil from taking place as there are allowing it to continue. We convince ourselves that evil is contagious—indeed, in its own way attractive—and that once it manifests itself in one place, it will inevitably spread elsewhere; yet far from being universal, evil nearly always shows its face in local situations. Most important of all, we are never quite sure whether we have truly won a campaign against political evil or have been defeated in our efforts, preparing the way for even more evil in the future.

Finding better ways of responding to political evil, in short, is more than a matter of improving airport security procedures or recruiting better informants; it also requires training in political philosophy and experience with political wisdom. It is this lack of serious reflection about the nature of political evil that explains why Western governments, far from bringing it under control, all too often enable it to spread. This is certainly the case when, determined to take the hardest possible line against evildoers, they engage in evil acts themselves, whether by relying on torture, suspending basic legal procedures, or turning a blind eye as others torture for them. But they are just as clumsy when they declare wars against terrorism as a way of containing terrorists or refuse to negotiate with leaders who in reality thrive the more they are isolated. Blinded by the rage that evil induces, leaders all too often respond with either inaction or overreaction. Some countries manage to develop better political approaches to political evil than others. But none of them have found the right combination of moral indignation and practical wisdom. And the two countries most threatened by political evil in the modern world—the United States and Israel—have been especially woeful at understanding its political causes and have therefore been unable to successfully combat it. Political evildoers are not so diabolical that they can anticipate just how self-defeating the responses will be to their acts. They have learned that with few exceptions the consternation and hysteria they unleash expand their opportunities to engage in political evil once again.

If we do not find a way to think more clearly about political evil, and if we continue to respond to it so ineffectively, the world we will inhabit will look very different from the one to which we are accustomed. It is not just that we will face new campaigns of extermination and religiously inspired violence; those things have long been part of the human condition. Political evil is no great problem when people expect nothing less. When almost no one is free, slavery seems less criminal. When it is simply assumed as a matter of course that leaders will oppress their own people, the existence of tyranny does not shatter human confidence. When all states are aggressor states, none of them are worse than others. It is only when we have gotten a glimpse of what it means to hope for a better world that political evil in this world shocks us.

A recognition of political evil serves as a reminder that we need not be ruled by it. Most people try to honor the moral codes of their religion, live in peace with their neighbors, learn to respect and tolerate those with whom they disagree, and refrain from urging their leaders to impose vengeance on their enemies. This makes the fact that others do not, that they instead break free of all moral restraint and participate actively in the cruelest actions known to man, all the more startling and all the more unacceptable. At stake in the question of political evil is not just whether we can bring an end to the death and destruction it inflicts, however important it is to try. Also hanging in the balance is the question of whether we are purposeful beings capable of creating a more just and humane world or are instead subhuman creatures engaged in an endless struggle for survival in which all the advantages go to the most ruthless. If that does not make political evil the fundamental question of the twenty-first century, nothing does.

WARMHEARTED BUT CLEAR-EYED

TWO SOMEWHAT CONTRARIAN approaches follow from focusing on political evil in particular rather than evil in general—and they are best acknowledged up front. The first calls attention to the dangers of misplaced empathy. Evil, the basest of all human motivations, strikes powerful chords deep inside those moved by a sense of compassion. Learning of genocide in distant lands or witnessing what innocent victims of terror have suffered, people with strong humanitarian instincts will identify with those victims and, in the case of those inclined to be politically active, seek to mobilize campaigns on their behalf. When people are dying, activists such as these find it unseemly to parse definitions, to quibble over categories, or to argue over appropriate historical analogies. Intellectuals splitting hairs seem wildly inappropriate when killers are cracking heads. We have seen evil triumph before, their sense of empathy tells them, and we must be vigilant never to allow its victory again. Our hearts must be touched before our brains kick into thought.

Such instinctive empathy, alas, despite its humanitarian wellspring, is not enough when dealing with actual cases of political evil. Political evil is distinctive; it comes in many different forms. Combating political evil demands what responding compassionately to evil in general discourages: making comparisons, thinking critically, questioning assumptions. We need to be careful before we can be effective, taking each case of political evil on its own terms to avoid lumping them all together as if the lessons learned from one automatically apply to the others. Because both Rwanda and Darfur are in Africa and have witnessed horrendous violence, we are inclined to see what happened in the latter as a replay of what took place in the former; yet the situation in Rwanda proved to be an example of genocide, while the conflict in Darfur grew out of an effort to put down an insurgency, and the difference matters. It may not appear particularly sensitive to those Israelis victimized by the terror unleashed by Hamas and Hezbollah to point out that each has its own reason for existence, or even to raise the question of whether the actions of Israel's leaders in the past and present have contributed to the terror facing its citizens, but these are questions that must be asked if Israel is ever to live without terror. The same risk of seeming indifferent is run if we conclude that the campaigns launched by Serbs against the other ethnic groups with whom they shared the Yugoslav federation were matched in ugly intent by the victims of Serbian aggression with whom we are more likely to identify, but in truth no side in the former Yugoslavia was innocent of the charge of political evil. Who cares if genocide and ethnic cleansing are not the same thing? Why does it matter that the moral and strategic issues raised by suicide terrorism are very different from those presented by terrorism from which the perpetrators walk away unscathed? If someone is shooting at you, is it really important whether he is an alienated high school student oblivious to the larger world around him or a religious believer motivated by a commandment from God? Asking questions in the wake of satanic acts seems, even to the nonreligious, somehow blasphemous.

Still, asking questions and making distinctions are things we must do if we are to understand and combat political evil. Even if it may appear—and I certainly hope it does not—pedantic and unfeeling to clarify concepts and make comparisons in the aftermath of horrors, we have to know what we are up against at any time but especially when we are dealing with actions that shock the moral conscience. We do not serve compassion by offering empathy while withdrawing constructive analysis with an eye to the future. The best way to help political evil's victims is to grasp why they are being victimized. We should not lose our heads just because people lose their lives.

Second, when we talk about evil in general, we frequently make the mistake of treating it as larger than life, as if those who kill en masse, precisely because they commit the worst of human acts, must be motivated by a cause equal to the enormity of their deeds. The twentieth century was an ideological one, and it is therefore no surprise that in its aftermath there exists a widespread inclination, depending upon the political views of the observer, to invoke such large-scale movements as fascism, communism, colonialism, radical Islam, Zionism, or global terror as explanations for the persistence of political evil. Treating evil as part of some larger worldview seemingly prepares us for the long, hard struggle against it. Those who stoop so low as to rain terror upon the innocent or to kill out of racial, religious, or ethnic hatred, it is widely believed, must be so blinded by a fanatic commitment to a cause that attributing their acts to specific conditions borders on justifying what they do. The end of the cold war, this way of thinking holds, has not brought about the end of grandiose dreams. If anything, we witness frequent clashes of civilizations in which violence deployed on behalf of one way of life leads to fatal collisions with others.

This tendency to find larger reasons for political evil is also a temptation best avoided. Evil in general may be free-floating, but political evil occurs on the ground—often on the most specific and contested pieces of ground—and to understand and combat it requires paying attention to local causes and concerns. The tyrant Saddam Hussein may have had fascist leanings, but he was an Iraqi Ba'athist, not a Nazi. Communism was one of the great failed gods of our time, but it did not cause ethnic cleansing in the former Yugoslavia; the determination of the leaders of noncommunist independent nations to redraw their boundaries to include more people like themselves did. Tribal conflicts escalating throughout Africa have been exacerbated by the artificial divisions Westerners imposed on their former colonies, but those conflicts also have indigenous roots. Hezbollah and Hamas refuse to renounce terror, but their militancy has little to do with something called radical Islam and everything to do with the immediate politics of the Middle East, just as Israel's determination to strengthen its security is motivated by considerations of state-building and is not part of some Zionist effort to control the world. The contemporary era contains more than its share of clashes, but not all of them are civilizational. We must meet political evil where it matters most, and that is where it makes its home. Ideologies do not kill people; local political leaders do.

None of this should lead to the conclusion that the struggle against political evil ought to be stripped of its moral passion. I, for one, find myself in awe of those humanitarians who have made the protection and advancement of fundamental human rights the major cause of their lives. The dedication shown by relief workers who give up the conveniences of Western life to bury the dead and save the wounded is well beyond my far more modest capacities. I can easily identify with all those who were appalled by the crimes Saddam Hussein had committed against his own people. Once the reality of political evil grips you, it does not let go. You hear about what innocent people experience in any of these hot spots, and you want to do everything in your power to punish those responsible so that other malevolent leaders will be stopped from carrying out similar atrocities.

Still, I believe that something has gone wrong in the way we understand and combat the political evils of our time. I am among those Americans who came to political maturity at the same time that my country decided to wage a war in Vietnam for no good reason and in a way that took countless lives. Like so many others of my generation, I developed such a strong reaction against the misuse of U.S. troops abroad that I could not imagine any circumstance that would justify American intervention into the affairs of other people. This, I later came to learn, was a serious mistake: it did not follow that because American forces were used badly in Vietnam, they should never be used at all. Ultimately appalled at the naïve leftism I saw around me, I resigned from the editorial board of *The Nation,* a magazine that in my view was publishing all too many simplistic attacks on America's role in the world, and began to write for its rival publication, *The New Republic,* known for its harder-line foreign policy positions and willingness to defend the use of American power to promote freedom and democracy. A critic of what we in the New Left had once called "cold war liberalism," I had become something of a post–cold war liberal myself. It especially pleased me that the magazine with which I was identified published intellectuals who wrote about our responsibility never again to allow the evils associated with totalitarianism to go uncontested. They struck me as among the most morally serious thinkers of our time.

I wrote this book because I have begun to have second thoughts—call them third thoughts if you are persuaded that I cannot make up my mind—about the wisdom of rushing to judgment about political evil and assuming that reliance on military power is the best way to combat it. It is not as if I find once again attractive the isolationism born of the fear of American power that took on such prominence in the years after Vietnam. Nor can I ever imagine that I will become an unfeeling realist who believes morality has no role to play in foreign policy decisions. The mass horrors revealed by genocide, ethnic cleansing, and terrorism prompted me to turn my attention away from the humdrum of domestic elections and policy to questions of moral philosophy and political theology. I still prefer the ideas of those intellectuals who view themselves as heirs to the liberal anticommunism of the earlier days of the cold war to those who blame America first for whatever global problem comes to their attention.

Yet it has become clear to me in recent years that there is often a thin line between moral seriousness and moral posturing. Those on my side of the political fence who twisted themselves into supporting the Bush administration's invasion of Iraq should have thought longer and harder about the immoral implications of preventive war. When I hear talk of a new Islamic conspiracy meant to take over the world, one bearing striking similarity to the Nazi threat of the mid-twentieth century, I shudder at the wildly inappropriate comparison between faith and fanaticism. Political philosophers I deeply admire who write about unjust wars, yet also seem to find wars undertaken by countries with which they identify invariably defensible, strike me as having lost their analytic edge. A decision to invade another country in order to free its citizens from the oppressions visited upon them by their own leaders will surely be required from time to time. But when every case of overseas violence is treated as an example of genocide demanding the deployment of more U.S. troops, something has gone seriously wrong with both the analysis and the recommendation. Newfound cold war liberals appealed to me because of their willingness to courageously confront complacency and cliché. Now I find many of them—their names will become apparent as my argument proceeds—formulaic and conventional. Like them, I continue to believe that we in the West have an overwhelming moral obligation to come to the defense of those victimized by evil irrespective of where they live. The important question is not whether we should but how we can be effective. There is no purpose served by posturing. Experience counts for nothing unless we learn from it.

Although we must continue to make the problem of political evil central to our concerns, we must also be willing to deal with its complexity. It does not benefit the victims of political evil anywhere if, anxious to come to their assistance, we fail to understand precisely what led to their suffering and therefore try to help them in wrong, if not counterproductive, ways. In nearly all the cases of political evil we witness in the contemporary world, the good guys are not always good, the motives of the bad guys may not be what we (or they) claim, and the failure to understand the motives of both may lead to decisions that wind up increasing suffering. It is for all these reasons that being warmhearted can only be accomplished by being clear-eyed. The risk of treating political evil with dispassion is that one appears not to be taking evil seriously. But making evil central to everything we do allows political evil space to grow. Paradoxes and complexities do not disappear just because our intentions are good. We should be liberal and idealistic enough to identify political evil and do everything in our power to limit its reach. We should also be conservative and realistic enough to recognize that doing so will never be simple and can easily backfire.

Although I will be critical in this book of some of the more hyperventilating campaigns against genocide, and even though I will also distance myself from apocalyptic thinking denouncing terrorism, I hope my readers understand that I respect everyone who makes fighting political evil a priority. If I did not feel as powerfully as they do that we must respond when political evil raises its head, I would not have undertaken the task of attempting to show why I believe they are trying to do the right thing in the wrong way. Some ways of thinking about political evil are more helpful than others. Some ways of combating political evil work better than others. If we are to do our best to limit the consequences of political evil, we cannot rely on sloppy historical analogies, amateurish psychological speculations, discredited theological apologetics, political oversimplifications, rigid ideological categorizations, and tired moral platitudes. We owe the victims of political evil more than our compassion. By lowering our sights we can raise their hopes.

PART ONE

What It Is

CHAPTER ONE

The Distinctiveness of Political Evil

FOUR VARIETIES OF POLITICAL EVIL

POLITICAL EVIL is all around us. Just a couple of decades ago, scholars were declaring the end of ideology, the inevitability of secularism, the benefits of modernity, and the triumph of liberal democracy. Now they are talking about not only the clash of civilizations but cosmic war and future jihad. Modernity has not taken the teeth out of political evil but has instead put new weapons into its hands. The political evils of today thus force us to rethink the optimism of yesterday. One of the best-known books written when evil seemed a thing of the past was the literary critic Andrew Delbanco's *The Death of Satan,* published in 1995. In subsequent years Delbanco has had second thoughts about the devil's continued presence among us. "I myself feel that it's not possible to live as glibly as we did before Sept. 11," he told the PBS television program *Frontline.* "The preoccupations that I had, that I saw in the television, that I saw in the popular press before Sept. 11 were put into a new light by that event."

For all the hopes we may once have had of a better world, the events of September 11 were by no means the only example of political evil we have witnessed in the past few decades. In terms of the sheer numbers of people singled out for harm and for dramatizing a lack of respect for basic human dignity, four distinct kinds of politically evil acts have grabbed the greatest amount of our attention: terrorism, ethnic cleansing, genocide, and a reliance on means such as torture to fight back against evil. Here I want to briefly consider and define each one before going on to argue that however dissimilar they are from each other, they possess a common political nature. So many of the ways we think about evil downplay politics in favor of either individual psychology or a focus on millennial visions. If we are to understand and respond effectively to the political evil so prominent in the world today, we ought not to confuse it with other forms of malevolent behavior that are motivated by no larger cause whatsoever or are driven by causes so large that no political means exist to realize them.

Terrorism, while subject to many conflicting and imperfect definitions, can generally be viewed as *the use of violence by nonstate actors to inflict death and destruction on innocent bystanders in order to publicize a cause.* Terrorism surely belongs on any list of the most visible and murderous forms in which political evil manifests itself. It is not just what happened to the World Trade Center and the Pentagon. Madrid, London, and Mumbai (and, unfortunately, so many other places) have experienced devastating terror attacks of their own—and all the savagery that accompanies them. Similar violence throughout Israel, planned and put into operation by zealots determined to wipe that country off the map, was the work of those who belong to Israel's own "axis of evil," composed, as Major General Aharon Ze'evi-Farkash, former head of the Israeli Military Defense Directorate, put it, of Hamas, Hezbollah, and al-Qaeda cells supported by Iran. In some parts of the world, merely sipping coffee in a café can make you the target of people determined to end your life once and for all.

If frequent terrorist bombings are not enough to place terrorism in the highest ranks of political evil, and if the additional prospect of terrorists acquiring nuclear weapons does not send a chill through one's bones, suicide terrorism, in which the perpetrator transforms himself into a weapon against which there is almost no defense, is especially outside the universe of morally permissible acts. The world's most common theater for suicide terrorism in recent years has been Iraq, where women wearing bombs attached to their belts, sometimes recruited from the ranks of the mentally handicapped, carried out their missions in cities such as Baghdad and Mosul already torn apart by the brutal tactics of ruthless insurgents. But the use of suicide terrorism is more widespread than that; in Lebanon, Moscow, Sri Lanka, Pakistan, Israel, and beyond, suicide terrorism has been used whenever less dramatic means of calling attention to a cause have failed.

A world characterized by terrorism in so many places and of so many kinds, which ours unfortunately has become, is a world where political evil becomes a constantly looming presence, influencing our actions and reactions even when it finds itself in abeyance. Because of the threat posed by terrorism, political evil has a face, a home, and a message. We can declare a war against it, but winning that war, if by that we mean eliminating terrorist threats from the world, is all but impossible. Terrorism will continue so long as people are willing to kill others, or to kill themselves, to further an ideology, a faith, or a people. Although traceable to the French Revolution and the tactics of nineteenth-century anarchists, terrorism, as the political philosopher Michael Walzer has written, "in the strict sense, the random murder of innocent people emerged as a strategy of revolutionary struggle only in the period after World War II." Given even more recent innovative technologies of destruction and mass communication, this kind of terrorism shows no sign of abating.

Ethnic cleansing is the second form of political evil worth singling out for attention. "The intention of ethnic cleansing," writes the Stanford University historian Norman Naimark in his definitive study of the phenomenon, "*is to remove a people and often all traces of them from a concrete territory. The goal, in other words, is to get rid of the 'alien' nationality, ethnic, or religious group and to seize control of the territory they had formerly inhabited*" (emphasis added). Although the term "ethnic cleansing" is relatively recent—a translation of the Serbo-Croatian phrase *etnicko ciscenje,* it came into popular parlance in 1992 to characterize what was taking place in Bosnia—the phenomenon has occurred throughout all of history. But it has been especially visible in the last century: the expulsion of Germans from Poland and Czechoslovakia after World War II, the removal of South Asians from Uganda during the regime of Idi Amin, and the Indonesian attacks against the people of East Timor can all serve as examples.

Two powerful political forces have made ethnic cleansing especially prevalent in our times. One is the demise of old-fashioned colonialism. The withdrawal of Western powers from their overseas outposts left the borders of too many nations up in the air. As a result, some ethnic cleansing undoubtedly took place when what was once British India became the three distinct nation-states of India, Pakistan, and Bangladesh; Africa is awash in violence as a by-product of efforts to redesign the territories of the nation-states bequeathed to the continent by foreign intervention; and the map of the Middle East was radically redrawn along religious and ethnic lines after Britain and France gave up their mandates in the area. The end of Western colonialism is a good thing. The ethnic violence that has followed in its wake is not.

In addition, ethnic cleansing is unfortunately associated, as the UCLA sociologist Michael Mann has shown, with the spread of democracy. When a nation becomes politically independent and its leaders consumed with populist forms of chauvinism, pressures to engage in ethnic cleansing intensify. So long as demagogic leadership styles retain their appeal, ethnic cleansing and the horrors that accompany it, including roundups, relocation camps, theft, rape, and confiscation, are unlikely to disappear. A world made safe for democracy is all too often a world ripe for ethnic violence.

Killing people for reasons of race, ethnicity, or religion instead of displacing them transforms ethnic cleansing into *genocide,* the third of political evil's many forms in the contemporary world. Genocide existed before the Nazi regime put it into practice in its most extreme form; deny it as insistently as they like, the Turks committed genocide against the Armenians during and immediately after World War I. It has also continued after Nazism's demise; there is no reason to question the appropriateness of the term with respect to the situation in Rwanda in 1994, where upwards of a million people were killed because of their tribal affiliations. Our age and century have been characterized as genocidal, and not without reason. We cannot grasp the ubiquity of political evil in the contemporary world without recognizing that genocide is still capable of causing untold suffering.

Both ethnic cleansing and genocide are politically evil, but the latter, because its ultimate objective is death, ups the ante. Reflecting on Stalin's campaigns against the people of Chechnya in the 1940s, the prizewinning *Washington Post* journalist Anne Applebaum wrote that "for the first time, Stalin had decided to eliminate not just members of particular, suspect nationalities, or categories of political 'enemies,' but entire nations—men, women, children, grandparents—and wipe them off the map." Applebaum is convinced that Westerners pay less attention to Stalin's evil than to Hitler's, and she is determined to correct the imbalance. Yet even she concludes that "perhaps 'genocide' is not the right term for these deportations, since there were no mass executions."

The question Applebaum raises is one that prompts strong disagreement; Naimark, for example, has recently argued that Stalin's overall treatment of his presumed enemies *was* genocidal in nature. How we respond to this question matters, in large part because Stalin himself, during the debates over the 1948 Genocide Convention, played a role in restricting the legal definition to killing carried out for racial and ethnic reasons rather than political ones. Yet even Naimark qualifies his argument in the course of making it by arguing that Stalin's treatment of the kulaks was "murderous if not genocidal." No one can doubt Stalin's murderous brutality or indifference to human suffering. It nonetheless remains the case that famines and labor camps are not the same as yellow stars and extermination camps. Stalin was the supreme master of ethnic cleansing, even before we had a term to describe his acts. His genocidal acts, in contrast to those carried out by the Nazis, were less thorough in application and not as central to the very definition of his regime. With the opening of once-closed archives, moreover, we also know that the Stalinist regime killed fewer people than the Nazi one. Both regimes were evil, even radically evil, yet they were different from each other. Stalin's ethnic cleansing frequently crossed the line into genocide. Hitler's actions were genocidal from start to finish.

The final form of political evil we see around us can best be described as *counterevil,* which I will define as *the determination to inflict uncalled-for suffering on those presumed or known to have inflicted the same upon you.* George W. Bush's decision to fight back against the September 11 terrorists was both justified and accorded widespread support around the world, but the methods his administration adopted included a number of highly immoral tactics and policies, among them the rendition of suspects to countries with no regard for human rights and the use of torture at Abu Ghraib and Guantánamo Bay. Along similar lines, political evil undoubtedly took place when innocent Israelis in towns such as Sderot became the target of rocket attacks launched by Hamas militants located in the Gaza Strip; no one can visit that town, as I did in June 2010, and come away without an appreciation of what it means to hear the red-alert warning of an imminent attack and have roughly fifteen seconds to decide how to protect your children or where to seek shelter. But having responded to Palestinian acts of terror by launching an invasion of Gaza that resulted in significant death and suffering to innocent people, imposing a blockade on one of the most densely populated places in the world in ways suggesting collective punishment against all the residents of Gaza in retaliation for the actions taken by their leaders, and later attacking a flotilla of ships attempting to break the blockade and killing even more innocent people along the way, Israel lost whatever moral advantages it once had over its terrorist enemies. It is anything but a new insight to recognize that evil begets evil; throughout history, victims of terrible crimes have sought appropriately proportioned revenge. Still, when leaders of a war presumably fought against evil use a 1957 U.S. Air Force study of Chinese Communist methods as the source of their interrogation tactics, as took place at Guantánamo, we know that a dangerous line has been crossed. Enter into that territory and the things you do will be judged by history accordingly.

Even if terrorism, ethnic cleansing, and genocide become less common in future years, the debate over counterevil will surely continue in those democratic societies that have employed it. A reliance upon the techniques of counterevil inevitably raises questions about the most fundamental values of those societies: Are they committed to the rule of law? Have they become morally indistinguishable from those who commit evil acts against them? Are they in violation of international treaties? Does it matter if they are? Will they give peace with their enemies a chance? How can those who employ such tactics be brought to justice? For liberal democracies, counterevil leaves a stain that can never be erased. Whenever it appears, the mark remains not only on its victims but on its perpetrators.

The four forms of political evil that have caused so much death and suffering in our midst cannot substitute for one another. Suicide terrorism is not on the same moral plane as forms of terrorism launched from more distant locations. While many examples of ethnic cleansing lead directly to genocide, others stop short. Even the most brutal of genocides do not transform themselves automatically into holocausts, let alone the Holocaust, a term generally reserved for the attempt by a powerful Nazi state using the most modern technological and bureaucratic means available to exterminate all of world Jewry. As deplorable as the tactics used by the Bush administration to fight the war on terror have been, and as disproportionate as the Israeli invasion of Gaza was, there is a major difference between an evil movement or regime and a reliance upon an evil tactic by governments that are otherwise law-abiding. Because political evil so violates our most fundamental notions of right and wrong, there always exists a temptation to conflate the particular forms it takes. Yet, as the world discovered when the United States went to war against Saddam Hussein citing examples of evil he never committed—Saddam was an ethnic cleanser and a tyrant but not a sponsor of the September 11 terror attacks—mischaracterizing the motives for mass killing all too often leads to the tragedy of even more killing.

At the same time, practitioners of political evil in any form are neither insane nor delusionary. What makes the wielders of political evil so frightening is in fact their very rationality; they engage in political activity to achieve their ends much as other kinds of leaders do. It cannot be emphasized enough that most leaders of states or movements do not unleash violence against innocent people the way terrorists do, but even liberal democracies recognize that violence, even the kind that results in what is euphemistically called collateral damage, can be appropriate in times of war. A determination to create an ethnically pure nation comes at far too high a cost for most societies if it includes removing people from their homes or killing them because of who they are, but people in those societies also appreciate the attractions of ethnicity and frequently look with suspicion upon those considered strangers. Genocide is far outside the range of what Americans consider permissible, but deep in their past are institutions such as slavery and practices such as Indian removal that bear an uncomfortable resemblance to today's mass atrocities. Western societies see their share of protests when leaders respond to evil by engaging in evil acts themselves, but because they are viewed as *our* leaders fighting to realize *our* values, there will always exist a deep reluctance to put them on trial or to hold them responsible as we do with enemies.

Political evil, in short, comes with its own shock of recognition. Acknowledging this in no way means that we are all complicit in evil; because there is a world of difference between pursuing one's goals through the ballot box or the mass media and killing everyone standing in the way of realizing them, we must resist any temptation to conflate the motives of political evildoers with our own. Yet we also need to recognize that although the methods of those who engage in political evil are horrific, their motives are familiar. It is the way they seek their goals, not necessarily their goals themselves, that defines them as the moral monsters they are. Denouncing them as demonic lets them off the hook, allowing us to forget that they are human, all too human, with all the good and bad that implies.

EVERYDAY EVIL

NOT ALL EVIL is political evil. While all forms of evil produce needless suffering, some of them are motivated by no cause at all. Philosophers use the term "category error" to describe the way we sometimes put things into boxes in which they do not belong. Conflating those who harm others for no particular reason with those whose reasons constitute the major motive of their actions is such a category error. One way to get a sense of what makes political evil distinctive is to contrast those who kill or maim because they are integral parts of political movements or states with those who do the same thing but make no effort to become leaders, do not pursue specific goals, and therefore engage in no strategizing. Nonpolitical evil can itself take many forms: piracy, pedophilia and its repeated cover-ups, sexual slavery, environmental degradation, and, for certain religious believers, abortion are among the most frequently named. For my purposes here, school shootings offer a near-perfect example of evil that lacks any political character whatsoever.

On April 20, 1999, two young men, Eric Harris and Dylan Klebold, opened fire on their fellow students at Columbine High School near Littleton, Colorado, killing thirteen and injuring twenty-four before taking their own lives. Harris and Klebold were as morally indifferent as they were ruthlessly cold-blooded. That their victims had their whole lives before them was irrelevant to them. The never-ending pain they would inflict on the families of their victims barely registered in their minds. "I want to tear a throat with my own teeth like a pop can," one of them, Harris, wrote in his journal. "I want to grab some weak little freshman and just tear them apart like a fucking wolf, strangle them, squish their head, rip off their jaw, break their arms in half, show them who is god." Harris and Klebold were as evil as evil can be.

Any of the great thinkers of the past who dealt with the problem of evil would have recognized the Columbine killers. Whatever language of evil one speaks, their acts apply. The stain of their sin was indelible. They used others as means to their twisted ends. By killing so many innocent people, nearly all of them in the prime of youth, they demonstrated no respect for the most basic of human rights, the right to life. And, as if reflecting some widely shared flaw in human nature, they were not alone. Their deed, in fact, was one in a series of horrific murders that have dominated the headlines in recent times: Richard Speck, destroyer of nurses; Jeffrey Dahmer, obsessive cannibalizer; the Son of Sam, David Berkowitz, tormented by demons; Theodore Kaczynski, the Unabomber, who killed three people and injured twenty-three; John Allen Muhammad and Lee Boyd Malvo, highway sharpshooters; Susan Smith and Andrea Yates, mothers who disposed of their children; and Seung-Hui Cho, the Virginia Tech purchaser and user of easily available guns. The conservative former congressman and Republican presidential candidate Newt Gingrich absurdly singled out one of these cases—Susan Smith—and tried to blame the Democratic Party and its commitments to liberalism for her acts. Similar, if not quite as far-fetched, were those who pointed their fingers at the absence of gun control to account for the crimes of Seung-Hui Cho. But the urge behind all such efforts at explanation was not misguided at all. When horrible things happen, we want to know why.

It is not clear that we ever can. The circumstances surrounding the acts carried out by all these killers were the stuff of everyday life. Places familiar to us all—bathrooms, hospitals, highways, employment centers—were used as murder sites. If actual grievances motivated these killers, and in most cases they did not, they were difficult to decipher. All of them were common criminals rather than holy warriors. There lay within them no conception of a glorious crusade and no anticipation of heavenly martyrdom. There would be no lessons to be drawn from accounts of their acts left on websites for the next generation to read and ponder. Their names remain in our memory because we gasp at the savageness of their deeds, yet in the long term they will be remembered as answers to trivia questions rather than as historically transformative characters.

In spite of the purposelessness so often associated with killers of this sort, commentators from time to time, shocked by the violence or motivated by ideological convictions of their own, insist that they must be part of a much larger cause. The neoconservative writer Daniel Pipes, for example, quickly came to the conclusion that the Beltway sniper John Allen Muhammad was not just another tortured soul but was driven by an ideological commitment to militant Islam. But Muhammad, who, unlike the typically verbose political protester, chose to remain silent at his Virginia execution in 2009, lacked a coherent political or religious outlook on the world. The same applied to the Columbine killers: despite breathless reports at the time of their rampage that they admired Hitler, their writings, which also contained attacks on racism, were too jumbled to focus on any particular political grievance. It is true that at least one of the best-known of these killers, Theodore Kaczynski, offered a seeming rationale for his crimes in his Unabomber manifesto, but his ramblings bordered on the incoherent. In none of these cases, and even less so with respect to Jeffrey Dahmer and Richard Speck, was there any attempt to lead a movement or to rally people to an idea. Killing of this sort is entirely apolitical. It is aimed at no end save death itself. This is not to say that such killing lacks planning; one has to worry about timing, security guards, sufficient ammunition, and coordination. Yet these killers devote obsessive attention to means while paying almost no attention to ends. For them it is all tactics and no strategy.

Because they are so apolitical, practitioners of everyday evil detest large groups and prefer to keep matters close at hand. The largest movement they typically build are parties of two: Harris recruited Klebold, and Muhammad found Malvo. Others are the clichéd "loners," people who distrust everyone except themselves. Seung-Hui Cho, like the hermit Kaczynski, fit the bill perfectly. In the multimedia presentation he prepared for NBC News before carrying out his actions, Cho praised "martyrs" such as Harris and Klebold and seemed to be attacking American society for its materialism. But most of what he had to say was a paranoid rant as unfocused on anything specific as it was a distillation of his own anger: "You had a hundred billion chances and ways to have avoided today," he proclaimed. "But you decided to spill my blood. You forced me into a corner and gave me only one option. The decision was yours. Now you have blood on your hands that will never wash off." As a Virginia judge held, and a panel created to investigate the shooting found, Cho was mentally unbalanced. Cho's cause was entirely his own; by putting the blame on an unspecified "you," he was simply finding a way of calling attention to himself.

Lacking a cause, apolitical evil remains a mystery. The evil perpetrated by these individuals was, as Samuel Taylor Coleridge said of Iago, a "motiveless malignancy"; it aimed at no particular goals, neither for themselves nor for their victims. Those victims, moreover, except for the children killed by their mothers, were chosen at random; like California wildfires that destroy one house while the one next to it remains intact, some students died because they majored in English rather than geology, and some commuters never made it home alive because they drove down one freeway rather than another. Try as we might to figure out exactly why these killers went on their sprees, we come up short. Because so many of them were mad, their acts were meaningless. The sheer lack of any explanation for what they did, in fact, is why we call them mad, for "madness" is a term that substitutes for the incomprehensibility of their acts. Whenever such killing takes place, experts rush into television studios to instruct the rest of us on what this means for the way we raise our children, organize our schools, relate to strangers, glorify violence, worship (or fail to worship) our gods, or fill our leisure time, but there is little to be learned from them. Even if so many of these killers had not killed themselves, thereby depriving us of the ability to find out more about what motivated them, there would still remain unanswered questions.

The most widely read and discussed treatment of the problem of evil in our time is Hannah Arendt's *Eichmann in Jerusalem.* By introducing the term "banality of evil" in the very last sentence of her book, and by leaving the meaning of the term ambiguous, Arendt ignited a firestorm that rekindles every time the world uncovers a new set of evil acts. I will have much to say about Arendt's concept shortly, but in this context it is worth noting that however bizarre it may be to apply a term such as "banal" to a man responsible for as many deaths as Adolf Eichmann, there *is* a certain level of banality associated with killers such as Harris and Klebold. To avoid the controversies associated with Arendt's term, I use the phrase "everyday evil" to characterize killers of this sort. Although no act of evil can by definition be an everyday affair—evil always takes place outside the boundaries of what we call routine—we can all recognize in these kind of killers someone who, save for a mind malfunction, is on the surface like us, a neighbor or colleague gone off the deep end. The deaths for which they are responsible dramatize their acts, but as individuals there is little or nothing dramatic about them.

Those who carry out acts of political evil could not be more different. The term "senseless," so often applied to the acts of random killers, ought never to be applied to those motivated by a political cause. People who engage in political evil generally kill in far greater numbers than those who shoot their fellow high school students or stab nurses to death. But this is not what makes them distinctive. However twisted those who carry out acts of political evil may be, they are in pursuit of a goal, no matter how delusional. Whether or not we agree with their goal depends upon who we are and what views we hold; all too many people have a way of downplaying the evil of those who happen to share their outlook on the world. But we will fail to understand the most important thing about those who are politically evil if we do not recognize that the acts they carry out make sense to them because they view them as part of a plan to realize their objectives. Even if they kill serially, political evildoers are not serial killers. Their primary purpose is to call attention not to themselves but to their aims. When we analyze what makes them tick, we need to stop thinking of people such as Harris and Klebold. The mental derangement of particular individuals does not help us understand the strategic motivations of those who kill for a purpose.

OUTSIZED EVIL

SUPREME MASTERS of evil exist at the opposite end of the spectrum from killers such as Harris and Klebold. Anything but colorless individuals who but for their deeds would have been completely obscure, the totalitarian dictators Adolf Hitler and Joseph Stalin were larger-than-life historical figures. No one can doubt that they were obsessed by causes that led them to concentrate power in their hands and to use that power to destroy those they considered their enemies. Yet they too should not be compared to today's practitioners of political evil. It is not that they lacked political goals; of those they had more than their share. But the goals they sought could never be achieved in the world in which they actually lived. Being determined to pursue goals that can never be realized shares one thing in common with having no goals at all: in both cases the evil that results is resistant to any political means of stopping it and can only be brought to an end when it extinguishes itself in its own frenzy or is met head-on by massive force. Cosmic ambition is as irrelevant to the political evils of our time as personal delusions of grandeur.

The special qualities that made Hitler and Stalin the extraordinary leaders they became were obvious to all from the start. Even before he chose a life of revolution, while financing his activities by robbing Georgian banks, Joseph Dzhugashvili (Stalin's real name) had begun to attract slavish followers such as Simon Ter-Petrossian, otherwise known as Kamo, who was always present when the dirtiest deeds were carried out. One of Stalin's main rivals for power, Leon Trotsky, was as brilliant and capable a revolutionary as the world has ever known, yet Trotsky would never make the slightest dent in Stalin's consolidation of power. Stalin's personality, underestimated by rivals who dismissed him as crude and ignorant, combined petty cruelty with supreme ambition. Once in power, Stalin played a role in just about every aspect of Soviet life. When it came to the show trials that destroyed his rivals, as the historian Robert Gellately notes, "he helped phrase the charges, decided on the slate of defendants, crafted the evidence, and prescribed the sentences." When war followed shortly thereafter, he appointed himself supreme commander and moved battalions and civilians around at will. There was no one like him among his comrades, and there has been no one like him since.

Hitler's evil was outsized as well, if not more so. The Führer not only mesmerized people with his speeches delivered to massive audiences but could, through his piercing eyes and sudden outbursts, leave those in his immediate presence speechless. "The levels of hero-worship," writes his most accomplished biographer, Ian Kershaw, "had never been witnessed before in Germany. Not even the Bismarck cult in the last years of the founder of the Reich had come remotely near matching it." Hitler too was underestimated, especially by those members of the German aristocratic elite who never quite understood how much he had marginalized them. He made himself indispensable to the regime whose evil he embodied. The term "charismatic" can be overused, but it easily applies to a man like Hitler. A large part of what he did can be explained by who he was. Like Stalin, Hitler transformed and at the same time seemed to transcend history. It will be impossible ever to forget either of their names.

Even if they had not possessed remarkable personalities, both Hitler and Stalin would have benefited from a propaganda apparatus that transformed them into magical figures in order to survive and flourish. "The success of the two cults of personality," as the British historian Richard Overy explains, "relied on the active and willing participation of millions, who suspended their disbelief and endorsed and magnified the overblown personalities constructed by the authorities." Totalitarianism created a fantasized reality as far outside the boundaries of everyday politics as its leaders were outside the realm of everyday people.

Killing there would be, but not in places where people congregate to take classes or mail their letters.

Instead, totalitarian evil was carried out in distant locations, out of sight and potentially out of mind. Despite the planning of the Final Solution undertaken at the Wannsee Conference, no documents survive linking Hitler directly to the extermination camps. (Hitler frequently "prophesized" the ultimate fate of the Jews, as if fate rather than his own decisions and actions would be responsible for their extermination.) Soviet citizens must have known about the gulag—how could they not when so many people suddenly disappeared?—but no public pronouncements about it were made; all the seagulls near the Solovetski Islands, the story goes, were killed so that no one could send a message out by carrier pigeon of what took place there. Just as day-to-day life was built on a fantasy of harmonious ideals, concentration camp life crossed the border of brutality. Death came to millions in these camps, but we would never describe those responsible for them as random killers. There is far too much blood on their hands to compare them to those who kill blameless innocents.

The camps may have been hidden behind shrouds of secrecy, but the totalitarian leaders' reasons for having them in the first place were not. Hitler and Stalin were all too clear about what they wanted to do. They explained their plans at great length in their written works and did their best to accomplish the goals they had so publicly announced. The problem, if anything, was that their intentions were so up front that people at the time could not bring themselves to believe that Hitler really did want to rid Europe of its Jews or that Stalin's commitment to a classless society in theory would lead him to try to kill off the kulaks, or wealthier peasants, in practice. Both leaders knew themselves and their grandiose objectives, knew the people they ruled, and knew their antagonists. Single-mindedness played as much of a role as ruthlessness in getting them to the top of the totalitarian heap and keeping them there.

Practitioners of everyday evil may be apolitical, but those responsible for the evils of totalitarianism were political in the extreme: as heads of state, Hitler and Stalin were in positions to assume all the means of violence that states have at their command. Politics consumed their lives; neither man had much time left over for anything else. One reason they were so successful at staving off challenges from others was their mastery of the art of playing potential opponents against each other. Machiavelli's *The Prince,* the world's greatest manual for leadership, had little to teach them; on the contrary, they could have taught the Florentine philosopher a thing or two.

Yet if politics means pursuing a goal that can be achieved, neither Hitler nor Stalin was political in this sense at all. Not even an evil genius such as Hitler could have made the world *Judenfrei.* (The Nazi regime killed roughly two-thirds of European Jewry and about one-third of the world's Jews.) Much the same could be said for the Marxist goal that gave the Soviet system the rationale for its existence; try as he might, Stalin never created a classless society. The unrealizable ambitions of Stalin and Hitler ultimately destroyed the states they spent so much time building up, as if states served no purpose and had no reason to exist without their leaders' presence.

The goals of outsized evil leaders come closer to eschatology, or what the faithful call the end-time, than to politics, for to reach them totalitarian societies demand an end to human history as we have understood it. Arendt saw as much when she wrote of the Nazis: "Here, there are neither political nor historical nor simply moral standards but, at the most, the realization that something seems to be involved in modern politics that actually should never be involved in politics as we used to understand it, namely all or nothing—all, and that is an undetermined infinity of forms of human living-together, or nothing, for a victory of the concentration-camp system would mean the same inexorable doom for human beings as the use of the hydrogen bomb would mean the doom of the human race." It is somehow fitting that both Hitler and Stalin had little sympathy with organized religion and viewed the churches of their countries as potential enemies; as the historian Michael Burleigh has emphasized, they were offering a competing system of meaning preoccupied with eternal questions of salvation and sacrifice.

The best-known term used to characterize the evil of the totalitarian dictators was once again utilized by Arendt. Neither the theology of Saint Augustine nor the philosophy of Kant, which in her view represented the two most profound moral traditions in the West, allowed for the possibility of "radical evil," she argued in *The Origins of Totalitarianism.* Augustine viewed Satan as a fallen angel and for that reason at least partially good. Kant, although he coined the term "radical evil," expressed wonder at the moral law within as well as the heaven above and therefore stopped short of saying that human beings would always be irredeemably bad. But the Nazis, Arendt continued, turned all this confidence in human nature on its head. "There is only one thing that seems to be discernible," she wrote of the experience of totalitarianism. "We may say that radical evil has emerged in connection with a system in which all men have become equally superfluous." History is filled with examples of human beings killing other human beings. But, according to Arendt, never before had a regime tried to kill the idea of humanity itself. This is what the Nazis sought to accomplish. In doing so, they transcended all previous historical experiences with evil and brought man's capacity for wickedness to an entirely new level.

It is the very unachievability of their objectives that makes outsized evil leaders so radical. Since the struggle to obtain their goals can never end, the power of those who proclaim them never ceases; radical evil can never be satisfied but always demands more. If by some miracle a totalitarian regime did achieve its goal, it would have to find another or go out of business; the worst thing a totalitarian system can do in terms of its own survival is to solve a problem it had previously identified as the reason for its existence. Because Hitler loved Wagner, it is common to describe the last years of the Third Reich as a *Götterdämmerung*, or twilight of the gods. Yet this was the only one of Wagner's operas that was not honored on the fiftieth anniversary of the composer's death in 1933; there would have been no twilight of the Nazi gods had Hitler had anything to do with the matter.

Defenders of Arendt have gone out of their way to explain how totalitarianism's evil can be banal and radical at the same time. Their explanations are not very credible, for the two terms she used as modifiers reflect entirely different sensibilities about one of the most important of human phenomena. Just as the evildoers of Columbine and Virginia Tech approached the banal in their ordinariness, the evil of Hitler and Stalin was truly beyond comprehension. On this latter point, if not on the other one, Arendt got it right, even if she subsequently told the Jewish scholar and mystic Gershom Scholem that "it is indeed my opinion now that evil is never 'radical' " and chose not to use the term again. She should have stayed with her original insight, at least as far as the great dictators were concerned. Totalitarianism may not have succeeded in destroying human nature. But it did kill huge numbers of people in a systematic way and with ruthless efficiency. One always hates to say that something is unprecedented, but sometimes something is. Totalitarianism, as I will try to show later, is one of them. People as evil as Hitler and Stalin have existed throughout history but lacked the means these men had at their disposal. Those motives may remain among leaders who possess an exaggerated sense of their own mission, but today's evildoers can never carry out as much damage. We want a term that marks the deeds of the totalitarian dictators as unique, and "radical evil" at least does that.

In his search for the origins of Hitler's evil, the writer Ron Rosenbaum offers readers a guide through every conceivable explanation—Was Hitler diabolical or eminently rational? A sexual pervert or totally asexual? A reflection of inherent German anti-Semitism or a shaper of it?—only to conclude that Hitler in some fundamental sense remains unexplained. Perhaps this is because in a very basic sense Hitler did not inhabit the same world we do. Hitler and his fellow Nazi leaders not only created a new hell for their victims but built a Valhalla for themselves in which, or so they maintained, they were purifying their world. It is one thing to understand killers who know that they kill. It is another to come to terms with mass murderers who think of themselves as purveyors of progress. This is why Hitler, in spite of the fact that he made his goals so transparent, nonetheless remains mysterious to us. For him to have been on the side of the angels, as he believed he was, everything we know about the role of devils would have to be turned upside down. If it is difficult to understand how a serial killer can be moved to shoot people for nonexistent motives, it is impossible to understand how a totalitarian dictator can kill millions for a dream so malevolent.

The uniqueness of what the totalitarians of the 1930s and 1940s wanted to do, as well as the utter grandiosity of their efforts to do it, makes them distinctly different from today's politically evil leaders. Contemporary terrorists and ethnic cleansers such as Osama bin Laden and Slobodan Milosevic learned something from the radicalism of a Hitler or a Stalin. They may have been just as bloodthirsty, and their tactics were just as immoral. But they did not seek to bring about a world so radically transformed that it would be unrecognizable to us. Lacking the sheer audacity of Hitler and Stalin, they pursued goals that could be realized—and, alas, all too often were. It is as much a category error to conflate them with Hitler and Stalin as it is to compare them to killers such as Harris and Klebold. They may have wanted to liken themselves to the greatest evildoers of our time—lacking in ego they were not—but this is one gruesome test they failed.

POLITICAL EVIL'S DUAL NATURE

NEITHER an everyday occurrence nor a radical attempt to transform human nature, political evil is at once a violation of all that modern people hold dear *and* a continuation of normal politics by other means. Political evil slips back and forth between two different worlds, one ugly, dark, and vicious and the other public, discursive, and familiar. If we are to understand political evil, and therefore be in a better position to control it, we must appreciate both its this-worldliness and its otherworldliness. It does not do us any good to denounce political evil as so beyond the moral pale that no engagement with it can be countenanced. Nor is it helpful to treat political evil as if those who choose it just happened to have picked one way of realizing their goals rather than another. Political evil has a quality all its own. The challenge it presents lies in the paradoxes it represents. We have little choice but to engage with political evil if we want to stop it, even as we acknowledge that its practitioners must be brought to justice for the atrocities they perpetrate.

Nothing better characterizes the dual nature of political evil than the objectives it seeks. There is, for those attracted to it, something glorious about the goals their violence is meant to produce: not for them the run-of-the-mill politics associated with negotiation, compromise, and diplomacy. As bad as it is, political evil offers its followers a grotesque conception of the good life. Obviously, terrorism, ethnic cleansing, and genocide can never be reconciled with any credible account of moral conduct. But the leaders of politically evil movements and states would not attract significant followings if they did not hold out some ideal found appealing by large numbers of people. Their politics, at least when they get started in the business of evil, are "visionary."

This taste for goals capable of moving masses explains why so much of the political evil we witness in the world today is so closely linked to religion. Especially among the September 11 terrorists, faith, evoking as it did powerful images of God's wrath at apostates while promising redemption and moral wholeness for those who choose his path, provided the inspiration for their acts. Those killers were, of course, Muslims, and Islam has ever since received the bulk of the attention when the relationship between religion and evil is discussed. But any religion can be used as the justification for evil acts. In his book *Terror in the Mind of God*, the sociologist Mark Juergensmeyer finds prominent examples of political evil in five different religious traditions: Islam, Buddhism (the sarin gas attack on the Tokyo subway), Judaism (Baruch Goldstein, the Brooklyn-born physician who killed twenty-nine Muslims in the city of Hebron), Christianity (the Oklahoma City bombing and abortion clinic murders), and Sikhism (Indira Gandhi's assassination).

Political movements inspired by religion are unique in their capacity to make the appeals of martyrdom attractive; religion nearly always comes in a form that rejects the human world as corrupt in favor of an ascetic retreat from everyday life, including, if not especially including, politics. Practitioners of political evil understand full well the importance of seeming to reject the secular world and the temptations of money, power, and sexual gratification it offers. Followers seduced by worldly things, in their view, can never become the soldiers for God that the visionary nature of political evil requires. The eyes of those followers are on the prize, but the prize is to be found not in this world but in the one that awaits.

Yet for all the talk about how religion radicalizes its followers, in reality practitioners of political evil constantly find themselves diverting from their religious origins as they seek to realize the political causes that mean so much to them. The acts analyzed by Juergensmeyer illustrate the point. Timothy McVeigh, who attacked the federal office building in Oklahoma City, was as motivated by his extreme right-wing political views as he was by any faith commitments; it was his hatred of government more than his love of God that led him to do what he did. To one degree or another, the same is true of Juergensmeyer's other examples; even Aum Shinrikyo, for example, guided by a Buddhist tradition of spirituality hostile to any form of politics, carried out the subway attack in Tokyo near the Kasumigaseki station, close to a number of government buildings. Only when politics matters does one consider going well beyond the killing of innocents to assassinate heads of state.

The fact that such groups are political as well as religious means they frequently wind up engaging in the very kinds of negotiation and compromise they start out by rejecting. Some of the best examples of this transformation come from the Muslim world. Despite cries of alarm in the West that radical Islam loves jihad and burns with hatred toward apostates and heretics, Islamist movements that began as fundamentalist have frequently moderated their goals as they sought political power. Realizing this, the French scholar Olivier Roy urges that we drop the term "radical Islam" and replace it with the expression "political Islam" in recognition of this pattern; Roy cites as examples the Turkish Refah Partisi (Welfare Party), Pakistan's Jamaat-e-Islami, Algeria's Islamic Salvation Front, elements of the government in Sudan associated with the National Islamic Front, and the best known of all, especially after the 2011 uprising in that country, Egypt's Muslim Brotherhood. In some of these cases, such as the Turkish one, these movements transformed themselves into or were replaced by legal political parties that completely abandoned earlier commitments to violence. But even where violence remains part of a group's repertoire of tactics, it does so for reasons having to do with gaining this-worldly authority. As Roy explains, "the main reason for the retreat of the Islamist movements is that they have been secularised by the very process of politicisation. Political logic won over the religious, instead of promoting it." Political religion is always two-faced, as much a force for such earthly goals as national solidarity or anticolonial resistance as it is preoccupied with piety and purity.

Once politically evil movements combine religion and politics, the goals they pursue, however detestable we may find them, become all too depressingly achievable. The best example is offered by ethnic cleansing. If the aim of those who engaged in ethnic cleansing in Yugoslavia was to replace Marshal Tito's multiethnic state with many states organized along their particular ethnic lines, the reliance on political evil there would have to be considered a success. Ethnic cleansers try to change maps, and because the borders on those maps frequently change, they typically view themselves as midwifing a process that is already taking place. Ethnic cleansing happens so often because it works so well. Although the media frequently portray ethnic cleansing as a by-product of ancient hatreds and rivalries, and hence irresolvable and bound to continue until the end of time, in nearly all cases of ethnic cleansing traditions are invented, histories revised, and memories manipulated in order to secure immediate political goals.

Terrorists too seek goals that they can realize. This is especially the case with those operating locally rather than globally, such as the Abu Sayyaf group active in the Philippine island of Mindanao and the Pakistani Harakat-ul-Mujahedeen based in the disputed region of Kashmir. Terror of this sort is aimed at the task of creating a new state independent of an occupying power and in that sense is similar to such earlier forms of terror as those sponsored by the Irish Republican Army or the Basque separatists. Yesterday's terrorist can become tomorrow's political leader, a phenomenon witnessed many times in the course of twentieth-century political life, as the experience of Israel's Menachem Begin or Ireland's Gerry Adams testifies.

Although a number of today's Islamic-inspired terrorist groups are frequently denounced as the very essence of evil, the same attempted movement from violence to leadership is also characteristic of them. Yasser Arafat's Fatah, which included in its constitution a commitment to the destruction of the state of Israel, has been transformed into a political actor participating with Israel in the search for a two-state solution to the Middle East imbroglio. Hezbollah has not moved nearly as far in the direction of a nonterrorist political organization as has Fatah, but it participates actively in Lebanese elections and its leader, Hassan Nasrallah, became a key power broker in that country. Even Hamas, which for Israelis is the true embodiment of evil, runs charities and sponsors a wide variety of activities in Gaza, and while these acts can be interpreted as offering covert financial support to terror, they are also designed to increase the organization's political clout. (However much one may protest Hamas's tactics, it came to power in Gaza by winning an election, in large part because, in contrast to Fatah, it was not viewed as corrupt.) All of Israel's enemies engage in evil acts. But while for some violence is an end in itself, for others violence is directed to achieve political goals whose attainment would significantly lessen the violence in which they engage. That is a difference worth noting.

Of all the terrorist groups often associated with radical Islam, only al-Qaeda advances goals that come anywhere near the unattainability of Hitler's and Stalin's; its grievances are endless, and its ultimate goal, to return to a state of Islamic purity associated with the earliest days of the religion, is as unrealizable as ridding the world of Jews. Yet in many of its messages, al-Qaeda demands the removal of foreigners from the two holy cities of Saudi Arabia, which is clearly a political demand that could, at least in theory, be realized, and no one can doubt al-Qaeda's success in winning converts by mobilizing resentment against the West. Whatever al-Qaeda's original intentions, moreover, it has become fractured into local cells, many of which, such as al-Qaeda in Iraq or Jemaah Islamiyah in Indonesia, were spawned by local conditions and are either unable or unwilling to spread terror globally. No one can possibly know what the future holds for al-Qaeda. But the pursuit of goals so utopian that they can never be realized on this earth is unlikely to continue to attract martyrs willing to sacrifice their lives for a dream.

One consequence of the fact that political evil is simultaneously this-worldly and otherworldly is that it has a beginning and an ending. Politically evil movements and states offer no promises of a Thousand-Year Reich or the withering away of the state. On the contrary, most forms of contemporary political evil rather rapidly exhaust themselves. The Serbian leader Milosevic died while his war crimes trial was taking place, but the mere fact that he was on trial symbolized the containment of the ethnic cleansing and genocide he did so much to unleash; nowadays, Serbia's president, Boris Tadic, is a leader who welcomes foreign investment, seeks eventual membership in the European Union, repudiates extreme nationalism, and is highly regarded in the West. The genocide launched by the Hutus in Rwanda was devastating to the rival Tutsis, but it is the latter who came to power in that country; so intense was the Rwandan genocide that it burned itself out with astonishing speed. The evils associated with genocide, terrorism, and ethnic cleansing are so horrible that we instinctively want to think of them as timeless, as if nothing less will honor the memory of the victims. By so doing, however, we attach an aura of eternity to actions that, as horrible as they are, remain temporal. In this way we lose sight of the fact that the causes that inspire political evil are the same causes that can bring it to a conclusion.

Political evil's dualistic nature also influences the way those who engage in it think and act. Writing in 1999, the distinguished historian of terrorism Walter Laqueur predicted that "there will be for the foreseeable future individuals firmly convinced that, in the words of Goethe's Mephisto, all that comes into being is worthy of destruction. Neither madness nor fanaticism will vanish from the world, even if the current terrorist frenzies give way to more sober trends." Fanaticism certainly did seem to be on display two years after Laqueur's book was published when the twin towers of the World Trade Center fell. Whenever we witness political evil, we tend to see fanaticism: one of the world's leading students of Islam, Michael Sells, points to the fanaticism inherent in Christianity to explain Serbian genocide against the Bosnian Muslims. For those concerned about Israel's national security, the terrorism associated with Hezbollah and Hamas is viewed as having Qur'anic injunction; as Meir Litvak of the Moshe Dayan Center for Middle Eastern and African Studies at Tel Aviv University puts it, Hamas "is a clear case of ideological fanaticism as far as its perception of the Middle East conflict, demonisation of the enemy, its aspired end-goal, and the means to achieve it are concerned." Despite the fact that Osama bin Laden was by all accounts a shrewd organization man and Saddam Hussein was a cunning political survivor, images of evildoers as wild-eyed and crazed have persistent staying power.

If by "fanaticism" we mean passionate devotion to a cause, practitioners of political evil certainly qualify. But if the use of the term leaves the impression that those who engage in acts of political evil think in ways so blinded by hatred that nothing, not even self-interest, will stand in their way, the term should be used more carefully. Although at one level ethereal if twisted idealists, the overwhelming majority of those who engage in contemporary political evil are also deliberate strategic calculators. In his controversial book *Dying to Win*, the University of Chicago political scientist Robert A. Pape argues that even as repugnant an act as suicide terrorism has its own strategic rationale. "Terrorists, like other people, learn from experience," he claims. Analyzing thirteen major cases of suicide terrorism between 1980 and 2003, he concludes that seven were successful in changing the behavior of the targeted states. Suicide terrorists, in other words, can be as coolly Benthamite in their utilitarianism as they are Werther-like in their death wish. We see evil in suicide terrorism—and we are right to do so. Those who engage in it see something else: a technique that is more likely to achieve its objective than to fail. If the intention of the nineteen terrorists who sacrificed their lives on September 11 was not only to rain death and destruction but to force the United States into overreactive acts of folly, their strategy has to be considered a success.

The reason for the controversy over Pape's book is not difficult to understand: once we view terrorists as strategic thinkers, we can no longer denounce them as diabolical figures beyond all reason. But there is also a positive side to Pape's analysis: the evil carried out by those seeking achievable goals can never be radical in the way Arendt used that term to characterize the insatiable Nazis. Suicide terrorism sends chills down our spines when it works. But when it no longer works, as it has not for some time in Sri Lanka, where the government was finally able to win its war against the terrorist group known as the Tamil Tigers in 2009, the entire rationale for its use collapses. Remove or blunt the cause motivating political evil through a peace treaty, the creation of a new state, the defeat of an insurgency, or, in Israel's case, the construction of a security fence, and it dissipates or disappears.

Careful strategic thinking also extends to how practitioners of political evil choose their victims. We rightly consider the Nazi extermination of the Jews as carefully planned and thoroughly carried out. But the entire process was also clearly mad, rooted in an absurd racial reading of history, based on racial distinctions that amounted to hogwash, and fueled by conspiratorial paranoia incapable of standing up to reason. Because the entire rationale for Nazism was so otherworldly, the extermination of the Jews, however systematic, was if anything the opposite of strategic; the Nazi regime sacrificed time, money, and personnel to the Final Solution that more rationally should have been deployed in the war effort. (Along similar lines, Stalin's paranoia, directed in the first place against colleagues loyal to both him and his cause, eventually became so pronounced that it lost whatever purpose it may have served in identifying and terrorizing enemies of his regime.) Hitler did not kill the Jews because doing so would strengthen Germany or contribute to the longevity of his Reich. He killed Jews because he hated Jews.

The way contemporary practitioners of political evil select their victims certainly has one important thing in common with the Nazi and Soviet regimes: those victims are innocent of any crimes they are said to have committed. But because political evil seeks goals located in the world around them, its victims are chosen with strategic calculation very much in mind. Consider the terrorist attack of September 11, 2001. Those killed on that day were ordinary people going about the business of everyday life, had no particular interest in or knowledge of any of the causes motivating the attackers, and in some cases even shared their faith. But their innocence, unlike the innocence of the Jews under the Nazi regime, was not a by-product of the obsessions of the leaders determined to kill them. The victims of September 11 were attacked not in spite of their innocence but because of it. The terrorists who took their lives did not hate them but chose them because it worked strategically for them to die. Terrorists' acts are designed to be shown in endless loops on television sets around the world and to furnish headlines for newspapers and posts for bloggers. Terrorists wish to send a message, literally so in the case of the many videotapes distributed by al-Qaeda. Because terrorism aims to strike fear as well as to strike down, it requires that its victims be innocent; the more innocent, the better. Killing people who are complicit in the causes that motivate terrorists would never have as much impact as killing those who have nothing to do with them.

This same calculating approach toward victims can be seen in other forms of political evil besides terrorism. Hitler wrote *Mein Kampf* to declare his hatred of the Jews and that the world would be better off without them. Although he was frequently compared to Hitler, Milosevic wrote no comparable book announcing his disgust with the Croats, the Albanians, or the Bosnians. The speeches he gave in Kosovo in his earliest efforts to stir up trouble in the Balkans, as Naimark writes, "were nationalistic but hardly Hitlerian in content. Nor was there any of the nasty racism or exultation of violence that was to characterize the wars of the 1990s." As the Serbian campaign to dominate the region intensified, the rhetoric would become far uglier and camps bearing a depressing similarity to ones established by the Nazis would be built. But as Samantha Power, no friend of the Serbs, points out, "the camps of Bosnia were not extermination camps, though killing was a favorite tool of many of the commanders in charge. Nor could they really be called death camps, though some 10,000 prisoners perished in them. Not every Bosnian Muslim was marked for death as every Jew had been in the Holocaust." Milosevic and his Bosnian Serb allies were barbaric and sadistic in the way they treated their victims. Milosevic, however, was not an ideological fanatic so much as a bureaucratic schemer capable of shifting his political convictions from Marxism to nationalism as conditions changed. His evil cannot be doubted. But neither can the absence of an all-consuming rage accompanying it be ignored. He was at all times working toward an achievable goal.

The role of strategic thinking in political evil even extends to the act of rape. Killing takes life away. Rape can do the same, but even when it does not, it leaves its victims demeaned, tormented, and in many cases facing the equally horrific prospects of either an abortion or the birth of a child conceived out of hate. In cases of genocide and ethnic cleansing in particular, women (and to some extent children) make inviting targets for rapists because political evil so frequently takes place in times of war, when men are off at the front lines doing the fighting. As a result of activism on the part of women's groups primarily in response to the Bosnian horrors, rape is now recognized as central to the experience of contemporary political evil. In June 2008, the United Nations Security Council adopted Resolution 1820, which says that "rape and other forms of sexual violence can constitute a war crime, a crime against humanity, or a constitutive act with respect to genocide."

In the context of political evil, rape, in addition to its horrid emotional and psychological impact, becomes a strategic tool. Sexual aggression does not typically represent some uncontrollable outbreak of fervent passion, or even the physical frustration so often associated with war, but is intentionally carried out to cause humiliation among a people held to be inferior. In the memoirs of many of the survivors of the Soviet gulags, as Applebaum writes, one finds "improbable tales of camp love, some of which began simply out of women's desire for self-protection." But no considerations of sexual attraction on the one hand or racial purity on the other entered into the minds of contemporary practitioners of political evil such as the Janjaweed who ran roughshod in Darfur or the Bosnian Serbs who took such joy in tormenting Muslim women. In comparison to what occurs under radical evil, they killed less but raped more—and more brutally.

Political evil's dual nature creates ongoing confusion since we never quite know whether we are dealing with Strangelovian madmen or Metternichian realists. Yet for all the uncertainty that its dualistic nature induces, political evil has specific features that can be individually analyzed and understood. Treating it as something other than a manifestation of fanaticism enables us to use our reason in confronting it. Appreciating that its strategic character is just as important as its utopian designs prompts us to develop strategies of our own to respond to it. Most important of all, recognizing that evil can have a political character reminds us that politics is, and always will be, the best means of dealing with it. The last thing we should do is compare political evil to forms of evil that lack all those characteristics.

RESPONDING TO REASONS

EVIL IS BY its very nature transgressive; it seeks to break with established morality and custom, to violate the law, and to outdo itself in the havoc it can inflict. However much they differ from each other, Eric Harris, Adolf Hitler, and Osama bin Laden all took unseemly pleasure in the harm they caused others. Politics, by contrast, generally takes place according to custom and is bound by rules. Reducing evil to the level of politics seems to cheapen it. Evildoers deserve their own place in the inferno.

But the truth is that politics and evil are frequently linked. Shakespeare's Richard III, that paradigmatic evildoer, not only was deformed and malevolent but also commanded an army:

> For conscience is a word that cowards use,
> Devised at first to keep the strong in awe.
> Our strong arms be our conscience, swords our law.

> (act 5, scene 3)

So, by the way, did Satan, at least according to Milton; his war council in book 2 of *Paradise Lost* was offered as a commentary on the interminable parliamentary debates of the time. Political leadership magnifies evil, bringing it to our attention in ways ordinary evildoers never quite can.

Especially today—when there are more sovereign nation-states than at any other time in history, when ideas spread so rapidly around the world, and when the market in weaponry has become global—divorcing politics from evil distracts our attention from the reasons we are interested in political evil in the first place. Calling the practitioners of terrorism, ethnic cleansing, and genocide political does not somehow make them less evil than they truly are. Instead, it enables us to focus on how they select their targets, choose their means, acquire their capabilities, and realize their intentions. These are people who kill for a reason. We have to respond to their reasons if we are to deprive them of their rationales and in that way bring their actions under control.

CHAPTER TWO

Widespread Evil Within

EVIL BEGINS AT HOME

ADAM STERLING, director of the Sudan Divestment Task Force, is one of the prominent activists working on behalf of the victims of the mass killings that have recently taken place in the Sudanese region of Darfur. Members of his family escaped the Holocaust, but, as he tells viewers of the film *Darfur Now,* "it always wasn't real for me." A class in college introduced him to the events in Rwanda, another African country that has experienced mass violence—and that class changed his life. "It's mind-blowing," he says. "You learn about what's happened in the past, what happened in Nazi Germany, what happened in Rwanda, and here we've got a chance to make it right." The trouble, he believes, is that people simply are not sufficiently engaged, and as a result the killing in Darfur continues. Hence his verdict: "As we sit here today, we are all complicit in the genocide. Indifference is complicity." The *Oxford English Dictionary* defines "complicity" as "a consenting or partnership with evil." Sterling's charge is a serious one indeed.

The notion that we are all complicit in evil is one of the most common responses to the mass atrocities that have taken place since the end of World War II. To some writers, in fact, Sterling's way of expressing the charge does not go far enough. It is not merely that in standing by we allow terrible things to happen to others. The bigger problem in responding to the horrors of our time, they argue, is that we all have a touch of evil within us. Examples of this way of thinking are numerous. Here are two. Jonathan Glover, a London-based medical ethicist and moral philosopher, contemplating the political catastrophes unleashed in recent times, writes that "we need to look hard and clearly at some monsters inside us." The sad truth, as the American psychologist James Waller puts the same point, is that "ordinary people are capable of committing acts of extraordinary evil." Like charity, evil is said to begin at home.

People are attracted to thinking this way because of its apparent profundity: rather than avoiding responsibility for the bad things that happen in the world, we are forced to be introspective and emphatic by understanding our indifference or even our attraction to evil. I will nonetheless argue here that universalizing political evil in such a way sends us down the wrong path. Asking whether we all have an innate capacity for evil turns our attention from where it truly belongs—on those who because they control levers of political power have the capacity to cause massive suffering and death—and focuses it instead on ordinary people who, however imperfect they may be, are not in the habit of organizing bands of followers to pillage, kill, and rape to advance their vision of how the world ought to work. If anything, significant numbers of people resist as best they can leaders who ask them to cross widely accepted moral lines and even at times come to the aid of those singled out for destruction. If the rich are different from you and me, as F. Scott Fitzgerald famously put it, so are those who engage in political evil.

The idea of widespread evil within did not spring full-blown into the minds of contemporary writers and thinkers. On the contrary, it has a long and fascinating intellectual history. Recounting that history—with all its problematic reasoning, imperfect methodology, and inapplicability to the contemporary world—is a necessary first step in the process of coming to terms effectively with the political evils surrounding us. The lesson that history teaches is straightforward: to combat the evil of others, we must not be so hard on ourselves.

AUGUSTINE'S PEAR TREE

THE IDEA OF widespread evil within began in the fourth century with an African religious seeker who, along with a group of friends, decided to steal some pears. He was not just any troublemaker, one hastens to add, but would go on to become one of the most influential theologians ever produced by the Christian tradition, Saint Augustine of Hippo. The pear tree in question was nothing special, "loaded," as Augustine put it in his *Confessions,* "with fruit that was attractive neither to look at nor to taste." But looking and tasting were not the issue; Augustine and his fellow ruffians wound up feeding the stolen pears to a bunch of pigs. The issue instead was the theft itself. "It was the sin that gave it flavor," said Augustine of the pears. He recognized that as sins go his was not among the most vile. If it were—if, for example, his sin had been one of pride or ambition—it would have possessed "the shadowy, deceptive beauty which makes vice attractive." Because the sin lacked beauty of any sort, even that of a more vicious crime, Augustine concluded that "as it was not the fruit that gave me pleasure, I must have got it from the crime itself, from the thrill of having partners in sin."

Augustine was under no illusion here: he knew that because he had stolen, he had committed evil. Worse, he was attracted to it: "The evil in me was foul, but I loved it. I loved my own perdition and my own faults, not the things for which I committed wrong, but the wrong itself." Thinking back on what had tempted him, he realized that because he "loved evil even if it served no purpose," evil's attraction to him could easily become all-consuming. That he finally overcame it, that he had learned to reflect upon his misconduct with appropriate self-scrutiny, was due entirely to God's power: "I will love you, Lord, and thank you, and praise your name, because you have forgiven me such great sins and such wicked deeds. I acknowledge that it was by your grace and mercy that you melted away my sins like ice."

It was at this point that Augustine's restless mind led him away from just giving thanks to God, which any Christian ought to do, and to ask instead a question that theologians have never ceased posing—and have never conclusively answered. This is known as the problem of theodicy: If God is so powerful, if he is capable of seeing into the evil in our hearts and forgiving us for our sins, and if God is also good, then why did he put evil there in the first place? For Augustine, God is the creator of the world and everything it contains, including himself. Must God then have been the cause of the malevolent deeds that he carried out? "Who made me?" he asks in the *Confessions.* "Surely it was my God, who is not only good but Goodness himself. How, then, do I come to possess a will that can choose to do wrong and refuse to do good, thereby providing a just reason why I should be punished? Who put this will in me? . . . If it was the devil who put it there, who made the devil?"

Anxious for answers, Augustine turned first to the astrologers and, quickly tiring of their irreverence, then to a sect founded by a third-century Persian prophet named Mani, who viewed the world as a constant struggle between the forces of good and those of evil. (Mani's followers were called the Manichees, and his ideas, especially when they took political form, are known as Manichaean; I will have a lot more to say about them in the chapter that follows.) The Manichees, unlike Christians, were dualists, or believers in two different and competing cosmic forces. "So convinced were they that evil could not come from a good God," writes an Augustine biographer, Peter Brown, "that they believed that it came from an invasion of the good—the 'Kingdom of Light'—by a hostile force of evil, equal in power, eternal, totally separate—the 'Kingdom of Darkness.'" Since both kingdoms were present from the very beginning, the evil that Augustine found within himself would have been viewed by the Manichees as not very mysterious at all: the bad God put it there and the good one was helpless to stop it. The existence of evil, the Manichees believed, led to the conclusion that God cannot be perfect and omnipotent simultaneously.

This was not a solution that Augustine, who eventually broke with the Manichees and became their most famous critic, was prepared to accept. As he pondered the questions that consumed him, he realized that he had been searching for the origins of evil in the wrong way—indeed, in an evil way. Instead of beginning with what he had done and asking why God would allow him to do such things, he needed to begin with the existence of God and from that think about why he had gotten such pleasure out of his disobedience. Once he did that, he came to understand that because evil is bad and God is good, evil itself has no real substance. (So much for the Manichees.) Evil is nothing, literally nothing; one can search the world for it forever and never find it. Augustine's metaphysics owed a considerable debt to Plato, who spoke of forms of justice or goodness or beauty that the philosophers know exist but that the rest of us can never fully grasp because the world in which we live makes available to us only the shadows of such forms and never the forms themselves. This is exactly what evil is *not* like. It has no perfect form, no essence, no quality of what later philosophers would call a thing-in-itself.

Augustine also argued that a potential for evil—even though not out there—very much lies within human beings themselves. He reasoned that God could have made us perfect creatures; being perfect himself, it would seem natural for God to have chosen to do so. This is precisely what God at first did do—before the Fall. But God realized that if human beings were perfect in everything they did, their worship of him would follow automatically from their pure hearts and in that sense would be too unreflective, too lacking in reason, for a God who was truly great. So God instead created rational beings who were exposed to choices and had to think carefully about which ones they should make. Alas for the human race, the first choice, the original choice, was made by Adam in the Garden of Eden and proved to be one that violated God's commands. We human beings have been imperfect, stained by sin, ever since. The conclusion, once Augustine came to it, seemed obvious: when he created the world, God did not create evil; he created us, and we chose evil instead.

Evil, it follows, is located in our hearts—or, as Augustine put it, our will. As the Cambridge University historian Gillian Evans explains Augustine's views, evil "arises in the will of rational creatures and makes itself felt by clouding their reason and making it impossible for them to think clearly or to see the truth." This is why Augustine's first efforts to explain evil were themselves evil; anything that takes us down a false path, that leads us away from the recognition of God's goodness, represents the wrong use of our reason. Evil occurs when we fall victim to our desires or our appetites: God created the pears that Augustine stole, but he did not create the desire on Augustine's part to steal them. Augustine cannot find any explanation of why he stole them because his act was so trivial as to defy explanation. This is precisely what makes evil so insidious: our will is most evil when we act with no sense of purpose, when we desire something for itself and not for any end it might serve. Evil is therefore more like a propensity than an action. As the theologian Charles Mathewes puts it, "Evil action is a kind of action which fails, in an important way, to be action at all: it is ultimately folly—irrational, inexplicable, as much a causal hiccup as a willed, intentional act."

Locating evil in the flawed will of rational human beings posed a difficult problem for Augustine. If evil is the product of our flawed will, and if we are rational creatures, why can't we use our reason to rid ourselves of the evil within us? This was the question raised by an important thinker of Augustine's era, the monk known as Pelagius, whose *Commentary on the Epistles of St. Paul* is most likely the oldest surviving work written by a British author. (Saint Jerome, the scholar and translator, said that Pelagius was stuffed with porridge; porridge was found in Britain; ergo . . .) Like Augustine, Pelagius was attracted to the idea that evil lacked any real substance. But for that very reason, he believed, rational creatures have the capacity to keep it at bay or even to triumph over it. Pelagius rejected the idea of original sin and the entire apparatus Christians had erected against the human tendency toward wickedness. To be sure, Adam and Eve had sinned in the Garden of Eden, Pelagius reasoned, but that does not mean that their sin will be visited on every subsequent generation. God created human beings with the potential to achieve perfection, and reach it they are capable of doing. Like the Manichees, Pelagius viewed good and evil as engaged in a contest for supremacy. But for Pelagius the struggle between these forces takes place not in the outer world but within ourselves. When good wins, it is because human beings have willed it to win. We have inclinations to be evil, but they are not inherent. Evil is not a stain; it is a flaw. And God gave human beings the power to correct their flaws.

When Augustine came into contact with the ideas of Pelagius, he quickly realized that if they were followed to their logical conclusion, human beings would have little or no reason to call upon God's assistance to overcome their weaknesses. His reaction was to paint an even more dire picture of the ascendancy of evil in the will of human beings than he had provided in his earlier writings. No longer did Augustine view the will as torn between a longing to do good and an inclination to do evil. Now he committed himself to a strict form of predestination; as Evans summarizes Augustine's post-Pelagian views, "Adam's sin so flawed the very nature of man, that the free will God gave him is no longer in balance; man can no longer turn his will Godwards, and allow God to enable him to do good; he can only turn his will away from God, towards nothing, and thus he can only do evil. Only when God intervenes directly and compels the will of man can man do good."

Three problematic conclusions, all relevant to the way we think about political evil today, follow from Augustine's theology. One is that evil will always be the default position. From an Augustinian perspective, it is impossible to imagine the relationship between good and evil as what statisticians call a bell-shaped curve, with one extreme including those who are good and the other those who are evil and with everyone else, the major portion of the curve, neutral between them. Evil instead is everything that is not actively good; it includes the entire curve save for a slight if not imperceptible tail at one end containing those who give themselves over to God. It follows that the most dangerous are not those who know full well how evil they are but rather those who mistakenly believe themselves in the middle. "What is reprehensible," Augustine once wrote, "is that while leading good lives themselves and abhorring those of wicked men, some, fearing to offend, shut their eyes to evil deeds instead of condemning them and pointing out their malice." Indifference to evil, for Augustine, really is complicity in it.

Second, Augustine was the first of many thinkers to psychologize evil. The *Confessions* is a remarkable book because Augustine, unusually for his time and place, wrote about himself. Stealing the pears was the least of it; readers of Augustine are given a frank account of his sexual attractions, glimpses into the torments he experienced as he struggled with his worldly ambition, accounts of friends being seduced by the bloodlust of violent games, and treatments of his ambivalence toward such sensual pleasures as music and food. So personal is the tone of the *Confessions* that even God comes across not as a distant and awesome power but as a conversation partner Augustine addresses as if he were in the room beside him. Conventional wisdom correctly holds that Augustine invented autobiography.

Given these inward predilections, it is no wonder that Augustine, at least in his *Confessions*, treats evil as a private matter rather than a public or political one. As he put it in *On True Religion*, "Vice in the soul arises from its own doing; and the moral difficulty that ensues from vice is the penalty which it suffers." In thinking about the problem of evil, the last place to turn is to actual political events in the real world, such as the pain and violence rulers inflict on their own people or their ambition to occupy by force the territories they covet. Politics is one of those very this-worldly activities that seduce us into false thinking. One can read Augustine's autobiography from beginning to end and not have a clue that in the years immediately preceding its publication the Roman Empire had established Christianity as the official religion of the state, the Visigoths had increased their attacks on the Roman Empire, and the center of political gravity within the empire had begun its shift to Constantinople. The *Confessions* focuses so much on the trials and tribulations of one man, and a somewhat provincial one from North Africa at that, that it ignores what is happening to the great majority of people in the empire into which he was born.

The same is not true of *The City of God*, Augustine's other great treatise, which was inspired by Alaric's sacking of Rome in A.D. 410. But this work illustrates the third unfortunate legacy of Augustine's treatment of the problem of evil: an unwillingness to make sharp distinctions between those who perpetrate it and those who find themselves victimized by it.

Parts of *The City of God* are remarkably compassionate in their sensibility. For example, Augustine asked whether those Roman women who had been raped by the barbarian invaders had sinned—and concluded that they had not. Chastity, he argued, was a state of mind, not a physical condition. When violent rape takes place, the evil lies with the rapist and not with the victim: "As long as the will remains unyielding, no crime, beyond the victim's power to prevent it without sin, and which is perpetrated on the body or in the body, lays any guilt on the soul." Augustine's reasoning does not conclude that women, following in the footsteps of Eve, are so seductive that they share responsibility for the evil of rape with those who attack them. It is strikingly more modern than a Taliban-like shunning or even stoning of rape victims for bringing dishonor upon themselves and their families. In Augustine's treatment of rape under conditions of occupation, one finds neither accusations of harlotry nor finger-pointing condemnations: "If to be the unwilling victim of violent rape is no unchastity, the punishing of a chaste woman is not justice."

Augustine's generosity toward victims of rape stands out because there is so little compassion in his attitudes toward all the other Romans victimized by the sack of their city. Knowing full well that his God was the only true God, Augustine had nothing but contempt for those Romans still attracted to their many—and, from his perspective, all-too-often ridiculous—gods. (If they have gods and goddesses for such daily pleasures as hunting and wine, Augustine sarcastically pointed out, their conception of the deity could never become truly magisterial.) Sounding a bit too much like Jerry Falwell for contemporary ears, Augustine admonishes the Romans for their hedonism. "Depraved by prosperity and unchastened by adversity," he tells them, "you declare, in your security, not the peace of the state but liberty for license. . . . Though crushed by the enemy, you put no check on immorality, you learned no lessons from calamity; in the depths of sorrows you still wallow in sin." Today we would call this blaming the victim. The responsibility for what happened to the Romans, Augustine is arguing, lay within themselves. God gave them a choice, they ignored him, and they therefore deserved their fate. This is a truly black-and-white view of the problem of evil; as even some of his contemporaries observed, Augustine's break with the Manichees was never as complete as his vehement debates with them would suggest.

Despite the role the sack of Rome had in inspiring Augustine to write his treatise, it plays little part in his analysis. On Rome versus the barbarians, Augustine is decidedly neutral. "When it is considered how short is the span of human life, does it really matter to a man whose days are numbered what government he must obey?" he asked. "So far as I can see, it makes no difference at all to political security or to public order to maintain the purely human distinction between conquerors and conquered people." Both the Romans and their enemies belonged to the secular City of Man rather than the heavenly City of God, and while in the former we go about taking care of our daily lives, in the latter "there reigns that true and perfect happiness which is not a goddess, but a gift of God—toward whose beauty we can but sigh in our pilgrimage on earth." Compared to the perfections of the City of God, the evils found in the City of Man are inconsequential. It is true that Rome experienced its share of sacking and pillaging—and that the innocent suffered along with the guilty. But such is God's way. Had God punished only the guilty, people would be tempted to seek his mercy for the purely instrumental reason of saving their own lives. The granting of God's grace should have nothing to do with such earthly matters. The only city that matters is the one that beckons in a future world.

Augustine lived at a time when even seemingly recondite theological questions were addressed as if the fate of the world hung on the correct answers. And if historical longevity is the appropriate measure of insight, his answers were the right ones because many of his opponents' have long been forgotten. Despite Augustine's great skills as a thinker and polemicist, however, his treatment of the problem of evil, as widely read as it still is, remains too strict for all but the most sin obsessed of contemporary theologians. For modern people confronting the problem of political evil, Augustine has everything backward: if we take his theology seriously, the horrors taking place in Bosnia or Rwanda provide the ring in which we wrestle with our own demons. This may be a perfectly appropriate way of thinking about the problem of evil if one believes that it has no substance. But if we believe that there really is such a thing as political evil, and that it is caused by identifiable tyrants and zealous warriors who choose the most horrific means available to them to pursue their goals, we must possess a greater confidence in our ability to distinguish ourselves from evildoers than he allows.

Nor is Augustine's understanding of the will especially helpful in dealing with political evil in the contemporary world. Augustine believed that while God created us to be rational creatures, we are at the same time slaves of our will. If our will is inherently corrupt, something to be distrusted irrespective of what it seeks, our very efforts to reduce or eliminate political evil in the world are not only hopeless—we cannot abolish what does not exist—but extensions of our pride and ambition; the very conviction that we ought to do something about political evil is a manifestation of the evil to which our wills are prone. All of Augustine's paths lead back to God. But once people develop the conviction that they have it within their power to make the world less evil, they will have little choice but to rely on the very will that Augustine so distrusted. In the modern world failures of will cause more political evil than flaws of the will. When dealing with the problem of political evil, it matters little whether we are bad people stained with sin or good people who will always do right. What matters is that leaders somewhere else in the world are literally getting away with murder.

EICHMANN REVISITED

SEARCHING FOR A suitable topic for her doctoral dissertation at the University of Heidelberg in the 1920s, the twenty-year-old German-Jewish scholar Hannah Arendt might have chosen to write about Kant, Hegel, or any one of a number of pathbreaking European philosophers. Instead, she decided to devote her dissertation to Augustine. Augustine and his era, in fact, were very much on the minds of German-Jewish philosophers in the first decades of the twentieth century. Arendt's friend and later colleague at the New School for Social Research in New York, Hans Jonas, wrote his first book on Augustine and showed a lifelong interest in both the Pelagians and the Gnostics, who, like the Manichees, were strongly dualistic in their spiritual outlook. Clearly something in the life, times, and ideas of this austere theologian attracted thinkers living through the turmoil that was Germany in the years following the catastrophe known as World War I.

Arendt's debt to Augustine over the course of her intellectual life proved to be enormous. Her posthumously published magnum opus, *The Life of the Mind,* is divided into three parts—"Thinking," "Willing," and "Judging"—and the second of these, as one might expect from the importance Augustine attached to the will, devotes a chapter to the

Bishop of Hippo. In *The Human Condition,* Arendt spoke of "natality," which she defined not only as our biological birth but as our ongoing capacity to experience the world anew; the process of self-creation as she describes it overlaps with Augustine's focus on God as the creator of the world we inhabit. Although Arendt was not always consistent in how she used the term "social," her search for ways in which human beings can act together began with her discussion of *caritas,* or the love of God, and through him of one's neighbors, which Augustine had compared unfavorably to *cupiditas,* or the love of worldly things. When she searched for models of how people could engage in authentic politics, in conduct enabling them to lead a genuinely active life, she turned to the Greek city-state, or polis, as her ideal, thereby relying upon a secular, indeed pre-Christian, version of Augustine's City of God standing in sharp contrast to the daily chores—what Arendt once called the drudgery of labor as opposed to the creativity associated with work—taking place in the City of Man. Arendt's dissertation was thoroughly apolitical and in that sense quite different from the ideas that engaged her after the Nazis took power in her homeland. But there is nonetheless a clear link between many of her mature ideas and her youthful inquiries.

Of all the many subjects treated by Arendt, the one that owed most to Augustine was the same one that transformed her from an obscure academic into a worldwide intellectual celebrity: the problem of evil. In 1961, *The New Yorker* asked Arendt to cover the trial of Adolf Eichmann, a key official in the Nazi effort to round up and exterminate the Jews, who had been captured in Argentina and brought back to Israel to be tried for crimes against humanity. Her articles and subsequent book *Eichmann in Jerusalem* promulgated the single most intense intellectual controversy of the twentieth century. The Israelis, and in particular the chief prosecutor at the trial, attorney general Gideon Hausner, had portrayed Eichmann as a monster and a sadist. Something in Arendt reacted against the whole idea. "Eichmann was not Iago and not Macbeth," she wrote in a postscript responding to the controversies she had stirred up, "and nothing would have been farther from his mind than to determine with Richard III 'to prove a villain.'" Arendt wanted to treat Eichmann as the ordinary human being she believed him to be. "The trouble with Eichmann was precisely that so many were like him, and that the many were neither perverted nor sadistic, that they were, and still are, terribly and terrifyingly normal."

To make her case, Arendt found Augustine's arguments about the nature of evil, with which she had wrestled in her dissertation, indispensable. Eichmann, needless to say, killed Jews rather than stole pears. But for this very reason Arendt's decision to portray Eichmann as normal proved so troubling to her critics. One of Arendt's strongest defenders, the philosopher Richard Bernstein, argues that Arendt's "portrayal of Eichmann is much more damning than simply characterizing him as some sort of demonic monster." His reason for thinking so reiterates the conviction of those activists and writers who hold to the thesis of widespread evil within. "Totalitarianism, whose legacy still haunts us," Bernstein writes, "shows that very ordinary people motivated by the most mundane, banal considerations can commit horrendous crimes." In adopting the Augustinian aspects of Arendt's analysis, Bernstein ignores the downside of her approach: by paying more attention to the criminal than to the crime, she never gave her readers a full account of what in fact made Eichmann's actions so horrendous. Arendt certainly does not equate what Eichmann did with pear stealing. But while she calls Eichmann "a new type of criminal" who "commits his crimes under circumstances that make it well-nigh impossible for him to know or to feel that he is doing wrong," her portrayal is one of a deeply flawed human being whom Augustine—or, for that matter, any serious Christian—would immediately recognize as fallen.

Rather than emphasizing what Eichmann did, Arendt spent too much time analyzing who he was. Like Augustine, she psychologized evil; no one, not even Arendt, could ever claim that the acts Eichmann carried out were "banal," even if she was determined to show that the man himself was. Eichmann never wrote his own *Confessions,* but Arendt, in a sense, wrote them for him; the whole idea that Eichmann could have a biography—that he was born in Solingen, famous for its scissors; that in his early years he led "a humdrum life without significance and consequence"; that he finally achieved his potential as a governmental bureaucrat—appeared to Arendt's critics as an absurd digression, a displacing of the public and political evils committed by Eichmann onto his personal and private life. The man was on trial for the deaths he caused, not the life he led.

Along similar lines, Arendt shared the inclination of Augustine in *The City of God* to place the evils taking place in the political world in the background and the internal tribulations of evildoers in the foreground. This was not true of *The Origins of Totalitarianism;* in that book, Arendt paid considerable attention to the organization and structure of the concentration camps in both Nazi Germany and the Soviet Union, the development of the leadership principle that made it possible for totalitarian states to transform themselves into dictatorships, and the crucial importance of ideology and propaganda in convincing the masses to obey their leaders. In *Eichmann,* by contrast, Arendt treated the death camps and the Final Solution not as ends but as means to understand how individual Nazis thought about themselves and their acts. We learn how Eichmann conceptualized what it meant to be law-abiding and how he conceived of his duty; indeed, we are even told that "it was not his fanaticism but his very conscience that prompted Eichmann to adopt his uncompromising attitude during the last year of the war," as if Eichmann, like every other normal person, had a conscience to begin with. Arendt finally did conclude that Eichmann was evil. But by calling his evil "banal," she once again developed a variation on her Augustinian theme: Eichmann's evil lay not in his active political decision to commit horrendous crimes but in his passive refusal to stand out from the crowd and do good. He was right there in the middle of the Nazi bell curve, more evil by indirection than by intention.

Nor does *Eichmann in Jerusalem* escape the Augustinian temptation on display in *The City of God* to blame the victims for the evils heaped upon them. Arendt's decision to analyze Eichmann psychologically was controversial enough, but for many critics it paled in contrast to her brutal portrayal of the Jewish councils, organizations used by the Nazis to recruit Jewish leaders to help them in their campaign of extermination. The term "complicity" rarely appears in Arendt's discussion of the role Jews played in causing death to their own people, and when it does, it is accompanied by the adjective "involuntary." But the word "cooperation" does, and on many occasions. The most famous usage was this one: "Wherever Jews lived, there were recognized Jewish leaders, and this leadership, almost without exception, cooperated in one way or another, for one reason or another, with the Nazis." Such unbending language did not help Arendt's cause, and neither did her charge in the very next sentence that "if the Jewish people had really been unorganized and leaderless, there would have been chaos and plenty of misery but the total number of victims would hardly have been between four and a half and six million people." This was blaming the victim with a vengeance.

Arendt's fascination with the Jewish councils, like her preoccupation with the problem of evil, reflected long-standing philosophical and moral interests; she viewed councils in general as opportunities for genuine politics and was shocked to see the Jewish ones used for such blatantly immoral ends. For Arendt such phenomena as bureaucracy, leadership struggles, position papers, and the formulation of public policies were corruptions of politics and not those forms of deliberation and decision making associated with the ancient philosophers. Inspired by an ideal vision of what politics ought to be that left little room for imperfect if not tragic choices and less than ideal solutions, she was unable to focus on the actual dilemmas facing the leaders of the Jewish councils. Arendt's loftiness, however inspiring in other contexts, seems completely out of place in a discussion of Eichmann's life and times; the leaders of the Jewish councils were too busy trying to deal with unprecedented evil to ponder Aristotelian conceptions of the polis.

Such moral perfectionism led Arendt to harsh judgmentalism. As a secular Jew, Arendt was no believer in original sin, but her condemnation of the Jewish councils comes as close as one can imagine to Augustine's equally harsh judgment that the hedonism of the Romans helped bring about the sack of their city. As with the thinker who so preoccupied her, Arendt's treatment of the victims of evil is demonstrably lacking in compassion: she nowhere manifests in *Eichmann* the compassion toward them that Augustine showed to the Roman women victimized by rape. "To a Jew," she wrote, "this role of the Jewish leaders in the destruction of their own people is undoubtedly the darkest chapter of the whole dark story." But why should that particular aspect of what took place in Germany under Hitler assume such importance? Surely the decision to exterminate the Jews in the first place was far darker than anything done by Jewish leaders in response.

Arendt's reply to her many critics was to assert that her only interest in the Eichmann affair was to further the cause of justice. From her perspective, "the German people in general, or anti-Semitism in all its forms, or the whole of modern history, or the nature of man and original sin" were not on trial in that courtroom in Jerusalem; only

Adolf Eichmann was. Unlike Gideon Hausner, she was determined not to treat Eichmann as a symbol of something far larger than himself, even if this seemed to put her on the side of Eichmann and his lawyers, who had argued that Eichmann was a mere "cog" in a vast machine and therefore not engaged in criminal acts. There are people in the world, Arendt claimed, "who will not rest until they have discovered an 'Eichmann in every one of us.'" She insisted that she was not one of them: "I need scarcely say that I would never have gone to Jerusalem if I had shared these views."

Of all the claims made by Arendt in her book, I find this one especially disingenuous. Of course she was treating Eichmann as something far larger than the man himself; it is no discredit to Arendt to claim that she had a story to tell—and that she spent much of her intellectual life telling it. "Eichmann," as the British theologian David Grumett writes, "is not a revelation for Arendt but an opportunity for her to test and develop a concept she already possesses." If for Hausner Eichmann was a symbol of Nazi hatred of the Jews, for Arendt he was symbolic of what can happen when individuals fail to live up to the high standards for thinking, judging, and willing she believed human beings capable of. In *Eichmann in Jerusalem*, Arendt found a case—as dramatic a case as one can find—of someone who was trapped in a world of bureaucratic conformity and hence unable to develop his own intellectual capacities. Eichmann's evil was banal because everyday life is banal; that his evil produced such dramatic results was incidental, not fundamental. Arendt seemed determined to normalize the evil of the Holocaust, much as Augustine normalized evil in general. It is impossible to accept that such an approach reflects only an interest in the narrower questions of justice raised by the trial of one man. Arendt was always a generalizer, a thinker who moved from concrete cases to dramatic conclusions about the human condition, and her reflections on Eichmann's trial had the same intent.

Because of her remarks about the Jewish councils, Arendt's book aroused a furious reaction among Jewish commentators. "Self-Hating Jewess Writes Pro-Eichmann Series for New Yorker Magazine," screamed the headline of the *International Jewish News*. "In place of the monstrous Nazi," wrote Norman Podhoretz in *Commentary*, "she gives us the 'banal' Nazi; in place of the Jew as virtuous martyr, she gives us the Jew as accomplice in evil; and in place of the confrontation between guilt and innocence, she gives us the 'collaboration' of criminal and victim.'" Hausner traveled from Israel to New York to rebut Arendt's arguments. Even Arendt's friends reacted negatively to the book. Gershom Scholem called her "flippant" and "malicious" and claimed that she had no love for the Jewish people. Hans Jonas refused to speak to her, and when they reestablished contact some time later, they agreed never to discuss what she had written about Eichmann. Hannah Arendt's life—and American Jewish life—would never be the same.

Yet if *Eichmann in Jerusalem* was not well received by Jewish critics, Christians, perhaps recognizing her debt to Augustine, were more forgiving. Because of her own lack of deep religious convictions, Arendt can never be entirely satisfying to a devout Christian; she writes about such topics as original sin and eternal judgment without speaking of Jesus Christ. Yet there is no denying that the themes she explored in *Eichmann in Jerusalem* were not only theological in nature but were more in accord with Christian theology than with any other faith— one reason why her books are taught at a number of evangelical colleges and her ideas discussed by prominent Christian scholars. One thinker in particular who recognizes his debt to Arendt is James Waller, the psychologist who insists that ordinary people are capable of committing acts of extraordinary evil. (Waller was the director of a seminar called "Deliver Us from Evil: Genocide and the Christian World," held at Calvin College, a conservative Protestant institution, in the summer of 2009.) In his book *Becoming Evil,* Waller writes that "Arendt, correctly in my view, reminds us that perpetrators of extraordinary evil are not that fundamentally different from you and me. She suggests that the commission of extraordinary evil transcends groups, ideology, psychopathology, and personality." Arendt may not have thought she was arguing for the existence of an Eichmann inside of everyone, but this is exactly the message that many contemporary Christians, searching for examples of the evil that can lurk in the heart of man, found in her book. Like no other twentieth-century writer, Arendt took the idea of original sin and made it part of our everyday vocabulary. Only now, we—Christians and non-Christians alike—refer to it as the "banality of evil."

The twentieth-century Jewish author Harry Golden was close to an exact contemporary of Arendt; he was born in 1902, four years before her, and he died in 1981, six years after her. As down-to-earth and humorous as Arendt was high-minded and serious, Golden, who lived much of his life in Charlotte, founded and edited *The Carolina Israelite.* (Golden also traveled to Jerusalem to cover the Eichmann trial, in his case for *Life,* and although he too thought Eichmann "a bland and colorless little functionary," he later became one of the critics who called Arendt a self-hating Jew.) Golden's columns, the best of which were collected in *Only in America,* his best-selling 1958 book, spoke of the miracles of Jewish success in the New World: handsome Jewish policemen; a Methodist housewife winning a North Carolina cooking contest with chopped liver and schmaltz; or the fact that the lyricist Irving Caesar and the composer George Gershwin created a hymn to the American South with "Swanee." Despite Golden's hostility toward Arendt, even he should have recognized that the reception given to her book constituted an only-in-America moment. Here was a secular Jewish member of the German academic elite writing a best-selling American book first published in a glossy magazine about the situation facing European Jews whose lessons would reinforce the core convictions of American Christians. Only in America indeed.

PSYCHOLOGIZING EVIL

If we are to psychologize evil, the task may best be left to psychologists. Stanley Milgram, the American social psychologist who lived from 1933 until 1984, fit the role perfectly. Milgram's experiments, which featured white-cloaked authority figures urging naïve subjects to administer fake electric shocks to ordinary people despite the latter's screams of protest and pain, are by now the most famous psychological experiments ever conducted. So many people complied, and often with so little remorse, that Milgram concluded in *Obedience to Authority,* his reflections on his experiment and its meaning, that "human nature, or—more specifically—the kind of character produced in American democratic society, cannot be counted on to insulate its citizens from brutality and inhumane treatment at the direction of malevolent authority." Not very many psychologists have had their last names transformed into an adjective, but Milgram—as a Google search for "Milgramesque" will quickly attest—is one. Nor do many get to be played by William Shatner and Yves Montand in two different films, have a rock star such as Peter Gabriel record a song based on their findings, or witness the publication of a dog-training manual derived from their experiments.

Milgram came up with the ideas driving his research in 1960, before Arendt's *New Yorker* essays were published. Yet the very summer in which he settled on his topic coincided with the abduction of Eichmann from Argentina by Israeli agents, and, as Milgram's biographer has noted, "it's certainly possible that this was the event that crystallized the obedience research in Milgram's mind." Whatever the original motive for his research, Milgram left no doubt about his debt to Arendt—and, through her, to Augustine. "A commonly offered explanation is that those who shocked the victims at the most severe level were monsters, the sadistic fringe of society," Milgram wrote, as if Augustine's *Confessions* was sitting beside him. But, he continued, "if one considers that almost two-thirds of the participants fall into the category of 'obedient' subjects, and that they represented ordinary people drawn from working, managerial, and professional classes, the argument becomes very shaky." Milgram then discussed the vendetta against *Eichmann in Jerusalem* before adding his own view: "After witnessing hundreds of ordinary people submit to the authority in our own experiments, I must conclude that Arendt's conception of the *banality of evil* comes closer to the truth than one might dare imagine."

Milgram's experiments were conducted while he was teaching at Yale. Psychology, his academic discipline, was at the time of his research completing its transformation from a humanistic to a scientific enterprise. The presumed experts ordering the shocks, when questioned by increasingly concerned subjects, spoke about how the experiment required that they continue. Augustine had been a theologian, and Arendt a political philosopher; however controversial their conclusions, neither could claim the authority of science to buttress them. Milgram, though, could—and did. *Obedience to Authority* is replete with formal models of human behavior, some expressed mathematically; technical jargon, including terms like "agentic shift," which refers to the process by which a person comes to view himself as carrying out the wishes of another; references to what at the time were cutting-edge disciplines, such as cybernetics; and statistical presentations of results. When Milgram concluded that 65 percent of us had evil in our hearts, he was likely to be treated not as having engaged in metaphysical speculation but as having discovered real-world facts. His bell curve of evil was a real bell curve.

Despite his pretensions to science, Milgram's work generated more controversies than it resolved. A major share of the criticism directed against him focused not on what he discovered but on how he discovered it: ironically for a student of human wickedness, Milgram was charged with relying upon unethical practices in his experiments. Subjects who responded to an ad, for example, drew straws when they first came into the laboratory to determine who would administer the shocks and who would receive them, but the drawing of the straws was fixed so that the subjects always wound up sitting at the controls. Although the subjects themselves frequently made clear their unease with what they were being asked to do, they were instructed to continue doing it, a way of conducting research that would never get past contemporary concerns with protecting human subjects from abuse. In many ways, the true victims of Milgram's experiment were those who were being asked to victimize others; the people receiving the shocks would always come out unharmed, which was not necessarily true of those applying the voltage. In today's cultural environment, Milgram would be guilty of professional malpractice.

Criticism did not stop with ethical issues; scholars in the field also offered substantial critiques of Milgram's methodology. No matter how ingeniously designed and well carried out, Milgram's experiments contained a built-in fatal flaw. It was crucial for Milgram to simulate reality in such a way that his subjects really did believe they were causing severe pain to those whose screams they could easily hear; without such audible evidence of anguish, subjects could not be certain that their actions were harmful, let alone evil. Yet Milgram could not risk allowing the experiment to come to an end, which would likely happen once a person administering the shocks was persuaded that real harm was being done. Faced with this dilemma, Milgram modified the seeming cruelty of the situation. "The shocks may be painful but they are not harmful," a subject named Gretchen was told by the authority figure asking her to increase their intensity, while another (unnamed) subject was told after he protested that "there is no permanent tissue damage." (Despite the disclaimers, both Gretchen and the other subject terminated their participation.) Much the same thing happened when Milgram, seeking to raise the tension, had the victim—or, as Milgram calls him, the "learner"—scream out that he was suffering from a heart problem. "I did not wish to make the 'heart problem' so serious," Milgram later wrote, "that it would disqualify the learner from participation but merely to raise a suggestion of a problem." Because Milgram's subjects were being simultaneously instructed to inflict cruelty and reassured that their actions were not cruel at all, his experiment does not tell us anything about man's capacity for evil however much they say about his willingness to be obedient; other psychologists concluded that Milgram's subjects were able to divine fairly quickly that they were not really harming anyone and, anxious to advance the cause of science, simply gave the experimenter what he was asking for. It was not the power of authority to compel obedience that Milgram had demonstrated but the desire of people to be considered cooperative.

Milgram's interpretation of his findings was also open to question. Intent on demonstrating how readily people follow orders, he paid relatively little attention to those who refused to go along—by his own count slightly more than one-third of all the subjects. When he did discuss them, moreover, especially when he was confronted with a case of determined resistance, he flat out refused to modify his conclusions. In one particularly telling example, a professor at a prominent East Coast divinity school is asked to administer the shocks. (To protect his subjects, Milgram never provided their real names; in this case, the subject was Brevard Childs, an internationally prominent Old Testament scholar at Yale and the holder of its most distinguished endowed professorship.) Soon after starting, Childs protests. When told that he must continue, that no permanent damage is being done, and that in any case he has no choice, he responds by saying, "If this were Russia, maybe, but not in America." He then raises questions about the ethics of the whole procedure, pointing out that the person being shocked says he does not want to go on and demanding that his wishes be respected. When the man who had ordered Childs to inflict the punishment realizes that Childs is determined not to continue, he stops the experiment and tells him that it was designed to teach us about resistance to authority, at which point the professor says that he gets his authority from God. To any reasonable observer, Childs's refusal to be ordered to commit presumably cruel acts is testimony to a deeply etched moral integrity derived from his faith and his equally strong adherence to principles of social justice. But not to Milgram. Professor Childs, he concludes, was not resisting authority at all but transferring authority from himself first to the victim and then to God. He therefore was as obedient as all the other subjects.

Like Arendt, who could so often be haughty in her judgment of others, Milgram treated the people he studied, once he became convinced they lacked the will to resist authority, with naked contempt. Although a woman he calls Elinor Rosenblum, described as a housewife, protests all along at shocking people, she nonetheless conforms and finally administers the highest level of shock to the victim—three times, no less. Milgram is appalled at the contrast between her self-image as a moral and caring person and her willingness to pull the switch. He finds her narcissistic, hysterical, conventional, and—this is the early 1960s—excessively feminine. Why did she fail to resist authority? "Mrs. Rosenblum is a person whose psychic life lacks integration. She has not been able to find life purposes consistent with her needs for esteem and success. Her goals, thinking, and emotions are fragmented." Poor Mrs. Rosenblum: believing she had volunteered for a psychological experiment, she found herself being psychoanalyzed. Sitting in his seat of judgment, Milgram looked down with disdain on ordinary people. In his version of the heavenly city that awaits us, science rather than God rules, and we all act out of principle rather than conform to arbitrary authority.

Arrogant toward others, Milgram was also arrogant in the claims he made for his research. As the fate of his experiments became increasingly intertwined with the fate of Adolf Eichmann, Milgram became more and more convinced that he had unlocked the secret of the Holocaust: the Nazis were evil because we all have a capacity for evil. The distinguished psychologist Gordon Allport had called Milgram's study "the Eichmann experiment." Milgram did not disagree; he just wanted readers to appreciate how truly significant a claim this was: "The 'Eichmann experiment' is, perhaps, an apt term, but it should not lead us to mistake the import of this investigation. To focus only on the Nazis, however despicable their deeds, and to view only highly publicized atrocities as being relevant to these studies is to miss the point entirely. For the studies are principally concerned with the ordinary and routine destruction carried out by everyday people following orders." This is Milgram at his most Augustinian: since obedience to authority is built into the human condition, any one of us could be a Nazi if given the opportunity. In a (never published) draft for a German translation of his book, Milgram wrote: "It is fitting that this book be translated into German, since it has a special relevance to the Germans. Obedience is, after all, their favorite alibi." But then he went on to broaden the charge to include everyone else: "My guess is, after conducting the experiments reported in this book, that if the same institutions arose in the United States—the concentration camps, the gas chambers—there would be no problem finding Americans to operate them." Milgram was not about to allow the structural differences between a totalitarian dictatorship and a liberal democracy to interfere with his predetermined conclusion that both are inhabited by people weak in will.

The Milgram experiment has become a permanent feature of American lore, trotted out anytime the problem of evil comes up for discussion. Pennsylvania State University has developed *Great Minds of the Twentieth Century: Stanley Milgram,* a DVD featuring clips illustrating his experiment, along with materials from the subsequent work Milgram conducted that led to the play and film *Six Degrees of Separation.* A number of high schools throughout the United States have created materials and lesson plans to teach about the Holocaust that highlight the experiment and the conclusions we presumably should learn from it. Psychologists have replicated the experiment in more recent times (after modifying it to downplay potential cruelty to the subjects) and come to the same conclusion Milgram reached. Each time they do, the media invariably pick up the story, as Adam Cohen of *The New York Times* did in 2008, reflecting, once again, on what Milgram has to teach us about preventing future holocausts. The findings of these kinds of experiments, Cohen concluded, "should be part of the basic training for soldiers, police officers, jailers and anyone else whose position gives them the power to inflict abuse on others." No matter how flawed Milgram's work and no matter how unsupported his conclusions, the notion that ordinary people are quite capable of inflicting terrible harm on innocent others when pressured to do so by respected people in authority has become so widely accepted that nothing is ever likely to shake it. We are, or so we are told, all part of genocide now.

AFTER MILGRAM

As a teenager, Stanley Milgram attended James Monroe High School in the Bronx, where for the yearbook he wrote two-line couplets below the photographs of the members of the graduating class. About one of the most popular of his classmates Milgram had this to say:

> Phil's our vice president, tall and thin,
> With his blue eyes all the girls he'll win.

"Phil" would go on to conduct the second most famous social psychological experiment of recent years; his last name was Zimbardo, and his Stanford Prison Experiment would also be featured in films and on television and would be discussed in one of Malcolm Gladwell's best sellers, *The Tipping Point*.

Zimbardo's idea was to place student subjects into the roles of prisoners and guards in a simulated penitentiary environment. As they played out their roles, the subjects went through remarkable transformations. Strong and self-directed individuals in the role of prisoners became weak and obedient. Pacifist types chosen as guards became violence-oriented bullies. For Zimbardo, the conclusion was self-evident: when good dispositions meet bad situations, the latter win. Whereas Milgram found that people who thought they were good could easily succumb to the commands of authority, Zimbardo concluded that oppressive institutional settings can change human behavior for the worse. "The line between Good and Evil," as he wrote, "once thought to be impermeable, proved instead to be quite permeable."

Although planned a decade later than Milgram's experiments, Zimbardo's work was also carried out in the shadow of Arendt's *Eichmann in Jerusalem*. Zimbardo does not share the Augustinianism so prominent in both Arendt and Milgram; in his view evil does not lie within but is caused by the social roles people adopt. Eichmann, or so he mistakenly interpreted Arendt to be arguing, represented a near-perfect case of this process, and for this reason he concluded that Arendt's book has become "a classic of our times." Not only does the prison experiment teach us about what Eichmann did then, Zimbardo wrote, it contains lessons for what we do today: "Arendt's phrase 'the banality of evil' continues to resonate," he stated in a book explaining and defending his experiment, "because genocide has been unleashed around the world and torture and terrorism continue to be common features of our global landscape." To ensure that we not miss the point, and in so doing to trumpet his own importance, Zimbardo offered numerous examples: "We will examine genocide in Rwanda, the mass suicide and murder of Peoples Temple followers in the jungles of Guyana, the My Lai massacre in Vietnam, the horrors of Nazi concentration camps, the torture by military and civilian police around the world, and the sexual abuse of prisoners by Catholic priests, and search for lines of continuity between the scandalous, fraudulent behavior of executives at Enron and WorldCom corporations." The important issue for Zimbardo is not whether evil is located within or without but whether ordinary people are susceptible to committing evil acts. Give them the right situation, he insisted, and they will be. We are not inherently Augustinian; we are made that way by society.

Zimbardo's work has been subject to withering criticism. Not only have the ethics of his research been questioned and his methodology attacked in ways similar to the responses to Milgram, but his use of students in his experiments has raised questions of what social scientists call selectivity bias, because students are not representative of the population as a whole. Even more serious, Zimbardo himself played the role of prison superintendent, thereby compromising his objectivity by giving him a vested interest in how the experiments turned out. It is always difficult to generalize from controlled and artificial psychological experiments. But at least Milgram, aware of some of the potential problems of bias, moved his experiments off campus and recruited subjects from nonstudent populations.

Zimbardo called his book *The Lucifer Effect;* in our increasingly secular age, it somehow seems appropriate that psychologists are the ones who raise the question of Satan's presence among us. The fact that we live in secular times does not mean that we live in peaceful ones, however, and every time mass atrocities come to our attention, we are tempted to turn to experiments like those conducted by Milgram and Zimbardo to understand why such terrible things happen. But even if Milgram's and Zimbardo's experiments had been ethically and methodologically flawless, it is questionable how much relevance they have either to the Holocaust or to the many examples of political evil that have followed in its wake. The gap between the laboratory and real life is simply too large to bridge.

In real-life situations of political evil, the whole idea is to inflict maximum pain upon the person you believe to be your enemy: the emotions are too raw, the need to make quick decisions too pressing, the fog of conflict too thick, and the threat of punishment for disobedience too omnipresent for any experimenter, no matter how ingenious, to replicate in a laboratory. The subjects of these experiments always knew they were in a university or in a building not far away. The person telling them what to do was not an armed tribal warlord known for his violent temper and reputation for brutality but a calm reciter of a prewritten script. He may have had the authority of science behind him, but he did not have charismatic authority. The subjects never witnessed blood spurt from their victims or contemplated the prospect of innocent children dying at their hands. They were not motivated by any racial, ethnic, or religious resentments. They were, in the case of Milgram's participants, people offered payment for their services or, in Zimbardo's, students worried about a grade. However cruel and sadistic their behavior may have appeared to be, no one knows how they would have acted if faced with an actual dilemma of protecting an innocent in a situation of mob violence, refusing to serve on a firing squad when ordered to do so, or participating in frenzied efforts to burn down the house of a neighbor, whether or not there were people inside it.

In spite of the questionable relevance of these experiments to real-world conditions, scholars frequently cite them for shedding light on the most puzzling, and therefore contentious, issues raised by situations of evil in the modern world. Perhaps the best-known example is offered by the historian Christopher Browning in his book *Ordinary Men,* a study of Reserve Police Battalion 101, which was charged with the task of killing some fifteen hundred Jews in the Polish village of Józefów. The men who carried out such dirty business constituted a cross section of people who would never make it into Germany's higher circles; as Browning writes, they "were from the lower orders of German society. They had experienced neither social nor geographic mobility. Very few were economically independent. Except for apprenticeship or vocational training, virtually none had any education after leaving *Volksschule* (terminal secondary school) at age fourteen or fifteen." Because they had no special training in military tactics or methods and had never been recruited by the Nazis to serve as storm troopers or enforcers, he concluded that such men were not natural killer material. The fact that they killed anyway therefore demonstrated to him just how evil ordinary people can be.

Seeking confirmation of his conclusions, Browning turned to both

Zimbardo and Milgram. "Zimbardo's spectrum of guard behavior bears an uncanny resemblance to the groupings that emerged within Reserve Police Battalion 101: a nucleus of increasingly enthusiastic killers who volunteered for the firing squads and 'Jew hunts'; a larger group of policemen who performed as shooters and ghetto clearers; . . . and a small group (less than 20 percent) of refusers and evaders," he wrote. There simply was no evidence that unusually cruel and sadistic men emerged out of a process of self-selection to volunteer for the task of killing Jews, he argued. Just as people take on social roles in a prison situation, they do the same thing in a genocidal situation. Jew killers are made, not born.

Although Milgram emphasized the notion of widespread evil within far more than Zimbardo, Browning finds the former helpful in resolving another issue: Why was there so little disobedience among the men serving in Reserve Police Battalion 101? "Was the massacre at Józefów a kind of radical Milgram experiment that took place in a Polish forest with real killers and victims rather than in a social psychology laboratory with naive subjects and actor/victims?" he provocatively asks. Noting that the two situations are very different, he continues. "Nonetheless, many of Milgram's insights find graphic confirmation in the behavior and testimony of the men of Reserve Police Battalion 101." Although they had never thought of themselves as killers when they joined the unit, they did kill, and one of the reasons, if not the major reason, was the very same combination of authority and conformity that Milgram had uncovered in his experiments in Connecticut, Browning argues. The parallels that Browning posits between his findings and those of Milgram are so striking to him that he even provides his own version of Milgram's treatment of Brevard Childs, the professor of divinity who refused to shock the "victim." Some of the men in the police battalion Browning studied refused to join the firing squad. But rather than dissenting from authority, he argued, they were only conforming: "Insidiously, therefore, most of those who did not shoot only reaffirmed the 'macho' values of the majority—according to which it was a positive quality to be 'tough' enough to kill unarmed, noncombatant men, women, and children—and tried not to rupture the bonds of comradeship that constituted their social world." From this particular version of hell there was indeed no exit.

If the men of Reserve Police Battalion 101 were not sufficiently immortal after Browning brought them to life, they became even better known when Daniel Jonah Goldhagen published his best-selling *Hitler's Willing Executioners* in 1996. Goldhagen famously argued that Germans killed Jews "because of a set of beliefs that defined the Jews in a way that demanded Jewish suffering as retribution, a set of beliefs which inhered as profound a hatred as one people has likely ever harbored for another." To provide empirical support for his thesis, he turned to the same unit studied by Browning, and there he did not find confirmation for the idea that these men—or any other Nazi exterminators, for that matter—killed "because they were coerced, because they were unthinking, obedient executors of state orders, because of social psychological pressure, because of the prospects of personal advancement, or because they did not comprehend or feel responsible for what they were doing, owing to the putative fragmentation of tasks." Far from being ordinary men, they were sadistic killers who not only took the lives of innocent people but congratulated themselves for their acts, invited their wives and others to witness their deeds, and fondly kept and later brought out photographs of their accomplishments. Browning's interpretation of their actions, as well as Milgram's findings about evil in general, are "untenable," claims Goldhagen. These men killed because they had swallowed the poison of German anti-Semitism and hated Jews enough to slaughter them.

Since Browning and Goldhagen reached such different conclusions about the same men, a debate between them became inevitable. It took place on April 8, 1996, at the U.S. Holocaust Memorial Museum in Washington, D.C. There, in tones characterized as "intense, at times even harsh and bitter" by Michael Berenbaum, the museum's director at the time, Browning and Goldhagen explored their differences on such questions as whether the killing had one cause or many, whether those who carried it out were or were not automatons, and how much coercion was applied to them. Needless to say, Goldhagen never changed Browning's mind and vice versa.

For all their differences, however, Goldhagen and Browning agree that the evil that broke out at Józefów can be explained in Augustinian terms. Because he was so in debt to Arendt and Milgram, Browning's Augustinianism is reflected, as the title of his book suggests, by the fact that the killers were "ordinary men." But in significant ways the title of Goldhagen's book is even more Augustinian; in searching for the best adjective to describe what the killers did, he came up with the crucial term "willing." "Germans," as Goldhagen reminds us, "could say 'no' to mass murder. They chose to say 'yes.'" The Nazis, Goldhagen contends, were, as Augustine said of humans in general, rational beings; their actions were "voluntaristic" and "they took initiative in the brutalizing of the Jews." Being weak of will, however, they used their reason for perverted ends, ultimately giving in to the sin called anti-Semitism and its temptations. Goldhagen's Augustinianism is not universal; what he says applies to Germans and Germans only. But there is no doubting the theological, and explicitly Christian, tenor of his analysis; in his own words, "the universe of death and torment into which the Germans hurled the Jews finds its closest approximation in the portrayals of hell contained in religious teachings and in the art of Dante or Hieronymus Bosch." One writer, Browning, speaks of ordinary men. The other, Goldhagen, speaks of ordinary Germans. But both find evil lurking within, a by-product of the autonomy we have in theory but all too often fail to exercise in practice.

That writers who could come to such radically different conclusions can nonetheless agree that evil lurks in the hearts of men suggests just how long is the shadow cast by Augustine's reflections on evil. Augustine appealed to the young Hannah Arendt and her circle in the Weimar Republic, and he similarly remains attractive for those pondering the lessons of political evil eight decades later. Confronted with examples of evil without, we react by searching for it within. It makes a certain amount of sense to psychologize evil because we live in confessional times. But just as Augustine in his *Confessions* paid little attention to the political realities of his era, any conviction that ordinary people are capable of extraordinary acts of political evil fails to recognize that what makes political evil extraordinary has little to do with the predispositions of those who engage in it. It is instead made possible because, as heads of state or leaders of mass movements, they have available to them means of mass violence beyond the reach of other people, ordinary or not.

POLITICAL EVIL'S ABNORMALITY

ONE REASON the notion of widespread evil within continues to attract adherents is that its advocates include witnesses who experienced firsthand the greatest evils of the twentieth century. "If only it were all so simple!" observes Aleksandr Solzhenitsyn in *The Gulag Archipelago*. "If only there were evil people somewhere insidiously committing evil deeds, and it were necessary only to separate them from the rest of us and destroy them. But the line dividing good and evil cuts through the heart of every human being." Solzhenitsyn, of course, was writing about the Stalinist variety of evil, but other literary figures of equal moral depth have drawn similar conclusions from the Nazi version. In his well-known essay "The Gray Zone," the Italian chemist and writer Primo Levi, who spent considerable time in Auschwitz, warned against drawing black-and-white conclusions from what took place there. Newcomers to the camps, he writes, "whether young or not; all of them, with the exception of those who had already gone through an analogous experience, expected to find a terrible but decipherable world, in conformity with that simple model which we atavistically carry with us—'we' inside and the enemy outside, separated by a sharply defined geographic frontier." It therefore came as a shock to discover that the reality of the camps was far more complex: "The enemy was all around but also inside, the 'we' lost its limits, the contenders were not two, one could not discern a single frontier but rather many confused, perhaps innumerable frontiers, which stretched between each of us."

Despite the unquestioned moral prestige of these authors, something important about political evil is lost if we proceed along the lines they suggest. Even if we were to grant, as I do not believe we ever should, that every single person has internalized a capacity for evil, it does not follow that every single person also possesses an equal calling for politics. The camps into which both Solzhenitsyn and Levi were thrown were not constructed out of the rough materials of human nature; they were built by regimes using the power of the state to implement policies meant to divide the population into those considered normal and those considered unwanted and to spare the one and kill the other. Carrying out such a task required a remarkable combination of bureaucratic skill, long-range planning, willingness to overcome obstacles, and tenacious determination. When it comes to political ability at that level of perverse achievement, few are called and even fewer are chosen. One of the most important lessons taught by the experience of the camps is that no matter how kind or cruel any one of us may happen to be, evil lies in the fact that some are in command of the state's instruments of coercion and others are not. Radical evil is not some spontaneous outburst from below fueled by the psychological rage of ordinary people. It takes very special circumstances to bring it into being and highly specialized experts to achieve its deadly effects. However "normal" Eichmann may have been as a person, his accomplishments as a bureaucrat make him unique indeed. Very few people can ever be quite as successful as he was in moving men and machines to achieve his purposes.

It is nonetheless true that very ordinary people will sometimes involve themselves enthusiastically in the business of mass murder. The most impressive documentation of their willingness to do so comes not from Browning's *Ordinary Men;* the people he studied, however humdrum their occupations, were still Nazis and therefore had already chosen evil as a way of life. (On that point, at least, Goldhagen has the better argument.) Far more chilling is the murder of the Jewish population of Jedwabne carried out by their Polish neighbors and brought to life in painful detail by the historian Jan Gross. Those who rounded up the town's Jews, herded them into a barn, and then watched as they died in the flames were, as Gross suggests, truly willing executioners. "Though there were sadistic individuals who, particularly in camps, might force prisoners to kill each other," he writes, "in general nobody was forced to kill the Jews. In other words, *the so-called local population involved in killings of Jews did so of its own free will.*" These killers were neither soldiers nor policemen but civilians. Theirs were not acts of war but acts of evil, pure and simple.

Yet it would be incorrect to conclude from what happened at Jedwabne that any people at any time can be transformed into mass murderers. For one thing, Poland in the 1940s lay in the very heart of that part of Europe the Yale historian Timothy Snyder has called the "bloodlands," the area, squeezed between Nazism on the one side and Stalinism on the other, that witnessed the greatest amount of violence in modern times. The conditions brought about by any war are devastating enough, but those who experienced World War II in the bloodlands, especially Jews but gentiles as well, were exposed to such a total upending of anything resembling normality that it is difficult to conclude that any such thing as normal people could be found. This is by no means intended as an excuse for the systematic murders of innocent Jews in Poland. It is rather meant to suggest that such horrific actions can occur only under the most extreme of conditions.

An additional reason not to draw hard-and-fast lessons about human nature from the experience of Jedwabne is that although the killings that took place there were not planned by the Germans, they were nonetheless planned. On the morning of July 10, 1941, Polish officials called all adult men to the town hall and then ordered the Jews to assemble as well. After the violence was unleashed, those officials "monitored progress and made sure at crucial junctures that the goal of the pogrom was advanced." Gross points out that the violence certainly had its spontaneous aspects, as violence nearly always tends to. But in Jedwabne the masses did not push their leaders toward extremism; if anything, it happened the other way around. Local politics, in short, is still politics. Without organization and leadership, not as many Jews would have lost their lives.

When it comes to the forms of political evil present in today's world, the same lessons about the importance of organization and leadership apply. Many of us may be tempted to steal pears, but very few of us have a taste for the rigors, frustrations, and ultimate rewards of a life of pursuing political ends through evil means. Politics by its very nature divides the few from the many. There is no Osama bin Laden inside all of us, and not just because he was a killer of innocents and the rest of us are not. Above and beyond his ruthlessness, bin Laden possessed an ability to organize to which most of us can never aspire. Political evil happens when unusually determined and politically talented individuals grab hold of a special opportunity and mobilize large numbers of followers to engage in acts of malevolence to realize the cause that they were the first to foresee.

Proponents of the idea of widespread evil within respond to this criticism by claiming that however unusual evil leaders may be, the great masses of people who follow their orders, much like the gentile citizens of Jedwabne, are much more like you and me. Yet this too is a proposition that falls apart upon closer examination. Those who carry out the orders of politically evil leaders in the contemporary world are not some sample of a local population chosen at random on the principle that since everyone has the same potential for evil, anyone can be relied upon to carry out evil acts. On the contrary, political evil recruits those attracted to brutality, motivated by a burning sense of victimhood, anxious to right what they believe to be long-standing wrongs, and in extreme cases willing to die for their beliefs. It is not easy to qualify for political evil. The September 11 hijackers were carefully selected after rigorous screening. Only the truly sadistic became Janjaweed militia carrying out their unspeakable cruelty in Darfur. However much the Palestinians may resent Israel, recruits for Hamas-led terror against Israel remain limited. The kind of sadism required for political evil to flourish is generally in short supply. As one study of the psychology of political evil concludes, "There is good evidence that those who carry out genocidal massacres have to be motivated and trained to overcome any scruples that would otherwise hinder their activities."

Practitioners of political evil know full well that they cannot trust everyone. Those anxious to be recruited will sometimes be found too unstable, others who seem to burn with zeal may turn against the cause, and one can never know which recruit has infiltrated the group prepared from the start to reveal its secrets. Lest those in charge of political evil be tempted to stretch a bit and bring within their ranks people marginally qualified to carry out their deeds, they have the examples of inept shoe and underwear bombers to remind them of the importance of careful procedures for selection and promotion. No one in the business of political evil would ever conclude, as a Stanley Milgram did, that just about everyone can be made to conform to authority. Even if it were true that 65 percent can, one can never succeed in the business of political evil if 35 percent of your followers will not toe the line.

If our inclination is to democratize evil to the point where it includes just about everyone, we will no longer possess the words we need to characterize those kinds of politically evil acts that bring special havoc to their victims. For all his reminders that the evils of Auschwitz took place inside a gray zone of moral ambiguity, Primo Levi ultimately concluded that it would be a mistake to confuse himself with those who terrorized him: "I do not know, and it does not much interest me to know, whether in my depths there lurks a murderer, but I do know that I was a guiltless victim and I was not a murderer. I know that the murderers existed, not only in Germany, and still exist, retired or on active duty, and that to confuse them with their victims is a moral disease or an aesthetic affectation or a singular sign of complicity." That way of thinking, not confused talk about gray zones, is the best way to come to terms with the distinctiveness of political evil today.

Possessed with Levi's insight, we ought to conclude that those who commit acts of political evil are not responding to flawed wills or merely conforming to authority. Call them ruthless, denounce them as butchers, seek to disrupt what they do—but don't confuse them with ordinary people. Neo-Augustinians are so intent on finding evil within that they downplay the fact that ordinary people spend considerable amounts of time loving one another, bringing children into the world, doing good things for others, and even, as studies of Germans and Poles who helped the Jews under the Nazi regime suggest, committing extraordinary acts of altruism. So fascinated are these thinkers by extreme cruelty that they neglect not only those who save lives and honor their conscience but those who learn from history and are determined to avoid the mistakes of the past.

In reality a willingness to commit politically evil acts is not a normal property of mankind. They are acts undertaken by people who lack the fundamental respect for human life the rest of us have—and who, even more important, know how to manipulate others and control the levers of power to transform their fantasies into reality. Saint Augustine held that all but a tiny few are marked by evil within. The lesson of our time is that, save for a tiny few, most humans cannot even imagine doing what the practitioners of political evil routinely do. The most important thing to know about political evil is how unusual are those who carry it out.

CHAPTER THREE

Unrelenting Evil Without

FROM ONE EXTREME TO THE OTHER

NOT EVERYONE SHARES the conviction that evil lurks within each of us, just waiting for its chance to burst out in acts of intentional cruelty or indifference to mass atrocities. The idea of widespread evil within, in fact, finds itself in strong competition with the opposite notion of unrelenting evil without. Solzhenitsyn is a figure much to be admired, advocates of this latter point of view hold, but his claim that there is no firm dividing line between good and evil is dangerously wrong. Worse, such a conviction distracts us from the task of taking firm action against evil leaders, including going to war if they become too aggressive to ignore. Neutrality in the face of evil represents not merely complicity with it but an open invitation to the world's worst tyrants to continue causing their damage without interruption. There *are* monsters in the world, lots of them and very dangerous, but they exist outside, not inside, us.

That monsters really do exist in this world is beyond doubt. But as tempted as we may be to respond to their acts by drawing the sharpest possible lines between them and us, such a response suffers from one fatal flaw: like its opposite way of thinking, it conflates evil in general with political evil in particular. Political evil comes into being for specific reasons and goes out of existence once the conditions that feed it change. By portraying political evildoers as the product of dark satanic forces, we place them in a world beyond reach, depriving ourselves of tools we need to combat the very real harms they cause.

Those who divide the world into good and evil—and who then view their own society as embodying the former and their enemies as inevitably corrupted by the latter—draw on a tradition of intellectual history not unlike the one guiding neo-Augustinians committed to the idea of widespread evil within. That history too must be recounted if we are to appreciate just how little value this way of thinking offers us as we try to respond to the brutalities of contemporary terrorism, genocide, and ethnic cleansing. Whether or not opposites attract, political evil ought neither to be broadened to include just about everyone nor confined only to those who are not like us at all.

MANI'S UNEXPECTED LEGACY

NO OTHER FIGURE of our time is more associated with the notion of unrelenting external evil than the former president of the United States George W. Bush. Bush explained the rationale for his foreign policy actions many times, including, as a coda to his years as president, in his farewell address to the nation delivered in January 2009. "I have often spoken to you about good and evil," he said on that occasion. "This has made some uncomfortable. But good and evil are present in this world, and between the two there can be no compromise. Murdering the innocent to advance an ideology is wrong every time, everywhere. Freeing people from oppression and despair is eternally right." In the battle between good and evil, our best approach lies with what the president repeatedly called "moral clarity." Guided by firm moral convictions, he said, the United States must stand for unwavering moral ideals: "The battles waged by our troops are part of a broader struggle between two dramatically different systems. Under one, a small band of fanatics demands total obedience to an oppressive ideology, condemns women to subservience, and marks unbelievers for murder. The other system is based on the conviction that freedom is the universal gift of Almighty God and that liberty and justice light the path to peace."

To his defenders, George W. Bush will be vindicated by history because he stood up to tyranny and oppression. To his critics, he will always be remembered for moral caricature rather than moral clarity. Prominent among the latter is the philosopher Peter Singer, who sarcastically dismissed Bush as "the president of good and evil." According to an analysis Singer carried out, Bush mentioned the word "evil" in 30 percent of the speeches he gave in his first two years in office, and roughly 80 percent of the time he used the term as a noun rather than as an adjective. "This suggests," Singer concludes, "that Bush is not thinking about evil deeds, or even evil people, nearly as often as he is thinking about evil as a *thing,* or a force, something that has a real existence apart from the cruel, callous, brutal, and selfish acts of which human beings are capable." Singer cannot know if Bush was sincere. But he argues that it hardly matters: Bush was "handicapped by a naive idea of ethics as conformity to a small number of fixed rules" and as a result was "unable to handle adequately the difficult choices that any chief executive of a major nation must face."

Bush drew so easily upon the language of evil because he was one of the most religious of America's presidents. It should not be surprising, therefore, that his language resembles the following passage addressing the question of what those who truly believe in the Heavenly Father should do when confronted, as inevitably they will be, by their enemies: "Endure persecutions and temptations, which will come to you, fortify yourselves in these commandments which I gave you . . . that you may avoid the evil end of the deniers and blasphemers who have seen the truth with their own eyes and have turned away from it. They shall come unto the Place of Punishment at which there is no day of life. . . . The wind and the air shall be taken from them, and from them they shall receive no breath of life from that hour onward." Like so much said and done in the second or third centuries after the crucifixion of Jesus Christ, these words condemning evildoers to everlasting hell were attractive to huge numbers of followers who tried to live as best they could in accordance with the teachings of their prophet.

These particular admonishments, however, do not come from any of the Gospels that proclaim the core convictions of the Christian faith. They are instead the words of the prophet Mani, who, according to Saint Augustine, "was not only ignorant of the subjects which he taught, but also taught what was false, yet was demented and conceited enough to claim that his utterances were those of a divine person." (Augustine also said of Mani's followers: "I ought to have disgorged these men like vomit from my over-laden system.") For all his talk of the importance of Jesus in his life, President Bush's way of formulating the problem of evil actually owed most to a man that one of the most prominent early church fathers denounced as a heretic. No Augustinian, for one thing, would have used the term "evil" so frequently as a noun because, as we saw previously, Augustine did not believe that evil had any real substance. Nor would Augustine have divided the world in such a radically dualistic manner; the really important struggle in which Christians must engage lies not in defeating external evil but in recognizing the capacity for evil we have inside ourselves. We are right to view President Bush's foreign policy pronouncements in the wake of September 11 as expressions of a religious outlook on the world. We are also right to ask that the religion be the correct one.

Manichaeism has all but disappeared as a faith, its key surviving texts are few and incomplete, and what remains suggests a cosmology riddled with implausibility. Still, it once exercised a powerful hold over the theologians prominent during Augustine's lifetime, including, as noted earlier, the young Augustine himself. It is important to understand why Augustine was both attracted to and eventually repelled by the cosmology developed by Mani if we are to appreciate why George W. Bush's approach to the problem of evil not only failed to make the world a better place but left so much chaos in its wake.

Like Gnosticism, brought back to life not long ago by the Princeton University religion scholar Elaine Pagels, as well as a number of by-now obscure sects such as the Bogomils and Cathars, Manichaeism posited the existence of an evil kingdom fully as powerful as the good one. Even more significantly, it also treated the individual human being dualistically: goodness resided in our uncorrupted soul, while earthly matter, especially our bodies, save for rare and precious rays of light, was all dirt and darkness. Struck by the sheer amount of wickedness in the world, Mani and his adherents believed that evil, in its struggle with the good, holds the upper hand. It does not come as a complete surprise that the young Augustine would be attracted to such a way of thinking. Desperate for answers to questions that tormented him, he found in Manichaean ideas not only an explanation of why the human world was so filled with disgust but also an understanding of why his own will was so tempted by it.

At the same time, Augustine's appreciation of divine authority would eventually give him every reason to condemn Mani's speculations. For Christians, Jesus Christ, simultaneously divine and human, was sent by God as a savior to mankind. The Manichees, by contrast, viewed Jesus not as having taken human form—how could he have when the body is so corrupt?—but as a spirit capable of gathering up whatever small amounts of light survived the darkness and transferring them back to the sun. By renouncing the temptations of this world, a few people of exceptional purity—Mani called them the elect—would help speed up the process, attracting followers (the hearers) who, if somewhat less rigorously than the elect, also aimed to lead lives of purity. Eventually the forces of light would be gathered together, but only in heaven. The universe's fate is not so joyous. It would eventually burn itself out of existence, and once it had, evil would no longer threaten the good. As the British medieval historian Steven Runciman explains, dualistic eschatology "was a religion of pessimism. It held out no hope for individual men and their salvation. Mankind should die out, that the imprisoned fragments of Godhead should return to their home."

Any religion convinced that humanity has no real future is unlikely to value bringing new human beings into the world, one reason why dualistic sects had such extreme views about sexuality. If evil in the here and now is going to triumph, there is no reason ever to be good; one side of dualistic doctrines viewed efforts to control our carnal lust as hopeless, thereby putting no brakes on sexual licentiousness. Yet for Mani's elect, chastity and the rejection of marriage were held to be essential steps to the eventual gathering up of the light. In either case, whether in the form of uninhibited sexual gratification or strict abstinence, those guided by dualistic views of the world typically repudiated marriage and the sexual reproduction associated with it. "Dualism," Runciman concludes, "necessarily disapproves of the propagation of the species. It therefore disapproves of marriage far more than of casual sexual intercourse, for the latter represents merely one isolated sin, while the former is a state of sin. Similarly sexual intercourse of an unnatural type, by removing any risk of procreating children, was preferable to normal intercourse between man and woman."

Although capable of appealing to those preoccupied with the problem of evil, dualism nevertheless wrote its own epitaph: a faith without hope is one that cannot grow. Augustine's rejection of the Manichees made not only theological but sociological sense. The debate between Augustine's and Mani's followers offers a classic case of what the contemporary thinker Robert Wright calls "the evolution of God." Mani's system was too gloomy to reproduce and survive. Convinced that the world would die, he could not explain why anyone would choose to live. Offering no hope of salvation, he could provide no source of inspiration. Mani's relative obscurity is thus well deserved. The darkness he saw everywhere ultimately enveloped him. His understanding of how the world works amounted to sacrificial suicide for the ideas in which he believed.

Yet the issues that dominated theological discourse centuries ago continue to preoccupy us today. However much Manichaeism may have failed as a religion, it has succeeded in modern times as secular gospel, especially in the realm of foreign policy. Manichaeism flourishes in questions involving national security because it rallies the people at home to confront their antagonists abroad, frames global conflicts not as struggles for economic influence or military power but as battles over correct ideas and moral absolutes, and calls upon idealistic yearnings to make the world safe from harm. Singling out our enemies as the very embodiment of everything that we more honorable creatures are not does not demand of statesmen that they explain nuance or require them to justify cooperating with distasteful regimes. In ways similar to Mani's once considerable appeal, it offers an easy-to-grasp explanation of how evil can persist in a world that is otherwise good: forces of darkness are always lurking out there and will triumph over us unless we prepare ourselves rigorously for the cosmic struggle that awaits. Bush, a conservative in domestic policy, surely never realized that he was borrowing his foreign policy worldview from a religion that praised homosexual sex. But for him, as for anyone who views the world as a never-ending struggle between those who do good and those who are stained with evil, the attractions of dualism made it close to impossible to resist.

Secular Manichaeism, however, must be resisted. Like its religious counterpart, secular Manichaeism is a political creed doomed to fail because it offers neither hope nor purpose. For all his efforts at moral clarity, George W. Bush was incapable of inspiring the West to take the problem of political evil seriously. His faults lay not in himself but in his system. When the forces of darkness are that powerful, our good intentions can never be that sufficient. Secular Manichaeans want to assure us that in the long run goodness will win out. But in the short run they so inflate the evil we are fighting that we lose our zest for the struggle. To understand and combat political evil requires something more than a doctrine of defeat.

TOTALITARIAN PERMANENCE

THE HISTORY of the contemporary world's attraction to secular Manichaeism begins in the 1930s and 1940s, when democratic societies had to face the challenge posed by totalitarianism in both Nazi Germany and Stalinist Russia. It was precisely during these darkest of years that the one American thinker who happened to be as conversant with

Christian theology as he was about American foreign policy, Reinhold Niebuhr, wrote his major books. Niebuhr's influence, then as well as now, testifies to the way long-ago theological debates can have surprising contemporary relevance. In Niebuhr's case, the task was to urge the United States to adopt a form of Augustinian realism premised upon a rejection of Manichaeism and everything for which it stood.

Niebuhr's most passionate work, *The Children of Light and the Children of Darkness*, was published in 1944, a year in which the Nazi regime was still capable of putting up a fight and in which Stalin was starting to plan for the cold war to come. The title Niebuhr chose for his book seems to evoke Manichaean imagery. But he actually borrowed it from the Gospel according to Luke, specifically what is called the parable of the unjust steward (Luke 16:1–8). In this portion of the New Testament, a rich man learns that his steward may be engaged in mismanagement and asks him to account for his actions. Worried that he will lose his job, the steward calls in the rich man's debtors and asks them how much they owe his master. When they tell him, he urges them to cut the amount down as a way of winning their favor; if the master fires him and he loses his home, he reasons, the tenants to whom he has just given a break may allow him to live with them. Discovering what his steward has been up to, the master, instead of denouncing him for his dishonesty, commends him, saying that "the people of the world are more shrewd in dealing with their own kind than the children of the light."

The parable of the unjust steward has been called by the theologian Dennis J. Ireland "one of the most difficult of all of Jesus' parables to interpret." It not only seems to give a seal of approval to a dishonest action but also endorses the actions of a pragmatic deal maker. Yet it is because the parable confounds our expectations of what Jesus would do that Niebuhr chose it. Niebuhr argued that when it comes to dealing with evil regimes, we ought to be wary of those, the children of light, who approach the world with innocent intentions; he knew his fellow Christians well, and he detected, especially among some of the more sanctimonious of them, a preference for sentimental idealism completely inappropriate to a dangerous world. At the same time, the world contains "moral cynics," as Niebuhr characterized the children of darkness, "who declare that a strong nation need acknowledge no law beyond its strength." Although Niebuhr was perfectly prepared to call the latter evil, he also believed that demonic forces have something important to teach us: "The preservation of a democratic civilization requires the wisdom of the serpent and the harmlessness of the dove. The children of light must be armed with the wisdom of the children of darkness but remain free from their malice."

Children of Light brought to a general audience some of the more technical theological issues with which Niebuhr had wrestled in his Gifford Lectures, published as the two-volume *The Nature and Destiny of Man* in 1941 and 1943. This work returned to the debates that so preoccupied Saint Augustine and his circle and drew out their implications for the way we think about evil in more modern times. Niebuhr, for one thing, expressed considerable disdain for the Pelagian view that human beings possess a sufficient measure of free will to overcome the effects of original sin. Both Catholicism and most forms of mainline Protestantism, which he characterized as semi-Pelagian, are, in his view, "too intent to assert the integrity of man's freedom" to realize that "the discovery of this freedom also involves the discovery of man's guilt." We may believe that we are masters of our fate, Niebuhr argued, but the whole idea is an illusion. We are free only when we realize that we live in a world in which, as fallen creatures, our inclination to sin is inevitable. Legend has it that members of the Harvard faculty once created an Atheists for Niebuhr club. True or not—it sounds apocryphal to me—Niebuhr, as theologians go, was as orthodox as they come; grace never came cheaply for him.

For all his distaste toward the Pelagians, however, Niebuhr also came to distrust Augustine's more literal-minded disciples. If the former err in assigning too much free will to human beings, the latter make the mistake of enslaving them too much to their capacity for wickedness. "Augustinians," Niebuhr wrote, "have been so concerned to prove that the freedom of man is corrupted by sin that they have not fully understood that the discovery of this sinful taint is an achievement of freedom." Any doctrine positing human beings as subject to forces completely outside their own control "is as clearly destructive of the idea of responsibility for sin as rationalistic and dualistic theories which attribute human evil to the inertia of nature." We therefore need a way of thinking that allows considerable room for at least some free will because without it individuals cannot be held accountable for the choices they make. God, after all, did not just create inanimate objects like trees and rocks; he created human beings as well. Because "man is the only animal which can make itself its own object," freedom of the will can be as vital as it is destructive; we should never become so pre-occupied with the danger of anarchy that we lose sight of the human potential for creativity. Niebuhr, Charles Mathewes has written, "is the greatest twentieth-century Augustinian psychologist of sin." This is true, but only in a partial sense. Niebuhr has much in common with the Augustine who could marvel at human reason and very little in common with the strict adherent of predestination for whom free will primarily meant the will to err.

Niebuhr continued to produce major works in the 1950s and early 1960s. As he did, he turned his attention from the Nazis, who in his earlier books had represented the quintessential children of darkness, to the evil omnipresent in the Soviet Union. Because he so thoroughly rejected pacifism and believed that theologians had to be grounded in this-worldly realities, Niebuhr's support for American foreign policy during the cold war made him a darling of those liberals who wanted to see the United States meet the challenge posed by Stalin's aggressive foreign policy head-on. But Niebuhr, who appreciated irony and distrusted any form of black-and-white reasoning, never became a full-fledged member of the cold war liberal club. In the early years of the cold war, as Richard Fox, one of his biographers, points out, Niebuhr worried that the United States would too arrogantly try to impose its ideology on the free world and questioned excessive reliance on military power. "Humility was strength, self-examination was preparedness," as Fox characterizes his views. "He repudiated any simple dichotomy between an evil Soviet empire and a virtuous American democracy—even when, in moments of crisis, he escalated his rhetoric against the Soviet 'tyrants.'" Niebuhr had read too much Augustine to ever become a Manichaean. Dividing the world into forces of good and evil was always for him the first step toward being tempted in the direction of the latter. The search for moral clarity can all too easily obscure.

An avid student of American history, Niebuhr was aware of the tendency of his country to pursue its foreign policy goals with moralistic zeal; it was, after all, John Quincy Adams who in 1821 in his capacity as secretary of state wrote of his country that "she goes not abroad, in search of monsters to destroy," as if knowing full well that this is precisely what the United States would do unless warned otherwise. Yet despite his best efforts to protect the United States against the tendency foreshadowed by Adams, Niebuhr's attempts to bypass Manichaeism in the years after World War II produced limited results at best. As the cold war escalated, more and more thinkers began to paint the conflict between the United States and the Soviet Union as a religious battle for the soul of man in which one side or the other had to be chosen. It was during those years that Mani's approach trumped Augustine's, and the world suffered as a result.

Political conservatives took the lead in framing the emerging cold war in Manichaean terms. One of the most insistent of them was the conservative polemicist James Burnham. Schooled in the realpolitik tradition of political thought, Burnham saw the world as engaged in a struggle for power rather than involved in a war of ideas. Yet even though he lacked a religious sensibility—born Catholic, Burnham returned to the church before he died in 1987—Burnham's writings immediately after World War II nonetheless held that nothing less than the future of civilization was at stake in the cold war. "It may be," as he said in 1947, "that the darkness of great tragedy will bring to a quick end the short, bright history of the United States—for there is enough truth in the dream of the New World to make the action tragic." All the key elements of a Manichaean worldview were on display in Burnham's book *The Struggle for the World;* not only was the world divided into light and dark, but the lights were always just about to be turned off.

Burnham's Manichaeism was widely copied among his ideological soul mates. One of them, the writer and former communist Whittaker Chambers, once dismissed by those on the left as a self-important buffoon, is now, thanks to the biographical efforts of Sam Tanenhaus and Michael Kimmage, taken seriously as a writer and truth teller. Still, there is no denying that Chambers—characterized by the intellectual historian Abbott Gleason as "utterly and crudely dualistic, self-confidently and rigidly moralistic"—presented secular Manichaeism to the widest possible audience. "I see in Communism the focus of the concentrated evil of our time," Chambers proclaimed at the start of his best-selling memoir and confession *Witness,* published in 1952. While Burnham's writings were apocalyptic, the man himself was not. The same could never be said of Chambers. His conspiratorial air, dramatic stories of espionage, and impressive testimony before Congress did as much as his actual writings to convince Americans during the 1950s that the conflict in which they were engaged was a herculean struggle. From a

Manichaean perspective, it is vital to explain how bad people manage to triumph over good ones. Figures such as Chambers, or the even more dualistic Senator Joe McCarthy, had a ready answer: evil by nature, our enemies, ruthless and unprincipled, take advantage of our goodness to impose their will upon us. What the historian Richard Hofstadter once characterized as the "paranoid style" in American politics was really just another term for free-floating Manichaeism.

Throughout the 1950s, Manichaean thinkers had a ready answer for everything. Because communism was the embodiment of evil, communism would have to be fought—everywhere it existed. This, conservatives like Burnham and Chambers insisted, was something liberals would never do. Although the Truman administration had promulgated the Marshall Plan and announced its intentions to defend Greece against Soviet meddling, conservatives believed it was unwilling to take on the required fight in any serious way. Truman, they were quick to point out, did nothing to stop the communist takeover of China and could not defeat the Red menace in Korea. Searching for a figure more supportive of their views, right-wingers were attracted to John Foster Dulles, son of a clergyman, an elder in the Presbyterian Church, and the likely pick for secretary of state in any future Republican administration. "There is a moral or natural law not made by man which determines right and wrong," Dulles had preached in a 1952 essay in *Life*. "This law has been trampled by the Soviet rulers, and for that violation they can and should be made to pay." Called upon to draft the foreign policy sections of the 1952 Republican platform, Dulles responded with language a Manichaean would not necessarily agree with—his words were too optimistic for any confirmed dualist—but would nonetheless understand. "We shall again make liberty into a beacon light of hope that will penetrate the dark places," he wrote. "It will mark the end of the negative, futile and immoral policy of 'containment' which abandons countless human beings to a despotism and godless terrorism."

Dulles became secretary of state and is remembered to this day for his moralistic views about the evil posed by communism. To the consternation of many conservatives, however, he appeared to have little influence upon the actual foreign policies of the president he served, Dwight D. Eisenhower. A realist who knew the horrors of war from firsthand experience, Eisenhower was not about to replace containment, which sought to limit the Soviet threat, with what conservatives

of the time called rollback, or the notion of reducing and finally eliminating it. When Hungarians rebelled against their Soviet occupiers in
1956, inspired by a determined Roman Catholic cardinal named József
Mindszenty, the Russians responded by putting down the rebellion by
force. Conservatives were shocked when Eisenhower refused to consider military intervention. The Republican Party, their own party, had
made the very accommodation with evil that Burnham and Chambers
had warned against. Their reaction was to mix their Manichaeism with
cries of betrayal, a particularly shrill if seemingly inevitable combination. In 1958, the conservative activist Phyllis Schlafly, along with her
husband, Fred, created the Cardinal Mindszenty Foundation to keep
alive the spirit of the Hungarian resistance. Their actions were part and
parcel of the attraction Manichaeism held for all those right-wingers
distrustful of the influence of moderates within the Republican Party.
"We are at war with an evil," as presidential candidate Barry Goldwa-
ter put it at the 1964 Republican National Convention, "and the evil is
communism."

With conservative Republicans gaining political advantage from
their reliance on Manichaean imagery, liberals and Democrats were
often anxious to join them. But not all of them did. One important
postwar Democrat, Truman's secretary of state Dean Acheson, in fact
specifically repudiated such ways of thinking. "Today, you hear much
talk of absolutes ... that two systems such as ours and that of the Russians cannot exist in the same world ... that one is good and one is
evil, and good and evil cannot exist in the world," he told an audience
at the Naval War College in 1949. Yet, he went on, "good and evil have
existed in this world since Adam and Eve went out of the garden of
Eden. ... That is what all of us must learn to do in the United States: to
limit objectives, to get ourselves away from the search for the absolute."
In the context of the time, Acheson's remarks stand out for their refusal
to conform to the hysteria upon which Manichaeism insists. Acheson
was not alone in urging realism over moralism. Another who thought
along similar lines was George F. Kennan, otherwise known as Mr. X,
whose July 1947 essay "The Sources of Soviet Conduct" did so much to
bring America's attention to Stalin's global ambitions. These were figures who recognized the existence of a Soviet threat and sought to make
American foreign policy more muscular in response. They also believed
that picturing the world as a relentless conflict between good and evil

would deprive foreign-policy makers of the flexibility they needed to meet the dangers posed by the spread of communism.

Liberals would find it difficult to maintain the right balance between a realistic appreciation of the Soviet Union's power and the dramatic language proclaiming the cold war as a struggle between two irreconcilable ways of life. One reason for their problem lay in the popularity of a term coined in part by the writings of the other great twentieth-century thinker besides Niebuhr inspired by Saint Augustine: Hannah Arendt. Arendt was no conservative (she was no liberal either). But the concept of totalitarianism she helped formulate contributed to an emerging sense in the United States that the struggle against totalitarianism was like no other known to man: *The Origins of Totalitarianism,* after all, contained her analysis of radical evil, a concept meant to call attention to the absolutely unprecedented nature of the horrors of Nazism. Arendt's concept, as I argued earlier, captured something real about Nazi rule. But when later applied to American foreign policy, it revealed how at her most Manichaean she was when she wrote *Origins.* No doubt Arendt herself understood this. Just like Augustine, who eventually rejected Mani, she too gave up on such dualistic thinking when she settled on the concept of the banality of evil in *Eichmann.*

Arendt may have begun *Origins* with the Nazis foremost in her mind, but as the cold war hardened, she found herself adding material on the Soviet Union after the book was published in 1951. In this, she was very much part of the immediate postwar zeitgeist, for, as Gleason explains, "the totalitarian idea—that the Communists were the successors of the Nazis and closely connected to them—was the most powerful political idea of the late 1940s." By equating the evil of the one with the evil of the other, the concept of totalitarianism contributed to an atmosphere that made it difficult for policymakers to treat the Soviet Union in this-worldly terms. Without the concept of totalitarianism, the struggle between democracy and communism would have been viewed as the stuff of territory, money, and power. With it, it became the latest chapter in the eternal struggle between good and evil. By relying so much upon it, both liberals and conservatives had come to support the American side in the cold war for ideological and moralistic as well as geostrategic reasons.

Manichaeism can have its time and place, and the United States in the late 1940s was one of them. With the eventual revelation of Nikita

Khrushchev's 1956 denunciation of the crimes of Stalin, the world came to understand just how far Stalin, the West's ally against Hitler in World War II, had gone down the road of political evil during the 1930s and 1940s. Evil can take many forms, and when it takes its worst form—when it kills in the millions, seeks to expand its reach, unleashes the furies of racial and ethnic hatred, and can only be brought to an end by military action—intellectuals, much as Niebuhr argued, make fools of themselves when they try to explain it away or seek an accommodation with it. That Stalin had been America's ally in defeating Hitler does not change the fact that his regime resembled Hitler's in its capacity for radical evil.

The problem was that the theorists of totalitarianism, because they ignored the constraints imposed on evil leaders by changing political realities, believed that once a regime became totalitarian, it would always remain so. In the second and expanded edition of *Origins* published in 1958, Arendt included an epilogue reflecting on the Hungarian revolution and Khrushchev's assumption of power. "No one, least of all probably Mr. Khrushchev himself, can know what the course of his future action will be," she wrote. Nonetheless, Arendt went on, Khrushchev had available to him all the means of terror that Stalin had possessed, and given the brutal suppression of the Hungarian freedom fighters, the prospects for liberalization did not appear to be great: "One wonders," as she put it, "if the hopes of some Western observers for the emergence of some 'enlightened totalitarianism' will not turn out to be wishful thinking." Arendt, who saw little prospect for reform from within, never even contemplated the possibility that the Soviet Union, or any of its satellites, would collapse due to popular protest. Her conception of totalitarianism was too timeless, too rooted in the philosophical conceptions that guided it, to allow for on-the-ground political realities that might have moderated it.

The idea that totalitarian regimes would never wither away united nearly all of those who believed that the events in the Soviet Union were a replay of what the world had experienced in Nazi Germany. Unlike Arendt, political scientists Carl J. Friedrich and Zbigniew Brzezinski did contemplate the prospect that internal forces might rise up against totalitarian elites—only to reject it. "One possibility should be excluded, except in the satellites: the likelihood of an overthrow of these regimes by revolutionary action from within," they wrote in *Totalitar-*

ian Dictatorship and Autocracy, first published in 1956 and revised in 1965. "Our entire analysis of totalitarianism suggests that it is improbable that such a 'revolution' will be undertaken, let alone succeed." Such a conclusion is, after all, what the term itself implies: if the control exercised by a regime is total, and if it includes both the means of terror and of propaganda, then no space exists for challenging it. By viewing totalitarianism as frozen in place in some countries while expanding its reach in others, respected political scientists ironically found themselves completely downplaying the importance of politics. Their conception of totalitarianism had room for everything but the emergence of new, more liberalizing conditions.

Far from imagining that totalitarianism could moderate itself, thinkers of this era believed that it would prove attractive enough to spread well beyond its German and Russian base. The most favored nation for this particular destination proved to be China. Throughout the 1950s, China—or, as it was then known in popular parlance, Red China—was frequently charged with carrying forward the worst aspects of the Nazi and Soviet systems both domestically and internationally. It was in these years that the term "brainwashing" came to be associated with the Chinese Communists, reinforcing the notion that totalitarian regimes had developed ominous new techniques for suppressing human yearnings for freedom and perpetuating the rule of evil leaders. Since totalitarian regimes were by definition expansionist, moreover, China was viewed as inevitably poised to take control over other countries, particularly Korea and Vietnam. For all the horrors associated with Stalin, the United States fashioned an alliance with the Soviet Union and continued to recognize it diplomatically during the height of the cold war. But for many Americans at that time, China was considered so evil a society that one administration after another persistently refused to offer it diplomatic recognition.

Despite the once broad popularity of the term, totalitarianism proved to be a short-lived reality. The Nazi regime bet on winning World War II but lost; once the war ended, so did the quest for a Final Solution. Long before the Soviet Union collapsed completely, it had already evolved into something still authoritarian but clearly no longer Stalinist. China proved to be as pragmatic as the conservative American president Richard Nixon, who initiated diplomatic talks with that country. Historians continue to be fascinated by the evil regimes of the 1930s, and many remain prepared to draw comparisons between them, but, as the University of Georgia's David D. Roberts concludes, "the earlier totalitarian model, long recognized as unsustainable, is a dead horse that no longer requires flogging." The concept of totalitarianism is now more interesting to intellectual historians than political and diplomatic ones; it is the decision by so many writers to use the term, and not merely the phenomenon itself, that continues to attract their attention. Not only is it a product of the past, the particular conditions that made it possible, as I will argue in the next chapter, are unlikely ever to be repeated.

Yet, as if a powerful concept will trump reality anyway, especially for the ideologically inclined, totalitarianism simply refused to disappear. No other group of thinkers has been more responsible for keeping it alive than the neoconservatives, nearly all of whom were former leftists who moved to the political right during the 1980s. Strongly anticommunist, the neoconservatives took the lead in viewing the Soviet Union as the inheritor of Nazi evil in the years after World War II when so many others found the comparison no longer helpful. Indeed, the late Irving Kristol, the most prominent neoconservative of them all, had in his younger days reached the conclusion, surprising for a Jew concerned with anti-Semitism, that the Soviet Union was *more* evil than Nazi Germany. At the very time the Nazi regime was exterminating the Jews, Kristol denounced leftists who urged stepped-up actions against Germany for their "near hysterical insistence upon the pressing military danger" and for supporting "an abstract war against Hitler." Trotskyites such as Kristol had twisted themselves into an ideological position in which both the United States and the Soviet Union represented evil forces that had to be condemned. Kristol's early views were touched with Manichaeism, but it was one that allowed little place in its explanatory scheme for the emphasis that neoconservatives, just a few decades later, would place on the unbreakable link between evil and hatred of the Jews.

The antipathy toward the Soviet Union manifested by Kristol early in his career formed the backbone of his views as he moved into the Republican Party and influenced the policies of its leading figures. Ronald Reagan—whose 1983 speech to the National Association of Evangelicals, which became famous for his use of the term "evil empire," linked the themes of Manichaeism with those of totalitarianism in an unforgettable performance—was one of them. Reagan cited Whittaker

Chambers for his observation that Marxism-Leninism was actually a religion springing directly out of man's original sin, a position representing literal rather than figurative Manichaeism. He also criticized misguided if unnamed people for their "historical reluctance to see totalitarian powers for what they are," just as, he insisted, liberals had done in the 1930s. Filled with language emphasizing the presence of sin and evil in the world, Reagan's speech also offered words of hope, but in contrast to the more optimistic tone he struck in so many of his other public appearances, in this speech even his hopefulness was surrounded by Manichaean gloom. "Let us pray for the salvation of all of those who live in that totalitarian darkness," the president advised, and especially "pray they will discover the joy of knowing God. But until they do, let us be aware that while they preach the supremacy of the state, declare its omnipotence over individual man, and predict its eventual domination of all peoples on the Earth, they are the focus of evil in the modern world." His audience loved it. Had Niebuhr been alive to remind them of the nuances of their own Christian heritage, which frowns on an outlook so pagan in tone and substance, they might have reacted with a bit more skepticism.

Manichaeans live in perpetual disappointment. Once let down by Eisenhower, they would also discover Reagan wandering far from the apocalyptic rhetoric associated with his 1983 speech; in his second term Reagan softened his views toward the Soviet Union considerably and even considered a plan for the United States and the USSR to engage in mutual nuclear disarmament. Despite all this, neoconservatives did their best to keep alive the idea that the Soviets constituted a radical, and radically dangerous, empire of evil. As the forces gathered that would result in the ascendancy of Mikhail Gorbachev and the popularity of Boris Yeltsin, they continued to publish warnings that the Soviet Union was incapable of political change. After a revolution from below succeeded in toppling Communist Party rule on top, they argued that Reagan's willingness to increase the U.S. defense budget, thereby forcing the Russians into an arms race they could not afford, had brought about its end, as if the people who had actually lived under Soviet rule had played no part in its demise. In their ongoing praise for Reagan, they all but ignored the visionary side of the man, preferring to keep alive the memory of the cold warrior who saw evil in the world and was prepared both to name it and to fight it. Disappointment only fueled their cause. Manichaeism, like its vision of the enemy it combats, never gives up.

As had the defeat of Nazi Germany before it, the collapse of the Soviet Union seemed once again to put the concept of totalitarianism to rest. It was one thing to insist on totalitarian permanence even as the Soviet Union had entered its decrepit stage. It was quite another to keep talking about it when the Soviet Union no longer existed. The end of the cold war deprived Manichaeism of its very reason for existence; it was no longer necessary for the children of light to be engaged in an ongoing and frequently hopeless campaign against the children of darkness when the latter themselves had begun to see the light. Yet although the political conditions that had once made the concept of totalitarianism seem useful had changed so radically, the idea that the world was fundamentally divided between good and evil, and the corollary proposition that the United States must always be on the side of the former, despite its having experienced a temporary setback during the Nixon administration, would be revived full-bore in the twenty-first century. Manichaean ways of thinking had simply become too entrenched in American life to disappear just because the conditions that had given rise to them had changed.

THE MACHIAVELLIAN ALTERNATIVE

MACHIAVELLIANISM has for centuries offered the best defense against Manichaeism. Post–World War II Americans did not need a crash course on *The Prince* to appreciate the Renaissance Florentine's calculating amoralism; they were presented with a living example of its premises in the career of Henry Kissinger, Richard Nixon's secretary of state and national security advisor. Both Kissinger and Nixon were cold-blooded realists who prized global stability and who sought to cut deals as much as to fight wars. Manichaeism's zeal was precisely what they distrusted about it. When confronted with evil regimes, it made far more sense either to offer them incentives to reform or to wait them out. "Time drives everything before it," Machiavelli had written in his masterpiece, "and is able to bring with it good as well as evil, and evil as well as good." Take the long-term view, establish and reestablish the balance of power, avoid excessive moralizing—such, Machiavellians believe, are the responsibilities of wise statecraft. In December 2010, it was revealed that Kissinger had once told Nixon it would have been no concern of the United States if the Soviet Union had decided to send its Jews to the gas chambers. That is how far Machiavellian realism can go and it is no place that foreign policy should ever be taken.

Kissinger-like realism, even if in a more moderate form, offered one alternative for conservatives after the evil empire known as the Soviet Union went out of existence. Some intellectuals and policymakers tried to keep it alive. One of the most interesting was Jeane Kirkpatrick, an adviser to Reagan during his 1980 campaign for the presidency and his choice to be the U.S. ambassador to the United Nations. Kirkpatrick, a former Democrat, had obvious neoconservative sympathies, including the fact that she was an unabashed anticommunist. Her reflections on totalitarianism had in fact been Soviet-centric: to the degree that she discussed Hitler at all, she did so by reading back into the Nazi experience what she had learned about Marxism and communism. Like the other neoconservatives, moreover, she was convinced, even as the Soviet Union was crumbling, that it was as powerful as ever. "During their six decades in power," she wrote just seven years before the revolution against communism began, "Bolshevik leaders have succeeded in developing a strong government, a military technology and strength that is second to none, and an empire that stretches from the Berlin Wall to the Sea of Japan, from Mozambique to Mongolia." When it came to predicting the future, neoconservatives were never very adept.

Nonetheless, Kirkpatrick was a realist as well as a neoconservative; her treatment of the Soviet Union avoided any moralistic condemnation of the regime as embodying the essence of evil and focused instead on political power and its opportunities and constraints. When she turned her attention to the Third World, moreover, Kirkpatrick's views proved to be decidedly Kissingerian. Kirkpatrick had come to Reagan's attention because of an essay she had written in *Commentary* elaborating a distinction between totalitarian and authoritarian regimes. The former would always remain totalitarian, but "right-wing autocracies," as she put it, "sometimes evolve into democracies—given time, propitious economic, social, and political circumstances, talented leaders, and a strong indigenous demand for representative government." Kirkpatrick acknowledged that authoritarian leaders could be corrupt and cruel. She accepted the fact that under their leadership the masses remain in poverty. She even called some of them "bestial," such as Uganda's Idi

Amin or Haiti's François "Papa Doc" Duvalier. Still, she went on to say, such authoritarian regimes are more traditionalist than revolutionary in character and thus their existence is not a great threat to global stability. One of the worst things we can do, she argued, is precisely what President Jimmy Carter did: we should not get on some kind of moral high horse and lecture other societies for their failure to honor human rights. Instead, we should recognize that even if the hands of these authoritarian leaders are dirty, they can nonetheless become our friends.

Kirkpatrick had two such autocrats in mind: Reza Shah Pahlavi, the last occupant of Iran's Peacock Throne, and Anastasio Somoza Debayle, once the ruler of Nicaragua. Out of a misplaced idealism that confused democracy with goodness, she argued, the United States had helped topple both men, only to bring revolution, chaos, and Soviet influence in their wake. So intent was the United States on furthering democracy everywhere that it failed to realize that "the only likely result of an effort to replace an incumbent autocrat with one of his moderate critics or a 'broad-based coalition' would be to sap the foundations of the existing regime without moving the nation any closer to democracy." Patience would have worked better than intervention. If we had only taken a longer view and helped these regimes reform themselves, both Nicaragua and Iran might have transformed into more stable democracies on their own.

Kirkpatrick's distinction between totalitarian and authoritarian regimes ultimately made little sense; one communist society after another turned to democracy, while many a right-wing autocrat, through sheer intimidation of opponents, managed to retain power as long as he lived. Her realism, moreover, while acknowledging the cruelty tyrants are capable of wreaking, was tone-deaf to the suffering of those upon whom they worked their will; Kirkpatrick, like so many realists, was not the kind of thinker moved by the plight of helpless and innocent people. Yet, as impractical as some of Kirkpatrick's distinctions were, she was right to make political distinctions. President Jimmy Carter talked frequently about his faith and often cited Niebuhr, but he was in fact a near-perfect illustration of a Christian child of light for whom Niebuhr showed such disdain. Kirkpatrick, Carter's fiercest critic, may have avoided talk of religion, and she did not share Niebuhr's nuanced perspective on the world, but she at least avoided simplistic moralizing. Balancing America's ideals with its interests was her main objective.

Because her views represented such a mixture of neoconservatism and realism, Kirkpatrick's reactions to the political evils of our times never followed along party lines. She believed that the United States was right to go to war against such mass killers as Slobodan Milosevic and Saddam Hussein—so long as we did so in the right way and for the right reasons. Saddam's invasion of Kuwait was the first major intervention into the affairs of another country since the cold war ended, and the United States could not allow his act to go unpunished. Milosevic, she reminded her readers, although now a Serbian nationalist, was nonetheless a former communist who relied on the party's once formidable organization and tactics and had to be stopped. When leaders of their ilk attempt to upset the balance of power, the balance of power must be restored. In both these cases, her views would classify her as a hawk, even as many of her fellow Republicans, carefully taking note that the campaign against Milosevic was being led by the Democratic president Bill Clinton, actually at the time were willing to sound like doves.

Anyone who viewed Kirkpatrick as a dyed-in-the-wool neoconservative, however, would have been surprised by her opposition to George W. Bush's attempt to finish what his father had started in Iraq. "Throughout my career," Kirkpatrick wrote toward the end of it, "I have been careful not to criticize any sitting president." Actually, she had attacked Jimmy Carter, and now she would offer some brutally honest remarks about George W. Bush. The key question for her was not whether Saddam was evil. It was instead whether Iraq could ever be transformed into a democracy. She held that it could not. "The administration's failure involved several issues," she wrote, "but the core concern is that they did not seem to have methodically completed the due diligence required for reasoned policy-making because they failed to address the aftermath of the invasion. This, of course, is reflected by the violence, sectarian unrest, ethnic vengeance and bloodshed we see in Iraq today." Kirkpatrick, a conservative, viewed the war in Iraq as a liberal war, too ambitious in scope, too careless with respect to means, too idealistic in intent. We cannot intervene every time a sovereign leader oppresses his own people. If we are to intervene, moreover, sanctions and diplomatic pressure may be better measures than force. The United States must reserve its use of military force for situations where its national interests are threatened, and Saddam constituted no such threat.

Kirkpatrick's views did more than suggest that conservatives could dispense with Manichaeism. They also implied that excessive use of the language of good and evil was hostile to a conservative preference for prudence. Had Republican politicians chosen to follow her advice, they might have developed a more credible foreign policy than the one that eventually emerged under George W. Bush. Such a policy would still have been severely flawed, especially with respect to the problem of political evil. Kirkpatrick's double standard, for one thing, led the United States to support dictators such as the shah, a disastrous decision in retrospect because when he was removed from power, an all but inevitable outcome given his unpopularity, the corruption and brutality of his regime fueled the emergence of the very Islamic Republic in Iran that has become such a threat to American interests in the region. Nor, given her indifference to human suffering, can we imagine a Kirkpatrick-style national security policy responding effectively to mass atrocities anywhere in the world. Kirkpatrick's cynicism all too easily led to inaction.

Still, Kirkpatrick was smart enough to recognize the dangers of excessive Manichaean zeal. The same cannot be said of others whose neoconservatism was never tempered by realism. In their 2003 book *The War over Iraq*, William Kristol, Irving's son, and his coauthor, journalist Lawrence Kaplan, first made the case that Saddam had to be removed from power because of his domestic reign of terror; only then did they go on to discuss any threat he might pose to the United States. (Kaplan, unlike Kristol, would later come to question some of the neoconservative assumptions that guided him when he coauthored this book.) Saddam, Kristol and Kaplan wrote, "epitomizes—no less than Osama bin Laden—sheer malice. Here, after all, is a man who has imposed a violent, totalitarian regime on the people of Iraq. He is at once a tyrant, an aggressor and, in his own avowed objectives, a threat to civilization." Saddam tortured children, relied on terror, and engaged in "virtually genocidal" acts. However awful his actions against fellow Arabs, his campaigns against the non-Arab Kurds were even more savage. George H. W. Bush, praised by Kirkpatrick, was in their view right to punish Saddam. But his failure to bring the matter to a close by toppling Saddam, they argued, was a disastrous mistake.

The War over Iraq dismissed Kirkpatrick's Machiavellian alternative out of hand. Kristol and Kaplan viewed the Arab world in particular as awash with petty tyrants not unlike Somoza and the shah. "The idea that the United States can 'do business' with any regime, no matter how odious and hostile to American principles, is both morally and strategically dubious," they wrote. In the early years of the twenty-first century, in their view, the United States was in an even better position to apply the lessons of cold war foreign policy than it had been during the cold war. Then, democracy had not yet proved its global appeal. Now, with the collapse of the Soviet Union, we know how much people around the world want democracy for themselves, and it is therefore America's obligation to help them achieve it even if doing so requires military intervention to remove from power their own leaders who stand in the way. "A century of fighting fascist dictators in Germany, Italy and Japan, communist dictators in Korea and Vietnam, neofascist dictators in the Balkans and Iraq, and for that matter a narco-trafficking dictator in Central America has alerted all but the most obdurate policymakers to the fact that the character of regimes—not diplomatic agreements or multilateral institutions—are the key to peace and stability." If Kristol and Kaplan had their way, the United States would be in the business of replacing leaders of bad character with those who had passed some kind of moral intentions test. Following the logic of their analysis would take the United States back to the era of totalitarianism, when Western leaders and foreign policy intellectuals, consumed by Manichaean gloom, paid little or no attention to actual political developments in those societies with which they viewed themselves at war.

In an interview with the conservative magazine *National Review* shortly after their book was published, Kristol and Kaplan were asked by the journalist Kathryn Jean Lopez if there was any group that they ought in particular to try to convince of their arguments. "Liberals," they replied. "Not liberals at *The Nation* or *The American Prospect*, who can always be counted on to favor tyranny over anything that strengthens American power, however marginally. But liberals who supported the American interventions in Bosnia and Kosovo—humanists, in short. For if ever there was a humanitarian undertaking, it is the liberation of Iraq from a tyrant who has jailed, tortured, gassed, shot, and otherwise murdered tens of thousands of his own citizens." Actually, Kristol and Kaplan did not need to engage in all that much persuasion. When it came to seeing evil incarnate in Saddam's Iraq, a number of prominent liberals were already convinced.

During the early years of the cold war, conservatives were the first to adopt Manichaean language of good and evil, and it was only after they had occupied that ground that liberals ultimately joined them. When it came to Saddam, the directional arrow went the other way. A thinker who played a particularly prominent role in applying the language of totalitarian evil to Saddam was the Iraqi dissident Kanan Makiya, whose cosmopolitan outlook and humanistic sensibility marked him out as liberal. Written with the same theoretical acumen and sense of moral passion as was *The Origins of Totalitarianism*, Makiya's *Republic of Fear*, first published in 1989, drew numerous parallels between the evils once embodied in Stalin and Hitler and those on display in Baghdad. On the one hand, the Ba'ath Party led by Saddam relied on the kind of techniques—terror, gulags, secret police, control of the press—that had characterized Nazi Germany and Stalinist Russia. On the other hand, there was the personality of Saddam himself, "marked by this calculated, disciplined, and above all effortless resort to violence genuinely conceived to be in the service of more exalted aims. His language is therefore a reflection of his personality—as opposed to professional training—in which violence and vision, through party organization, got distilled into a volatile mixture."

As the case for waging war against Saddam was built, Makiya's writings had a major impact on conservatives such as Kristol and Kaplan. But they would have an even bigger influence on liberals, especially the writer Paul Berman, one of the leading enthusiasts for war against Saddam. Berman took the Manichaeism implicit in Makiya's analysis and made it explicit. For the Iraqi dissident, Ba'athism, with its toxic combination of socialist ideology and Arab nationalism, was the problem. For this American liberal, Ba'athism, a secular ideology, although evil in itself, paled in comparison to the even greater insidiousness of radical Islam. In his book *Terror and Liberalism*, Berman described Islamic radicalism in the "wide arc from Afghanistan to Algeria, and beyond" in the following terms: "Piety spread. Religious devotion deepened. Women hid behind their veils. And as piety, devotion, and patriarchy bloomed, in every country a new kind of politics came into flower. It was the politics of slaughter—slaughter for the sake of sacred devotion, slaughter conducted in a mood of spiritual loftiness, slaughter indistinguishable from charity, slaughter that led to suicide, slaughter for slaughter's sake. It was a flower of evil. And this new politics, in its bright green Islamist color, proved to be sturdy."

As this passage illustrates, Berman, who was as passionate as he was poetic, uses language in a fashion that Whittaker Chambers would have appreciated. One can read sections of *Witness* dealing with communist evil and sections of *Terror and Liberalism* dealing with Islamic evil and not have any idea which author was responsible for which passages. For the one writer as for the other, the enemy was not only evil in itself but a force that had developed an entirely new form of politics and possessed seemingly unlimited strength. *Terror and Liberalism* was an anguished cry from the heart, a work seamlessly blending historical and political analysis with personal confession and a sense of coming doom. Berman's book was a *Witness* for the left.

If Berman's case for war against Saddam sounded like Chambers, the one made by the Middle East specialist Kenneth Pollack was a liberal version of James Burnham. Burnham's late-1940s arguments for confronting communism had not been written with emotional fervor. His books were clinical, almost legalistic, in tone, with bullet points rather than flowery metaphors dominating his prose. The case he made, moreover, was not based on the Soviet Union's military prowess. Unlike later conservatives who would go out of their way to exaggerate the Soviet threat, Burnham had written that "technologically, the weaknesses in the Soviet economy and culture are reflected in the armed forces. With some exceptions, the quality of weapons and equipment is relatively low." But rather than take such weaknesses as an indication that perhaps the Russians were not so threatening after all, Burnham argued quite the reverse. It was not the military capacity possessed by the Soviet Union that ought to have worried us, he suggested, but its intentions. Guided by a messianic ideology, the Soviet Union was determined to dominate the world. "Unfortunately, we do not get rid of cancer by calling it indigestion," Burnham wrote in one of his rare metaphoric moods. Disease had to be stopped early, before it metastasized. Sitting around and waiting would only allow the Russians to develop the capabilities that would enable them to realize their evil aims.

In *The Threatening Storm*, a book whose Churchillian title evoked the earlier struggle against totalitarianism, Pollack, following in Burnham's footsteps, urged the West to focus not on what Saddam could do—his actual capabilities were not known to us—but instead on what he hoped to do. Saddam, Pollack pointed out, thought of himself as the latest in a line of Middle Eastern strongmen such as Nebuchadnezzar, Saladin, and al-Mansur (the ruler of Córdoba who waged war against the Christian West). We knew what the man wanted, Pollack wrote: he aimed to transform Iraq into a global power, become the major figure in the Muslim world, and lead the fight against Israel, all of which would have been "disastrous for the United States." The fact that he could not actually do these things made him not less dangerous but more so. Relying on the work of the American psychoanalyst Jerrold Post (who, needless to say, had never sat Saddam down on a couch), Pollack concluded that while Saddam's regime did not threaten the United States directly the way Hitler's had in the 1930s, Saddam himself "does share some of Hitler's more dangerous traits, and one of them is his propensity to take colossal risks." Since evil can never be trusted to act rationally, to protect itself the United States had to shut him down immediately because it could never be sure what threats his delusions of grandeur could pose in the future. Pollack was the strategist turned moralist, just as Berman was the moralist become strategist. It was as if James Burnham had come back to life dressed in liberals' clothing.

The war in Iraq thus returned Manichaeism to where it had been in the late 1940s—and brought with it many of the same problems. Conservative Manichaeism in the early years of the cold war had transformed anticommunism from a geopolitical outlook to an obsessive mania, leaving the West too insecure, defensive, and moralistic to recognize that, far from monolithic, communist regimes were politically divided in ways that could be effectively exploited. Communism is now almost gone, but many examples of political evil remain. Liberals who opt for a Manichaean approach to dealing with them risk misunderstanding the nature of the political evil we face today in the same way conservatives who once saw the Soviet Union as the moving force behind every event that took place in the world did. Once again, in urging us to ignore politics and to place our focus on evil instead, they lead us in a self-defeating direction.

Consider the very case of Saddam, which did so much to inspire contemporary Manichaeism. As early as the first Gulf War, Saddam had been viewed by prominent American strategists and thinkers as the essence of evil. Illustrative of them is Peter Galbraith, a diplomat long identified with the cause of the Kurdish people. "Hitler, when he took power in 1933, did not have a plan to exterminate all the Jews in Europe," Galbraith pointed out in 1988. "Evil begets evil." His words, along with those of writers such as Berman and Pollack, or for that matter Kristol and Kaplan, certainly had a ring of truth. Saddam's actions against the Kurds, most notoriously during the Anfal massacre of 1987–88, really were genocidal. He used chemical weapons. He jailed and tortured his political opponents. Saddam's crimes, to be sure, never approached the scale of those of Hitler and Stalin. Under pressure from the rest of the world, moreover, he had softened some of his policies, abandoning, for example, his plans to acquire and use weapons of mass destruction. Yet as tyrants go, he was a major one. What harm could come from refusing to coddle him, as a Machiavellian might have urged, and instead seeking not only to call as much public attention as possible to the evil he represented but also his overthrow by military force?

A good part of the harm came from the fact that leaders who oppress their own people, even in the most evil of ways, are not necessarily threats to other people. As I will soon argue, the link between domestic ugliness and foreign policy aggressiveness, however appropriate to the totalitarian leaders of the 1930s and 1940s, rarely applies to the politically evil leaders of today. Against the Kurds, Saddam stopped at nothing. Against the Iranians, he launched an aggressive war. But against the rest of the world, he was no threat. We can trace both the military and the diplomatic failures of the George W. Bush administration's efforts in Iraq directly to its mistaken diagnosis of the kind of evil Saddam represented. Bush was so convinced that Saddam was a reincarnation of Hitler that as president he was never able to understand the differences between Sunni and Shia, the way the U.S. occupation of Iraq would be perceived by its residents, or the necessity of co-opting former members of the Saddam regime, no matter how complicit in evil they may have been, into the process of reconstructing Iraqi society. It was not a flawed military strategy alone that doomed the American efforts in Iraq but flawed ways of thinking about evil.

Saddam and his cruelty, to be sure, are gone, and there may come a day—although with every new horror in that country it becomes less likely—when the cost will be viewed as having been worth it. In the meantime, the attempt by those to treat Saddam as evil incarnate persuaded the rest of the world that whatever tactics might be used to combat terrorism, relying on the United States to accomplish the job by itself is not the right way to go. About the only good thing that emerged from the United States' response to the evils represented by Saddam was that mistakes so egregious are likely to be avoided in the future—unless, of course, Americans somehow find themselves persuaded that the very same way of thinking about evil that failed in Iraq should be applied to its neighbor, and longtime enemy, Iran.

WHY MANICHAEISM INEVITABLY FAILS

THE REASONS SECULAR Manichaeism rarely succeeds in eliminating or even reducing the evil it finds so prevalent in the world can best be appreciated by returning to the period in which early church fathers such as Saint Augustine wrestled with the Manichaeans among them. The seemingly obscure theological issues they fought over then have direct relevance to the failure of black-and-white thinking now.

Manichaeism in world affairs raises the same problem it does in matters of the spirit: If evil is indeed so powerful and omnipresent, can the forces of goodness ever truly conquer it? As I emphasized earlier, Manichaeism, pessimistic to its core, as a faith offered its adherents little reason to hope. Much the same is true of those who adopt a similar, if by now secular, viewpoint on terrorism, genocide, and the other forms of political evil that currently surround us. There can be no doubt that they are correct to bring the problem of evil to the world's attention. But by doing so through a constant search for unrelenting evil everywhere but here, their program leaves evil in place or may even expand its reach.

For one thing, and a most odd one for an outlook that prides itself on its determination, Manichaeism is inevitably accompanied by defeatism. Although promising to treat political evil harshly, leaders attracted to a Manichaean outlook on the world rarely tell us that its practitioners are fractious, error prone, or myopic. Instead, they go out of their way to emphasize their guile, inflate their capacities, overestimate their appeal, and expand their ambitions. Manichaeans proclaim that anyone who is not on the side of the good is on the side of the evil in the hopes of rallying the neutral to their cause, but they wind up turning off potential allies who do not view the world in such dramatic terms. They may talk about putting "an end to evil," yet for the true

Manichaean, evil can never end so long as the world is dominated by Hobbesian struggles for power. Once a Manichaean perspective identifies one particular tyrant as embodying evil, it is not long before it finds others resembling him. Although it often does, a Manichaean temperament need not become evil itself—Mani, who so far as we know lived in accordance with his own teachings, did not—but it does invest in a futures market for wickedness; without evil, the fight for the good loses all meaning. Ultimately, a Manichaean foreign policy becomes gloomily unable to anticipate a brighter global future, just as third- and fourth-century Manichaean views toward human sexuality could not imagine reproductive families. Manichaeans find it impossible to escape from the dilemma that awaits them. If evil is not as strong as it appears to be, we do not need to engage with it in a global contest for supremacy. But if it really is as strong as we say, the global contest becomes one we have little chance of winning.

Another reason to question the efficacy of secular Manichaeism is that it undermines the notion that people are responsible for their own acts. There are many reasons Augustine came to reject the Manichees, but one of the most important concerns the question of free will. Peter Brown, Augustine's biographer, explains the theological differences between the Bishop of Hippo and Mani's followers this way: "It was a matter of common sense that men were responsible for their actions; they could not be held responsible if their wills were not free; therefore, their wills could not be thought of as being determined by some external forces, in this case, by the Manichaean 'Power of Darkness.'" From Saint Augustine's perspective, the Christian God ought never to be viewed as equal in every respect to Satan. One wanted human beings to live with the consequences of their acts; the other wanted them to be a slave to passions they could never control. Augustine therefore chose God, and with him free will, for a reason. To be sure, Augustine's appreciation of free will was always hedged by his conviction that, as a result of Adam's original sin, the will of human beings had become distorted with evil. But as harsh as Augustine's theology may sound to contemporary ears, it is joyous and spontaneous when compared to the darker vision held by Mani.

If Augustine was ambivalent toward the idea of free will, contemporary Manichaeans, in both their religious and their secular manifestations, are decidedly hostile. When Manichaeism dominates the mind of a foreign-policy maker, the enemy has no will at all, not even a distorted one; he is viewed as a lunatic and a criminal, consumed with irrational rage and primitive longings. Because he is in the grip of his own ideology, he is never free to exercise his reason. Lacking the most basic of human motivations, the evildoer may be treated with all the force at one's command because he knows neither mercy nor charity. He is simply outside our moral universe, a beast in human form. There is no standard to which a radical evildoer can be held. Any attempt to bring him within the community of human beings will reward his evil, and that we simply must never do.

The irony of this way of thinking is that when secular Manichaeans deny free will to their enemy, they simultaneously deny it to themselves. The neo-Manichaean viewpoint holds that we are fighting because we believe in freedom and our enemy does not. Yet the very effort to fit foreign policy views into a neo-Manichaean framework denies our side as well as the enemy's the freedom to escape from a very tightly organized Manichaean outlook. Demonizing others as evil strips from the demonizer the choice of treating his antagonists as people with whom he can negotiate or as members of political movements with goals of their own. Once we view our enemies in Manichaean terms, we lose the option of thinking about why they act the way they do or believe in the causes that attract them; in such a way we strip ourselves of the capacity to respond strictly and effectively to the political elements of the evil they represent. Determined to confine our enemies, we limit ourselves. Unable to distinguish between evil in general and political evil in particular, we take constant aim at an evil we can never eradicate while leaving in place a political structure and ideology whose contours, if we thought about the problem differently, we might be able to change.

No sooner do we identify perpetrators of political evil as Manichaean, furthermore, than it becomes all but impossible to avoid finding ourselves in the same category. They divide the world dualistically and so must we; the only difference between them and us is how we view the duality—which side is good and which is bad? We are at war with evil; they are at war with the West, Zionism, Christianity, secularism, or simply outsiders, all of which represent their own axis of evil. Everything then comes down to which side one is on, as if both sides take it for granted that there can only be two sides from which to choose. In such a way is our free will further confined: so long as the

Manichaean spirit is accepted, enemies can only act—and those who fight them can only react. No wonder the United States has had so little success fighting its enemies on Manichaean terms. When secular Manichaeans characterize the all-or-nothing outlook of communists in the 1950s or radical Muslims today as paranoid and suspicious, they are simultaneously describing their own way of thinking.

Finally, the neo-Manichaean search for unrelenting external evil and the Augustinian notion of radical evil within all of us bring us to similarly unsatisfying results. Neo-Augustinians such as Stanley Milgram make inflated claims about the extraordinary evils that ordinary people, in their willingness to be obedient, commit. Secular Manichaeans such as George W. Bush and other foreign policy hawks make far too grandiose assertions about the capacities and intentions of their enemies. If reducing the amount of political evil in the world is one's goal, it makes as little sense to compare one's own side to evildoers as it does to equate petty tyrants and corrupt crooks with Hitler or Stalin.

Broadening evil to include everyone and restricting it only to one's enemies therefore produce far too much moralizing and far too little talk of the difficult political trade-offs required to make foreign policy work. Never quite taking proper aim at the evil both points of view think they are firing at, they constantly miss their targets. Each falls victim to a self-fulfilling prophecy, one claiming that the evil within can never be eliminated, while the other insists that evil can only be defeated, if at all, after years of arduous struggle. Whether inside us or out in the world, evil cannot be tolerated, yet, unless we are capable of either transforming ourselves into sinless creatures or rendering the entire world anew, evil will have to be tolerated. When dealing with political evil, we need to be clear about what we can achieve and what we cannot, and this is precisely what neither the followers of Augustine nor the followers of Mani can offer us.

Augustine was wrong to deny that there is no such thing as evil in the world, for surely we have seen too much of it by now to deny that it has real substance. Mani and his disciples, however, were wrong to find so much evil that it constitutes half the world. From John Quincy Adams to Reinhold Niebuhr and George Kennan, warnings against Manichaean tendencies have been plentiful in American political discourse. The fact that the United States continues to search out monsters to destroy indicates just how frequently their words have been ignored. Whether one is

liberal or conservative, romantic or realist, fundamentalist or antifun-
damentalist, the temptation to divide the world into good and evil, and
to view oneself as occupying the good corner while one's enemies stand
in the bad one, is a temptation that must be resisted. Political evil can
never be defeated by adopting its own perspective on the world.

CHAPTER FOUR

The Misuses of Appeasement

AN ANALOGY SPUN OUT OF CONTROL

"WHEN GREEDY Mr. Hitler started taking over other countries, people at first thought 'give him a little more, then he will be satisfied,'" wrote one concerned American to his senator. He might have been referring to the need to take a firm stand against the Soviet Union in the early days of the cold war, stopping the spread of communism in Southeast Asia during the Vietnam era, or the struggle against Islamic-inspired terrorism today. Instead, he was employing the by now familiar reference to appeasement in response to Martin Luther King Jr.'s plan to lead a march in the Marquette Park area of Chicago in 1966. "Give greedy Mr. King a little more freedom then he will stop. Isn't that what we are being told today?"

Forty-two years later, an American president addressed the Israeli Knesset. "The fight against terror and extremism is the defining challenge of our time," George W. Bush told his hosts. Noting that "some"— he offered no names—preferred negotiation with extremists to confrontation, Bush added that "we have heard this foolish delusion before. As Nazi tanks crossed into Poland in 1939, an American senator declared: 'Lord, if only I could have talked to Hitler, all of this might have been avoided.'" Only one conclusion was possible: "We have an obligation to call this what it is—the false comfort of appeasement, which has been repeatedly discredited by history."

Both the bigot and the president were relying upon the most common way of thinking about political evil available to us today. In 1938, the British prime minister Neville Chamberlain went to Munich and gave Hitler a free hand to take control over the German-speaking areas of Czechoslovakia known as the Sudetenland. His decision, one of history's all-time great blunders, not only was a cowardly and shortsighted act but led directly to the massive global conflict that followed in its wake. Put evil of that magnitude together with gutlessness of that scope and the conclusion appears obvious: never again shall a rapacious dictator be appeased.

For more than half a century now, a willingness to invoke the failure of Munich has come to define sober statesmanship. Leaders who proclaim that peace in our time is a goal transcending all others are dismissed as naïve idealists unprepared to deal with the hard facts of political life. Those courageous enough to stare evil in the face and insist on their determination not to cede an inch to its malignancy, as Chamberlain's political antagonist Winston Churchill did in response to the 1938 events, are taken by both press and people to have passed all the requisite tests of political acumen. It matters not a whit whether such leaders are inexperienced or seasoned, liberal or conservative, men or women. Evildoers, we are told, prey on weakness. Confronting evil demands guts. So long as there is a politician anywhere in the West even tempted by appeasement, evil will be given free rein to expand its reach.

Such a way of thinking about evil may be deeply ingrained, but it is severely misguided. No other legacy of our confused ways of responding to political evil is more dangerous than our constant attempts to create new Hitlers on the one hand and to overcompensate for Chamberlain's mistake on the other. Just as Churchill then quite rightly urged war against Hitler, political leaders today need the courage to stand up to the charge of appeasement if they are to make the world in which we live that much less prone to political evil. Invoking appeasement under inappropriate conditions suffers from more than historical inaccuracy; it is an act of supreme irresponsibility and gross negligence. In the years since the end of World War II, more people have died because political leaders were determined not to give in to threats they denounced as Hitlerian than would have had those leaders realized they were actually dealing with petty tyrants whose thirst for conquest was in reality quite limited.

The appeasement analogy contains two problematic assumptions. The first is that the horrors of totalitarianism do not lie just in the past but can make a reappearance in the contemporary world. Since a number of today's nastier regimes have available to them weapons of destruction more powerful, and means of extermination more sophisticated, than Hitler had available to him, leaders must be that much more prepared to confront potential evildoers before they can assemble the vast military apparatus they are seeking. The second assumption holds that the enemy one is facing is so aggressive by nature, and therefore so intent on expanding his power, that if he is not stopped in one place, he will have to be confronted at greater risk and cost in another. Whenever a tyrant uses brutal methods to oppress his own people, he is viewed as having global designs as well.

Neither of these assumptions makes sense when dealing with contemporary forms of political evil. The totalitarian regimes of the 1930s and 1940s gained the power at their disposal because of unique historical factors unlikely ever to be repeated again. Furthermore, acts of political evil, whether their effects are felt in Darfur, Haifa, Srebrenica, or Mumbai, are invariably local in nature, not fueled by global ambition but aimed to address specific grievances by attacking particular people. Greedy Hitler undoubtedly was. But while he has certainly not been brought back to life in the persona of Martin Luther King Jr., neither has he been embodied in the form of Slobodan Milosevic, Osama bin Laden, or the terrorists who threaten Israel. We can no longer afford to give Hitler the honor of bequeathing to him so many successors. What happened in Munich deserves to stay in Munich.

WHY TOTALITARIANISM WILL NEVER HAPPEN AGAIN

THE CONCEPT of totalitarianism that became so popular in the years after World War II was based on the historical experience of three countries: Italy, where the term had been invented, and then Nazi Germany and the Soviet Union. The theorists who formulated the concept, including Hannah Arendt, Carl Friedrich, and Zbigniew Brzezinski, held that a combination of pernicious ideological thinking, dictatorial accumulation of state power, ruthless methods of propaganda and terror, charisma and the adulation of leadership, and aggressive foreign policy intentions had created an entirely new political reality. The books elaborating this concept became contemporary classics. But not only did their authors lack access to documents that have since become available, they were too close to the horrors just past to have sufficient perspective on their ultimate meaning. As a result, they failed to anticipate the collapse of the Soviet Union and could not foresee how thoroughly postwar Germany—indeed, all of postwar Europe—would turn its back on the twentieth century's history of violence.

A new generation of historians has emerged challenging the assumptions of the totalitarian model. The basic conclusion of these historians can be summarized as follows: far from being the wave of the future, as both the defenders and the critics of the totalitarian regimes themselves frequently asserted, both Nazi Germany and Stalinist Russia were created at a time when a number of highly unusual conditions came together to shape the specific form both states took. This finding could not be more relevant to the way we think about political evil today. If the conditions that brought about totalitarianism cannot be replicated, straining to avoid the appeasement of evildoers could not be more self-defeating. We find ourselves face-to-face with a number of depressing realities when dealing with contemporary forms of terrorism, ethnic cleansing, and genocide. Fortunately, any return of totalitarianism is not among them.

Totalitarianism, first of all, was a direct result of World War I. "The First World War made Hitler possible," writes Ian Kershaw, and the same could be said for Lenin or Mussolini. None of the leaders who took their nations to war in 1914 realized just how long and bloody that conflict would be, and it was the peculiar political genius of the totalitarian dictators to exploit the resulting resentments for their own ideological purposes once the war finally came to an end. Totalitarianism constituted a reaction against the spirit of liberal optimism that had dominated much of the late nineteenth century. Populations that had seen irrationality on so huge a scale in the trenches could not be surprised by politicians preaching fear and creating campaigns of mass hysteria in peacetime. Totalitarianism required extensive psychological preparation, and the futility of World War I provided it.

Militarily speaking, World War I was like no other war before it. In previous European wars, one hoped for a quick defeat of the enemy, after which conditions would return to normal. World War I, by contrast, radicalized the whole idea of warfare. This war, the historian Alan Kramer writes, was geared "towards systematic, total exploitation of enemy civilians and the resources of the conquered territory. From cultural destruction, in the sense of the deliberate targeting of cultural objects, the war moved to a 'culture of destruction'—the acceptance of the destruction, consumption, and exploitation of whatever it took to wage the war." The totalitarian state's coercive capacity, from this perspective, was not created out of thin air; it was built upon a state that had already come into existence to fight as ruthlessly as possible.

"The most spectacular and terrifying instance of industrial killing in this century was the Nazi attempted genocide of the Jews," another historian, Omer Bartov, concludes. "Neither the idea, nor its implementation, however, can be understood without reference to the Great War, the first truly industrial military confrontation in history."

As in Germany, so in Russia. "The First World War brought communism into being," as the late Martin Malia put it in his book *The Soviet Tragedy*. Not all that popular, possessing an ideology wildly inappropriate for actual Russian conditions, and excessively conspiratorial and sectarian, Lenin and the Bolsheviks never could have assumed power in any kind of open competition. But World War I and its aftermath created conditions perfect for their methods. "Normal politics were suspended, the economy was nationalized and militarized, culture was turned to propaganda, and private life was eclipsed by public purpose," Malia went on. "No nation's social order could survive such intrusion unaltered, and that of fragile, rickety Russia least of all. Her economy, her society, and her political system alike were radically transformed from what they had been in 1914." It was, moreover, not just at its start that the shadow of World War I loomed over the Soviet system. Knowing full well that communism's triumph was made possible only by Russia's defeat in one world war, Stalin was determined to prevent another catastrophic military defeat in the coming one, and he continued the Soviet Union's militarization and industrialization unabated.

For something like totalitarianism to happen again, something like World War I would have to happen again. It is certainly possible that the world could experience another truly global war: conflicts between nations spilling over into violence are unlikely ever to disappear. But the pernicious effects on political life evident in so many countries in the aftermath of World War I were not due to the violence of the conflict per se, or even to the defeats suffered by Germany and Russia. It was the very senselessness of the war, the unexpected number of casualties, the inability to make visible progress on the front, that did so much to produce the apocalyptic style of politics in which totalitarian leaders thrived. *That* kind of war is impossible to imagine happening again, if for no other reason than the existence of nuclear weapons. Obviously, nuclear weapons create the potential for horrendous political evil; the prospect of their use in the Middle East or over disputes between India and Pakistan is too frightening to contemplate. Yet because of their sheer destructive power, nuclear weapons make protracted trench warfare, and its particularly irrational legacies, obsolete. Either nuclear weapons will deter such a war from being fought in the first place or they will—hopefully never—produce a war whose huge number of casualties will be predicted because they will be so expected.

If the kind of war that started totalitarianism is unlikely ever to be repeated, so is the one that ended it. World War I is remembered for its irrationality. World War II will always be recalled for the sheer scale of the destruction it caused. The Jews, of course, were the primary victims of Hitler's murderous obsessions. But World War II produced death and destruction everywhere; Snyder estimates that as many as twenty-one million people were killed as a result of war, starvation, and genocide. If anyone doubted the cost in human lives necessary to bring the era of totalitarianism to a close in the 1930s, they knew by the 1940s just how extensive those costs could become. This is not to suggest, as the American writer Nicholson Baker has, that the costs were too high. But it does serve as a reminder of the havoc that totalitarianism could wreak.

It is surely worth emphasizing, therefore, that in Europe, where so much of the carnage of World War II was felt, the desire to go to war has been all but extinguished. In the years since totalitarianism's passing, Western European societies gave up their imperial ambitions, formed first a commercial and then a political union, demilitarized themselves, aided and supported democratic movements in the Eastern bloc, survived domestic terrorism without completely abrogating liberal democratic procedures, and made clear their skepticism toward America's reliance on doctrines of preventive warfare in Iraq. "In the first half of the century," writes Stanford University historian James Sheehan in his book *Where Have All the Soldiers Gone?*, "European states . . . were made by and for war. . . . In the century's second half, European states were made by and for peace." To the American neoconservative writer Robert Kagan, Europe's skepticism toward militarism represents the victory of naïve Venus over tough-minded Mars; no better proof of the attraction of appeasement exists than this general European failure to recognize the need for a strong national defense. But another interpretation of Europe's aversion to militarism is more persuasive. Given the historical experience of totalitarianism, it makes far more sense to view postwar Europe as evidence of just how much Europeans have learned from their totalitarian past—and how determined they are to avoid reproducing the conditions that gave rise to it. It is difficult to know which to admire most: postwar Europe's success with democracy or, with the admittedly significant exception of the Balkans, its experience of peace.

The economic circumstances that gave rise to the era of totalitarianism were almost as unusual as the military ones. One of them was the rapid hyperinflation that gripped the Weimar Republic in 1923, the same year in which Hitler conducted his Munich putsch; prices at the peak of the inflation doubled every forty-eight hours. Economically speaking, hyperinflation all but destroyed the German middle class. If one believes, as many political sociologists do, that a strong middle class is a prerequisite for a well-functioning democracy, hyperinflation's immediate political consequence was to fuel the rise of extremist political parties of both the right and the left. But the psychological and cultural effects of hyperinflation may have been greater than either its economic or its political effects. Just as World War I's futility contributed to the sense that the world lacked any sense of order, hyperinflation undermined bourgeois ideas of prudence, long-term investment, and merit. "People just didn't understand what was happening," wrote the publisher Leopold Ullstein at the time. "All the economic theory that had been taught didn't provide for the phenomenon. There was a feeling of utter dependence on anonymous powers—almost as a primitive people believed in magic—that somebody must be in the know, and that this small group of somebodies must be a conspiracy." When currency loses meaning, everything loses meaning. Although hyperinflation was eventually brought under control in Weimar Germany, its contribution to the rise of fascism cannot be underestimated.

Even more devastating than hyperinflation was the U.S. stock market crash in 1929 and the subsequent worldwide depression. In the years after the crash, unemployment in Germany expanded dramatically; roughly one-third of all Germans were without work in 1932, and the percentages were even higher in the major industrial areas. The political effects registered almost immediately. "As Germany plunged deeper into the Depression," writes the British historian Richard Evans, "growing numbers of middle-class citizens began to see in the youthful dynamism of the Nazi Party a possible way out of the situation." They may not have been good ones, but Hitler did have answers to the economic catastrophe. He blamed Jewish capitalists for its persistence. He pursued autarkic economic politics that promised to end Germany's dependence on foreign investors. He sponsored rapid remilitarization of the country in ways that would create jobs and stimulate further economic growth. The crisis atmosphere spawned by a badly functioning economy fostered a crisis atmosphere in politics; without the chaos represented by idle workers, food and product shortages, and unused industrial capacity, it is hard to imagine the Nazis even getting an electoral foothold, let alone rising to the highest levels of power and retaining that power as long as they did.

Hyperinflation and depression, in short, when added to the pot already brewing in the aftermath of World War I, increased people's receptivity to the idea that strong-armed ruthlessness offered the only path to stability. "The Great Slump almost inevitably increased social and political tensions everywhere," Volker Berghahn, a German historian, points out in *Europe in the Era of Two World Wars.* "Violence that had become part of daily life during World War I and the years thereafter returned, and with it reappeared men who had a vision of the future that was different from the civilian one of the mid-1920s. . . . The most radical elements came to believe that the struggle could only be won by the ruthless annihilation of the internal enemy." There is no direct line from the Great Depression to the extermination camps, but there is an indirect one. Extremist politics requires crisis conditions, and the economic collapse of the early 1930s provided more than its share.

In the context of today's world, any return to the combination of hyperinflation and depression that gave totalitarianism its breathing room is about as unimaginable as any war on the scale of the twentieth century's two world wars. Hyperinflation can still happen; Chile, Yugoslavia, and Zimbabwe have all experienced it in recent years. But not only is it rare, its chance of recurring in heavily industrialized countries is close to nonexistent. The closest the United States has ever come to hyperinflation in recent years was the 18 percent rise in prices under Jimmy Carter, but in the long history of hyperinflation, this was less than a blip. America's bout with excessive inflation did have its political consequences; Ronald Reagan was elected in 1980 in large part because of it. Although the entire episode was accompanied by talk of the Latin Americanization of the economy, the United States, like all advanced capitalist democracies, had in place fiscal and monetary tools unavailable to political leaders in the 1920s. Before long the inflation of the

1970s was brought under control without any damage to the structure of democratic politics.

These days policymakers worry more about deflation than hyperinflation. While methods exist to prevent prices from rising too rapidly, there are no especially helpful ones available to government when prices decline too fast; once interest rates are lowered to zero in the hopes of stimulating aggregate demand, they cannot be lowered any further. Deflation could therefore have dangerous effects on democratic forms of government if it persists too long. But the most serious case of deflation in recent years, Japan's, lasted for decades and, despite the fact that liberal democracy did not have deep historical roots in that country, did not result in a turn toward totalitarianism. Because of what happened during Weimar, we have a pretty clear understanding of how hyperinflation can create the conditions for political extremism. No one knows whether prolonged periods of deflation, should they spread from country to country, would have similar political consequences. But even if deflation were to reinforce economic stagnation and political gridlock, as it did in Japan, it would be highly unlikely to contribute to the same sense that the world is spinning hopelessly out of control that prevails when prices increase hour by hour. Hyperinflation leads to a politics of fervid enthusiasm. Deflation is more likely to produce a politics of sullen despair.

Toward the end of 2008, the United States and other countries around the world began to experience the worst recession of the post–World War II era. Comparisons to the Great Depression were not long in coming. Yet even though the effects of the recession were severe and could be felt everywhere, nothing quite like the truly devastating events of the 1930s has taken place. The reason may well lie in the ways both economics and politics have changed since the late 1920s and early 1930s.

The initial U.S. response to the deteriorating economic conditions of the 1930s, for one thing, was protectionist. In more recent times, despite the domestic unpopularity of free trade, as well as the severity of the recent recession, U.S. politicians from both parties remain committed to an open world economy. In large part this may be due to the lack of any reasonable alternatives; for all the passion of the demonstrations led by antiglobalization forces, no one has developed a credible model for promoting growth along autarkic political lines in a capitalist world as interconnected as today's has become. Nor are more radical solutions all that attractive, for, as the economic historian Harold James points out, "the obviously political types of reaction against globalization—fascism, Stalinism, and their economic manifestations in managed trade and the planned economy—are forever discredited." Given the magnitude of the Great Recession, economic policymaking remained remarkably conventional. Even though the recovery has been uneven, with unacceptably high rates of unemployment continuing, the Obama administration's bailout program, denounced by his Republican opponents as radical and socialistic, was actually rather moderate. Wall Street did not have to deflect full-scale attacks on its privileges; if anything, the bankers who did so much to bring about the crisis were soon once again receiving bonuses from their firms, complaining about their unfair treatment, and being welcomed into the halls of power.

Politics in the aftermath of the 2008 recession also stopped well short of the demagoguery and extremism of the 1930s. To be sure, the most significant political force to emerge in its wake, the so-called Tea Party movement, proved itself conspiratorial, given to hyperventilation, and susceptible to the charge of racism. Its political success suggests that the United States can expect a considerable amount of political extremism in the years to come, as unemployment and deficit spending persist while government remains too deadlocked to do anything much about them. But political gridlock, however frustrating, offers in its own way a protection against extremism; it discourages reaction as well as action. There is no reason to believe that liberal democracies for the foreseeable future face a threat to their continued existence anything like that posed by the attractions of totalitarianism during the 1930s.

There is still another reason to doubt the return of totalitarianism: one totalitarian system existing all by itself is something of an impossibility. Because all three of them came to power in the aftermath of World War I and faced similar challenges in the drastic economic conditions of the 1920s and 1930s, the totalitarian leaders watched each other carefully and applied the lessons of the other regimes to themselves. "The Bolshevik Revolution and the first phases of Soviet practice radically changed the political situation in Italy and Germany, not least in affecting what could now be imagined, what seemed to have become possible," writes the historian David D. Roberts. "Lenin influenced Mussolini, Mussolini and Stalin both influenced Hitler, and the advent of Nazism changed the situation for the Stalin regime in the Soviet Union.

Indeed, there is plenty of evidence of mutual admiration and influence, rivalry and fear, all constituting a kind of web connecting the three regimes." Ideologically dissimilar, totalitarian regimes were operationally similar. Each system required terror because the other system had terror. Propaganda had to be organized and systematic in one because it was organized and systematic in the other. Totalitarianism required an enemy, and when the enemy was itself totalitarian, the existence of one regime made possible the continued existence of the others. Little or nothing about totalitarianism was predetermined, but the unique political atmosphere of the 1920s, 1930s, and 1940s, by strengthening totalitarianism in one place, strengthened it in all.

The fact that totalitarianism existed on the extreme right as well as the extreme left during the 1930s and 1940s made democracies such as Great Britain, France, and the United States feel doubly threatened; no matter which way they turned, there was a vicious dictator facing them. Yet because the totalitarian regimes were so interdependent, the collapse of one unexpectedly prepared the ground for the collapse of all the others. The defeat of the Nazi regime required the military might of the Soviet Union, and when World War II ended, it seemed as if the Stalinist regime had been strengthened by its victory. Quite the opposite proved to be the case. Without Hitler's dictatorship, Stalin's was doomed; the Soviet Union went out of official existence in 1991, but it had already lost much of its totalitarian character even before Stalin's death in 1953 and had lost it completely by the time of the Twenty-second Congress of the Communist Party in 1962. With no totalitarian enemies to sustain it, the Soviet system turned in on itself, producing more than its share of corruption, assaults on civil liberty, and meddling in the affairs of other countries, but little or none of the sheer everyday terror of the Stalinist period. Although American foreign-policy makers continued to emphasize the Soviet threat during the last two decades of the Soviet Union's existence, persuaded that a society that had become a totalitarian dictatorship would always remain one, the leaders of those last few years, now all but forgotten, were in no position either to threaten the West or to contain the longings of their own people for a fresh start.

Totalitarianism came into existence when the countries attracted to it were undergoing rapid militarization and industrialization without many of the features of modernity already in place. Germany and Italy were among the last in Europe to become unified nation-states, and the borders of the Soviet Union were never fixed. In both Italy and the Soviet Union, some lived traditional lives not unlike the peasants of the feudal period while others embraced futurism in art and politics and worshiped the avant-garde. None of these countries had had much experience with liberal democracy, and in one of them, Germany, the short and unhappy life of the Weimar Republic only contributed to liberal democracy's destruction. Totalitarianism, in other words, offered the lure of a quick journey into the modern world. Industrialization and militarization would take place at so fast a rate that liberal democracy would be put to shame.

Totalitarianism's inability to survive the conditions that brought it into existence has had the consequence of undermining its attractiveness to societies that are seeking the same goal of rapid modernization today. The most interesting case in this regard is China. Chinese leaders are determined to turn their country into a major industrial power and to exercise all the political influence that comes with that status. They have, in addition, no real interest in democracy; public opinion is carefully monitored, demonstrations against the regime are rarely permitted, the Internet is controlled, and nothing like free elections takes place. It is therefore quite striking that contemporary China, while certainly not democratic, cannot be described with any accuracy as totalitarian either. "Under conditions that elsewhere have led to democratic transition," writes the political scientist Andrew Nathan about the years since the death of Mao, "China has made instead a transition from totalitarianism to a classic authoritarian regime, and one that appears to be stable." To promote economic growth, its leaders have opened its economy to some degree to the world economy. The army has become more professionalized and less politicized. Party and state are increasingly differentiated. Less overtly communist in its ideological coloration and leadership styles, China is less threatening to the United States; by assuming out-of-control American debt, the Chinese are in fact supporting Americans in their lifestyles rather than threatening the West militarily. As a result, far from viewing the Chinese as an aggressive power the United States ought never to appease, American politicians routinely overlook Chinese violations of human rights in order to keep the Chinese market open for American products. China's recent history suggests that liberal democracy and totalitarianism are not the only paths to modernity. In the world as it currently exists, there are alternatives clearly on the authoritarian side, and the Chinese, as well as other societies including Qatar and Peru, are finding ways of relying upon them.

The evils of totalitarianism, in conclusion, were unique to a particular time and place. Policymakers and intellectuals inclined to see the prospects for totalitarianism in the actions of today's terrorists and tyrants therefore ought to think a bit more about the historical comparisons they throw so loosely around. There exists enough political evil in the contemporary world to turn anyone's stomach, and people truly as rotten to their core as Hitler and Stalin can find themselves holding state power. Many of them will use that power to oppress their own citizens, often in the cruelest of ways. If opportunities present themselves, some of them will seek to satisfy their ambitions to gain additional territory or interfere in the affairs of other states through whatever military force they can accumulate. But none of this bears even the slightest resemblance to what was appeased in Munich in 1938. No leader on the world stage today could ever create a political system as brutal and as expansionist as those that were fashioned by Hitler, Stalin, and their henchmen; the military, economic, political, and cultural conditions of the contemporary world would not permit it. Appeasement cannot happen again because there is nothing like totalitarianism left to appease.

APPEASEMENT'S FIRST TESTS

ALTHOUGH THE CONDITIONS that had made appeasement at Munich possible were and are unlikely ever to be repeated, it did not take long after World War II came to a close for Western leaders to see new Munichs in every crisis they faced. In fact, it took just five years. No sooner did North Korea invade South Korea in 1950 than the appeasement analogy began to solidify itself as a never-to-be-questioned truth about the way evil in the contemporary world works. The desire to avoid appeasement, in short, is not some recent innovation. It had already become a persistent feature of Western political life while those who witnessed the original sin of giving Hitler what he wanted were still on the world stage.

Flying back to Washington from a visit to his home state of Missouri shortly after the North Korean invasion, President Harry Truman had plenty of time to think about the events unfolding in that part of the world. "In my generation, this was not the first occasion when the strong had attacked the weak," he later recalled about what had preoccupied him during that flight. "I remembered how each time that the democracies failed to act it had encouraged the aggressors to keep going ahead. Communism was acting in Korea just as Hitler, Mussolini, and the Japanese had acted ten, fifteen, and twenty years earlier." Newspapers around the country agreed. Republicans were as persuaded as Democrats that not coming to the defense of South Korea would mean appeasing communism. When the British foreign secretary Ernest Bevin suggested that the United States, being a young nation, required the mature wisdom that Britain could provide in the crisis, General Douglas MacArthur, commander of U.S. forces in Korea, scathingly replied that he "needed no lessons from the successors of Neville Chamberlain."

Appropriate analogy or not, appeals to Munich did the United States little to no good in Korea; the war there proved to be a stalemate, with death and suffering aplenty. Because it did, the appeasement analogy faced no real empirical test. Since the war ended with South Korea still very much an independent state, one could claim that this time the West really did reject weakness as an option and showed its willingness to use force to stop totalitarian advancement. Yet because the North Korean leadership remained in place, one could also conclude that the West had given a green light to communist regimes to act aggressively, especially after Truman did not follow MacArthur's recommendation to launch full-scale war against the Chinese. Korea simply delayed the questions over appeasement for another conflict.

That conflict eventually took place elsewhere in Asia, specifically in Vietnam. The decision, now widely regarded as disastrous, to send a hundred thousand additional troops to that country, and thereby to transform the American mission there to one of the costliest wars ever fought by the United States, was taken at a June 21, 1965, meeting of the National Security Council. In the course of that meeting, the U.S. ambassador to South Vietnam, Henry Cabot Lodge, bristling with anger toward those he believed unaware of the gravity of the situation, expressed his frustration with these words: "I feel there is a greater threat to start World War III if we don't go in. Can't we see the similarity to our own indolence in Munich?"

One wonders why Lodge even had to pose his question. The fact is that he was not the only one to see a similarity between the challenge posed to the United States by Ho Chi Minh and the one faced by the West at Munich; just about every single decision maker at the time, with the exception of the State Department's George Ball and a few cautious generals, did as well. John F. Kennedy, while a student in London, had written a senior thesis that he later turned into the best-selling book *Why England Slept;* its original title had been "Appeasement at Munich: The Inevitable Result of the Slowness of British Democracy to Change from a Disarmament Policy." When Kennedy ran for the Democratic nomination for president in 1960, his major challenger, Lyndon Johnson, referred to the fact that JFK's father had been an isolationist during his tenure as ambassador to the Court of St. James's by announcing, "I wasn't any Chamberlain umbrella man." He certainly was not. Shortly after assuming the presidency after Kennedy's assassination, Johnson defended escalating the war in Vietnam on the grounds that "on history's face the blotch of Munich is still visible." After leaving office, he told Doris Kearns that "everything I know about history told me that if I got out of Vietnam and let Ho Chi Minh run through the streets of Saigon, then I'd be doing exactly what Chamberlain did." The man who served both Kennedy and Johnson as secretary of state, Dean Rusk, wrote in his memoirs that "the principal lesson I learned from World War II was that if aggression is allowed to gather momentum, it can continue to build and lead to general war." Lodge may have been a Republican while the administration he served was Democratic, but such bipartisan agreement underscored how widespread the consensus that had formed over Korea had become a decade or so later.

As it happened, however, there was a major difference between Johnson's approach and the one developed by the Republican administration that followed. Richard Nixon was well known for his lack of scruples, and his major foreign policy adviser, Henry Kissinger, a practitioner of realpolitik, was quite capable of saying one thing while doing another. No such cynicism colored Lyndon Johnson's approach to Vietnam. "Look, I know you don't agree with me," Johnson had told Kearns, "but you must know that I believe everything I've just said with every bone inside me. You must give me that." The appeasement analogy for LBJ was not just some exaggeration cooked up for public consumption. It was rather a matter of deep belief, an assumption never to be questioned lest history judge him as yet another leader willing to allow a vicious dictator to expand his reach. If Johnson had been merely using the Munich metaphor as a ploy, as a way of winning popular support for a war that Americans found difficult to otherwise justify, he could have gradually stopped speaking of the dangers of appeasement as he began to understand that neither the war itself nor the effort to win public backing for it was succeeding. Instead, for better or for worse, he actually believed that Vietnam was a major historical turning point and that he was another Churchill.

In retrospect, it is difficult to understand how so many bought into a comparison that was so divorced from reality. Hitler had been the head of one of the most powerful states in the world, and even though its military was weak as a result of the Versailles Treaty, he rapidly engaged himself in rebuilding it. He had announced his intentions openly. A risk taker, he had judged his potential opponents in France and Britain well and had concluded that they would not consider his takeover of one neighboring country after another as vital to their national interest. He was even prepared, as he showed the very year after Munich, to enter into a nonaggression pact with the Soviet Union, the one country in Europe that truly threatened his power. No one can ever know whether Hitler would have backed off had he been rebuffed at Munich. But we can be sure that had he been, he would have tried other tactics to get what he was determined to have.

Vietnam, by contrast, was located in a part of the globe not directly related to American national security. What American policymakers viewed as aggression is now widely understood as a civil war aiming to reunite a country that had been artificially divided by the French when they had been the colonial power in the region. The ism that motivated Ho Chi Minh was nationalism, not communism. Ho was no Hitler, and the South Vietnamese leader Ngo Dinh Diem was no Churchill. When the war was finally over and Ho's successors were able to confirm Johnson's worst fears by walking down the streets of Saigon, Western civilization managed to survive unscathed. Regions of that country once bitterly contested are now tourist destinations.

Right from the start, of course, U.S. policymakers claimed that it was not just the Vietnamese that constituted the threat to the West but the larger communist movement of which they were a part; in this sense, the Vietnam War was understood as a second attempt to do what the United States had not accomplished in Korea. But this claim as well made little or no sense. The split between the Soviet Union and China had already begun to appear when the United States made its commitments to Vietnam, and those commitments, if anything, delayed the eventual rupture between them. The Soviet Union was not nearly as powerful as many foreign-policy makers, intent on building up the American military, claimed. Communism in Asia had as much to do with economic development as with the creation of a classless society. Smart policymakers would have recognized that the communist world was divided and was beginning to crumble and would have sought ways to exploit its resulting vulnerabilities. Analogies to appeasement made it impossible for them to do so. As the military historian Jeffrey Record concludes, "The differences between Hitler's Germany of the 1930s and 1940s and Ho Chi Minh's Democratic Republic of Vietnam of the 1960s were so profound as to make Munich an enemy of sound judgment by the United States on Vietnam."

The United States, unlike with the stalemate in Korea, simply lost in Vietnam. It was therefore the latter war that proved to be the first sustained test of the relevance of the appeasement analogy to a situation far removed from the Europe of the 1930s and 1940s. The results of that test could not have been more debilitating. They go well beyond the extraordinary number of people killed on all sides. Inflation and other economic problems caused by the war's drain on the U.S. budget persisted for years. The divisions produced by the war within the United States could be felt decades later, as the attacks on Democratic presidential candidate John Kerry, himself a Vietnam veteran, in 2004 testify. The reputation of the United States as an honest player in world politics has never recovered. If there is any one lesson to be learned from Vietnam, it is to avoid flirting with false analogies. Unfortunately, America's subsequent response to other world events suggests how little of that lesson was absorbed.

APPEASEMENT IN THE BALKANS

As a result of America's ill-fated venture in Southeast Asia, American leaders were forced to ponder with more care the question of when and where troops were to be deployed. One form their skepticism took was associated with officials such as Defense Secretary Caspar Weinberger and Secretary of State Colin Powell, both of whom developed doctrines holding that because Americans had never given Vietnam their full support, the bar would have to be raised before the United States would commit troops to future conflicts in which no direct American national interest could be ascertained. In theory, their way of thinking did not rule out potential military intervention. In practice, military caution, isolationist inclinations, and the collapse of the Soviet bloc combined to produce a situation in which American intervention would be an option of last resort. The appeasement analogy had turned itself into the Vietnam syndrome. Once, we saw aggressive dictators even when they did not exist. The question for critics of Powell and Weinberger would be whether we would fail to see them even when they did.

The crucial test for these new doctrines was posed by the outbreaks of political evil that came to the world's attention in the 1990s, especially the Rwandan genocide and the vicious ethnic killings in Yugoslavia. At one level, these events, however devastating, appeared to be the product of conflicts all but unintelligible to outside observers unable to distinguish a Hutu from a Tutsi or unfamiliar with the complicated history of the Balkans. Knowing so little about places so remote, Americans saw no reason to shed blood on behalf of those being killed. The Powell and Weinberger doctrines were not intended to get them to change their minds. Let other people deal with their own affairs, the new ethic held. We would not repeat the mistakes of Vietnam in other parts of the world.

A number of prominent intellectuals and activist politicians found the hyperrealism of Powell and Weinberger repulsive. For them the lesson of Vietnam was not to turn our backs on the victims of oppressive leaders but to find more effective ways to offer assistance. It did not follow that because communism had collapsed evil had come to an end. On the contrary, evil was the general phenomenon and communism the particular form. It is inherent in the nature of evil, they insisted, that it tries to spread its wings; if we allow it to succeed in one place, dictators elsewhere, persuaded that they can murder without being punished for their acts, will absorb the lesson and more easily embrace evil themselves. From the perspective of those who thought along these lines, the appeasement analogy was not a way of conducting foreign policy but a method of moral reasoning. One Holocaust was enough. Any other potential one must be stopped in its tracks by force, lest malevolence spin wildly out of control.

It would not be long before those who thought this way were offered a chance to apply their analysis. The Balkans, given the region's location in Europe, provided the place. "The Bosnian catastrophe that began in 1992," Alan Steinweis, a historian at the University of Nebraska, has written, "was the first international crisis during which the American foreign policy debate routinely invoked Holocaust imagery and analogies." Although the number of deaths produced by the events in Bosnia never came anywhere near the mass extermination of the Jews during World War II, comparisons to the Holocaust began to appear everywhere. The leading Jewish organizations in the United States sponsored an ad appearing in *The New York Times* claiming that "to the blood-chilling names of Auschwitz, Treblinka, and other Nazi death camps there seem now to have been added the names of Omarska and Brcko," referring to the camps set up by Serbia in Bosnia. Pictures showing in graphic detail the results of the atrocities taking place in the former Yugoslavia called to mind the pictures that caught the world's attention in the wake of the Nazi defeat. The Bosnian conflict happened just after the cold war had come to an end and therefore served as a reminder of what the world was like before the cold war began. When these factors were combined with the increased determination on the part of those victimized by previous genocides to recall what had happened to them, the result guaranteed that the events in Bosnia would be viewed through the framework of the totalitarian experience.

All this is fair enough; the outbreak of ethnic violence in Europe really was shattering and bound to evoke memories of the Nazi horrors. But where there is a Holocaust analogy, must there be a Munich one? There is no logical reason why there should be: it does not follow that because Chamberlain's actions gave Hitler free rein to take over Czechoslovakia, domestic tyrants will always transform themselves into potential world conquerors. Still, a remarkable number of influential thinkers held otherwise. In *The New York Times* the liberal columnist Anthony Lewis, after calling President George H. W. Bush a "veritable Neville Chamberlain," attacked the idea of negotiating with the Serbian leader Slobodan Milosevic by writing, "You can't do business with Hitler." *Time* put the same point this way: "The ghastly images in newspapers and on television screens conjured up another discomfiting memory, the world sitting by, eager for peace at any price, as Adolf Hitler marched into Austria, carved up Czechoslovakia." On the crucial question of whether military force ought to be deployed to stop Milo-sevic's ethnic cleansing, an editorial in *The New Republic* in May 1993 reminded the magazine's readers that "the British and French are as pusillanimous now as they were in a far greater but similar crisis in the 1930s." In direct contrast to those historians who had come to view the era of totalitarianism as unique, these writers and thinkers all believed that once history happened one way, it was bound to happen again the same way.

Conservatives as well as liberals found use for the appeasement analogy during the Bosnian crisis. There were some, especially Robert Dole in the Senate, who, much like Anthony Lewis and the writers for *The New Republic*, strongly supported a forceful American response to the Serbian aggression because of a determination to prevent another Holocaust. His more conservative colleagues in the Congress, however, raised the Nazi specter in a quite different, and far uglier, manner. For them, refusing to stand firm against the threat of totalitarianism con-tinued to be a dangerous course to be avoided—except that it was not the strength of America's enemies but the presumed weakness of its own leaders that drew their attention. The situation in Bosnia, Repub-lican House Speaker Newt Gingrich pointed out in the halls of Con-gress, was "the worst humiliation for the western democracies since the 1930s"—not because Milosevic was so evil but because Bill Clinton was too Chamberlain-like to confront him. (In 2010, Gingrich followed up on this line of reasoning in his book *To Save America*, in which he made clear the implicit charges of treason against American leaders at which he hinted during the Bosnian crisis. "Treason" may seem like a strong term, but what else is one to make of Gingrich's proclamation that a "secular-socialist machine"—his name for the Democratic Party under Obama—"represents as great a threat to America as Nazi Germany or the Soviet Union once did," and "comes from a movement that funda-mentally rejects the traditional American conception of who we are." For Gingrich then and for Gingrich and his right-wing allies now, the Holocaust was not so much one of the great evils of all time but a con-venient club with which to beat Democrats and liberals over the head. A historian by training, Gingrich deserves a special place in the Hall of Shame reserved for those who misuse the totalitarian experience.)

Unlike Gingrich, those more responsible intellectuals and policy-makers who urged strong action against Milosevic genuinely believed that he was another Hitler and that it was only a matter of time before he too tried to conquer Europe—or as much of Europe as he could control. Yet, much as was true of Lyndon Johnson and Dean Rusk, their use of the appeasement analogy also proved to be misguided. Milosevic may once have been a communist, but he had morphed into a nationalist invoking manifold Serbian grievances against Croats, Muslims, and Kosovar Albanians in a bloody struggle for land and power. Hitler wanted Czechoslovakia and Poland so that he could dominate Europe and then the rest of the world. Milosevic wanted Bosnia (followed by Kosovo) to make possible the creation of a Greater Serbia. Both situations were about "living space," as the Nazis had characterized their drive for expansion. There the similarities come to an end. Ethnic cleansing, as the term implies, because it appeals to those who belong to a specific group, is the very opposite of global ambition. It results in wars to form or strengthen nations, not to create a new Reich. What was at stake in Bosnia was evil but not expansionism. Even the most ruthless Serbian and Bosnian Serb leaders had no designs on the nearby Czech Republic or any other country in Eastern Europe that contained no Serbs.

More than any other event of our era, the Bosnian crisis should have taught us that domestic viciousness is not always accompanied by foreign policy ruthlessness. But so captivated had so many become by the appeasement analogy that during the Bosnian crisis they were no longer capable of understanding the nature of the enemy with which they were dealing. The problem was not some widespread unwillingness to denounce Milosevic as evil. It was instead a failure to understand the kind of evil he represented. History should have taught us that conflicts in the Balkans are difficult enough to resolve; they had, after all, led directly to the outbreak of World War I. Of course liberal intellectuals believed that in a situation of uncertainty it made the most sense to apply a worst-case analysis to Milosevic. But by imposing upon him so inappropriate an analogy, Western intellectuals inflated a regional conflict into a moral tale of twentieth-century tragedy. Later I will discuss some of the problems that followed from the NATO efforts to use military force to put a stop to Milosevic. For now it is important to emphasize that as horrific as the events in the Balkans were, putting them into a Holocaust context proved to be counterproductive. It goes without saying that mass death is always a horror to be condemned. But to mitigate the effects of mass killing and curtail the tragedies that accompany it, comparisons to the Holocaust confuse the picture. In Bosnia, the United States had a chance to finally put the Munich analogy to sleep. Instead, and with equally unfortunate consequences, it simply prepared its use for the terrorism the West was soon to face.

APPEASEMENT'S REMARKABLY LONG LIFE

IF CONTEMPORARY TALES of political evil had stopped with the Yugoslavian tragedy, efforts to find new parallels to Munich would eventually have run their course. But no sooner did genocide and ethnic cleansing make their reappearance on the world stage than a new round of terrorists began to unleash their fury. A moment's reflection might have allowed Western policymakers to see that the evils of terrorism are so different from the evils of totalitarianism that equating the two is precisely the wrong thing to do. Terrorists, for one thing, are typically stateless. They may have followers but they control no troops and use violence to furnish the statehood they lack. Given such distinguishing features, they cannot use their control over one piece of territory to take control over others. War as we usually understand it is not their objective. Terrorists would rather kill their enemies than occupy their countries. The term "expansionism" as we have understood it since Hitler's conquest of his neighbors simply does not apply to them.

At the same time, however, the concept of terror was a crucial ingredient in the theories of totalitarianism that gripped the Western intellectual imagination in the years after World War II. Leaders such as Hitler and Stalin, we were told then, carried forward the terror associated with the French Revolution in even more brutal ways by first spying on and imprisoning potential critics and then simply disposing of them. Because terror of that sort unquestionably existed during the age of totalitarianism, it seemed to follow that those such as al-Qaeda who use terror to achieve their ends are the logical inheritors of the dictators who preceded them. "Terrorism is the new totalitarianism," the British foreign minister Jack Straw told the Labor Party's spring conference in 2004 in a typical formulation, adding that "we cannot and must not be slow to recognise the dangers of the new totalitarianism today." Straw was determined not to prove himself a Chamberlain. Instead, he revealed himself as a terrible historian. Straw was merely one of many who wrenched what happened at Munich wildly out of context to apply it to the events of September 11 and afterward.

Views such as those expressed by Straw, for example, were even more pronounced in the United States. An extreme illustration was provided by the conservative essayist Victor Davis Hanson writing in *The Wall Street Journal* in 2004. "The 20th century," he argued, "should have taught the citizens of liberal democracies the catastrophic consequences of placating tyrants. British and French restraint over the occupation of the Rhineland, the *Anschluss,* the absorption of the Czech Sudetenland, and the incorporation of Bohemia and Moravia did not win gratitude but rather Hitler's contempt for their weakness. Fifty million dead, the Holocaust and the near destruction of European civilization were the wages of 'appeasement.'" Yet when faced with the challenge of militant Islam, Hanson continued, as if aiming for the world's record in applying the appeasement analogy to as great a number of leaders as possible, not one but *four* American presidents had chosen to be Neville Chamberlains. It began with Jimmy Carter, who refused to threaten a devastating military response to the Iranian hostage crisis. Ronald Reagan then withdrew American troops after a terrorist attack in Lebanon. Appeasement continued under George H. W. Bush, who coddled the Saudis in the hopes of gaining access to cheap oil. Bill Clinton's response to the terrorism on his watch was to treat it as a criminal matter rather than the war it was. Thus was built up what Hanson called "the consensus for appeasement that led to Sept. 11," as bin Laden—Hitler reincarnated—understanding that he could get away with murder, chose to do exactly that. For a conservative, Hanson's accusations were refreshingly bipartisan; he included two Republicans and two Democrats in his litany of weak-willed leaders. But this only made his historical acumen even shoddier than Straw's.

Hanson and those who think like him have been and are strong admirers of the foreign policy of George W. Bush. They believe that he was right to punish al-Qaeda by fighting a war against the stronghold that, in their view, it had established in Iraq. To them—and to the president himself—Bush was a reincarnation of Churchill. Because of his firmness and moral clarity, for once the United States had not responded to aggression by seeking to appease the aggressors. Finally a president had come along who understood that when it comes to evil, talk is cheap and military action required. At least one country in the world, and one determined leader, his supporters felt, had drawn the right conclusions from Munich.

Unfortunately, in their view, the same was not true of the Europeans. Munich, after all, had been an entirely European affair: the appeasers were British and French, and the immediate victims of their cowardice were Czechs and Poles. These conservative intellectuals were therefore not surprised to discover that in today's world it was European leaders who chose to be irresolute in the face of militant Islam. Borrowing his title directly from the appeasement-inspired best seller written by John F. Kennedy decades previously, the American journalist Bruce Bawer entitled his effort to call attention to the violence associated with militant Islam *While Europe Slept*. Kennedy, it must be said, wrote only one book about appeasement, whereas Bawer has written two. Returning to the subject in 2009, when sufficient time had passed since September 11 to make it clear that not all Muslims living in the West were harboring violent fantasies but were in fact trying to move up in the world and raise their families in peace, Bawer published another book, this one called *Surrender*, repeating his charges that all too many Westerners were complacent in the face of the looming threats against them.

Indictments such as these require actual terror attacks to sustain them, and such attacks did come. After Islamic-inspired violence broke out in Madrid (2004) and London (2005), criticisms of European leaders for their presumed dillydallying became even more shrill. "Neville Chamberlain, en Español," proclaimed a *Wall Street Journal* op-ed by the Spanish journalist Ramón Pérez-Maura dealing with the policies of the socialist leader José Luis Rodríguez Zapatero, who was elected prime minister shortly after the March 2004 attack in his country. "Are Europeans prepared to grant much of al-Qaeda's conditions in exchange for a promise of security?" asked Robert Kagan about the same event. "Thoughts of Munich and 1938 come to mind." Those who live on planet Venus, all these writers believed, are not prepared to confront evil with sufficient determination. European leaders could write off Czechoslovakia's fate in 1938 because for them Prague was far away. So craven are Europe's leaders today, the critics charge, that they turn away from evil even when their own citizens come under attack.

Contemporary invocations of Munich go well beyond terror attacks. Unlike those who targeted civilians in London or Madrid, Iran's president Mahmoud Ahmadinejad is a head of state. It would be difficult to find a leader more unrepentant than he is and a regime more brutal than his. Iran gives support to terrorists who threaten Israel's right to exist. It is in the process of acquiring nuclear weapons. Ahmadinejad's willingness to engage in Holocaust denial and to accuse Israel of the grossest of crimes does not win him many friends outside the more radical circles within the Middle East. His actions in working with his country's mullahs to suppress dissent and deny legitimacy to opposition parties, finally, clearly make him an enemy of democracy in any sense of the term.

It cannot come as a surprise, therefore, that no other leader in the world today raises the specter of Munich more than this man. Many examples of the use of appeasement rhetoric to characterize Ahmadinejad could be supplied but perhaps one can suffice. After he denounced Israel at the Durban II conference in Geneva in April 2009 as "a cruel and repressive racist regime," speeches or interviews comparing Ahmadinejad to Hitler were immediately made by acting Israeli prime minister Ehud Olmert, Deputy Prime Minister Silvan Shalom, President Shimon Peres, Republican presidential candidate Mitt Romney, Ohio senator George Voinovich (who for good measure made fun of his name), Italian president Silvio Berlusconi, and German chancellor Angela Merkel. As is nearly always the case when such comparisons are invoked, the purpose was to focus not on Ahmadinejad's plans for his own people but on his foreign policy objectives. "The world must open its eyes before it is too late," as Peres put it. "Many times in history it was too late to prevent horrors and bloodshed, for instance with Stalin and Hitler. We are nearing a similar turn of events with Ahmadinejad. We must not ignore Iran's aspiration to become a religious, extremist Persian empire that would rule the entire Mideast."

Yet as unpleasant as Ahmadinejad's rhetoric may be, and as destructive as his and his colleagues' rule has been to the genuine aspirations of the Iranian people, Ahmadinejad is no Hitler, determined to expand his reach into as many countries as possible. Ray Takeyh of the Council on Foreign Relations has pointed out that "it is a peculiar American fascination to continually look for the next Hitler. Josef Stalin, Mao, Ho Chi Minh and even Saddam Hussein were all touted at one time or another as Hitler incarnate. Ahmadinejad is simply the latest figure to be contemplated for that role." Ahmadinejad's rhetoric is bone-chilling, but so were the comments of Nikita Khrushchev about burying us—and we found a way to negotiate with him. Other Iranian leaders with whom the United States now cooperates, Takeyh observes, have said similar things about Israel and the Holocaust. Iran seeks to acquire nuclear weapons, but other states, including dangerous ones like Pakistan, already have them. Ahmadinejad's support for Hamas and Hezbollah is real, he continues, but it is based on strategic calculation more than a bloodthirsty love of violence. Ahmadinejad is not even, as Hitler undoubtedly was, the undisputed leader of his country; in fact, the position he holds is more a symbolic than a policymaking one, and he has been able to retain his job, in the aftermath of a hotly disputed election in 2009, only through chicanery and the support of his country's religious establishment. Both the United States and Israel have good reason to distrust him. Neither has any rational reason to invoke Munich in talking about him.

The case against applying the appeasement analogy to Iran does not rest just on the fact that Iran is not Nazi Germany. There is also the fact that only a decade or so ago, American policymakers were applying the exact same incorrect analogy to another leader in the region, Saddam Hussein, who, unlike the Iranian president, had actually attacked neighboring countries. Since Saddam's Iraq and Ahmadinejad's Iran have had a long history of mutual hostility and have even gone to war with each other in the recent past, any sensible foreign policy, just as was true of the split between Russia and China during the Vietnam years, would have sought to widen the rift between the two countries. Charging that both were led by would-be Hitlers, thereby raising the prospect of appeasing not one but two mad aggressors, was hardly the best way to achieve that objective. It ought to be clear why the United States failed so badly in the war in Iraq and shows little sign of knowing how to develop a workable foreign policy with respect to Iran. It is difficult to win a war when you confuse the actual enemy you are fighting with a dictator from another time and place.

Each time the appeasement analogy has been raised in the years after World War II, it has been done with increasingly less conviction. Lyndon Johnson and Dean Rusk, as we have seen, really did believe that we were facing another Munich. Those who saw Hitler reborn in the form of Slobodan Milosevic were principled opponents of genocide. All these thinkers and policymakers were sincere even if they were wrong. Their great mistake was simply the misuse of an analogy.

By the time the appeasement rhetoric was applied to Iran and Iraq, by contrast, the cynicism had become palpable. George W. Bush and Dick Cheney, because they spent so much time constructing the untenable case that Saddam Hussein must have had ties to Osama bin Laden, knew full well he was not part of a worldwide conspiracy to rain evil down on the heads of the innocent. Neoconservatives today who call for either an Israeli or an American war against Iran are equally promiscuous with their historical analogies; whatever Iran's level of anti-Semitism, it is not planning to try to wipe out the world's Jewish population, and no matter what its plans for any nuclear weapons it may be developing, its leaders are not so mad as to risk the ruin of their own people in a retaliatory strike. No one who invokes the appeasement analogy today can possibly believe in it. At best, it is meant as a helpful exaggeration. At worst, it is a lie. A certain amount of cynicism is a requirement of effective foreign-policy making. But when cynicism becomes a way of life, as it did during the Bush-Cheney administration, it renders one unable to see the world clearly.

When the Munich analogy is used so automatically with so little conviction and imagination as it has been in recent years, its retirement would seem to be inevitable. Yet the appeasement analogy has been pronounced dead before but managed to come back to life. It may well find new usage in the future. Israel, for one thing, seems certain to continue to invoke analogies to appeasement helpful whatever the United States does; as I will show soon, Benjamin Netanyahu, its leader as of this writing, is especially fond of comparing terrorists to totalitarians. Perhaps, given its history, Israel has special reasons for erring on the side of anticipating the worst rather than hoping for the best. Still, there is only limited value in treating the leaders of Hamas and Hezbollah as born-again Hitlers, denouncing those who supported the Oslo peace process as latter-day incarnations of Neville Chamberlain, and equating Jimmy Carter, the one recent American president most insistent on taking the needs of the Palestinians into account, with Lord Haw-Haw, the propagandist who broadcast pro-Hitler messages into England. Israel's enemies exist not in the past but in the present and not in Europe but in its own region of the world. So long as Israelis support hard-line politicians resolute in rejecting any viable paths toward a peace settlement, analogies to appeasement will never die. Yet the fact is, as former speaker of the Knesset Avraham Burg has argued, that analogies to the Holocaust, the event that played such a major role in the creation of the state of Israel, have begun to poison Israel's soul. Israel wants to be treated as a normal nation-state. That is unlikely to happen so long as it treats its enemies not as military and political antagonists but as new incarnations of events that happened long ago and far away.

Even in the United States, despite the efforts by the Obama administration to engage its enemies more diplomatically than its predecessor chose to, analogies to appeasement cannot be considered a thing of the past. Cries of appeasement always work better when those who are uttering them are out of power. Whatever actions Obama takes, in the Middle East or elsewhere, his policies will continuously be subject to criticism from conservatives and Republicans who find them insufficiently hard-nosed. Should chaos continue in Iraq or a new terrorist attack take place somewhere in the world, Obama will quickly find himself blamed for his Venus-like failure to stand up to Mars-like realities. In a society like the United States, in which history was once declared bunk, Munich is one piece of the past that everyone seems to remember. Perhaps we can learn not to take our historical analogies so literally.

POLITICAL EVIL ON ITS OWN TERMS

IN 1990, Mike Godwin, an attorney specializing in Internet law, coined his famous law stating that "as an online discussion grows longer, the probability of a comparison involving Nazis or Hitler approaches 1." Leaders in both Israel and the United States seem determined to prove that Godwin's law applies in places far removed from the Internet. During a 2010 Senate hearing into climate change, for example, skeptics of the notion of global warming were given a chance to have their say. "It reminds me in some ways of the debate taking place in this country and around the world in the late 1930s," responded Vermont's Bernard Sanders. "During that period of Nazism and fascism's growth—a real danger to the United States and democratic countries around the world—there were people in this country and in the British parliament who said 'don't worry! Hitler's not real! It'll disappear!'" Conservatives have no monopoly on false analogies to the Nazis. The most liberal member of the U.S. Senate showed himself willing to join them.

The most important lesson Godwin's law can teach us when we approach the political evils of our day is this: the moment comparisons to Hitler are made by our leaders, we know we are dealing with men and women who do not understand history, have given no serious thought to the actual crises they are confronting, care more about their domestic popularity than rectifying the evils they are denouncing, and have set their nations on a course doomed to fail. Intellectuals and policymakers who raise the specter of Munich every time a local tyrant appears on the world stage, or even when terrorists conspire to pull off an act as destructive as the September 11 bombings, are informing us that they are not to be taken seriously. Their use of one of history's most morally clarifying moments is no act of great political courage but serves as a reminder of their lazy unwillingness to make the most basic moral distinctions. They have forgotten or never knew what totalitarianism actually was. They talk about evil but know little about the depths of human depravity. They believe lessons of history simple that are, in fact, stunningly complex. When all is said and done, Dean Rusk's warnings about the communist menace in Asia and George W. Bush's vapid remarks to the Knesset are no different from those of the Chicago racist who hated the idea of Martin Luther King Jr. walking through his neighborhood or the over-the-top charges of Senator Sanders. None of these people seemed to have had any idea of what their words actually meant.

In the end, use of the appeasement analogy impedes our ability to fight political evil effectively. Invoking one of the darkest moments in world history as a way of avoiding any real inquiry into why today's practitioners of political evil are motivated to do what they do serves no possible good. In dealing with political evil, no step is harder to take than treating its outbreaks on their own terms, yet no step is more necessary. The sooner we learn to talk about such brutalities as genocide, ethnic cleansing, and terrorism by exploring their roots and causes independently of each other the better off we will all be.

PART TWO

How to Combat It

CHAPTER FIVE

Democracy's Terrorism Problem

DESTROYING DISTINCTIONS

FROM THE TIME of the early-twentieth-century French thinker Émile Durkheim, there has existed a rich tradition in the social sciences seeking to understand how societies function. One of that tradition's most important insights calls attention to the distinctions that guide people through what would otherwise be the randomness of time and space. All societies rely on such structured classifications. The clock is divided into day and night, with different expectations for each. Some spaces, one thinks immediately of churches or museums, are treated as sacred and with a reverence inappropriate for others, such as post offices or shopping malls, viewed as profane. We experience both private life and public life and value each. Without such distinctions—deviancy and normality, purity and pollution, rights and obligations—we would be rudderless. Civilization is made possible by routines, patterns, rules, and rituals that, in ordering the world, make it possible to inhabit it.

The insights of the Durkheimian school offer a way of understanding what terrorists seek to accomplish: their goal is to abolish the classifications that enable society to function. Terrorists make no distinctions among their victims, treating them all, whatever their age, race, gender, or nationality, as targets for attack. What most people might consider peace is to them just another phase of armed struggle. The more everyday the places in which people congregate, the more likely it is they will be chosen as sites for holy war; terrorists seem to have a special fondness for means of mass transit. Because terrorists select as victims individuals who wear no uniforms—or, if they do, who are not engaged in battle—they abolish the difference between the soldier and the civilian. Terrorists use ambulances to transport weapons, religious sites to urge violence, and hospitals as places to hide. They put bombs into baby carriages and strap them to pets. They recognize that social life is made possible because certain areas of existence are roped off as places where individuals can be safe from the dangers all around them, and they then try to make those places the most perilous of all. Sociology contains a field called ethnomethodology, based on the assumption that if the normal order can be disrupted, we can learn a great deal about the unseen mechanisms that hold society together. Terrorism is the most extreme possible form of that. If terrorists had their way, the very notion of civilization itself would be undermined. Terrorism aims squarely at the social contract that enables people to live in peace with each other, recognizing that when they live in fear, they are living at their most vulnerable.

So nightmarish are the conditions terrorists aim to produce that when confronted with their acts, we are tempted to respond by treating terrorists as fanatics as primitive as the state of nature to which they seek to return us. I will argue here that such a response, however understandable, must be avoided. Terrorism, for all its resemblance to war, is a *political* tactic that must be met *politically*. When it comes to combating terror, proposals abound for reorganizing intelligence agencies, improving the language skills of potential agents, using advanced electronic monitoring, and sharing data among allies. These are important matters, and the books that deal with them contain much that can be recommended. But underlying proposals for changes in policy is the even more important question of just what kind of evil terrorism represents. Terrorism, in short, is an intellectual as much as a policy problem. Unless we are clear about the nature of what we are fighting, we are likely to fight it in the wrong way.

SOCIOCIDE

"WHEN I CONSIDER a terrorist atrocity, I do not think of the perpetrators as evil monsters," writes Louise Richardson, vice-chancellor of St. Andrews University in Scotland and one of the world's leading authorities on the subject. Unlike her, I do. What makes terrorists evil is not just the indifference to life they exhibit through their murderous attacks, for many people—criminals, soldiers, psychopaths—kill and are not considered anywhere near as morally repugnant as those who engage in terrorism. It is not homicide that makes terrorism evil so much as sociocide. The aim of the terrorist is to kill the society that makes the free and rewarding life of modernity possible. The Israeli writer Yossi Klein Halevi recognizes as much when he writes that "the terrorists' goal has been to turn Israelis into a nation of shut-ins, fearing the most minimal gathering of fellow citizens as an inviting target, a mortal threat. In trying to deny Israelis their public space, the terrorists have aimed at unraveling our collective existence." Terrorists are not so radical as to want to destroy the idea of humanity itself. They would be content merely with attacking the social structures that enable people to rise above mere subsistence and cooperate with each other to achieve ends chosen by themselves.

How ought a society to respond to efforts to undermine so violently its social cohesion? Although I disagree with Richardson over whether we should view terrorists as evil, I think she is right to emphasize "how futile counterterrorist policies are likely to be when they are based on a view of terrorists as one-dimensional evildoers and psychopaths." As I have tried to stress, terrorism is a form of political evil rather than an embodiment of evil per se. Our challenge is to find a way to combine resolute moral condemnation of the evil terrorists carry out with clear-eyed political understanding of why they do it.

Especially in the aftermath of a vicious terrorist attack, we are often advised against responding to terrorism's political nature. "Terrorists," the political philosopher and ethicist Jean Bethke Elshtain has written, "are not interested in the subtleties of diplomacy or in compromise solutions. They have taken leave of politics. . . . It is violence that kills politics." For her, and for the many who think along similar lines, the evil carried out by terrorists is such that they live in a world beyond reason. Because they are haters of morality and all its obligations, in responding to terrorists we cannot, those of this persuasion believe, appeal to any universal values and standards, for toward these they will have nothing but contempt. It is useless to rely upon negotiation, Elshtain would argue, because bargaining presupposes rules and terrorists recognize no rules. The moment we acknowledge that terrorists are human beings with political goals of their own, we accord them, from this point of view, a legitimacy that they can never properly deserve. To protect ourselves, we must shun them as the moral lepers they are.

If Richardson is correct to insist that counterterrorist policies ought to be realistic but is not persuaded that terrorists are inherently evil, Elshtain's moral denunciation of terror rings true even if her refusal to recognize that terrorism is a form of politics leads nowhere. Not only do those who denounce terrorism in such strong moral terms lack a realistic plan for bringing it under control, in some cases, such as that of the well-known Harvard law professor Alan Dershowitz, they go out of their way to argue, quite incorrectly as it happens, that terrorists nearly always win. When dealing with terror, it is a mistake to engage in a form of realism so cynical that it accepts the killing of innocents as just another justifiable military tactic. But it is equally problematic to place ourselves on an elevated moral pedestal from which we refuse to deal with the political realities that, as much as we may find them unacceptable, lead terrorists to go on their killing sprees.

Because the aim of terrorism is sociocide, terrorists pay particular attention to the character of the societies they single out for attention. Due to the local nature of the issues that so often fuel terrorism, sometimes the people selected for attack will be chosen because of where they live rather than because of the kind of political system they live under: Russians are the target of Chechen terror because Russia is Chechnya's historic enemy. But when terrorists have a choice about what country they wish to terrorize—al-Qaeda, for one, prides itself on having such choices—invariably they attack democratic ones; Great Britain, Spain, India, and the United States can testify to that. Something about a democratic society attracts terrorists. Although democracies possess significant advantages in fighting terror—the vision of a life of freedom they hold out is ultimately far more attractive to people around the world than the violent conspiratorialism motivating terrorists—they do have one major disadvantage. Democratic societies find it difficult to separate the military task of fighting against terror in the short run from the political strategies needed to defeat it in the long run. Of all the distinctions terrorists seek to abolish, the one between militarism and politics may be the most important. Terrorists want their self-declared enemies to act violently, if for no other reason than to demonstrate the futility of normal political give-and-take. All too often the targets of terror do precisely that.

Two factors contribute to the problems democracies face as they try to balance military and political objectives in their response to terrorism. One is that democracies give pride of place to public opinion, a perfectly appropriate thing to do when passing domestic legislation but a far more problematic matter where terrorism is concerned. When attacked, citizens want their leaders to take swift and decisive action against those who would destroy their society, irrespective of whether such action can achieve its goals. Because being soft on terror is as politically effective a charge in the early years of the twenty-first century as being soft on communism was in the middle of the twentieth, leaders who urge more nuanced and potentially more effective political responses are likely to be punished at the polls. Relatively transparent, contentious, and media-saturated societies are hardly the best places to hold seminars on political evil, even if in the absence of deliberation the policies are unlikely to work.

In addition, Western democracies find themselves handicapped in their responses to terror because World War II and the cold war were won primarily by relying on the West's military advantages and it would therefore seem to follow that defeating terror will require the same approach. But this, as it turns out, is incorrect. Political evil, as I have been arguing throughout this book, is not the same thing as the radical evil of Hitler and Stalin, and the responses most effective for controlling the one will not be the same kind that helped defeat the other. Listening carefully to what Hitler wanted in an effort to cut off his political appeal, split his potential allies, and work toward an eventual diplomatic solution was precisely the wrong thing to do in the 1930s, so bent were the Nazis on gaining as much control over Europe, if not the whole world, as possible. But this does not mean that communication and diplomacy are always to be shunned. In an age of terror, responding with words is likely to wind up saving more lives than responding with arms. Even when both are required, it is foolish to give up one.

The last thing the citizens of democratic societies should do in the face of terror is to allow themselves to be terrorized. Unfortunately, this is exactly what they do when they give their support to those leaders who claim that terrorism is a form of unreconstructed evil that must be eradicated from the face of the earth through the mobilization of military might. When confronted with terror, democracies require leaders capable of something more complex than demanding an eye for an eye. The most violent terrorists in today's world are inspired by the vengeful words contained in sacred texts. That is no reason the rest of us should be.

ISRAEL'S EXAMPLE

No society in the world has had to confront more persistent attempts to terrorize its people than Israel. No society therefore offers more lessons for thinking about the best and worst ways of responding.

Because of its frequent experience of terrorism, Israel is in the unusual position of having among its preeminent political leaders Benjamin Netanyahu, who not only has twice been that country's prime minister but has published two books on the subject: *Terrorism: How the West Can Win,* a collection of essays by him and others from 1986, and *Fighting Terrorism: How Democracies Can Defeat Domestic and International Terrorists,* which appeared in 1995. "It is a certainty," Netanyahu wrote in the latter of these books, "that there is no way to fight terrorism—other than to fight it." Confronting terrorism requires above all else the will to do so. Alas, Netanyahu laments, leaders rarely possess sufficient quantities of such firm will. In his own country, he charges, politicians, especially during the Labor governments in the early to mid-1990s, tried to be reasonable by granting concessions to the Palestine Liberation Organization, then Israel's main terroristically inclined enemy, in the hopes of achieving peace with it. But the truth is that "terrorism has the unfortunate quality of expanding to fill the vacuum left to it by passivity or weakness." A firm believer in the appeasement analogy, Netanyahu is convinced that both Israel and the United States need to fight terror the same way the Western democracies once fought totalitarianism. "The salient point that has to be underlined again and again is that *nothing* justifies terrorism, that it is evil *per se*—that the various real or imagined reasons proffered by the terrorists to justify their actions are meaningless."

When Netanyahu wrote those words, he had been out of power and was considered something of an extremist. Now his views on terror and how to fight it, in the wake of Israeli disappointments over the breakdown of the Oslo peace process, put him squarely in the center of a national consensus. Ami Pedahzur, an Israeli national security expert teaching at the University of Texas, offers a helpful distinction relevant to that consensus. Counterterrorism policies can take three general forms, he writes: the war model, the criminal justice model, and the reconciliatory model. Under the assumptions associated with the first one, public officials treat terrorists as soldiers engaged in revolutionary war and believe that it is upon military force, as well as the intelligence agencies closely associated with the military, that society must rely in fighting them. Criminal justice approaches view terrorists as lawbreakers and call upon legal and police authorities to capture and punish them. The key proposition of the reconciliatory model is that terrorism is a form of politics and that the best venues for responding to it are through diplomacy and negotiation. Although Netanyahu refers from time to time to terrorists as criminals, his views are a near-perfect expression of the war model. The consensus in Israel around one or another version of his approach rejects negotiation as having failed and insists that terrorist militants are too motivated by zealous hatred ever to be reformed by punishment. If anything, the criminal justice approach, by forcing them into prison with like-minded lawbreakers, would likely make them even more determined killers. By default, if nothing else, only a military response can work.

In the context of Israeli history, it is not difficult to understand why Netanyahu came to these conclusions. Since its founding as a state in 1948, Israel has developed a very powerful military with a strong track record of success. Historically, however, its greatest victories have come in conventional wars against other nation-states. This record started with the 1948 war in which Israel came into being and continued through the Sinai War of 1956 and the Six-Day War of 1967; despite its small size and geographic vulnerability, Israel managed to administer severe defeats to its seemingly more powerful enemies in the Middle East. (The Yom Kippur War in 1973 produced a stalemate at best and a psychological loss for Israel at worst.) In nearly all of these cases, Israel benefited from the determination of its citizens to protect their new society, whatever the sacrifices required, as well as from a bold military leadership willing to take risks and from soldiers more than willing to serve. On the other side of the equation, both Egypt and Syria, Israel's main enemies at the time, were autocratic states whose military capacity not only proved to be weaker than Israel (and the rest of the world) imagined but whose citizens lacked any particular will to fight. No wonder that during this period of its existence, Israel was able to repel foreign attacks, expand its borders, and prevent its enemies from carrying out any plans to destroy its society.

This kind of military success, however, came to an end with the decision to invade Lebanon in 1982. Unlike Israel's previous wars, the

Lebanese invasion did not involve a conventional warfare situation in which one state engaged another. For Israel, the government of Lebanon was never the enemy. Instead, Lebanon was the site of the first major war Israel undertook against a terrorist organization, the PLO. Israel had launched its war in an effort to oust Yasser Arafat and his movement from Beirut; along the way, key figures such as Defense Minister Ariel Sharon and Prime Minister Menachem Begin had hoped to install a Christian, pro-Israeli government in that country. Some of Israel's military objectives were met; the PLO, for example, did leave the country. But otherwise the war proved something of a disaster. The brutal killings undertaken in the refuge camps of Sabra and Shatila, carried out by right-wing Lebanese Christians known as Phalangists who were supported by Israel, shocked the world's conscience. The assassination of Bashir Gemayal, Israel's (unreliable) ally among the Lebanese, caused massive political instability in that country. Efforts by the Israel Defense Forces, or IDF, to control areas of southern Lebanon made Israeli soldiers easy targets for their enemies. By occupying southern Lebanon for almost two decades, Israel, as the political scientist Zeev Maoz points out, defeated one terrorist enemy, the PLO, only to allow for the emergence of a deadlier one in Hezbollah, or Party of God, a Shiite-based terrorist organization with strong ties to Iran and firmly committed to Israel's destruction. The result was a politically unstable Lebanon in which Hezbollah had become a significant political force among the Shiite population, which in the past had not been all that hostile to Israel. Such a result proved to be more devastating for Israel's national security than a Lebanon in which the PLO had made its home.

The lesson of the Lebanon War ought to have been clear: a new kind of enemy required a new kind of approach. Yet in Lebanon, Israel found itself unable to adopt one. Instead of going to war defensively against another state's aggressive actions, Israel went on the military offensive against nonstate actors. Instead of its military power offering it advantages, it found itself stymied by guerrilla-like tactics. Instead of lightning strikes followed by quick withdrawals, it was unable to extricate itself from increasingly desperate situations. Instead of obedient troops, it had to deal with dissenting ones. Instead of a peace treaty, the war produced a prolonged military occupation of another country. And instead of a rapid victory reinforcing national unity, Israel, for reasons having more to do with immigration and religious intolerance than with military stalemate, became more politically divided than ever in its domestic life. In wars against terror, anything less than full-scale victory is a defeat. Before 1982, Israel won most of its wars. After 1982, it began to lose them.

As it happens, the next major loss also took place in Lebanon, this time in 2006. The Second Lebanon War, which lasted thirty-four days, began as the result of the kidnapping of two Israeli soldiers. This war's outcome proved as counterproductive as the first one's. Although the Lebanese government was furious at Hezbollah for instigating the war—the country's top leaders made little secret of their hope that Israel would undermine Hezbollah's military capacity—the massive bombing campaign against large sections of Beirut united the whole country, as well as much of world opinion, against Israel. "It is doubtful whether Israel ever went to war in so slapdash a fashion," the journalists Amos Harel and Avi Issacharoff later wrote. A once popular military response turned sour so quickly that an investigation was required. The Winograd Commission, which carried it out, was remarkably blunt. There was no "clear victory" despite the fact that Israel possessed "the strongest army in the Middle East," the portions of the report released to the public in 2008 pointed out. No effective action, furthermore, was taken against the terror attacks that provoked the war in the first place: "The barrage of rockets aimed at Israel's civilian population lasted throughout the war, and the IDF did not provide an effective response to it. The fabric of life under fire was seriously disrupted, and many civilians either left their home temporarily or spent their time in shelters." The Winograd Report did not result in the resignation of Prime Minister Ehud Olmert, who had ordered the second Lebanese invasion. But it served as an eloquent testimony to the limits of military action in dealing with threats that Israel faced from groups like Hezbollah that operate within a state but are not themselves state actors.

Israelis themselves, or at least significant numbers of them, do not believe that their wars against terror have been failures. They are, for one thing, impressed by the fact that after Israel built a barrier between itself and the Palestinians in the West Bank in 2003, terror attacks dropped by 90 percent and fatalities fell by 70 percent. There is, in addition, the case of the 2009 Israeli invasion of Gaza. Widely denounced for its brutality—an issue to which I shall return—the Gaza invasion, like the two Lebanese wars, constituted a significant setback to Israel's political standing in the world. Unlike them, however, it reduced terror significantly; in 2009, the most recent year for which data is available, not only did terrorist attacks against Israel decline dramatically from previous years, according to the Israel Security Agency, or Shin Bet, but those emanating from Gaza fell off as well. One of the reasons Israelis remain attached to firm measures is that tangible benefits can be attributed to reliance upon them. Any military action that reduces terror to such a level that something like everyday life becomes possible is considered by most Israelis, not without reason, a huge relief. The diplomatic blunders, declines in international support, and longtime strengthening of Israel's enemies that accompany such reductions are all but forgotten.

It nonetheless would be foolish to conclude that such a strong reliance on military means has helped Israel solve its terrorism problem once and for all. During my trip to Israel in the summer of 2010, I was repeatedly told by high-ranking military and political figures that the strong Israeli actions against Gaza proved that the use of massive force can function as a deterrent to prevent terror attacks. But it is also possible to draw the exact opposite conclusion, which is that Hamas decided on its own to agree to a cease-fire as a way of building upon the global support it received from those shocked by the Israeli invasion. So long as political conditions remain unstable in the Middle East and so long as Palestinians in either the West Bank or Gaza continue to resent Israeli control over the conditions of their lives, any cessation of terror will at best be an uncertain one. A lull should not be confused with a victory. Israel's terrorist enemies receive their support from states such as Lebanon, Syria, and Iran. Short of trying to destroy any or all of them through a nuclear attack—which a few Israeli leaders believe desirable but most consider impossible—diplomacy remains the only long-term solution for bringing terror under control. Yet so long as the Israelis can lead something resembling normal lives without rockets landing in their schools and hospitals, politicians have few if any incentives to pursue such longer-term objectives.

If military responses to terrorism cannot by themselves solve the problem of terror, why are they relied upon so often? In his critical analysis of Israeli security and foreign policy, Maoz suggests that deep structural problems in the dynamics of Israeli society are responsible for the dearth of alternatives to military approaches. Discussing the ill-begotten first Lebanon venture, he points out that neither the media nor the academic community engaged in any meaningful debate and discussion of the strategy and tactics of the IDF. There was little oversight of government policy exercised by the Knesset. Public opinion was not uniformly hard-line for, if anything, the public tends to turn quickly against failed military adventures, but public opinion at the start of the war—indeed, at the start of all of Israel's wars—was resolutely hawkish, creating an environment in which politicians are rarely rewarded for their caution. Leaders in Israel find it easier to build consensus around strong military measures than to challenge the notion that Israel must always be prepared to meet any threat by going to war. Domestic considerations of political popularity consistently trump effective foreign policy recommendations.

Israel's problems in dealing with terror, in short, are related to the problems it faces as a democracy. There are, to be sure, critics who do not believe that Israel is much of a democracy to begin with. The state of Israel, they point out, contains a number of citizens such as those from Russia or other Middle Eastern countries who have had little experience with and appreciation for democracy, treats its own Arab citizens as having fewer rights and privileges than its Jewish ones, and increasingly faces demographic pressures that will make it difficult to be both a Jewish and a democratic state simultaneously. Such criticisms, in my view, are not without merit; Israeli Arabs really are second-class citizens, and Israel's future as a democratic state is anything but guaranteed. In the main, however, such charges miss the target. Especially in comparison to nearly all of its neighbors, Israel has free elections, an open media, competitive political parties, freedom of speech, a vigorous tradition of parliamentary debate, and an economy open to an increasingly globalizing world. Israel's chief problem in dealing with terrorism is not the absence of democracy but the particular form it takes. If by "democracy" we mean frequent elections that bring to power those who best capture the popular taste for the violent retaliation terrorism inspires, democracy in Israel is working very well indeed. But if a democracy is defined as a system of government in which widespread input from a plurality of institutions works to expand the options available to leaders, Israeli democracy is not working well at all.

In their book *Democracies at War*, political scientists Dan Reiter and Allan C. Stam show how "those political institutions that hold democratic leaders accountable to the consent of the people," as well as "the spirit of democracy, with its emphasis on the development of individual rights, responsibility, and initiative," allow open societies to develop more powerful armies and greater public support for military actions than closed societies possess. Contrary to the views of many defeatists during the 1940s and the cold war, they show, democracies were able to win over two militaristic enemies, first Nazi Germany and then the Soviet system.

When it comes to wars against terror, however, many of the advantages Reiter and Stam cite can easily become problematic. In conventional wars, democratic societies choose to fight where and when they are most likely to win, but this is something terrorists seek to curtail by acting first, thereby forcing their enemies to respond on terms they establish. Because terrorists do not seek to occupy another country, democracy's ability to mobilize large numbers of its own people to rally around the defense of the homeland becomes less relevant. Democracies do an especially effective job producing better fighting troops than authoritarian regimes because those troops are given more initiative and have higher morale, but troops are only of limited use when their opponents avoid the battlefield in favor of hit-and-run tactics against civilians. The benefits democratic states have over authoritarian states disappear when the enemy is stateless; if anything, a condition of statelessness, whatever its disadvantages for terrorists in assembling manpower, yields benefits of elusiveness and flexibility that can make their campaigns more damaging. The purpose of fighting conventional wars is not to vanquish an enemy but to bring it to the bargaining table, a goal Israel was able to achieve with the Egyptians and may yet achieve with the Syrians. But such an objective, while still necessary, proves to be far more illusive when the external threat comes from a terrorist movement motivated at the start by ideology or religious passion. Unlike conventional wars, wars against terror need to be accompanied by smart public diplomacy among neutral or even sympathetic nation-states, while the defensive and confrontational mood required for domestic political support against terror frequently works against that objective. This is not to say that authoritarian states are better equipped to fight terror than democratic ones; the Russians have not proved themselves masters of the situation in Chechnya. But it does suggest, in direct opposition to the ideas of Netanyahu, that democracies cannot assume that the methods of mobilization and fighting that worked in World War II and the cold war can be adopted without serious modification in the battle against terrorism.

Many of the nonmilitary advantages democracy possesses in situations of conventional war also disappear under conditions of terrorism. Terrorism has more to do with the science of psychology than military science. Its aim is to instill fear, which is another way of saying that its purpose is to undermine reason. Wars against terror do not require major sacrifices from the society under attack, such as gas and food rationing or the imposition of a draft, which, however onerous, can help rally the country's morale and impress upon its citizens the seriousness of the situation they face. Since some of the most successful actions against terror are covert, they cannot be broadcast publicly as major victories on the road to eventual military success. There are times, moreover, when public opinion can go from strongly supportive of campaigns against terror to highly critical. As popular as aggressive tactics may be domestically, asymmetrical or nonconventional wars often are accompanied by the kinds of brutal incidents or highly publicized atrocities that so frequently accompany the occupation of a hostile country—My Lai and Abu Ghraib in the case of the United States, civilian casualties in Lebanon and Gaza in the case of Israel—that can quickly reduce the public taste for vengeance.

As the Israeli experience illustrates, democracies must be prepared to defend themselves unflinchingly if they are going to be successful at reducing terrorist threats against them. But that is the relatively easy part: especially in the aftermath of Munich, democracies produce all too many leaders willing to call on the military whenever they deem it necessary. The more difficult problem is for democracies to take a deep breath and react politically as well as emotionally when dealing with terror. Israel's experiences, and, as we shall see, the response of the United States in the aftermath of the September 11 attacks, demonstrate just how hard it can be for democratic societies to find such political leaders when they need them. This is by no means an impossible task: the reactions to terrorism in Spain and India, as well as the less flamboyant approach used by the United States since the election of Barack Obama, suggest that more effective methods are within the realm of possibility. The trick is to find them before military responses to terror become obstacles to longer-term political strategies that can reduce the incentives to engage in terror and thereby limit the damage it inflicts.

THE LOGIC OF AGGREGATION

ALTHOUGH THE United States has a distinctly different political system from Israel's, it too operates by democratic rules. Its responses to terror have therefore been quite similar to those of its Middle Eastern ally. Here, once again, both the successes as well as the problems of a predominantly military response to terror have been on clear display in recent years.

The George W. Bush administration, which had come to power shortly before the terrorist attack of September 11, 2001, was at first not predisposed to take terrorist threats very seriously. As the 9/11 Commission would later document, officials in the Clinton administration who had studied the work of al-Qaeda close up, such as Richard Clarke of the National Security Council, did everything in their power to insist on the seriousness of the threat during the presidential transition. "We *urgently* need . . . a Principals level review on the *al Qida* network," Clarke wrote in a January 2001 memo. (The Committee of Principals is an interagency group involving an administration's highest officials, thereby assigning major importance to the subjects it discusses.) The new administration's national security advisor, Condoleezza Rice, did not respond to Clarke's memo. Although the Principals Committee met in 2001 to discuss such issues as Russia and the Persian Gulf, it never addressed the question of Islamic-inspired terrorism. Convinced that the incoming administration, in his words, was not "serious about al Qaeda," Clarke requested a transfer to work on issues of cybersecurity.

However unprepared for terrorism the Bush administration may have been, it was extremely well prepared to reassert U.S. power in the world. One of the key components of its worldview had been that major threats to the United States would come from states with global ambitions. The other was that the best ways to meet such threats would be through a continued buildup of American military forces. Memories of the World War II victories over both Germany and Japan, as well as the collapse of the Soviet Union and the end of the cold war, predisposed policymakers in the Bush administration, much like Netanyahu in Israel, to view the world through the prism of the struggle against totalitarianism. Any victory meant military victory, and military victory was achieved through the accumulation and deployment of massive firepower. However unprepared the Bush administration may have been for terror, it was quite prepared for war.

The September 11 attacks may have been unprecedented, but the response came right out of the Nazi and Soviet period. Addressing a joint session of Congress nine days after the attacks, the president began to draw analogies between the threat posed by Islamic terrorism and the earlier horrors associated with fascism and communism. "We have seen their kind before," the president said of those attracted to al-Qaeda. "They're the heirs of all the murderous ideologies of the 20th century. By sacrificing human life to serve their radical visions, by abandoning every value except the will to power, they follow in the path of fascism, Nazism and totalitarianism. And they will follow that path all the way to where it ends in history's unmarked grave of discarded lies. Americans are asking, 'How will we fight and win this war?' "

Answering his own question, Bush then went on to outline the kind of war that the United States would have to fight to defeat the terrorists. This conflict, he said, would not resemble the one his father had led against the government of Saddam Hussein in Iraq. Nor would it be a limited campaign with minimal loss of life such as the one Bill Clinton had pursued in Bosnia. The stakes now were much higher than those posed by one nation's invasion of another or by the grim realities of ethnic cleansing. "This is not . . . just America's fight," the president declared. "And what is at stake is not just America's freedom. This is the world's fight. This is civilization's fight. This is the fight of all who believe in progress and pluralism, tolerance and freedom." With the stakes that high—indeed, with the stakes as high as they could possibly be—the war would have to be fought with every tool available to the United States. "We will direct every resource at our command—every means of diplomacy, every tool of intelligence, every instrument of law enforcement, every financial influence, and every necessary weapon of war—to the destruction and to the defeat of the global terror network." To accomplish that objective, the president made demands on the Taliban-led regime in Afghanistan in preparation for destroying the home base for al-Qaeda that had made the attacks possible. But this would be just the first step: "Our war on terror begins with al Qaeda, but it does not end there. It will not end until every terrorist group of global reach has been found, stopped and defeated." In many ways Bush's speech called for a *more* thoroughgoing response than the one the West adopted in the face of the totalitarian threat. During World War II, after all, the United States was willing to ally itself with one totalitarian state, the Soviet Union, in order to defeat another, Nazi Germany. In the war against terror President Bush was calling for the destruction of the evil of global terrorism in whatever form it took.

Because he rose so dramatically to the occasion, President Bush's September 20, 2001, speech is widely considered one of the great moments of his presidency. After initially stumbling in the days after the attack, the president used the prestige of his office to introduce al-Qaeda to the American people and to announce his intentions to hold them responsible for their acts. No one could doubt, when the president had finished speaking, that he had drawn upon some of the strongest moral and religious ideas embedded in the Western tradition to make his case that terrorism was evil, pure and simple. The president's goal was to rally his people and to reassure them; his strong words did precisely that. In the aftermath of this speech, the United States came together in ways quite at odds with its usual partisan and cultural bickering.

Yet Bush's speech, as well as his subsequent actions, also made clear the extent to which he was going to rely on a military rather than a political understanding of the threat posed by al-Qaeda. Treating your opponent politically implies neither giving in to his demands nor treating him with kid gloves; two sides with diametrically opposed visions of the world and possessed of a determination to defeat each other can nonetheless engage in political conflict. Politics encompasses searching for areas in which differences can be negotiated short of violence and, if that proves impossible, as it surely would have in the case of al-Qaeda, trying to win as many potentially neutral allies to your side in recognition of the fact that the violent struggle against your opponent is likely to be long and complicated. Despite what advocates of a military response to terror claim, terrorists themselves make political demands. Lacking statehood to press those demands one way, they rely on violence against innocents to press them in another. By proclaiming the war against al-Qaeda to be civilizational in such stark terms, Bush was effectively tying his own hands. It was as if he recognized the potential seduction of a political response to terror and was steeling himself against the possibility of adopting it.

The rhetorical strategy used by Bush to ensure that he would keep on a militaristic rather than a political course can be called the logic of aggregation. Aggregation represents the effort to bring together all the charges one can possibly make against the enemy one is going to fight. When aggregation takes place, details are less important than drama. The stakes are so high that they must be defined as clearly as possible. The job of a political leader is to build his case, and the best way to build it is to include an inclusive bill of particulars against the enemy. If exaggeration is required, so be it. The purpose of aggregation is mobilization. In war, public opinion counts, and aggregation usually constitutes an effective rhetorical strategy for shaping it.

Aggregation has its time and place. Conventional wars that call upon citizens to give up their lives in massive numbers, that demand that all of a society's resources be coordinated for fighting purposes, and that may likely see disproportionate numbers of defeats before victory becomes possible will be more winnable to the degree that the public's anger against the enemy is maintained at fever pitch. World War II, fought against the radical evil of Nazi Germany, was a war that required the rhetoric of aggregation. The crucial question is whether the war started by al-Qaeda is the same kind of war.

Bush's speech left no doubt where he stood on that question. The president linked all forms of Islamic terrorism together, portraying al-Qaeda as a worldwide movement capable of attacking anywhere and anytime. He included in his indictment against the terrorists the fact that the regime supporting them, Afghanistan's Taliban, oppressed women, banned televisions, and punished men for wearing their beards too short. He criticized the terrorists for lacking democracy. He charged that their version of their faith was a distorted one. He claimed that the terrorists who attacked the United States "want to drive Israel out of the Middle East" and "want to drive Christians and Jews out of vast regions of Asia and Africa." He even used the occasion to announce the creation of a new Department of Homeland Security. Americans have long been familiar with this kind of rhetoric; their own Declaration of Independence contains a long list of grievances imposed on them by the king of England. Alexis de Tocqueville famously wrote that when the spirit of equality dominates societies, wars "become more rare, but when they break out, they spread over a larger field." In President Bush's case, the field had become the entire world.

Despite the fact that the president justified his emphasis on aggregation by pronouncing the war against al-Qaeda as civilizational, the truth is that it never was. To be sure, *any* speech made in the direct aftermath of September 11 would no doubt have presented the wrong occasion to start discussing the nuances of terrorism. Still, the development of an effective campaign against terror capable of winning widespread public backing would require demonstrating at some point that terror, even in the form taken by al-Qaeda, is simultaneously local and global, religious and secular, and utopian and political. Unfortunately, the tutorial role of the presidency—or, as it is sometimes called, the "bully pulpit"—was never adopted by Bush; in his view of the world, moral clarity was incompatible with real-world complexity. As a result, Americans never learned the extent to which the logic of aggregation is inappropriate to situations involving terror. Taking the sting out of al-Qaeda was possible. Eliminating terror from the world is impossible. Only someone viewing himself as a military commander about to engage in an epic campaign could have confused one with the other.

To his credit, Barack Obama, upon assuming office, opted not to follow the same logic of aggregation that had captivated his predecessor. He nonetheless faced the same kind of decision Bush had to make about how best to protect the United States against any new attacks. For Obama, the question of terror and how to combat it came down to the problem of Afghanistan—or, more precisely, the border between Afghanistan and Pakistan known as AfPak—and what to do about it. "The U.S. failure to secure this region," writes the Pakistani journalist Ahmed Rashid, "may well lead to global terrorism, nuclear proliferation, and a drug epidemic on a scale that we have not yet experienced and I can only hope we never will." Even if Rashid's prognosis is an overstatement, the AfPak situation remained dangerously unresolved when Obama assumed office. Two general approaches were presented to the new president for how to resolve it: counterterrorism and counterinsurgency. The difference between them hinged once again on the question of whether the proper response to terror ought to emphasize political approaches or military force.

Those holding to a counterterrorism strategy, especially including Vice President Biden, argued that the United States possessed sufficient intelligence-gathering capabilities to monitor and destroy enough al-Qaeda cells in Afghanistan to prevent major attacks against the United States. In addition, they pointed out, the government of Afghanistan was too weak and corrupt to take on the burden of sharing with the United States a full-scale military effort designed to destroy the terrorists who had gained refuge in that country. America's goals in fighting terror should therefore be limited to controlling terror. The best way to do that, according to intelligence expert A. J. Rossmiller, is not by relying on the military but by seeking a political solution to Afghanistan's constant turmoil, even, if necessary, by trying to co-opt elements of the Taliban into a political coalition rather than by trying to destroy the entire movement. From this point of view the Taliban—at least elements within it—is more interested in holding power than in sponsoring terrorism. As evil as the Taliban's methods may be, its power in Afghanistan means it has to be engaged as a political force.

For those in the other camp, such as Republican senator John McCain and a number of key military officials, counterterrorism is never enough. The United States, in their view, will not be safe until the Taliban is defeated militarily and in that way rendered unable to protect any terrorist groups seeking its support. Counterinsurgency tactics, especially the so-called surge associated with General David Petraeus, ultimately worked in Iraq, they believed, and based on what the United States learned there, it should apply the same general approach to Afghanistan. Terrorists thrive where chaos and instability reign, and the United States has no choice but to bring to Afghanistan a sufficient level of basic security so that an insurgency such as the Taliban will give up the fight. The whole world is watching for signs of American weakness, making it essential to stop terrorism in Afghanistan as a way of stopping terrorism wherever terrorists might be lurking. As with all approaches based on the logic of aggregation, the idea is not only to win a war but to make a point. A crucial feature of the militaristic perspective on terror is what the strategist and lawyer Joshua Geltzer calls signaling: sending a message to your opponent that you will be relentless in your determination to use force in order to get him to desist.

Advocates of the counterinsurgency strategy were not quite correct to suggest it worked in Iraq; sectarian violence continued after the United States began to withdraw its troops, and it is by no means certain what the future of that country holds. Yet despite the commitments of money and manpower they require, militaristic strategies such as counterinsurgency remain difficult to resist in democratic societies such as the United States. Republicans are attracted to them, while Democratic presidents nearly always try to embrace them in order to inoculate themselves against the charge of weakness, one reason Obama took a strong position on Afghanistan during his campaign for the presidency that limited his options once in office. Military officers often have friends in the media and among lobbying groups willing to support their calls for more troops and hence willing to dramatize the danger posed by the Taliban. No matter how skeptical the public may be of new military adventures, they will reward any leader who engages in a successful one. In a democratic society such as the United States, the default position will be the position closest to what the military wants.

Ultimately, as Bob Woodward's book *Obama's Wars* documents in detail, the Obama administration resolved the tension between the militaristic and the political options by not making a choice; it sought to split the difference between them by simultaneously increasing American troops in Afghanistan even while setting an early target date for their withdrawal. Clearly the administration recognized that the surge analogy was not quite appropriate and that committing large numbers of troops for any extended period of time would be not only frighteningly expensive but unlikely to produce the promised stability in a country of Afghanistan's size and ethnic complexity. Just as clearly, Obama understood that decreasing troop presence from the start not only would have resulted in a confrontation with the military and its supporters but also would have run huge political risks, especially if another terrorist attack were to occur. The entire episode demonstrated the extent to which even presidents not inherently attracted to viewing the world as filled with evildoers who will only respond to force nonetheless find it difficult to downplay military responses to terror in favor of political ones. In recent years the United States has become programmed to respond to terror in one way and one way only, and changing the program has become all but impossible.

The initial returns on Obama's approach have not been encouraging. One year into the new effort, the general who had assumed command of U.S. forces there, Stanley McChrystal, had to be replaced after he publicly criticized Biden. Appointing Petraeus as his replacement helped insulate Obama from domestic criticism. But it also placed the fate of the Afghan campaign into the hands of a man with a sufficient power base to defy the president should he decide to reduce the American presence there as planned. While all this was taking place in Washington, moreover, the government of Hamid Karzai in Kabul remained hopelessly corrupt, Karzai himself began to tire of the American presence in his country, and the influence of the Taliban spread even more widely. In 2010, the Afghan war passed the Revolutionary War to become the second-longest war in American history. (Vietnam is the longest.)

Many of the same forces that pushed Israel in the direction of downplaying political responses to terror, in short, have been on full display in the United States as well. After a terror attack, policymakers must consider military options among the possibilities open to them. But even as they are deploying troops, they also must begin dealing with the political realities that bring terror into being and are responsible for its success. No one should conclude this will be easy, with the aim of terrorists to disrupt so thoroughly the normal workings of the societies they target. Still, a step in the right direction is to avoid inflating the deeds of evildoers beyond recognition, as the logic of aggregation tries to do, in favor of describing as specifically as possible what is at stake. "The only way to understand, explain, or respond successfully to either the IRA or al-Qaeda," writes Richard English, an Irish expert on terrorism, "is in fact to disaggregate: to know and to be clear about the specific, contextualized reasons for the violence occurring, rather than to lump together all such acts as 'terrorism' as though there were some generalized template of causation, impulse, and action which was universally applicable across the planet." Once the truth of that lesson is learned, the military temptation, no matter how well designed for public consumption in major wars, is something that decision makers ought to consider as a very last resort if they are trying to limit the damage from wars against terror.

THE BENEFITS OF DISAGGREGATION

AT LEAST FOUR different kinds of disaggregation would significantly improve the ability of democracies to develop political responses to terrorism. Each is based on the understanding that terrorism does not represent evil in general but is a specific form of political evil. Each therefore asks us, no matter how satisfied we may be in the wake of terror to respond with moral denunciation and military force, to look carefully at what terrorists actually do. Countries victimized by terror might still decide that war is the only appropriate response—or, more probably, they will learn that good diplomacy and targeted intelligence offer better political opportunities. But whatever they decide to do, they will be less likely to overreact.

One form disaggregation can take is *downsizing*. When an act as well organized and devastating as the one that took place on September 11 occurs, the first reaction is to assume that whoever carried it out had at their disposal a disciplined, effective, and centrally organized chain of command. This was certainly true in the era of fascism and communism, when the states that threatened the West were authoritarian, hierarchical, and intolerant of dissent. Surely, many believe, the same must be true today. Al-Qaeda, writes Walid Phares, a Lebanese-born political analyst for Fox News and a professor at the National Defense University, "has a highly centralized body, with international and also regional command centers, covering continents and vast regions. It has its own central units, deployed in many places. Before the removal of the Taliban in Afghanistan, al Qaeda enjoyed a safe haven where it was able to train, plan, fund-raise, communicate worldwide, and even produce new generations under the full protection of a jihadist regime." From this perspective, al-Qaeda not only can extend its control from top to bottom but is also capable of shifting from side to side. Like the Catholic Church or the Soviet Communist Party, its vertical structure is as solid as its horizontal reach is broad.

Phares belongs to what the political scientist John Mueller has called "the terrorism industry." Those who compose the terrorism industry—politicians interested in getting reelected, television networks seeking viewers, policy think tanks associated with the military, neoconservative pundits and journalists, conservative Christians suspicious of Muslims and (temporarily) in love with Jews, and all those contemplating contracts with the Department of Homeland Security—naturally prefer to portray terrorists as far more deadly and far more effective than they are. It never seems to occur to them that groups such as al-Qaeda could be lucky—or that, having pulled off a surprisingly successful attack, they might not be in a position to launch another one.

Outside the more conservative quarters of the terrorism industry, al-Qaeda is not treated as a centralized and hierarchical organization at all. Yet the desire to portray it as more extensive and coordinated than it actually is finds other ways of expressing itself. Acknowledging the irrelevance of the hierarchical model, the terrorism expert Jerrold Post looks to the corporate world for the appropriate organizational analogy for al-Qaeda. "Perhaps reflecting his training in business management," he writes, "bin Laden in effect serves as chairman of the board of a holding company, which can be termed 'Radical Islam, Inc.,' a loose umbrella organization of semi-autonomous terrorist groups and organizations with bin Laden providing guidance, coordination, and financial and logistical facilitation." This is a clear improvement over organizational models inappropriately borrowed from totalitarianism, but it still exaggerates not only al-Qaeda's global reach but also the ability of one man, in this case bin Laden, to impose his will on the group as a whole. Post simply cannot give up on the idea that al-Qaeda is far-flung and tenacious. Even when it was forced to reconstitute itself after losing the protection of the Taliban regime in Afghanistan, he writes that "al-Qaeda central," as he calls its core leadership structure, "has largely been reconstituted." The threat it represents is always there because the organization embodying the threat constantly finds new ways to reinvent itself.

A more trustworthy guide to these matters is Marc Sageman, a forensic psychiatrist and former Foreign Service officer. Al-Qaeda, he observes, "is not a specific organization, but a social movement." It has no headquarters but is composed of a series of cores, some more centralized than others, that evolve over time to account for new conditions. The best analogy to capture its structure is the concept of what Sageman calls a small-world network. Small-world networks contain fuzzy boundaries, are highly decentralized, encourage cliques, and avoid predictable routines. "This flexibility and local initiative of small-world networks and cliques contrast with the rigidity of hierarchies, which do not adapt well to ambiguity but are excellent at exerting control," Sageman writes. Small-world networks operate in a high-risk, high-gain environment. Lacking centralized coordination, some of their plots have to be called off, and others fail. But when they succeed, as they did on September 11, they do so spectacularly.

Once we begin to downsize our expectations of terrorism's organizational capacities, we can take the second necessary step of *localizing* terror. All political evil, as I have been arguing throughout this book, is local, terror included. Terrorists, as the RAND Corporation scholar Bruce Hoffman has pointed out, appear in every kind of stripe: ideologically, some are on the left and others are on the right; religiously, they cross every major faith tradition; geographically, they range from Latin America to East Asia; and tactically, some consider the killing of innocents justifiable and others do not. If we follow Hoffman's guidance, we should talk about terrorisms rather than terrorism. What works in one theater may not work in another.

Those in the terrorism industry such as Phares, while perhaps willing to acknowledge terrorism's local nature in places such as Peru or Northern Ireland, insist that when it comes to Islamic-inspired terror, jihadism is by its very nature global in scope, seeking nothing less than to wage holy war against the West and its entire way of life. In this he is by no means alone. One of the more outspoken voices articulating this point of view belongs to the conservative commentator Daniel Pipes. Roughly 15 percent of the Muslim world, Pipes told an association of Coptic Christians in 2004, adheres to one or another form of militant Islam, which, as he defines it, "derives from Islam but is a misanthropic, misogynist, triumphalist, millenarian, anti-modern, anti-Christian, anti-Semitic, terrorist, jihadistic and suicidal version of it." Pipes, like all those who share his convictions, argues that radical Islam inherited its drive for world conquest from the totalitarian movements of the 1930s and 1940s. Indeed, there exists something of a cottage industry among neoconservative historians dedicated to showing direct links between the Nazis and Islamic jihadists. In their book *Icon of Evil,* for example, the historians David Dalin and John F. Rothmann argue that Haj Amin al-Husseini, the grand mufti of Jerusalem during the 1930s and 1940s, imbibed the anti-Semitism of the Hitler regime and returned to Palestine after World War II to infect the Arab world with his poison. Having established such a link, scholars and pundits of this persuasion feel free to rely upon the term "Islamofascism" to emphasize the degree to which Islamic terrorists seek worldwide domination. Despite the criticism this term has received for conflating a political ideology with a religion, the prolific British-born American intellectual Christopher Hitchens defends it on the grounds that "both movements are based on a cult of murderous violence that exalts death and destruction and despises the life of the mind." Islamic terrorists, all these writers agree, talk locally but think globally. When we combat political evil today, we are therefore engaged in a replay of the struggle against the radical evils of yesterday.

The truth, however, is that nearly all the terrorist movements motivated by their interpretation of what Islam demands of them are guided by local objectives more frequently than by global ambitions. This was clearly the case in the early 1980s, when jihadists were almost exclusively concerned with trying to ensure that Muslim states lived in accord with their interpretation of Muslim law; their targets were governments in Egypt or Saudi Arabia that were deemed too secular in their goals or too close to the United States in economic and geostrategic terms. Osama bin Laden's break with them lay not only in the greater grandiosity of his vision but in the fact that he was willing to attack the "far enemy" represented by a country such as the United States, thereby seeming to confirm the notion that jihadism had gone global. In the years since then, however, all the major forms taken by Islamic-inspired terrorism have gone back to their local roots. The 2004 Madrid terrorist attacks, directed against an administration that had given its support to the U.S.-led war in Iraq, were timed to influence electoral outcomes in Spain. London's 7/7 bombings a year later, while inspired by al-Qaeda, were carried out by British Muslims acting on their own. Hamas and Hezbollah, although supported by regimes in the region, have no global ambitions but are preoccupied with the creation of a Palestinian state. Precisely because terror emerges from small-world networks, its goals are determined by local contexts.

Even the Taliban, which once provided the haven for al-Qaeda before its September 11 attacks, is no longer especially interested in far-off enemies. In the course of the Obama administration's debate over how to limit the reach of the Taliban, advocates of a counterterrorism approach insisted that the organization no longer had a global reach or was motivated by global causes. One official, a former marine captain and Foreign Service officer named Matthew Hoh, had been asked to find out why American troops had been sent to the remote Korengal Valley near the Pakistan border. Investigating the issue, he began to understand "how localized the insurgency was. I didn't realize that a group in this valley here has no connection with an insurgent group two kilometers away." Hoh, who resigned his position because he was persuaded that counterinsurgency strategies are doomed to fail, coined the term "valleyism" to suggest just how disconnected one segment of the Taliban had become from another. In his view, the term "localism," implying as it does a focus on one particular country, is still too broad to account for why terrorists engage in the actions they do. (In 2010, Hoh joined other critics of the war in formulating an alternative strategy for Afghanistan that would put more emphasis on a political solution for that troubled country.)

Although one would never know it from the way advocates of Islamofascism talk, terror campaigns, far from maintaining their militancy until all their goals are achieved, eventually come to an end. In recent years scholars of international relations have devoted increasing attention to the various ways in which terror campaigns lose their momentum. "Terrorist campaigns end," writes Audrey Cronin of the National War College, "when they are denied leadership, when negotiations redirect energies, when they implode, when they are repressed, when they descend to selfish ends, or when they transmogrify into the strategic mainstream." Historical experience, she suggests, warns against strong reliance on military methods in favor of "understanding the nature of the appeal of a campaign in the evolving international context." Without in any way detracting from the sheer viciousness of terror, we must remember that it is a tactic relied upon by the weak and that no terrorist campaign has ever gone on forever.

There is every reason to believe that the terror we witness today will meet the same historical fate. The amount of terror that will continue to be associated with Hezbollah and Hamas depends in the long run on how much progress is made in stabilizing the Middle East. The primary cause of Pakistan's soft spot for terrorism is that its intelligence services think of Islamic mujahedeen as potential allies in their country's conflict with India over Kashmir; addressing that issue more effectively through American diplomatic efforts could significantly reduce the amount of terror in the world. The withdrawal of American troops from Iraq will calm the anger that provides ever-newer recruits for terror, even if it is already fueling greater sectarian violence within Iraq as those troops depart. Should the people of Iran ever succeed in toppling the theocratic leaders who have governed them, Iran's ties to terror in other parts of the Middle East could well be lessened. The most violent group of all is of course al-Qaeda, yet, as Cronin concludes, it also possesses many of the same vulnerabilities that brought other terrorist movements to an end. The key, in her view, is that the United States should aim toward "dividing new local affiliates from al-Qaeda by understanding and exploiting their differences with the movement, rather than treating the movement as a monolith." Terror in the abstract will never be eliminated. But there can be successful ways of responding to various terrorisms. Wherever these ways have worked, it is nearly always because the political conditions that cause local conflicts to fester have been addressed.

A third form that disaggregation ought to take in responding to terror can be called *calming*. Despite the havoc terrorists seek to wreak, it nonetheless remains the case that, as English puts it, "the most serious danger currently posed by terrorists is probably their capacity to provoke ill-judged, extravagant, and counter-productive state responses, rather than their own direct actions themselves (which statistically continue to represent a comparatively limited danger)." As passionate as our reaction to terrorism may be, our response must be dispassionate. The use of terror ought not to mean the sacrifice of analysis. Leaders can, and no doubt should, treat the aftermath of a terrorist incident as an opportunity to rally the society under attack. But they must also refrain from easily manipulatable color-coded terrorist alerts, exaggerated statements that cross over into repeated falsehoods, and claims that unprecedented emergencies require radical breaks with established legal precedents. Terrorists gain advantage when we lose perspective.

Perhaps due to his temperament, or more likely the result of careful study of how best to respond to terrorism, Obama engaged in just such calming after assuming the presidency. This does not mean that he broke in any substantial way with the antiterrorism policies of the administration that preceded him. On the contrary, Obama's continuation of the program of extraordinary rendition (in which terror suspects are sent to other countries where they are likely to be tortured), as well as his backing off from a commitment to hold civilian trials for terror suspects, suggests, much like his reliance on military force in Afghanistan, the lingering power of hard-line approaches to terror in American political culture. Still, rhetoric is important—consider the role it played in the Bush preference for the logic of aggregation—and the less Manichaean rhetorical style of Obama is one of the few hopeful signs that the United States could possibly shift to a more sensible way of thinking about the threat that terrorism represents.

In urging calm as a response to terror, President Obama was joined by others. After the December 2008 terrorist attacks on Mumbai, India's prime minister, Manmohan Singh, was under considerable pressure to take aggressive military actions against Pakistan. Instead, as the prominent economist Amartya Sen has pointed out, he chose a "deliberate" approach designed to "ease the tension." If Pakistan's objective was to put barriers in the way of India's emergence as a global economic and military power, Singh was determined not to give them what they wanted. Although domestic opinion in the immediate aftermath of a terrorist incident such as the one in Mumbai generally favors revenge, patience can produce political rewards; Singh and his Congress Party were reelected in May 2009. Much the same happened in Spain, where José Luis Rodríguez Zapatero, who was first elected right after the 2004 Madrid bombings, was returned to power in 2008.

This cooling of passion is an essential feature of an effective antiterrorism strategy because at some point terrorists have to be engaged. Those who inflate the capacity and ambition of terrorists obviously disagree. Dershowitz, for one, claims that "our message must be this: even if you have legitimate grievances, if you resort to terrorism as a means toward eliminating them we will simply not listen to you, we will not try to understand you, and we will certainly never change any of our policies toward you." In speaking this way, he reveals his myopia. Even though democratic states such as the United States and Israel do in fact negotiate with terrorists—only by such means do cease-fires, hostage releases, and prisoner exchanges become possible—they like to persuade themselves that because negotiation with terror only rewards it, they must always resist the temptation to do so.

This is advice we should not follow. Dershowitz seems to believe that in refusing to listen to terrorists, he is acting out of firm moral principle. In fact, his point of view suggests a flight from moral responsibility: any terrorist who took Dershowitz seriously would conclude that he now has a free hand to be as evil as he wants because he will meet neither intellectual nor political resistance from those he targets. Terrorists generally do pretty well with weapons and pretty badly with persuasion. Reacting hysterically to them shifts the terrain to where they are most comfortable. It is important, indeed vital, to stand on principle when dealing with terrorists. But the principle upon which we must stand is that we will never give them the luxury of isolation. The statesman's duty is to save lives, and more are saved when terrorists are brought within the universe of politics than when they are excluded from it.

Finally, disaggregating terror requires a certain degree of *contrasting*. Democracy's great disadvantage in fighting terror, as I have said, lies in the overwhelming public support for retaliatory violence, which only fuels more terror. Finding a better approach does not mean that democracies ought to be passive. On the contrary, democracies ought to devote as much attention to political competition between themselves and the terrorists as they have habitually devoted to military victory. People all over the world yearn for freedom, which is why those who live under tyrants try their best to rebel and those whose futures are bleak seek out new opportunities no matter how costly to them and their families. In contrast to the violence and chaos of terror, the advantages of free and open societies are considerable. Democracies have everything to gain by contrasting themselves to authoritarianism.

Such contrasting, of course, is precisely what President Bush did in his many speeches justifying his approach to terror. Unfortunately, the rhetoric of aggregation he pursued undermined his case. Having pronounced terrorism the very embodiment of all that was evil in the world, the president was convinced that democratic societies had no choice but to suspend their usual ways of doing business in order to respond effectively. The result was viewed by most of the world as one more example of how the United States refused to practice the democracy it preached to everyone else. Few people will remember Bush's words. Most people will never forget his reliance on torture, secrecy, intentional dissimulation, and other practices that violate liberal democratic norms.

Terrorists do not care what those who live in the West think of them. But there are large numbers of people around the world who, while distrustful of the West, also have qualms about terror and its effects. Terrorists are few. Those inclined to support their goals can be many. Reducing the number of the latter is crucial to limiting the damage inflicted by the former, and it is to that end that the strategy of comparing ought to be directed. Responding to terror by contrasting democratic politics with authoritarian politics is an effort to drive a wedge between the few who truly are politically evil and the many who are not. It befits a democratic society to appeal to the many rather than the few. In the years since September 11, al-Qaeda, far from solidifying its standing in the Muslim world, has lost considerable popularity, even in countries that were once viewed as seedbeds of global terrorism. Contrasting our way of life to theirs ought to be designed to make it lose even more. That can best be done by promoting the democratic way of life not as a rhetoric weapon in a long-term ideological struggle but as concrete proof that those who learn to live with differences by not killing those with whom they disagree have discovered a way of practicing politics that works better than any other available method.

DEMOCRACY'S DOUBLE DUTY — AND DOUBLE BENEFIT

IN THE AFTERMATH OF September 11, a great deal of attention was paid to the question of whether the steps necessary to combat terrorism were compatible with the commitments that liberal democratic societies have made to the rule of law, civil liberty, and separation of powers. In retrospect, there seems little doubt that many of the measures taken were not: the Bush administration in particular struck the balance between national security and individual liberty heavily in favor of the former. Clearly times of terror are a danger to democracy. Let leaders go overboard in their determination to protect national security no matter what the costs, and the freedoms democratic citizens have come to accept can be easily curtailed.

There is, however, another danger that terrorism poses to democracy. If democracy is understood to mean little more than the ability of leaders to gauge the public mood and then to offer the public what it wants, democratic responses to terror are very likely to fail. Any society that inflates the threat represented by terrorism, globalizes it in breathtaking ways, substitutes for calm reaction hysterical overreaction, and fails to make an effective contrast between its own political system and those of the attackers lacks sufficient insulation from the horror terrorism inflicts to develop effective means for limiting what terrorists are capable of doing. Democratic societies require something more than popularity contests posing as elections if they are to avoid the mistakes that have characterized the responses of both Israel and the United States.

Terrorism therefore imposes a double duty on democratic citizens. Right from the start, those victimized by terror do not need instruction on the evil represented by sociocide. Whether they experience terror themselves or watch its effects from afar, they quickly grasp that terror is not like other forms of warfare: this one takes place at home rather than in distant locales, aims to kill those within reach no matter what their status as a combatant, and threatens to bring all forms of social life to a halt. When society comes under attack, the defense of that society, and in particular the determined efforts to rebuild the norms, conventions, and distinctions that terrorists seek to abolish, becomes essential, and no one is in a better position to do so than the ordinary citizens at whom terror is directed. Those on the ground seeking to restore order play as heroic a role as those leaders who make the political decisions at the national level. By seeking to divide, those who rely on terror can unite. The fact that their target is not another army but a society in its entirety allows that society to rejuvenate itself.

At the same time, however, democratic citizens also find themselves in a position where, if they are to protect and preserve what is most valuable about their society, they also must resist the blandishments and simplifications of their own leaders. While this is a difficult task to pull off, especially in the aftermath of an attack, it is by no means impossible. The truth is that in both Israel and the United States, public opinion did eventually turn against wars that were launched against terrorists but that either were undertaken precipitately and without adequate justification or failed to achieve their objectives. Democratic citizens need to move up the timetable by thinking more about the long run even when they are pressured to respond in the short run. When their leaders demand action, it will be up to citizens to raise questions about whether those actions are proportionate to the crimes to which they are responding, have sufficient international backing, and are likely to work. In so doing, they may find, as Americans did during the initial phases of the war in Iraq, that the media are all too fond of cheerleading, that politicians rarely possess the requisite courage, and that the terrorism industry will be in full swing. But if they are careful, they will note the presence of truth-telling generals, realistic intelligence officers, objective scholars, and courageous on-the-ground journalists—all of whom existed in the buildup to the Iraq War as well. When leaders lose their heads, ordinary people must keep their wits. It is even possible, and in fact it happened in the United States, that citizens will finally tire of an administration committed to a long and no-holds-barred war on terror in favor of one that seeks approaches more rooted in the diplomatic cultivation of necessary allies.

If democratic citizens perform their double duty, they will receive a double benefit. Not only will greater reflection on their part help their leaders avoid overly militaristic actions that prolong the terror those leaders set out to control, citizens will revitalize the meaning and performance of democracy itself. Democracy is of course endangered by public policies that curtail civil liberty, protect secrecy, and centralize power in one place. But it is also damaged when people become too passive about the threats facing them and all too willing to give their leaders excessive leeway out of the belief that those leaders know how to keep them safe. The history of terror shows no such thing. It is because of a long-standing recognition that leaders make mistakes that democracy developed in the first place. A time of terror is not the time to forget that truth. If anything, the fact that terrorists aim to strike at the very nature of liberal democratic societies makes it all the more essential for those societies to maintain what is most liberal and democratic about them.

CHAPTER SIX

The Case Against Dramatizing Genocide

THE GREAT POLITICAL EVIL OF OUR TIME

GENOCIDE IS THE great political evil of our era. Although traceable to ancient times, indeed to primordial ones, genocide violates all the achievements in equality, liberty, and commitments to reason that modern people have come to appreciate. Nothing shocks the contemporary conscience quite like the unspeakable cruelties that one group, typically with the power of the state behind it, can impose on another that lacks the capacity to respond, or even to protect itself. If we are to maintain any pretense that we live in a world in which human dignity matters, we ought to do everything in our power to prevent genocide before it happens and to control it once it breaks out.

Genocide may be old but campaigns against it are relatively new. Appalled by the all too complacent reactions not only to the Holocaust but to the mass killings that followed in its wake, political activists and engaged intellectuals have done their best in recent years to bring public attention to the full scope of the horrors taking place in the contemporary world. The problem is so serious, and the tendency to deny or look away so pronounced, they believe, that it becomes necessary to dramatize the problem of genocide as vividly as possible. When such violence happens, people must be shaken out of their complacency. Shock and awe proved itself incapable of preventing an insurgency in Iraq, but shock and awe, many believe, is our best approach when political leaders take it upon themselves to murder as many people as they can get away with.

All this may sound reasonable enough, but I want to make an argument *against* dramatizing genocide. Far from arousing the world's conscience, for one thing, such an approach dulls its moral imagination; we become so overwhelmed by instances of mass murder that we find ourselves reluctant to intervene in any of them for fear that we will have an obligation to engage in all of them. For better or worse, most human beings, although not inherently stained by sin, can expose themselves only to a limited amount of hate. Offer them too much and they will change the channel. Such a response is lamentable. But it is also common. Pretending otherwise, convincing ourselves that people ought to care more than they do about every outbreak of violence that takes place somewhere in the world, can easily become an illusion. Illusions are the last thing we need when death is so frequent.

Genocide, moreover, is not just any kind of mass atrocity. All mass killing is immoral, but genocidal killings have a distinctive feature that increases the repugnance we feel toward them: their victims are chosen based on personal characteristics—their race, for example, or their ethnicity—that are ascribed to them independent of any identities they choose for themselves. When someone is determined to practice genocide against you, you are what they define you to be. Genocide takes away not only life but choice. Someone else's warped view of history, malignant conception of fate, or deeply ingrained hatred determines whether you will live or die.

Because genocide singles out its victims in such a distinctively immoral way, it is important not to blend all kinds of mass killing together. Suicide terrorism, which the political scientist Daniel Jonah Goldhagen labels "genocide bombing," is dreadful enough; it does not have to be characterized as something it is not. Ethnic cleansing, as I will soon discuss, is frequently distinguished from genocide for valid reasons. Civil wars and counterinsurgencies may be responsible for massive numbers of deaths, but they involve clashes over territory or struggles over ideological worldviews that lack a distinct racial, ethnic, or religious element. We are under a strong moral obligation to use the term "genocide" wherever it applies. But this does not mean it applies every time large numbers of people die. It may sound insensitive to the pain of the victims, but campaigns against genocide must be reserved for the truly genocidal.

The reason we need to be careful about how we define genocide has little or nothing to do with academic precision. On the contrary, saving lives, as I will show, hinges on getting our concepts correct. How we respond to mass violence depends on what we find. If what appears to be genocide is actually a civil war or political insurgency, the world community ought to remain neutral in an effort to get all parties to put down their guns. If it does not, if it takes sides and condemns and isolates only one party to the conflict based on the mistaken premise that it

alone is responsible for the violence, it increases the difficulty of achieving a cease-fire and eventually finding a political solution to the crisis.

Getting genocide wrong, in addition, stiffens the spine of those
engaged in political violence. If they are indeed genocidal, of course
they must be denounced for the crimes against humanity in which they
are engaged. But if they are not, labeling them as among the world's
worst criminals gives them just the excuse they need to deny humanitarian workers entry into their country or to justify the very sense of
persecution that, however misplaced it may seem to us, fuels their rage.
Genocide, like cancer, requires a proper diagnosis if it is to be attacked
effectively. It is precisely because genocide stands for the worst political
evil of our time that throwing around the charge too loosely can wind
up taking more lives than it saves.

Even when we do discover that genocide is taking place, moreover,
it is still important not to overdramatize. One does not have to be a
theologian or a philosopher to appreciate that genocide can serve as a
metaphor for the modern condition, forcing us to ask deep questions
about what went wrong in God's plan or in the process of history or
the complexities of human nature to have produced outcomes so ugly.
At the same time, no matter how hateful genocide may be and no matter how determined we are to punish those responsible for it, we must
always keep in mind that genocide is not just a metaphysical puzzle but
a political reality taking place at a particular time and in a specific place.
Genocide, like all forms of political evil, is primarily local in nature. The
world community can do only so much to transform human nature. It
can play a more active role in changing the political facts on the ground
to encourage members of one group from trying to exterminate those
who belong to another.

GIVING DEATH THE BENEFIT OF THE DOUBT

THE DRAMATIZATION OF genocide we witness today cannot be understood without an appreciation of the considerable efforts undertaken
by murderous regimes and their supporters in the past to deny their
crimes. The Turks, although softening slightly in recent years, are the
most notorious for this; they have been known to subsidize historians and hold conferences in efforts to whitewash the Armenian blood

they shed. But genocide denial is more common than that. Whether out of perversity, publicity seeking, or simple madness, every now and then a seemingly respectable intellectual—or even a prominent Catholic priest—will flirt with the idea that the gas chambers were a fraud or that far fewer than six million Jews lost their lives during the Nazi era. In response to such blatant distortions of history, we are tempted to conclude that exaggeration against bigotry can be no vice. The fact that its practitioners and apologists say that genocide does not happen means that we must insist on the fact that it does.

Daniel Goldhagen is perhaps the most persistent, as well as the most determined, of those who seek to counter claims of genocide denial. In his book *Worse Than War,* he illustrates one way of responding to the methods used by killers to cover up their crimes. His approach can be characterized as a politics of counting. Goldhagen points out that in recent years mass killings have taken place in most parts of the globe: Africa (Uganda, Nigeria, Burundi, Rwanda, the Congo, and Darfur), Latin America (Argentina, Guatemala, Chile, El Salvador), Europe (the former Yugoslavia and before that the victims of both Hitler's and Stalin's imperial ambitions), Asia (Indonesia, Cambodia, Bangladesh, Vietnam), and the Arab world (Algeria, Iraq, and Syria, among others). By taking the higher rather than the lower mortality estimates in these cases, and by arguing that even such a seemingly natural phenomenon as starvation should qualify as an intentional act of political murder on the grounds that elites can generally prevent it from happening if they really want to, he estimates that as many as 175 million people, or 4 percent of the world's population, can be included in the total number of those who have died for the sake of politics. "Our time has been an age of mass murder," he concludes. "By any reasonable accounting, mass murder and elimination have been more lethal than war." When it comes to political evil, death, in his view, should always have the benefit of the doubt.

So concerned is Goldhagen by the presence of political evil in the contemporary world that, despite his talk of genocide bombing, he is actually reluctant to use the term "genocide" for fear that it *underplays* the ubiquity of mass killing: he prefers "exterminationism" as an alternative. The same is decidedly not true of other intellectuals convinced that the problem of genocide ought to be rendered as vividly as possible. Since the adoption of the 1948 Convention on the Prevention and

Punishment of the Crime of Genocide by the General Assembly of the United Nations, we have the proper term for acts of mass killing, their argument runs, and we ought to be prepared to use it. Following the Columbia University political scientist Mahmood Mamdani, they can be viewed as engaged in a politics of naming rather than of counting.

One of the best-known individuals holding to this point of view is Samantha Power, a Harvard human rights professor turned Obama administration official, and author of the eloquent and highly influential book *"A Problem from Hell."* Even when regimes lack the single-minded determination to kill people because of the race, religion, or ethnicity to which they belong, she insists, we should not get bogged down in technicalities and definitional quibbles. Regimes that have prominent genocidal features ought to be treated as inherently genocidal in nature. Political leaders will avoid naming genocide whenever they can get away with doing so. Any society that takes genocide seriously must overcome such reluctance and call things what they are. Naming, like counting, is another way of giving death the benefit of the doubt. We cannot allow considerations of political correctness or the requirements of diplomatic niceties to stand in the way of shaming those who select out those they wish to kill and then promptly go out and kill them.

Compared to the negligence with which the Nazi Holocaust was treated around the world during the 1930s and 1940s, the passion shown by writers such as these is more than admirable; one can never dismiss them as indifferent to suffering. Yet if it is true that the world has not lived down the shame of its response to Hitler, it is also true that today's world is not as equally complacent in the face of political evil as it was then. Contemporary political leaders are still quite capable of turning their attention away from acts of mass killing—or even providing rationales that enable them to continue. Yet shaped by a concern for human rights, U.N. conventions and treaties, agencies working for international justice, a growing distaste for aggressive wars, and technologies that make it close to impossible for leaders to hide their crimes, our era is a very different one from that in which Hitler—or, for that matter, Stalin—rose to power. The question is no longer whether we are capable of naming genocide and counting its victims; in fact, as I hope to make clear here, we do both these days with considerable frequency. The real question is whether we can do so correctly. A review of some of the most prominent examples of recent mass killing—specifically those that have taken place in the African countries of Rwanda and Sudan—suggests why lives are at stake in getting the naming and counting right.

REAL GENOCIDE

No ATROCITY IN the modern world can ever offer itself as an exact replay of the Nazi era. Yet what happened in a few bloody months in Rwanda in 1994 comes strikingly close. "The genocide in Rwanda is the first attempted extermination since the Second World War to be genuinely comparable to the Holocaust," states Linda Melvern, a British journalist who has written extensively about the events there. The 1948 U.N. convention defined the phenomenon of genocide as "any of the following acts committed with the intent to destroy, in whole or in part, a national, ethnical, racial or religious group, as such: (a) killing members of the group; (b) causing serious bodily or mental harm to members of the group; (c) deliberately inflicting on the group conditions of life calculated to bring about its physical destruction in whole or in part; (d) imposing measures intended to prevent births within the group; (e) forcibly transferring children of the group to another group." By just about every one of these criteria, the events in Rwanda fit.

For one thing, the sheer amount of the killing was by any reckoning astronomical. Eight hundred thousand deaths, the generally accepted number of Tutsis and moderate Hutus killed, ranks well below the six million associated with the Nazis, but, then again, the Rwandan killing took place over months rather than years; at the rate of 333⅓ deaths per hour, or 5½ per minute, this genocide was the most intense in human history. It is true that the chosen instrument of death was the machete rather than the extermination camp, but this too makes the Rwandan genocide even more gruesome than the one to which it is so often compared, for the blood and suffering were visible to all and not hidden behind bureaucratic obfuscation and carried out in remote regions. If we are to give death the benefit of the doubt, there is no doubt when it comes to the Rwandan events that death was the omnipresent reality of everything that took place.

Those deaths, moreover, were the consequence of intentional acts by leaders who knew what they were doing. The frenzy of the killing should not distract us from recalling just how calmly deliberate was the planning that led up to it. The violence began in earnest when a plane carrying Rwanda's president, Juvénal Habyarimana, was shot down after a trip to Tanzania on April 6, 1994. (The president of neighboring Burundi was also killed.) For twenty years, Habyarimana had run a dictatorial state, carefully cultivating support from members of the Hutu tribe to which he belonged but at the same time resisting pressure from some hard-line Hutus to exterminate the rival Tutsis, many of whom were living in exile. Almost immediately upon his death, extremist Hutu militias undertook a campaign to kill not only the Tutsis but moderate Hutus considered insufficiently bloodthirsty. The slaughter took place so quickly, and with such thoroughness, that there can be little doubt that plans for it had been developed long before the plane crash. Not a full day had passed before the moderates from all factions in Rwandan politics were crushed; those who had not been killed fled or were in hiding, unable to mobilize against the regime and its supporters. Spontaneous violence this was not. As the political scientist Lee Ann Fujii points out, the events leading to the bloodshed were political in nature; the fighting took place "between those opposed to multiparty democracy and those firmly committed to this aim."

If the genocide in Rwanda began for political reasons, however, it soon became intertwined with the country's history of ethnic rivalry and hatred. Once the conflict spread from the capital of Kigali, the violence was no longer confined to one faction of the Rwandan government trying to kill its opposition but penetrated down to village, neighborhood, and family, bringing horrendous suffering to ordinary people. For many who have written about the Rwandan genocide, especially those who find it eerily parallel to the Holocaust, the resort to mass violence involved nothing less than race hatred, pure and simple: Hutus were determined to rid the country of Tutsis in much the same way the Nazi regime developed the Final Solution for ridding the world of the Jews. Such direct comparisons are not all that accurate, for in Rwanda the perpetrators of the violence, as Mamdani has pointed out, came from the lower ends of the social scale, while the victims were historically from the elite. Both groups, moreover, spoke the same language, shared common Christian beliefs, and intermarried with such frequency that the distinctions between them became blurred. To a considerable extent, finally, the tensions between them did not have ancient lineage but were manipulated by Belgium, the major colonial power in the region, which had followed a classic European strategy of dividing those it sought to rule. Every nation's ethnicity is different from that of every other nation, and for that reason Hutus were not Germans and Tutsis were not Jews.

Still, there is no denying that, in conformity with the U.N. Genocide Convention, ethnicity played a major role in the Rwandan genocide. Whether you were killed depended to a considerable extent on who you were—or, more properly, who your parents and grandparents were. Although killing took place on both sides of the conflict—Tutsis fought back, made their own contribution to the final death total, and eventually won the war of which the genocide was part and parcel—the Hutu militias who launched the attacks carried around lists of people meant to die and set out to kill them one after another. Hutus contrived to steal everything they could from the Tutsis they massacred, down to the doors and window frames of their houses. Checkpoints were established to corral Tutsis who were fleeing for safety with the intent of denying them the refuge they were seeking. Children of mixed-marriage parents were declared to have Tutsi blood and added to the body count. The idea, in a nutshell, was to find and kill every Tutsi there was. "Please don't kill me," Power writes about one three-year-old boy shouting to his tormenters. "I'll never be Tutsi again." His plea went unheard.

In one other way did the Rwandan genocide recall the Nazi experience: no one who might have intervened chose to do so, at least while the bulk of the killing was taking place. The story of the West's complacency has been told many times, but no matter how often one hears it, it retains its capacity to both numb and disturb. One of the most common words used in reference to the Rwandan genocide is "impunity." It is not merely that the West did so little to prevent it; far more gruesome was the fact that the *génocidaires* knew from the start that they were unlikely ever to be called to account for their crimes. It is as if Hitler's comment about how no one would remember the Armenians stuck in the minds of Rwanda's Hutu leaders—even though they had most likely never heard it.

Considering that there was no such thing as the United Nations, let alone a convention on genocide, when Hitler carried out his policy of extermination, the reluctance of the world community to take any serious action with respect to the Rwandan genocide is especially troublesome. From the start, major U.N. officials, including Secretary-General Boutros Boutros-Ghali, as Michael Barnett, a former political officer to the U.S. mission to the U.N., has written, "could see only civil war because that was what they were prompted to expect." The U.N. had established procedures for dealing with civil wars, and they involved maintaining neutrality and seeking power-sharing arrangements acceptable to both or all sides. Desperate pleas from those in the know, especially Roméo Dallaire, the Canadian general who headed the U.N. peacekeeping operation in the area, documented that Hutus were killing Tutsis for ethnic as well as political reasons. But U.N. officials, by fitting the events taking place there into their preexisting diagnosis of civil war, wound up empowering one side in its genocidal campaign against the other—for example, by threatening to withdraw U.N. forces, which was exactly what the extremist Hutus desired. Barnett's judgment is as devastating as it is fair: Boutros-Ghali "bears some moral responsibility for the genocide" because his failure to transmit information he possessed about the ethnic dimension of the conflict "might well have cost thousands of lives." Whatever one's political views, it is impossible to look back at the role played by the U.N. during the Rwandan genocide without feeling a sense of shame.

Because so much of the cost of the United Nations has been borne by the United States, the cowardly failure of the former to take the genocide in Rwanda seriously was linked to the unwillingness of the latter to do so as well. Less than two years before the outbreak of the Rwandan genocide, the United States had sent troops to Somalia in an effort to prevent mass suffering, only to be humiliated by the loss of eighteen American lives in the battle of Mogadishu. Somalia loomed so large in the minds of the Clinton administration's leading foreign policy figures that the possibility of U.S. military intervention in Rwanda was ruled out from the start. Whatever one thinks of that decision—I for one believe we need to be precise in defining genocide because when we find it we must be prepared to stop it—the simultaneous failure of the Clinton administration to consider nonmilitary methods of putting pressure on the Hutu leadership, such as by confronting France, which often acted as an apologist for the Hutus, or by trying to mobilize African opinion against them, is impossible to justify. Key policymakers in the West knew full well that genocide was taking place in Rwanda; their preferred response was to hope it would just go away.

Although policymakers did little to stop the killing in Rwanda, the events there produced an outpouring of activism and introspection that forced the question of genocide, and how best to respond to it, to the top of the world's moral agenda. Shame can play a considerable role in politics, and in this case it most certainly did. Philip Gourevitch, a writer for *The New Yorker,* brought the human cost of the genocide home to huge numbers of readers with his 1998 book *We Wish to Inform You That Tomorrow We Will Be Killed with Our Families.* So did the film inspired by the book, *Hotel Rwanda,* featuring the efforts by the hotel-keeper Paul Rusesabagina to save lives during the killing. Educational programs designed to teach students about the horrors of genocide, such as those sponsored by the Massachusetts-based organization Facing History and Ourselves, made the Rwandan events central to their efforts. It was as if thoughtful people the world over woke up from their long night of inaction and realized that despite repeated calls after the Holocaust never again to sit back and do nothing in the face of genocide, they had done exactly that. Inattention to genocide the second time around only doubled the resolve of those committed to stopping this most bloody form of political evil from ever happening again.

Despite this outpouring of concern, however, one question remained unanswered: Would those who realized that genocide had occurred in Rwanda, even as the world looked the other way, go to the opposite extreme in some future conflict and conclude that genocide was taking place even when it was not? The answer would be provided when violence in Africa once again came to the world's attention, almost ten years to the day after the outbreak of genocide in Rwanda. That answer proved to be far more complicated than many of those who involved themselves in the crisis had anticipated.

"THE MOST SUFFERING I'VE SEEN"

EVEN HUMANITARIAN WORKERS who thought they had seen it all had never seen anything quite like what had taken place in Darfur, the western region of Sudan. Violence broke out in the area in 2003 when insurgent groups, convinced that the central government in Khartoum was bent on the economic and political suppression of Darfur, took up arms against it. The response, led by Sudan's violence-prone strongman Omar al-Bashir and his allies, the camel-riding militia known as the Janjaweed, was especially bloody. An estimated two hundred thousand people died in the resulting violence. Conditions of extreme poverty and severe drought multiplied the horrors. Because the people of Darfur considered themselves African, while the Khartoum government identified itself as Arab, moreover, racial hatred seemed to enter the picture as well. The violence in Darfur shook the world. "I don't know if it is genocide or not," said one European humanitarian helper who wished to retain her anonymity for fear of reprisal. "But I've worked in a lot of post-conflict places—Iraq, Afghanistan—and this is the most suffering I've seen."

Not everyone shared this observer's reluctance to invoke the word "genocide"—or, for that matter, any of the other terms that have been used to characterize the worst horrors of the twentieth century—to describe what took place in this region of Africa. During the height of the conflict, *The Village Voice*'s Nat Hentoff put the matter this way: "Of course this is genocide. It is also pure evil. Mr. Bush is not afraid of that word. Let him, right now—unlike Bill Clinton turning away from Rwanda—save lives in Darfur." After reviewing a number of books detailing the cruelties imposed on the victims, Richard Just, now the editor of *The New Republic,* went even further. "Radical evil has become commonplace in Darfur," he concluded, citing Hannah Arendt's famous phrase from *The Origins of Totalitarianism*. "It is impossible to reach any other conclusion. There are simply too many government-sponsored men who show up in these narratives solely for the purpose of committing almost incomprehensible acts of cruelty. The sadism knows no bounds." Humanitarians concerned with this crisis reminded us that there are more ways than one for human beings to suffer, and in Darfur ways were found to combine them all.

Those who took up the cause of Darfur led a public campaign against political evil remarkable for the widespread attention it drew. Hollywood figures—especially *Hotel Rwanda*'s star Don Cheadle, but also Mia Farrow, Matt Damon, and George Clooney—played a crucial role in bringing the Darfur crisis to public consciousness. Along with the human rights activist John Prendergast, Cheadle published *Not on Our Watch,* which quickly became the manifesto of the antigenocide campaign while also giving rise to an organization of the same name devoted to using the appeal of Hollywood notables to raise funds for the cause. (*Not on Our Watch* contained a preface cowritten by two senators at the time, Sam Brownback, Republican of Kansas, and Barack Obama, Democrat of Illinois.) The Save Darfur Coalition, the leading activist organization dealing with the issue, brought together more than 180 faith-based and humanitarian groups to hold rallies, sponsor speakers, and bring pressure to bear on companies that profited from their investment in Sudan. Active in publicizing the atrocities in the region was the U.S. Holocaust Memorial in Washington, D.C., which featured a nighttime exhibit, *Darfur: Who Will Survive Today?*, consisting of images from the crisis illuminated by candles and displayed outside the museum's doors. Prominent Wall Street investment banks, major companies such as General Electric, famous intellectuals, and religious leaders from every imaginable denomination all joined the efforts to stop the violence. Had you paid a visit to a secular college campus—or even, for that matter, a Sunday megachurch service—in the aftermath of the worst periods of the war, you might well have come across signs and petitions protesting the cruelties in Darfur. There even existed a video game, *Darfur Is Dying*, sponsored by MTV and Reebok, as well as a Save Darfur black leather boot designed by Cheadle and marketed by the Timberland Company.

Jews in particular were determined to come to the aid of those being killed in Darfur. American Jews disagree among themselves on a wide variety of issues, from affirmative action to the war in Iraq; even Israel's wars in Lebanon and the Gaza Strip have provoked debate among them. But when it came to stopping what so many of them considered a replay of the Holocaust, they were united. Of the groups that made up the Save Darfur Coalition, thirty-nine were Jewish, more than any other single religion, and they included the American Jewish Committee, the Anti-Defamation League, the Conference of Presidents of Major Jewish Organizations, Hadassah, Hillel, the National Council of Jewish Women, the Religious Action Center of Reform Judaism, and the Union of Orthodox Jewish Congregations of America. "We know what it means to be victims of those who want to wipe another people off the face of the earth," proclaimed Robert Levine, president of the New York Board of Rabbis, to a 2006 rally organized to protest the events in Darfur. "It was only two generations ago when we looked around and wondered, where was everyone?"

It is not difficult to understand why so many groups made the cause of the victims in Darfur their own: just listen to what some of those victims had to say. "The Arabs arrived and asked me to leave the place," twenty-three-year-old Aisha Ali recalled, from her refuge in Chad, about the 2003 campaign that marked the most brutal period of the conflict. "They beat the women and the small kids. They killed a little girl, Sarah Bishara. She was two years old. She was knifed in the back." Not only did the Janjaweed kill, rape, brand, and pillage, they insulted and humiliated. "The Janjaweed were accompanied by soldiers," a victim of an August 2003 attack on the village of Jafal testified. "They attacked the people, saying: 'You are opponents to the regime, we must crush you. As you are Black, you are like slaves. Then the entire Darfur region will be in the hands of the Arabs.'"

For nearly all those who became involved in efforts to save Darfur, such accounts of attacks by Arabs against Africans, the one determined to enslave, the other forced to obey, suggested a repeat of the Holocaust. For example, Eric Reeves, a professor of English at Smith College and one of the most engaged and passionate of the Western writers who took up the cause of Darfur, wrote that the camps to which more than a million people were forced to flee "have become an African Auschwitz. Their purpose is human destruction. Those being destroyed have been displaced and concentrated in these camps because of who they are, because of their racial/ethnic identity." Analogies to the Nazi era appeared over and over again in the writings of Reeves: even the fact that Hitler welcomed the Olympics to Berlin in 1936 and the Khartoum regime's major ally, China, was host to the 2008 games were used to underscore his case. The world must do now what it so conspicuously failed to do then, he repeatedly urged. It must find a way to intervene before it is too late. Rwanda was the first place in Africa to experience the full force of genocide, and because genocide tends to spread, Darfur was next in line.

The evidence assembled by the campaign to save Darfur leaves no doubt: gruesome violence took place in that part of the world, enormous numbers of lives were lost, and many if not most of those killed had done nothing to bring about their own destruction. Also not open to question is the cruelty of al-Bashir and the Janjaweed; they killed with reckless abandon, indifference to any claims of conscience or rules of war, and contempt for international opinion. Yet for all that, it is still important to raise the question of whether the violence in Darfur ever rose to the level of evil associated with the Nazi Holocaust—let alone the genocide that undoubtedly did take place in Rwanda. It may appear to be unfeeling to develop a kind of litmus test for genocide, as if the deaths in one place somehow do not match the degree of immorality of those in another. But if we are to have a chance to stop genocide, we must define and identify it precisely in order to make clear exactly what we are dealing with so that we can tailor our responses accordingly. Rwanda taught us the error of treating a genocide as a civil war. Darfur raises the question of whether it is equally misguided to treat a civil war as a genocide. Details matter. Just because Rwanda and Darfur are both in Africa does not necessarily mean that what happened in the former offers an appropriate guide for what occurred in the latter.

The first of these details involves the all-important questions of race and ethnicity. Sudanese such as Aisha Ali knew what they meant when they talked of Arabs killing Africans. But these seemingly fixed labels have a different meaning in Sudan than they do elsewhere. The name "Sudan" stems from the Arabic *bilad al-Sudan,* or "land of the blacks," and those called "Arab" are just as black as those called "African." Because the former are more likely to be descended from the Islamic invaders of centuries ago, they may have different facial features from the latter. For this reason, Sudanese can be aware of even very subtle racial distinctions unobservable to non-Sudanese. It follows that, as the Sudanese-born, California-based historian Jok Madut Jok puts it, "the Sudanese citizens racially perceive of themselves and of each other in ways that differ dramatically from the way race is popularly perceived and talked about in the Western world." Taking race in the Western sense of the term into account, the conflict in Darfur is not between races but within one. Taking it in the African sense of the term, the same conflict is not between two but among many.

When people in Sudan use terms such as "Arab" or "African," they are not referring primarily to race, religion, or place of origin but to distinctions of class, occupation, language, and tribe. The term "Arab" can refer to any one of a number of groups; traditionally it was used to characterize those who were nomadic herders, in contrast to the "Africans," who were settled farmers—a difference that accounted for the frequent conflicts over land and water that occurred between them. In addition, "Arab" is used to denote those living in the vicinity of the Nile—the so-called riverine elite—who have dominated politics in Khartoum since they took power in a 1989 military coup. In this more contemporary usage, "Arabs" tend to be relatively better off economically and to live in the northern and eastern part of the country, whereas "Africans" are poorer and can be found predominantly in the more remote western areas, Darfur itself being an inland state roughly the size of France and equidistant from the Atlantic Ocean and the Red Sea. Ethnic and racial identities in Sudan are real and constructed, precise and diffuse, as shaped by history and geography as they are determined by biology, and undergoing a process of merging and blending. To view them as fixed by color or line of descent, as if one group has more in common with people in the Middle East while the other is native to the African subcontinent, is to distort the reasons so many in Darfur found themselves under such brutal attack.

It is, moreover, not just that ethnic rivalries caused the violence in Darfur. In addition, as the human rights scholar Alex de Waal has pointed out, violence was part of a process of refashioning and transforming ethnic identities. On the one hand, the Bashir government in Khartoum and the rightly feared Janjaweed militias exaggerated their "Arab" ethnicity as an excuse for suppressing threats to their power from the rebels in Darfur. On the other, the Darfurians reinforced their "African" ethnicity to win allies for their cause on the larger continent and to unify themselves against the invaders. "Darfur's is hardly the first case of cynical appeals to ethnic loyalty for the purpose of achieving political and economic ends, nor indeed of fading identities revivified against perceived threats," writes the British historian M. W. Daly. This is certainly a formula for horrors aplenty, but it is neither a holocaust nor a genocide, both of which involve attempts by one well-defined ethnic group to destroy another one in order to expropriate its land, possessions, or identity. Such conditions simply do not apply in Darfur, where identities are not fixed, so much of the population is poor, tillable land is in short supply, and there are almost no possessions to take over. In a situation as ethnically complex as this one, "Arabs" can be found killing other "Arabs," and rivalries can exist between tribes who all consider themselves "African." Ethnicity was in play during the Darfur crisis, but it played out in ways far more complex than our Hitlerian picture of genocide allows.

In one other way has the conflict in Darfur been understood as ethnic in nature, and this involves the tribal distinctions characteristic of the region. Darfur contains three major tribes—the Fur, Masalit, and Zaghawa—all of which were under attack by Khartoum. (*Darfur* in Arabic means "home of the Fur.") These tribes, most especially the Fur, have their own dialects and history, making them, for those who claim the presence of genocide in the region, even more inviting targets for extermination than the more ethnically similar tribes at war in Rwanda. Even if the conflict in Darfur were not between "Arabs" and "Africans," persistent tribal conflict has been viewed as the crucial factor in concluding that genocide took place there.

Yet when tribal differences intensified the violence in Darfur, as they did at the height of the conflict in 2003, the question nonetheless remained whether the killings were directed against the tribes per se or against the region of the country in which those tribes predominated. Darfur has what Rwanda lacks: well-defined regions composed of populations sufficiently different from the rest of the country that autonomy, if not independence, remains an option, however distant. (Rwanda, by contrast, is one of the most densely populated countries in the world; the fact that Hutus and Tutsis lived so close together and were unable to escape from each other helped fuel the genocidal nature of its violence.) Because of Sudan's pronounced regionalism, the Fur, unlike the Tutsis, were killed not only because of who they were but because of where they lived. African tribal violence, as two economists from the World Bank have shown, often has more to do with poverty, lack of natural resources, and weak political institutions than with ethnic hatred. This has been especially true in Sudan. Tribal differences not only are regional in nature but also overlap with the different forms of production specific to the climatological and geologic characteristics of those regions. When tribes kill each other for reasons of ethnicity, we have genocide. But if the violence is more related to matters of geography and economics, the situation is closer to civil war.

Religious differences were not in play during the Rwandan genocide; both sides were predominantly Christian. Religious differences, by contrast, do exist in Sudan, which has led some to suggest that genocide took place there in ways comparable to Hitler's Germany because the Nazi regime also singled out one particular group for extermination based upon its religion. To the degree that religious violence exists in Sudan, however, it involves not the war in Darfur but the earlier efforts by the Islamic regime in Khartoum to suppress an insurgency in the south, a region populated by many Christians and animists. Darfur, unlike the south, is universally Muslim in its religious affiliations, which means this particular conflict took place within one faith rather than between two or more of them.

Although both sides in the Darfur conflict are Muslim, they approach their faith in different ways. This has led to the argument that because the killing was orchestrated by militant and fundamentalist Muslims in Khartoum and was directed against more tolerant and peaceful Muslims in Darfur whose faith is Sufi-like in its spiritual intensity, genocide still took place there because intrareligious violence is little different from interreligious extermination campaigns. Daniel Pipes, the neo-conservative writer who believes that 15 percent of the Muslim world adheres to radical or fundamentalist versions of the faith, has singled out Darfur as one of two cases—the other is Algeria—in which radical Muslims identified as their major enemy not Christians or Jews but other Muslims who reject Islamism.

Such claims have an initial plausibility because the Bashir government was led by members of the National Islamic Front, which has its roots in the Muslim Brotherhood founded in Egypt. The NIF, moreover, imposed Sharia law on the country and made alliances with terrorist regimes around the world. But despite these developments, any effort to portray the crisis as a genocidal conflict between two different versions of the same faith also mischaracterizes what happened in Darfur. Although the regime in Khartoum was influenced by a radical version of Islam, for one thing, it was at the same time a force for modernization rather than reaction in the region; much like Protestantism did in the West, political Islam can encourage such forces as urbanization and education. Nor was the regime's radicalism associated indiscriminately with hostility toward the non-Islamic world; Sudan was actually removed from the U.S. terrorist watch list in May 2004 because its leaders had found a way, much like the government of Pervez Musharraf in Pakistan once did, to be on both sides of the war on terror. Meanwhile, the people of Darfur are among the most devout in the country. The Sufism in which many of them believe is more introspective and mystical than this-worldly and political, but it is also very traditional in its practices and cultural assumptions. To characterize it as somehow more tolerant or secular than radical Islam is to apply Christian analogies to Islam in ways that do not fit. Muslims were not killed in Darfur because they rejected literal readings of the Qur'an, encouraged their women to wear Western clothing, adhered to a liberal theory of jurisprudence, or were on the wrong side of the Sunni-Shia split. They died not because of their faith but in spite of it.

Whatever the reason that leads some people to single out others for death and destruction, the element of intentionality so present in Rwanda was also missing in Darfur. However high the number of deaths in Darfur—as we have seen, the consensus is two hundred thousand, or one-quarter of those in Rwanda—as many as 70 percent, according to an estimate from the Center for Research on the Epidemiology of Disaster at the University of Louvain, were caused by disease and starvation rather than by deliberately murderous actions such as those that characterized the Rwanda conflict. Those massacres that took place, in addition, were frequently combustible, spontaneous, and random, more the work of warlords and militias than governmental officials prepared with lists of potential enemies to kill. "The practice of genocide or quasi-genocide in Sudan," writes Gérard Prunier, a French expert on Africa, "has never been a deliberate well-thought-out policy but rather a spontaneous tool used for keeping together a 'country' which is under minority Arab domination and which is in fact one of the last multi-national empires on the planet." Chaotic violence may well be worse than coordinated violence, since it can be visited upon a person so arbitrarily in the wink of an eye, but for the human rights activists who developed the legal basis behind the concept, the key features of genocide, which the events in Darfur lacked, are planning, coordination, and control.

Because of all the complexities of race, ethnicity, tribe, religion, and region in Sudan, not everyone is as persuaded as humanitarian activists and engaged intellectuals that the question of whether genocide took place there is open-and-shut. In January 2005, the International Commission of Inquiry on Darfur released to the U.N. secretary-general a report that found that war crimes had taken place in the region, as well as what it called "acts with genocidal intent." Nonetheless, the report concluded, "the crucial element of genocidal intent appears to be missing, at least as far as the central Government authorities are concerned. Generally speaking the policy of attacking, killing and forcibly displacing members of some tribes does not evince a specific intent to annihilate, in whole or in part, a group distinguished on racial, ethnic, national or religious grounds." If intentionality is a crucial precondition for genocide, the commission did not find enough of it to support the charge.

One can dismiss the commission's findings as wishy-washy and politically correct, yet another depressing example of the failure of the United Nations to take a strong moral position when the interests of any of its member states are involved. This was certainly the conclusion of former U.S. ambassador to the United Nations John Bolton, one of the most hawkish figures in American foreign-policy making circles. Bolton denounced the whole inquiry as a sham; the "Euroids," as he indelicately called those who opposed him on one issue after another, were "getting out their wig boxes and preparing to go to court" instead of planning the needed military intervention. (In October 2005, Bolton, to make his disdain for the investigation clear, took the radical step of preventing a briefing to the Security Council on the extent of human rights violations there.) Yet in its defense, the U.N. report at least acknowledged the complexities of race and ethnicity in the region, something that Bolton, whose Manichaean outlook on the world typically disdained complexity, never did.

The U.N. commission's findings, moreover, received significant support in other quarters. Fabrice Weissman, the former head of mission in Darfur for the highly respected Doctors Without Borders, wrote in *Le Monde* in November 2006 that the region's "horrendous death toll appears directly linked to the brutality of Khartoum's counterinsurgency campaign—not to the implementation of a secret program of systematic extermination of part of the Darfurian population." In much the same fashion, John Holmes, the emergency relief coordinator for the United Nations, told *Newsweek* in January 2009 that he would not use the word "genocide" to describe the situation there and also let it be known that in his view groups like the Save Darfur Coalition that insisted on doing so were doing more harm than good. The caution these observers displayed in pronouncing Darfur a genocide had little in common with the world community's earlier failure to take action against genocide in Rwanda. These were thoughtful individuals with long experience in dealing with and responding to mass atrocities, not indifferent U.N. officials anxious to look the other way. Their unwillingness to judge the violence that took place in Darfur as genocide cannot be lightly dismissed. Weissman, Holmes, and others like them were not appeasers with their heads in the sand but humanitarian activists fully aware of the evils with which they were dealing—and worried that throwing irresponsible charges around could make the situation worse.

Considering these factors together, we must resist pronouncing every outbreak of violence as genocidal. Rwanda rightly reminds us of the Nazi era, so virulent was the racial and ethnic hatred and so single-minded were the killers. That comparison, however, fails in the case of Darfur. When we find genocide in too many places, we treat all stories of evil as if they were the same story; there is nothing new to learn about man's ugly nature because we have already learned in another context what we need to know in this one. Such an approach opens our eyes to evil while shutting our ears to the particulars of time and place. The problem of finding genocide in Darfur comes down to one major obstacle: genocide, at least as we understand that term in the aftermath of the Holocaust, did not take place there.

HOW EFFORTS TO STOP VIOLENCE
CAN END UP PROLONGING IT

NOTHING WOULD BE wrong with making an inaccurate case for genocide in Darfur if no harm came from doing so. But those who argued that Darfur contributed one more piece of evidence for the modern world's capacity for genocide did very little good and may have caused considerable harm. It is worth cataloging some of the major mistakes the campaign against genocide in Darfur made in the hopes of avoiding them in the future.

If terrorism shocks the collective conscience by deliberately aiming to disrupt the routines and conventions that make social life possible, genocide, as I have been arguing here, belongs in the category of political evil because the killing it launches is motivated by the gross and arbitrary stereotyping of the groups singled out for destruction. Yet in an ironic way, antigenocide activists engaged in more than their share of ethnic and racial stereotyping. The "Arab" side, as they portrayed the conflict, came to be viewed as violent, vengeful, and aggressive, while the "African" was portrayed as blameless and peaceful. Such stereotyping prevented activists from understanding that in this conflict, unlike the one in Nazi Germany, both sides were guilty of politically evil acts. Worse than that, it also fueled distrust of the Muslim and Arab world, an especially dangerous thing to do at a time when, in the wake of Islamic-inspired terrorism, greater public understanding of how diverse and multifaceted both those worlds actually are had become essential. Stereotypes always distort reality. When they are used on behalf of causes we believe to be good, they can still have consequences that we have to consider bad. In this context, the decision on the part of Jewish organizations to involve themselves so extensively in the campaign to save Darfur needs a careful look. At one level, Jewish organizations took up the cause of Darfur because Jews know what it means to be a victimized minority and are determined to ensure that innocent black Africans do not suffer a similar fate. Yet at another level their deep involvement in the Save Darfur movement revealed far less idealistic motivations. Israel is at war with its Arab neighbors. By reducing the violence in Darfur to a morality play in which evil Arabs were attacking helpless Africans, these organizations, consciously or not, were using violence in one part of the world to build a case for a cause important to them in another. In such ways can high moral principles reveal themselves as seemingly self-interested prejudices.

Western commentators who proved themselves guilty of stereotyping could especially be found among those who adhered to the concept of Islamofascism—the idea, discussed earlier, that Islamic radicalism has inherited Nazi Germany's plans to dominate the world. One of them was the well-known French philosopher Bernard-Henri Lévy. Displaying pictures he had taken during a visit to Sudan, Lévy, speaking along with Mia Farrow at the New York meeting of the PEN World Voices Festival of International Literature in 2008, asked his audience the key question: "Does what happened in Darfur deserve, if I dare say, the name genocide or not?" And he also supplied the answer: "I know that there is a polemic on this point. Some say that it is a genocide, others say that it is not quite a genocide. There is a sort of discussion similar to the discussion of the sex of the angels in the Middle Ages. [Laughter.] What I saw, what I witnessed, what you can see in this photo, what you can see in this one, what you can see in this one, what you can see in this one, makes this sort of discussion completely absurd and frivolous." For Lévy, the case for genocide in Darfur was not only clear-cut but also closely linked to jihadism. Pointing to the presence of Osama bin Laden in Sudan in the 1990s, Lévy argued that the attacks on the people of Darfur, although taking place in a remote part of Africa far from either the wars in Iraq and Afghanistan or the Israeli-Palestinian conflict, were all part of Islam's unfortunate affinity with radical evil. In this he had many allies. Christopher Hitchens, for example, described the events in Darfur as a "race-murder campaign against African Muslims" being carried out by Osama bin Laden's "pious Sudanese friends in Darfur." Genocide, for all these writers, was not evil enough; it had to be linked to September 11, much in the way George W. Bush treated the regime of Saddam Hussein, to show how truly evil it was. Nazi Germany, the attack on the World Trade Center, Hezbollah, Khartoum—a direct line was presumed to connect them all.

The problem with such a perspective is that it is difficult enough to end political violence when no racial or religious differences are at stake. If we instead try to take on an entire religion, or even just the 15 percent that Pipes believes to be supporters of Islam's radical wing, we doom ourselves to defeat from the start, especially when the religion in question has as many followers as Islam does. Darfur was at best a regional conflict involving such countries as Chad and Libya and, off in the distance, China. It was never part of anyone's global campaign. The attacks against its people had nothing to do with revenge for Saladin's victories during the Crusades, Arab-Jewish conflicts in the Middle East, suicide bombings, forced conversions to hostile faiths, either of the attacks on the World Trade Center, and the peregrinations of the grand mufti of Jerusalem, who, as we saw earlier, has been alleged by so many adherents to the concept of Islamofascism to be the missing link between the Nazis and the Arabs. (Both Lévy and Hitchens managed to include the mufti in their accounts of the violence in Darfur.) The last thing we should do in trying to end political violence is to define it in such a way that it can never come to an end.

An additional mistake made by the antigenocide movement lay in its insistence on inflating the death toll in the region. Intent on dramatizing the situation, Save Darfur, no stickler for accuracy, took out an ad in British newspapers publicizing a figure of four hundred thousand. This immediately brought a rebuke from the Advertising Standards Authority, which, responding to complaints by pro-Khartoum groups, ruled that such a number—twice as high as most other estimates—had to be presented as opinion rather than fact. Numbers, because they can become political weapons, are never as innocent as they may appear: by quite deliberately exaggerating the mortality figures, Save Darfur was attempting to maximize Western guilt in order to promote intervention. Yet even if it had succeeded in producing enough domestic pressure within Western countries to force a more interventionist response to the crisis, guilt is rarely a healthy foreign policy motivation. Once the guilt dissipates, which will happen quickly when people discover that the number of deaths was exaggerated in the first place, a strong desire to withdraw, whatever the consequences, becomes inevitable.

On top of all these mistakes, those committed to calling what took place in Darfur genocide displayed an annoying sense of moral superiority in which they portrayed themselves as the only people with insight and conscience sufficient to understand what was really taking place, while everyone else was seen as lazy, foolish, or morally craven. "This is genocide," wrote Reeves about the events in Darfur. "Let those who would deny explain why it is not." Eyewitness accounts of the destruction taking place there should, in his surprisingly violent imagery, "incinerate all agnosticism about what is happening in Darfur, and all doubt about whether this is genocide." Not only is such certainty arrogant to the point of contempt, it proved to be politically self-defeating; comparing those who may disagree with your diagnosis or who have questions about your methods to those who downplayed the Nazi horrors is not an effective way to build consensus for your position. It was also open to charges of hypocrisy because it singled out certain instances as genocidal while ignoring others; as Mamdani points out, far more people have died in the nearby Democratic Republic of the Congo than in Darfur but much less Western attention has been paid there. Genocide is so serious a matter that whether it is taking place deserves deliberate discussion. It is close to impossible to have such a discussion when one side is so certain of its conclusion that anyone else must be charged with indifference or cowardice.

By persuading itself that it occupied the moral high ground, the antigenocide movement never understood how it was perceived among those it was so desperate to help. Richard Just, the *New Republic* editor who saw radical evil operating in Darfur, has written that Western liberals are frequently caught between their respect for human rights around the world and their reluctance to have the West impose its own ideas about the right way to live upon those who may not share them. The dilemma is a real one. But those who called for radical intervention into the domestic affairs of Sudan in order to protect the people of Darfur against their own leaders never acted as if the dilemma were present. They certainly never recognized that their interventionism would be viewed as repugnant not only by tyrants in the Third World but even by pro-Western leaders trying to protect their citizens from other threatening outside forces such as economic globalization. Nor did they adequately understand that however much they may have supported humanitarian intervention but opposed the American invasion of Iraq, other people around the world saw both actions as two sides of the same coin. There is nothing wrong with liberals concluding that the protection of human rights ought to take priority over the claims of sovereignty made by Third World leaders, especially when those leaders are corrupt, brutal, or both. But intervention also requires the presence of outside force to be achieved. If that force is the United Nations, it may have a certain legitimacy, but it probably will not be militarily effective. If it is the United States, its chances of success may be greater—although the U.S. record with respect to intervention has not been all that successful—but it is also much more likely to be viewed as too tainted with neocolonialist evil to be widely accepted. This part of the dilemma as well was never subject to serious scrutiny.

The mistakes I have been describing were intellectual in nature, primarily involving the incorrect frameworks so many antigenocide activists developed to understand the conflict in Darfur. Unfortunately, conceptual failures can have real-world consequences. The most serious was this: dramatizing genocide, far from helping bring the violence in Darfur to an end, played a role in allowing it to continue. This is a harsh charge to make, especially against a movement intent on demonstrating its humanitarian intentions. Yet the charge nonetheless has considerable merit.

There was, for one thing, the false hopes that antigenocidal activism raised in the region. Stopping genocide involves a full-time commitment. Power illustrates the point when she writes that the United States "must respond to genocide with a sense of urgency, publicly identifying and threatening the perpetrators with prosecution, demanding the expulsion of representatives of genocidal regimes from international institutions such as the United Nations, closing the perpetrators' embassies in the United States, and calling upon countries aligned with the perpetrators to ask them to use their influence. . . . Given the affront genocide represents to America's most cherished values and to its interests, the United States must also be prepared to risk the lives of its soldiers in the service of stopping this monstrous crime." Power may well be correct that genocide must be met with military force if need be, but the fact is that no country, and certainly not the United States while waging two failed wars against Muslim countries in Iraq and Afghanistan, was prepared to risk the lives of its own citizens to stop the violence in Darfur. One can argue that those citizens were wrong, that they ought to have been just as willing to come to the aid of victims of mass murder who are poor, black, and foreign as they were to those who lived in Europe and were more like them. Yet one must also recognize that a nation can go to war just so many times. When it comes to genocide, a nation must be willing to put its troops where its mouth is.

By characterizing the situation in Darfur as genocidal even while knowing full well that military intervention was off the table, Save Darfur and other like-minded groups acted in a highly irresponsible manner. Conor Foley, a British human rights activist who witnessed how the best intentions can have perverse consequences during situations of extreme conflict, describes the consequences of their actions this way: "The idea that foreign troops could fight their way into Darfur and disarm the various militias by force was a fantasy, but as long as the rebel groups thought there was a chance of western military intervention—as happened in Kosovo—they had every incentive to keep fighting." When the rebels in Darfur intensified their side of the conflict, partly as a result of just such false hopes of Western intervention, the regime in Khartoum was anything but displeased. Not only could it respond violently in turn, it also saw an advantage in threats from the outside world to intervene (especially when no one actually was prepared to carry them out) because such threats could be denounced as a form of Western imperialism, thereby proving the "justice" of their cause in the first place. The term "genocide" is a loaded one, which is precisely why humanitarian interventionists invoke it. Loaded guns, however, can explode in the face of those holding them. By giving both sides reasons to keep fighting, the antigenocide movement wound up undermining its own humanitarian commitments.

A false diagnosis of genocide did more than keep the violence going; it also interfered with efforts to stop it. Sudan is a complex, multiethnic state with a long history of Western occupation and political instability, but most experts on the region believe that the Darfur crisis was the product, as Prunier has put it, of a political insurgency gone awry.

No one doubts the brutally violent proclivities of the Bashir government nor the fact that the Janjaweed militias accompanied their killing with vivid racial epithets. Yet because the conditions in Darfur resembled civil war more than they did genocide, responses designed to quell the violence of the one worked at cross-purposes with appropriate responses for the other. In reality, the lines between genocide and civil war are not always sharp. Still, it is important to get the gist correct lest the response do more harm than good.

On this point the tragic consequences of treating Rwanda and Darfur as twin examples of genocide came into full view. Determined to find a civil war in Rwanda when genocide was actually taking place, the United Nations conspicuously failed to point the finger of blame at the militant Hutus overwhelmingly responsible for the violence and even helped them along in their genocidal efforts. Chastened by their failure there, Western leaders decided to do the exact opposite in Sudan. In 2004, for example, U.S. secretary of state Colin Powell specifically used the term "genocide" to characterize the actions of Khartoum and the Janjaweed in testimony before the Senate Foreign Relations Committee. Three years later, George W. Bush, a president not well regarded for his humanitarian instincts, added this: "For too long the people of Darfur have suffered at the hands of a government that is complicit in the bombing, murder and rape of innocent civilians. My administration has called these actions by their rightful name: genocide. The world has a responsibility to put an end to it." Outside the United States, similar efforts at naming took place: the chief prosecutor of the International Criminal Court, Luis Moreno-Ocampo, for example, spent years working to fashion an indictment charging Bashir with the crime of genocide. The pleas of those working on behalf of the victims did not go unheard. Although the United States in particular did not follow up its discovery of genocide in the region with any forceful action designed to stop it, it did break with a long history, so well documented by Power, of shying away from ever using the g-word. When it came to Darfur, influential figures in the world community, even if haltingly, were going to make up for their earlier failures in Rwanda. This time there would be no fear of naming.

Yet because the conditions in Darfur were so different from those in Rwanda, identifying one side as genocidal was precisely the wrong response. This was certainly how many of the relief agencies actually working in the region felt. To gain access to the local areas where they can minister to the sick and the dying, relief workers, following in the tradition established by the Red Cross, prize neutrality. Those intent on making the case for genocide, by contrast, call on world opinion to punish the side that is responsible. Thus it was that groups such as Save Darfur, persuaded of the evils of the Bashir regime, urged the creation of a no-fly zone designed to inhibit Khartoum from carrying out its attacks. Yet, as the writer David Rieff has pointed out, such a policy would have made it impossible for relief workers to fly in supplies. As the struggle over this issue suggests, antigenocide activists seek above all else to avoid what they call complicity with evil; working with or refusing to condemn leaders they consider genocidal represents just such complicity. For relief workers, by contrast, dirtying one's own hands can be a precondition for saving the lives of others. When it comes to such mundane matters as caring for the sick and the dying, moral purity is an obstacle. It is simply a fact that certain leaders are in charge, and even if they are prone to violence and oppression, no humanitarian assistance is possible unless they are willing to cooperate.

When in March 2009 the International Criminal Court finally issued its indictments in the matter of Darfur, the same kind of dilemma arose. Rejecting Moreno-Ocampo's campaign to charge Bashir with genocide, the ICC instead ordered his arrest for war crimes and crimes against humanity. This decision was greeted with considerable derision by those persuaded that the attacks on Darfur amounted to genocide and nothing less. But humanitarian relief agencies faced a more immediate problem: in reaction to the ICC decisions, Bashir, finding even such halfway charges offensive, simply ordered them out of the country. It was for this reason that at least one prominent international lawyer, Antonio Cassese, the first president of the International Criminal Tribunal for the former Yugoslavia, had been as determined *not* to charge Bashir with genocide as Moreno-Ocampo was to do the opposite. It was not merely the power that Bashir exercised over relief workers that disturbed Cassese. Charges of genocide, he maintained, must meet "strict conditions." If they do not, and he left no doubt about that in Darfur, the consequence of nonetheless accusing leaders of genocide will be to stiffen their resolve and weaken the international political and diplomatic alliances necessary to bring the violence to an end.

Not only was the antigenocide campaign responsible for prolonging the past violence in Darfur, finally, but its efforts may come to harm peace efforts in the future. Although in theory *génocidaires* will not stop their bloodbath until every one of their intended victims has been killed, the war in Darfur did finally come to an end. In the summer of 2009, General Martin Luther Agwai, who had commanded the U.N.–African Union peacekeepers in the region, said that "as of today, I would not say there is a war going on in Darfur. Militarily, there is not much. What you have is security issues more now. Banditry, localized issues, people trying to resolve issues over water and land at a local level. But real war as such, I think we are over that." In his own way, Major General J. Scott Gration, President Obama's special envoy for Darfur, agreed; he described the situation in the region as "remnants of genocide," implying that it was no longer (if it ever had been) the real thing. In October 2009, the Obama administration unveiled its new policy for the region, and while it did use the term "genocide" to characterize what had taken place there, it also came down against hard-line efforts to isolate the Bashir regime, let alone take military action against it, by recognizing that "to advance peace and security in Sudan, we must engage with allies and with those with whom we disagree." Even Washington's Holocaust Museum, an institution that had done so much to promote the idea that genocide had been taking place in Darfur, changed its position; in August 2009 the director of its Committee on Conscience opted to place Darfur in the "genocide warning" category instead of its stronger "genocide emergency" category. One can never dismiss the possibility that violence may take place in Darfur at some point in the future, and even come complete with the reemergence of something like the Janjaweed, but at least for now, even in the context of troubled Sudan, Darfur is no longer the major problem. As with terrorism and other forms of political evil, this kind of violence does not go on forever.

A pronounced diminution of violence in Darfur ought to be treated as good news by everyone involved in the region. Yet General Agwai's assessment was greeted with considerable skepticism by antigenocide activists, including those whose humanitarian credentials were indisputable. Perhaps the most perverse reaction came from John Prendergast, who had coauthored *Not on Our Watch* with Don Cheadle. His view was that "it undermines international urgency in resolving these problems if people are led to believe that the war in Darfur is over." One can understand the concerns that led Prendergast to speak as he did. Having devoted so much of his life to the victims of violence in Darfur, he wanted to be absolutely certain that the violence had stopped before he moved on. At the time, however, his comment illustrated the major flaw that results from the dramatizing of genocide: a certain kind of peace activist becomes reluctant to pronounce war over in order to promote activism more than peace. The case against genocide requires genocide. When the violence comes to an end, the first instinct of some peace activists is suspicion. The problem is that what we call things helps shape what they become. We should not seek to keep the potential for genocide alive merely to make a point.

In retrospect, it seems clear that the campaign against genocide in Darfur was more about genocide than it was about Darfur. Crucial to the movement's understanding of the problem of political evil was the conviction that the West's leaders, obsessed in the past with realism and assertions of national self-interest at the expense of morality and a concern for human rights, had never taken genocide seriously and that as a result one petty tyrant after another learned that he could get away with mass murder. Darfur for them would be the place where all this would stop, where the West would finally muster itself to call genocide by its rightful name, protest vociferously against it, and bring those who had perpetrated it to justice. If the killing in Darfur could serve the higher cause of responding to genocide more effectively, perhaps it was not in vain.

The trouble was that events in Darfur persistently slipped out of the more general narrative designed to explain them. In their definitive history of the Darfur crisis, Julie Flint and Alex de Waal wrote that "the level of interest [by antigenocide political activists] increased Khartoum's suspicion of American motives, catapulted often incompetent rebel leaders out of obscurity and to a world stage awash in dollars, and created a simplistic moral fable that portrayed the crisis as a battle between good and evil." This was not the first time that good intentions had gone awry in some not-well-understood part of the world; Graham Greene had made the case in his 1955 classic *The Quiet American* and, lest the point be lost, Philip Caputo fleshed it out with respect to Sudan in his 2005 novel *Acts of Faith*. The fact that the dangers of well-meaning intervention had already been documented in print and on film made the naïveté of the antigenocide movement in Darfur that much more problematic.

In the end, dramatizing genocide, like the search for moral clarity in fighting terror, conflates evil in general with political evil in particular. Evil may well have contributed to the deaths of so many people in Darfur, but it was a conflict that had local causes and could be resolved only through local means. However different they may be from each other, humanitarian groups such as Save Darfur and the more militaristically inclined hawks such as John Bolton brought to their concern with Darfur a worldview in which local political events played no particular role. This is what melodrama does, and why it is important to resist it. Melodrama renders on-the-ground participants in a series of discrete events as players in a global drama. It avoids getting bogged down in the complexities and nuances of real life because the stakes in that drama are so high. Thinking in such black-and-white terms evinces compassion aplenty for the victims of violence in Darfur, but those victims are treated as pawns in larger struggles of which they are unaware. Those holding to this perspective did not wish to acknowledge the actual number of deaths in the region for fear that such a total would be viewed as too low to justify action. In their worst moments, they accused everyone who disagreed with their diagnosis of complicity with evil while never examining the morally compromising consequences of their own actions. Although done with the best of intentions, dramatizing genocide can result in painfully disturbing results. Rarely does it happen that just being well intentioned is enough. With respect to Darfur, this was a lesson that many liberals never learned and many conservatives managed to overlook.

SOMETHING UNHOPED FOR

BECAUSE GENOCIDE could happen again, the question of how best to respond to it remains. Next time, it will be important to do what the Darfur activists never did: to avoid sweeping generalizations about evil in order to focus on the local conditions that produced the violence. Interestingly enough, just such a local focus emerged in postgenocide Rwanda as the people of that country contemplated their past and future.

In part because the quest for explanation and understanding of the Holocaust led directly to the Nuremberg trials, one of the first steps taken in the aftermath of the Rwandan genocide was the application of international justice. In November 1994, just months after the killing had ended, the United Nations created the International Criminal Tribunal for Rwanda (ICTR). The motives for doing so reflected the early post–World War II humanitarianism represented by such figures as Eleanor Roosevelt and Lebanon's Charles Malik. No longer could the world sit by and allow tyrants to claim that respect for national sovereignty prevented outside interference into their domestic affairs. All people around the world were entitled to the same fundamental human rights. Those who violated such rights had to be brought to justice. Effective international institutions and a willingness to develop and apply norms of international law, it was and is widely believed, were the best way to do so.

The ICTR never lived up to the high hopes that accompanied its establishment. In its first fourteen years of operation, it tried only thirty-five cases—at the surprising cost of more than one billion dollars, much of which was eaten up by corruption and mismanagement. Some of those who participated in the genocide actually worked, under assumed identities, for the court, an especially egregious problem since it gave them access to the names of potential informants. Because the ICTR was located in Tanzania, witnesses to the genocide found it close to impossible to appear before the court to testify. One prosecutor, Carla Del Ponte, was dismissed because she insisted on trying Tutsis as well as Hutus and thereby ran afoul of Paul Kagame, the Tutsi leader who had assumed power in Rwanda after the genocide. Although the court had promised to complete all its work by 2008, it, on more than one occasion, asked for the deadline to be moved back. Some justice was no doubt achieved: rape was established as a serious crime, guilty confessions were induced, and some convictions were obtained. Still, disappointment with the ICTR was well-nigh universal.

Adam M. Smith, a former legal adviser for the U.S. State Department, has examined many cases of international justice in the wake of genocide, Rwanda included, and is not impressed by their results. *Génocidaires,* he points out, are selectively chosen for prosecution; for every successful prosecution, someone of equal or even greater guilt can go scot-free. Although genocidal conditions typically have deep historical roots, he argues, international courts focus on behavior at one particular point in time and in that way tend to downplay the long-term complexities behind the violence. As was especially true of the ICTR, the location of the court far from where the violence took place biases what the court is able to hear. International tribunals can pass judgment but they cannot imprison, raising the awkward question of who, in the aftermath of a guilty verdict, will accept the condemned. Charges that international tribunals represent Western neocolonialism have the ring of truth to him; the International Criminal Court, for example, which condemned the Bashir regime in Darfur, simply lacks the capacity to understand the cultures and conditions into which it intervenes. Most important of all, international tribunals remove the responsibility for judging genocide from the states in which it occurred, effectively "outsourcing" the problem.

As it happens, the aftermath of the Rwandan genocide produced an alternative to international justice. Never enthusiastic about the ICTR in the first place, Kagame in 2001 helped create a nationwide system of so-called *gacaca* courts, community-based institutions set up to deal with the huge numbers of prisoners the government had rounded up in the wake of the genocide. Building on traditions established in the sixteenth century, Rwanda's modern *gacaca* courts hold outdoor hearings—*gacaca* means "grass" or "lawn"—in which guilt or innocence is determined by judges elected by the villagers and with their active participation. Although prison sentences have been handed down in some cases, the system is primarily designed to uncover what actually happened during the killing. In part because Rwandans are overwhelmingly Christian—56 percent Catholic and 26 percent Protestant—the procedures of the *gacaca* courts bear a strong resemblance to the practice of confession. *Gacaca* is perhaps best understood as a cross between a strictly legal attempt to judge guilt or innocence and the more memory-healing Truth and Reconciliation Commission established in South Africa.

By generally agreed-upon standards of international law, *gacaca* falls well short. Lawyers, for one thing, are excluded from playing a role in operations. Due process as understood in the West does not exist. The direct involvement of President Kagame in the creation of these courts raises suspicion of bias in favor of Tutsis and against Hutus. Testimony often sounds contrived, if not prearranged, with copious tears and hugs appearing at just the right place in the proceedings. Those accused are usually unable to defend themselves. Meant to uncover the truth, the testimonies offered are frequently full of lies. When the system was initially being established, Amnesty International, in a 2000 report, pointed out that "fundamental aspects of the *gacaca* proposals do not conform to basic international standards for fair trials guaranteed in the international treaties which Rwanda has ratified." Although the laws governing *gacaca* have been modified many times since, the basic criticisms still hold. Anyone whose conception of a fair trial is based upon Western constitutional ideals is likely to be disappointed by the buzz, emotionality, and religious overtones of a *gacaca* process.

Still, there is reason to believe that however flawed *gacaca* may be, it possesses certain advantages that international tribunals lack. At first such a suggestion seems counterintuitive. Since genocide takes place between two ethnic, racial, or religious groups who hate each other, how can they be brought together to reach conclusions acceptable to both? Not only that, but genocide is a form of political evil that unifies all those on one side against those on the other: Hutus are just as unlikely to judge one of their own as having committed genocide against Tutsis as Tutsis are to do the reverse. A postgenocide environment, finally, because it can easily foster retaliatory violence, is not ideal for establishing the conditions of fact-finding and objectivity that justice requires. Kagame, for one, may well have blood on his hands. In 2010, the United Nations issued the results of an investigation showing that massive deaths in the Congo throughout the 1990s were the result of Rwandan forces attacking Hutus who, having lost the 1994 war, had fled across the border. In other words, despite the praise he has received for being a healer, Kagame is in all likelihood not above a little genocide of his own. When poverty, a lack of professional lawyers and judges, and the international pressures sought by both sides to help their cause are added to the picture, the possibility of rendering any kind of justice seems remote.

Yet local institutions such as *gacaca* are not about rendering justice so much as they are about promoting reconciliation. As I have said, Rwanda is such a crowded country, and its two main tribes live in such proximity, that reconciliation may be the only workable postgenocide alternative. "What can you say," asks the French journalist and the world's foremost authority on the daily lives of Rwandans, Jean Hatzfeld, "when a Rwandan fate, unique in contemporary history, requires the families of victims and the families of killers, leaders, and architects of the genocide to resume living side by side *immediately*."

To establish a system of formal justice and its resulting penalties under such conditions could easily lead to an effort to select guilty individuals with their victims watching intently hoping for revenge, a formula not conducive to preventing future genocides but laying the grounds for them. *Gacaca* does not offer a foolproof alternative: Hatzfeld's reports include many just going through the motions of reconciliation with little or no conviction. Still, Hatzfeld includes remarkable moments of understanding. Marie-Louise Kagoyire told him that she "didn't want to miss a single word. . . . I'd arrive at eight o'clock. And I listened: the killers' names, where people were cut, all the details about the murder of my husband, Léonard Rwerekana. Each of the killers spoke only a tiny truth, since they were under no obligation, but still, they told a small useful part. For us, that was already something unhoped for."

Ultimately, there may not be any choice but to accept local methods of preventing genocide. As Smith points out, creating effective international institutions capable of passing judgment on genocide cannot occur without some local political capacity in place, since someone must investigate what happened in order to find the accused and bring charges against them. Once such a domestic capacity exists, it may as well be used. In addition, as we saw in the Darfur crisis, winning the cooperation of local political leaders, however odious their conduct, is often a precondition for establishing any international overview of what took place in their country. No one can ever guarantee that a society which has experienced genocide is immune from experiencing it again. Still, Smith's conclusion is an apt one: "Supporting domestic rule of law has a far greater chance of encouraging true deterrence and cultural change that might prevent a repetition of violence than does the imposition of a paternalistic justice from afar."

The creation of a system of international law capable of passing judgment on history's worst monsters is a significant achievement worth celebrating. As important as such international institutions may be, however, they can also set back the struggle against genocide if they place the responsibility for judgment far from those who directly experienced it. No matter how we define genocide, and no matter where we find it, we must never become so preoccupied with the lessons it presumes to teach the world that we lose sight of the local reasons it happened and the local traditions and customs that might prevent it from happening again.

It is precisely the tendency to overlook or downplay such local conditions that renders efforts to dramatize genocide so problematic. Those who find in genocide some larger truth inevitably simplify what are complex local political realities. Goldhagen, for example, one of the most melodramatic writers on the subject of political evil we have, ends *Worse Than War* by posing a question whose answer he finds self-evident: "How can we *choose* not to take simple and effective steps to prevent future wars against humanity?" It is all, in his view, so open-and-shut. Killing is wrong. Mass killing is worse. Stopping it is our only option. We know everything we must know and our primary duty is to act.

The problem is that there is nothing either simple or obviously effective about stopping something as monstrous as political evil. Whenever it occurs, we have to answer a number of crucial questions, most of them difficult. Is what appears to be genocide in fact a civil war? Are race and ethnicity the reason for the killing or an excuse to carry it out? If we have to choose between them, do we shun tyrants or save lives? Is punishment more valuable than reconciliation, or the other way around? Genocide is not a conversation stopper but a window into the complexities posed when politics and evil work hand in hand. Patience may not seem the proper virtue to display when people are being killed. But we will be better off if we pause for a moment's reflection instead of leaping to the conclusion that all forms of mass violence are equivalent to the worst forms of mass violence.

CHAPTER SEVEN

Ethnic Cleansing's Seductive Attractions

QUASI GENOCIDE

ETHNIC CLEANSING IS frequently distinguished from genocide on the grounds that its purpose is to forcibly remove people from where they live rather than to kill them flat out. The fact that its intention is not mass death, of course, in no way excludes ethnic cleansing from the ranks of political evil. Killing in large numbers, for one thing, can and does occur during episodes of ethnic cleansing. The systematic slaughter of eight thousand Muslims by Bosnian Serbs at Srebrenica in July 1995, to cite one of the most graphic examples in recent years, is certainly frightening enough. Ethnic cleansing, moreover, is typically accompanied by rape, looting, compulsory labor, property seizure, family separation, humiliation, denial of medical treatment, and other indignities well beyond the pale of civilized conduct. When inhumane and degrading methods are employed against relatively defenseless people due solely to who they are and where they happen to live, those who carry out such acts deserve censure and punishment for the harms they inflict.

Since genocide can accompany ethnic cleansing, and because those features of it that do not result in fatalities are nonetheless exceptionally violent in their own regard, an influential number of thinkers insist that we should treat ethnic cleansers as the latest incarnations of Hitler and Stalin. Ethnic cleansing, from their perspective, may not go as far as genocide, but it exists on the same continuum of evil. Ethnic cleansing is therefore best characterized as a form of quasi genocide. Its intent is the same, even if the means chosen are different.

Those who hold to this point of view are correct on one point: there is no moral justification for ethnic cleansing however and whenever it takes place. Even when victims are left alive, the violent removal of people from their homes and families and the determination to ship them to far-off places must count as evil lest the concept lose all meaning. The world community cannot stand by and let ethnic cleansing happen, not, at least, if that community is to claim commitments to the protection of human rights and the advancement of human dignity.

At the same time, those committed to the proposition that ethnic cleansing is a form of quasi genocide make one major mistake. By urging us to treat ethnic cleansers as so horrific that no engagement with their political objectives ought to be undertaken, they strip us of the best available tools for responding to the crimes they commit. The most important thing in dealing with ethnic cleansing, after all, is not the indignation we muster but the lives we save. Viewing ethnic cleansers as the embodiment of radical evil interferes with the saving of life in two crucial ways. Because the objectives associated with ethnic cleansing are not as unambiguously evil as those that characterize genocide, portraying those who engage in it as the equivalents of a Hitler or a Stalin prevents us from understanding why they do what they do and thereby complicates our efforts to stop them. In addition, we must shun Manichaean accounts of the evil of ethnic cleansing because they stand in the way of taking the effective diplomatic and military action needed to control it.

Genocide, as I have just been arguing, is the very embodiment of political evil. What *génocidaires* aim to bring about—the elimination of an entire people—is evil by any moral standard to which people in the modern world commit themselves. Genocide violates the mature teachings of all the world's major religions. It contradicts the emphasis on human rights enshrined in international law. It is illegal under the charter of the United Nations. It is, and always will be, the supreme crime against humanity. We need not enter into the heads of those who commit genocide in order to understand why they do it. The doing of it is all we need. If anything, trying to understand *génocidaires* is the first step toward justifying their actions.

We may wish to believe that the same applies to ethnic cleansing, but in truth the moral clarity that exists with respect to genocide cannot be found when we deal with ethnic cleansing. The objective that ethnic cleansers seek, for one thing, the creation of an ethnically pure nation, while morally dubious in a world that praises diversity and pluralism, resonates sufficiently with the Wilsonian ideal of national self-determination to retain a certain democratic, and even at times idealistic, appeal. It is true that ethnic cleansers use unconscionable amounts of violence to reach their goal. But nationhood is an objective that has been shared by nearly all peoples in the modern world. This is why ethnic cleansers are perfectly capable of acknowledging their reliance on brutal means to achieve their goals. But over that, they will frequently claim, they have no monopoly. The societies of North America and Western Europe, in their view, not only have difficulties accepting the ethnic diversity that accompanies immigration in the immediate present but also removed indigenous people or redrew maps to their own advantage in the distant past. In this they are no doubt wrong; just because cruel things happened a century or two ago does not make them morally permissible now. Still, ethnic butchers can charge those who denounce them with hypocrisy in ways simply not available to *génocidaires.* They are aware of the widespread appeal of their ultimate objective and know how to manipulate it.

In addition, ethnic cleansing, unlike genocide, scrambles the question of victimhood. Those who carry out ethnic cleansing portray themselves on occasion as innocents at the mercy of the very people against whom they have violent designs, as a group of intellectuals did in an infamous 1986 memorandum of the Serbian Academy of Sciences and Arts. Such claims are laughable; the Serbs were preparing to attack Croats and Bosnian Muslims, not the other way around. But it is also the case that the victims of Balkan ethnic cleansing, unlike the Jews, gays, and Gypsies of Nazi Germany, were not without weapons of their own. The moment the Croats and the Bosnians were in a position to do so, they fought back. When ethnic cleansing takes place, if the former Yugoslavia is indicative, guilt may not be that difficult to establish but innocence is frequently open to question. Slobodan Milosevic and his Bosnian Serb allies, undoubtedly responsible for much of the violence that took place in the former Yugoslavia, were not responsible for all of it. If we find ourselves condemning the use of ethnic cleansing by some, especially in the context of mutual nation-building, we ultimately face it among many.

Western countries have relied on two major means to punish those who engage in ethnic cleansing: putting the aggressor parties on trial, as Milosevic was before the International Criminal Tribunal for the former Yugoslavia (ICTY), and taking military action designed to stop the slaughter, as NATO did in the Yugoslav province of Kosovo. The moral ambiguities of ethnic cleansing have interfered with the successful application of both. On the one hand, the trial against Milosevic became bogged down as the defendant used his position in the dock to lecture the West on its own failings. On the other hand, successful military intervention is made easier when public opinion is aroused against unambiguous evil. But in the case of Kosovo, Western governments, unsure of domestic support for their intervention, relied on airpower instead of troops, a decision that increased ethnic cleansing overall. Ethnic cleansing in the former Yugoslavia eventually did come to an end. But there is no evidence that treating Milosevic and his Bosnian Serb allies as radical evil incarnate sped the peace process along.

As if this were not problematic enough, understanding ethnic cleansers as the embodiment of radical evil also interferes with the steps the West can take to stop ethnic cleansing before it begins. One way to limit the breakout of ethnic cleansing is to encourage the strengthening of multiethnic states instead of recognizing ethnically defined nations too hastily. Another is for the international community to remain an honest broker between the parties threatening violence. Both approaches treat ethnic cleansing as a form of political evil seeking rationally chosen goals instead of a manifestation of radical evil run rampant. To limit the damage caused by ethnic cleansing, we must do our best to diffuse its attractions by responding to the political conditions that fuel it. But this is precisely what we cannot do when we view ethnic cleansing as little different from genocide. In 1993, Secretary of State Warren Christopher described Bosnia as "a problem from hell," a statement made famous by Samantha Power when she wrote her book on the contemporary world's descent into evil. The real horror associated with ethnic cleansing, alas, is not that it is a problem from hell but that it has become such a reality on earth.

HAS ISRAEL COMMITTED ACTS OF ETHNIC CLEANSING?

INTERNATIONAL TRAVELERS flying to Israel land at Ben-Gurion Airport in the city of Lod, twelve miles southeast of Tel Aviv. Roughly sixty-seven thousand people live in Lod, 80 percent of them Jewish and 20 percent Arab. Transportation is the city's major industry. Israel Aerospace Industries, the largest industrial exporter in all of Israel and a leading supplier of systems for aerospace and defense firms around the world, can be found there. Due mainly to its preponderance of poor and

disadvantaged people, Lod is not one of Israel's more attractive destinations; one can drive by it on the freeway from Jerusalem and, except
for the exit sign, barely know it exists. Still, Lod has a rich biblical and
Roman history and plays an important role in contemporary Jewish
life. A large number of the *olim,* Hebrew for "immigrants," receive their
introduction to life in their new country through the Jewish Agency
Absorption Center located in the city.

Until the middle of the twentieth century, Lod had been known as
Lydda, an Arab town famous for its gardens and olive trees. (It is also
where Saint George, the immortal dragon slayer, was born.) Because
of its location so close to Tel Aviv, Lydda, along with Ramla, not quite
two miles away, assumed unusual strategic importance during the
Arab-Israeli war that followed the British withdrawal from the Middle East in May 1948. David Ben-Gurion, the leader of the Yishuv, as
Israel was called before its achievement of statehood, developed what
the Israeli historian Benny Morris characterizes as an "obsession" with
the towns, writing in his diary of the need to "destroy" both of them
because they had become "two thorns" in the side of the emerging state.
He appointed future Israeli leaders Yigal Allon and Yitzhak Rabin to
carry out Operation Dani, an attack on the territory east of Jerusalem
that included the two towns, whose combined population, inflated by
refugees from nearby Jaffa, was then between fifty thousand and sev-
enty thousand. To the surprise of the Israelis, resistance, especially in
Lydda, was fierce. It was not until an aggressive young officer, Lieuten-
ant Colonel Moshe Dayan, entered the fray that Lydda was finally taken.

Violence did not come to an end after Dayan's raid. Israeli troops may
have gained control over Lydda, but, trained as they were in fighting,
they were inexperienced occupiers. Surrounded by hostile Arabs, the
three hundred to four hundred Israeli soldiers panicked when attacked
and, ordered to shoot anyone in plain sight, retaliated by killing innocent civilians, women and children included. The exact number will
never be known for certain, but the accounts of Western journalists in
the town, combined with research into the archives undertaken by a
later generation of Israeli historians, led to estimates of 250 killed in the
panic attack, raising the Arab casualties involved in the taking of Lydda
close to 400. (The number of Israeli dead was 3 or 4.) When the shooting was over, resistance faded away, leaving many anxious to escape to
areas under Arab control.

The Israeli political leadership was only too happy to accommodate their wish to leave. "What shall we do with the Arabs?" Allon asked Ben-Gurion. The future prime minister, as Morris writes, made a "dismissive, energetic gesture with his hand and said: 'Expel them.'" Although many, if by no means all, Arabs had agreed to go, the process of moving them proved heartless. Israeli soldiers went from house to house forcing the Arab residents out. The inhabitants of Lydda and Ramla lost not only their homes but, given the widespread looting, any valuables they had hoped to take with them. Mid-July is the hottest time of the year in the Middle East, furthermore, and many of those who made the trek from the two towns died of thirst or exhaustion along the way. Shmarya Guttman, an intelligence officer with the Israeli forces and a professional archaeologist, was stunned by the suffering involved. It reminded him of the exile once forced upon the Jews by the Romans, he later wrote. Lydda, emptied of nearly all its Arab inhabitants, also brought up uncomfortable memories of what had been left in the wake of the pogroms the Russians had launched against the Jews. To the death total already accumulated, another three hundred or so were now added.

Lod was only one of many towns and villages that saw their Arab population depleted during the 1948 war. Seven hundred fifty thousand were displaced in all, and the violence that took place in Deir Yassin, Abu Shusha, and Dawaymeh was especially noteworthy. What happened in Lydda—or in any of the other places whose Arab residents were expelled during the 1948 events—raises the question of whether Israel engaged in ethnic cleansing during its war for independence. Ilan Pappé, an Israeli historian currently living in England, argues that it did. Pappé points out that Ben-Gurion had been a longtime advocate of "transfer," the term used by the Israeli founding fathers to describe the process of creating a Jewish majority in those parts of Palestine that would eventually come under Israeli control. Hinting darkly about the possibility of a conspiracy among the Yishuv leadership, Pappé pays particular attention to Plan Dalet (*dalet* is the fourth letter of the Hebrew alphabet), finalized in March 1948. Developed by the Haganah, the militia that was in the process of turning itself into the Israel Defense Forces, Plan Dalet, according to Pappé, was a "blueprint for ethnic cleansing" that constituted "a master plan for the expulsion of all the villages in rural Palestine." In his view, Jewish soldiers were not merely responding to unexpected attacks upon them when they began the process of removing all the Arabs from towns such as Lydda. They were carrying out orders from on high that had been in place for some time.

Pappé is a controversial historian who has been accused of tailoring facts to suit his left-wing perspective. There is certainly merit to those charges. Yet the question of whether Israel engaged in ethnic cleansing during the period characterized by Israelis as their war for independence—and by Palestinians as the *nakba*, or catastrophe—really has only one possible answer: of course they did. At the same time, however, the 1948 events, as well as Israel's subsequent treatment of the Palestinians in the West Bank and Gaza, also teach us why it makes little sense to treat ethnic cleansing as an unspeakable radical evil equivalent to what took place under Hitler or Stalin.

The birth of the state of Israel, for one thing, illustrates the powerful attraction of nationhood to a people lacking it. Only such an attraction can explain why Israeli historians who passionately disagree with Pappé's political views and consider his scholarship superficial nonetheless accept the proposition that what took place in Lydda was planned, exceptionally violent, and disruptive of people's lives. Benny Morris is among them. Morris is anything but a dove; in recent years he wrote in favor of a preventive Israeli attack against Iran's nuclear capability and called for a ground invasion of Gaza as a follow-up to Israel's initial air strikes there. Still, Morris is as honest in his role as a historian as he is explicit in his political advocacy and is therefore under no illusions about what took place at Lod. In the revised edition of his book on the origins of the Palestinian refugee crisis, he writes, "From the start, the operations against Lydda and Ramle were designed to induce civilian panic and flight—as a means of precipitating military collapse and possibly also as an end in itself." A 2004 interview with the journalist Ari Shavit in *Haaretz* gave Morris the chance to elaborate his views. "So when the commanders of Operation Dani are standing there and observing the long and terrible column of the 50,000 people expelled from Lod walking eastward, you stand there with them? You justify them?" Shavit asked him. "I definitely understand them," Morris replied. "There are circumstances in history that justify ethnic cleansing. I know that this term is completely negative in the discourse of the 21st century, but when the choice is between ethnic cleansing and genocide—the annihilation of your people—I prefer ethnic cleansing."

Israel's founders, needless to say, did not view themselves as ethnic cleansers. Far from doing the work of the devil, they believed themselves on the side of the angels. Arabs in general and Palestinians in particular, they frequently pointed out, had once supported Hitler and in any case were given to virulent anti-Semitism. The chances of their creating a democratic and tolerant society, let alone one that would forever constitute a rebuke to evil, were in their view close to nil. By their going to war against them, and by taking over the land they had seemingly abandoned, the Israeli project of state-building came to be seen by them, and especially by Ben-Gurion, as promoting the ideals established by the United Nations and the world community in the aftermath of World War II. What others might view as ethnic cleansing became to these leaders not only a bitter necessity but a moral obligation. Choosing to forcibly remove people who they were certain were unable to appreciate the blessings of freedom in order to protect those who had been subject to the world's worst tyranny was for them an easy call. Israel's accomplishments, these men never doubted, would be remembered long after the fate of the Palestinians had been forgotten. They may well have known that they were inflicting pain. But they never believed themselves evil. How could they ever be compared to the moral monsters of the past when they thought of themselves as helping to prevent the emergence of new monsters in the future?

Such views today seem remarkably indifferent to the loss of land and property Israel's 1948 actions imposed on stateless Palestinians. But for the founders of Israel, the very fact that the targets of their violence were stateless somehow justified the actions taken against them. There are many reasons why Palestinians lacked statehood. The British controlled much of the Middle East before 1948, and as halfhearted as their support for the state of Israel may have been, they gave even less support to a potential new state of Palestine. Arab governments in the region had no particular incentive to create a new state that might at some time impinge on their own boundaries. Before Israel ever engaged in ethnic cleansing, Jews living in the area had bought considerable amounts of Arab land, weakening the chances for a stable government or ruling class to emerge there. The Palestinian leadership did not help its own cause by identifying so much with the Nazi regime and was in any case riven with factionalism. No international movement of sympathy and support existed toward the Arabs in anything like the way Zionism appealed to non-Jews. When we try to find reasons why the Palestinians lacked a state, there is no shortage of them to be discovered.

For the emerging Israeli leadership, however, one consideration mattered most: the fact that there *was* no Palestinian state became an explanation for why there *should be* no Palestinian state. It was one thing to fight armies trained and funded by Arab leaders; the second phase of the 1948 war included military action against four such states: Egypt, Syria, Iraq, and Transjordan. But the Palestinians, at least in the eyes of the leaders of the Yishuv, deserved no respect as honorable combatants because they lacked the ability to organize themselves politically. What now seems to be a clear-cut case of ethnic cleansing appeared to them as preparation for a wider war that would follow. The famous phrase that Zionism amounted to a "land without a people for a people without a land" was true in one sense. Clearly there were people living in the area known as the Palestine Mandate—all the early Israeli leaders were aware of that. But as Prime Minister Golda Meir said in 1969, there did not live there *a people,* that is to say, a nation possessed of its own sovereignty and marked by internationally accepted borders. In the process of creating a state themselves, Israel's emerging leadership persuaded itself that those lacking statehood were not entitled to recognition, making it that much easier for them to take their land and, if necessary, to kill them as they did so. Behind every citizen, I once wrote, lies a graveyard. The birth of the state of Israel offers no exception.

If there is little question that Israel engaged in ethnic cleansing in 1948, whether it continues to do so today is far more open to question. The charge that it does can frequently be heard; Mairead Maguire, the Irish peace activist who won the Nobel Prize in 1976 and who in June 2010 was on board the Turkish flotilla seeking to break the blockade of Gaza, is one who has made it. Pappé agrees; in an October 2006 interview with an American magazine, he argued that Israel's policies in the occupied territories, as well as its treatment of Arabs within Israel, "are all different ways for implementing the coveted goal of a complete ethnic cleansing of the Palestinians." In Pappé's view, such harsh actions happen when those who are determined to maintain Israel's Jewish character feel themselves threatened by rising birthrates among both its Arab citizens and those who live in its occupied territories. Pappé does not write about the events of 1948 as a disengaged historian. He believes that the way Israel treated the Palestinians then influences how it treats the descendants of those who survived that ethnic cleansing half a century later.

Israel today contains more than its fair share of politicians whose attitudes toward the Palestinians are strikingly similar to those of the early leaders of the Yishuv. No one has achieved more notoriety in this regard than the Israeli foreign minister as of this writing, Avigdor Lieberman. The infamous plan he developed in 2004, while ostensibly not forcing people to leave their homes, would have redrawn Israel's map along ethnic lines, concentrating Arabs outside the state, increasing the percentage of Jews within it, and requiring of Arabs who chose to remain in Israel the signing of a loyalty oath. Lieberman, moreover, speaks for many. The eviction of Palestinians from their homes in East Jerusalem and the West Bank to make way for Jewish settlers is only one example of an attitude similar to his; since the Palestinians consider East Jerusalem the capital of their future state, settler activity there is especially designed to offend. Broad-based hostility toward Israel's Arab citizens has risen sharply, much of it motivated by the sentiment that were they to emigrate they would not be missed. Many of the nonlethal features of ethnic cleansing, including family separation and denial of basic rights to a decent standard of living or to medical treatment, have become unfortunately routine in the way Palestinians under Israeli control are treated wherever they live and especially in the Gaza Strip. It is even possible to hear echoes of what happened at Lydda in 1948 in Lod itself. Consider Lod's Ramat Eshkol neighborhood, the poorest area of the city. When a right-wing yeshiva opened in this previously Arab-dominated area, ethnic tensions markedly increased. It was not long before Lod's Jews concluded that a 20 percent Arab population was still too high. Lod, proclaimed Yoram Ben-Aroch, a spokesman for the municipality, ought to be a "more Jewish town." Supporting the Orthodox who had opened their yeshiva, he added, "We need to strengthen the Jewish character of Lod and religious people and Zionists have a big part to play in this strengthening." If ethnic cleansing began in places such as Lod, it seems at first glance to be continuing unabated.

Despite all this, I do not think that contemporary Israeli approaches toward Palestinians rise to the level of ethnic cleansing. For one thing, there are not all that many Palestinians left to cleanse. Israel's problem these days is that it has overextended itself, prompting not the takeover of new lands but withdrawal from places such as Gaza, as well as the recognition that the occupied territories are as much a curse as a blessing. In addition, the Palestinians, although still lacking a state, are, at least in the West Bank, well on the way to building one and have far more of a national consciousness than they did in 1948. None of this is to deny that Palestinians remain the victims of violence directed against them by Israel—or that they respond with violence in return. But it is to say that however much current events remind us of the ethnic cleansing undertaken in 1948, we are dealing with a different phenomenon when we discuss Israel's demographic challenges today. Israel's current treatment of the Palestinians remains morally unacceptable and, in the opinion of many, including myself, antithetical to the state's long-term security. But however it is characterized, ethnic cleansing it is not.

The fact that hostility toward the Palestinians crossed into the territory of political evil in one period, while stopping short of that dubious marker in another, underscores the extent to which ethnic cleansing is political in nature. We can, if we wish, view ethnic cleansing as evil pure and simple, the kind of thing that happens when otherwise sensible people become gripped by a frenzied taste for blood that they purge their own or nearby countries of elements they consider alien. By that definition, Israel in 1948 did not engage in ethnic cleansing—but neither, then, with an occasional exception here and there, has anyone else. What Israel's emerging leaders did in Lod or in any of the other towns that lost their Arab residents was not primarily the result of a sadistic preference for inflicting harm. As has been the case since 1948, many in Israel today possess racist views about Arabs that no doubt lead them to explain away their actions toward them. Yet racism per se played, and continues to play, a minor role in Israel's treatment of the Palestinians when compared to desires for land and security. Ethnic cleansing, in short, happens when leaders use violence to create a state composed primarily of people who share a common ethnicity. It does not happen when they take actions that are discriminatory and unfair rather than immoral and lethal.

Since ethnic cleansing is nearly always undertaken as a political act, it cannot exist without choices being made. There can be no doubt that the choices made by the leaders of the Yishuv, because they caused so much harm to so many innocent people, were evil by design. Ben-Gurion and those who worked with him to establish the state of Israel opted for violence over diplomacy at nearly every juncture and expressed little or no remorse for the crimes they committed. For all that, however, the 1948 events teach us that societies that rely on ethnic cleansing, while engaged in political evil, are themselves neither inherently evil nor populated by evil people. This does not justify ethnic cleansing; nothing does. But the very fact that so many in Israel and the United States identify with such a goal should remind us why there is so little to be gained by treating ethnic cleansing as a form of quasi genocide. Creating a nation and exterminating a people are not the same thing. Israel's founders committed crimes aplenty in 1948. But they never approached the crimes against humanity associated with the regime whose Final Solution led to the creation of the state of Israel in the first place.

Israel's conduct in 1948 contains lessons than can be applied to subsequent acts of ethnic cleansing elsewhere in the world. We are right to be appalled by the horrors that Milosevic unleashed upon the other ethnic groups with whom he once shared Yugoslavia. Before we conclude that he was a modern-day Hitler, however, we need to think about the cruelties that Israel's founders imposed on the Palestinians. It is not a question of equating the two; every case of ethnic cleansing is different, and Milosevic killed more people in one Bosnian town than Israel did during the entire process of its birth. But the desire to link a people with a state was as powerful among those urging a Greater Serbia as it was to those convinced that Israel must be a country for Jews. We shall see momentarily how the West's responses to Milosevic's actions fell on deaf ears. There was a reason they did: all the participants in the Yugoslavia bloodbath knew that however much Western leaders may have condemned the means used by Serbs and Croats to achieve their goals, they would be more sympathetic to the goal of nationhood itself. Had Western leaders learned from the example of Israel why the creation of nations can be as powerfully attractive as it can be brutally ugly, they might have been less inclined to compare Milosevic to Hitler, recognizing that the latter's efforts to dominate the world were different in every significant respect from the former's determination to create an ethnically homogeneous nation.

TOO MANY STATES RATHER THAN TOO FEW

IN STRIKING CONTRAST to the Middle East, where the Palestinians have to this point failed to build a state, the furious ethnic cleansing that took place during the breakup of Yugoslavia resulted in the creation of seven: Serbia, Slovenia, Croatia, Bosnia-Herzegovina, Macedonia, Montenegro, and Kosovo. (An eighth would come into existence if the autonomous region of Vojvodina, now part of Serbia, were ever to become independent.) The Balkan wars did not represent a situation in which one party to a conflict used all of its power to build a state along ethnic or religious lines while trying to prevent the one next door from any opportunity to do the same. Here ethnic cleansing came about when an already existing multiethnic state crumbled, leading its major constituent parts to declare independence on their own.

While Balkan history is notoriously complex, the 1991 events that resulted in the region's ethnic cleansing are not that difficult to follow. Slovenia began the formal process of breaking Yugoslavia apart when in June of that year it declared its independence, and even though Serbia responded by sending troops into Slovenia, the resulting violence was brief. When Croatia followed with its own declaration hours after Slovenia's, however, Serbia reacted by proclaiming the establishment of the Republic of Serbian Krajina in the Croatian regions containing large numbers of Serbs and proceeded to cleanse them of their Croat population. The battles that followed were bloody from the start, none more so than the one at Vukovar, a city at the far eastern end of Krajina, bordering on Serbia, which set the norm for all the ethnic cleansing that would follow: the forced evacuation of the city's residents, the separation of men from women and the systematic slaughter of the former, the capture of a major hospital and the movement and killing of its patients. Vukovar has been described by two scholars of genocide as "possibly the most thoroughly devastated town in any of the wars in the former Yugoslavia between 1991 and 1995." Because Milosevic, the Serbian leader, was determined to take over as much of Croatia as he could, the siege of Vukovar contributed to the widespread impression in the West that he would stop at nothing to achieve his goals. If any party to the many conflicts that followed was guilty of starting the chain reaction that set them off, it was Serbia.

At first glance, what transpired at Vukovar appears to be a replay of the Lydda events, except with far greater levels of violence and a more pronounced manifestation of ethnic antagonism. Yet for all the destruction caused by the Serbian forces, Vukovar did not produce a victory for Serbia in the same way that Lod was part of a military triumph for Israel. In part, this was due to a serious disagreement between Milosevic and his army, the JNA. But the more important reason was that the fighting in Vukovar occurred over a period of time long enough to enable the Croats to form their own army capable of engaging Serbian forces on other fronts. Such are the advantages of statehood. After the battle of Vukovar, Serbia would continue its campaigns of ethnic cleansing. It would, however, meet stiff resistance along the way. Those living in occupied territories, such as the Palestinians, lacking armies, typically fight back using terror. Those living in independent states, including Croatia and later Bosnia-Herzegovina and Kosovo, can meet the force applied against them by relying on the armies that statehood enables them to raise. What Milosevic began, others would take upon themselves to finish.

Croatia's leader at the time of the Vukovar violence was Franjo Tudjman, the head of the Croatian Democratic Union (HDZ). Four years after the Serbian attack on that town, Tudjman finally brought the areas that the Serbs had transformed into Krajina back under Croatian control, forcibly removing some two hundred thousand Serbs in the process. It cannot be a surprise that the Croats would respond in ways so similar to those used by the Serbs, for on the question of political evil, Croatia had never been innocent. Tudjman, a fervent nationalist, welcomed the display of flags and other symbols that had been used by the Ustashe, a fascistically inclined terrorist movement that ultimately became indistinguishable from the Independent State of Croatia established by the Nazis during World War II. (While in power, the Ustashe had created concentration camps responsible for the killing of Serbs, Jews, Gypsies, and other groups deemed racially inferior or religiously unreliable.) An authoritarian in his own right, Tudjman did not lack for historical precedents when he assumed control over Croatia. The ground for relying on ethnic cleansing to respond to ethnic cleansing had been laid, and he was only too happy to occupy it.

In 1948, Israel's ethnic cleansing was frequently portrayed both there and in the United States as a victory of good people who had been singled out for destruction over bad people who were too disorganized and fanatical to deserve the blessings of statehood. Many in the West viewed the events in the former Yugoslavia as a similar struggle between an evil Serbia and the innocent victims it was determined to target. In reality, however, all sides to the Balkan conflict were prepared to use the ugliest of means to achieve their ends. This democratization of ethnic cleansing, already visible when the fighting took place between Serbia and Croatia, became even more pronounced when the next province, Bosnia, threatened to break away. Milosevic and Tudjman loved to compete with each other over who was the aggressor and who the aggrieved, but when it came to Bosnia, they were partners in crime; they had, for example, developed plans in a secret March 1991 meeting to divide up Bosnia between them. That they wanted to destroy each other was no obstacle in their mutual determination to destroy others.

Serbia once again played the leading role in the events that followed. One reason Milosevic had been willing to accept something far less than victory in Croatia was that he already had his eye fixed on Bosnia. When Bosnia-Herzegovina declared its independence in 1992, Milosevic turned over control of the JNA to Serbs residing within Bosnia, many of whom were even more bloodthirsty than he was. Without question the ugliest examples of ethnic cleansing during the wars of Yugoslav secession—if anything, the worst examples of ethnic cleansing in our times—took place as the Bosnian Serbs relocated some two million Muslims out of their own country, established the infamous concentration camps of Omarska and Brcko, carried out the notorious massacre at Srebrenica, and exploited and killed the residents of Bosnia's second-largest city, Banja Luka. Any list of the most evil figures in the years after World War II would have to include Ratko Mladic, Radovan Karadzic, Radislav Krstic, and Biljana Plavsic, all of them Bosnian Serbs. "For three-and-a-half years," writes the historian Norman Naimark, "Bosnia was to be the scene of the worst fighting and massacres in Europe since the Second World War."

To play a leading role is not to play the only role, however, and Tudjman was also anxious to get whatever part of the newly established state of Bosnia-Herzegovina that he could. Unlike Milosevic, who craved Bosnian land mostly in order to create a Greater Serbia, Tudjman was a virulent racist as hostile toward everyone outside his ethnic group as the Nazis, whom he had admired, had been toward the Jews. Tudjman, rather than Milosevic, was the true hater. It was he who thanked God that his wife was neither a Serb nor a Jew and characterized the leader of the Bosnian Muslims, Alija Izetbegovic, as "a fundamentalist, Algerian, and wog" presiding over "dirty stinking Asians." Tudjman's HDZ became extremely active in Bosnia, especially in those areas where large numbers of Croats lived, constantly on the lookout for conflicts it could exploit to its own advantage. The Croats too built concentration camps, such as the one at Kaonik, filled with their share of rape and abuse. They also engaged in ethnic cleansing, especially in the Lasva Valley of Bosnia, even if their most notorious campaign took place at the Herzegovinian town of Mostar. Not only were the Mostar Muslims rounded up to be deported to camps, but the landmark Turkish bridge that made Mostar famous was destroyed. Croatia added its own contributions to the list of war criminals produced by the conflict in the former Yugoslavia, none more dramatic than retired general Ante Gotovina, who was arrested while dining at a resort on Tenerife in the Canary Islands. The ethnic cleansing of Serbs in Krajina, for which Tudjman would be an enthusiastic advocate, had a trial run in Bosnia.

Although the category of victim fits the Bosnian Muslims better than any of the other parties to these conflicts—they were, after all, set upon by two ethnic groups rather than one—they too knew something about retaliation. Bosnian Muslims met the Croat attacks in the Lasva Valley by carrying out their own series of murders and setting fire to Croat-occupied houses. Their contribution to the burgeoning number of camps in the region was the one at Celebici, where under the eyes of sadistic wardens they engaged in rapes and executions. Had such events occurred anywhere else, they would easily be classified as ethnic cleansing. Because the Bosnian actions took place in the context of far greater horrors launched against them, however, they are often viewed, with some justification, as tactics used for purposes of self-defense. Bosnia-Herzegovina was the most ethnically blended of all the states that emerged out of Yugoslavia, and for that reason Bosnian Muslims did not have as much undisputed state authority as the other ethnic groups involved in these conflicts. Lacking more political power, they engaged in less political evil.

It would seem obvious that effective responses to ethnic cleansing should take into account the fact that guilt for it is often widely shared; the greater the number of leaders who engage in political evil, the more of it there is. Oddly, however, many intellectuals appalled by political evil and anxious to stop it reached the exact opposite conclusion. Not only did they convince themselves that one man, Milosevic, was singularly responsible for the violence in the region, they went out of their way to absolve his copractitioners of ethnic cleansing for any blood that wound up on their hands. For example, Thomas Cushman and Stjepan Mestrovic, in the introduction to their collection of essays called *This Time We Knew*, wrote that the Croats' attacks on Mostar were "contemptible and indefensible" but then excused them by arguing that their actions, in comparison to Serbian aggression, were not intentional and therefore not genocidal. Samantha Power went a step further; she simply ignored Mostar. For all her indignation at ethnic cleansers as *génocidaires* in the making, she too gave Tudjman a pass: the harshest term she used to condemn him, in the all too brief references she makes to him, was "fanatic." In her view, anything he or any of the leaders of Yugoslavia's other states may have done was due to the fact that "the repressive policies of the Serbian president left no place in Yugoslavia for non-Serbs." She does not mention that Tudjman's repressive policies left no place in Croatia for non-Croats.

Not only did these writers fail to include Tudjman among the ranks of those engaged in political evil, they found a way to denounce those who did as apologists for genocide. To blame Tudjman as well as Milosevic, Cushman and Mestrovic wrote, was to engage in "equivocation and relativism" as "rationalizations for nonintervention in Balkan affairs." Serbian leaders, and only Serbian leaders, they continued, "are responsible for genocide in Bosnia," and those who put the blame on all sides "have engaged in reproduction of some of the obfuscations, false-hoods, and other conventional wisdoms that circulate on the global information highway." Power makes the same point, if in less polemical style. In her view of the world, U.S. officials, and especially those associated with the Department of State, were always reluctant to intervene against genocide; blaming all sides became their perfect excuse for inaction. Power never contests that all sides were in fact guilty of political evil. But rather than viewing policymakers and diplomats who insisted on pointing this out as honest brokers, she treats them as mendacious hypocrites. They were desperate for arguments that would persuade them of the futility of intervention, she maintains, and finding guilt in more than one place gave them their excuse. To support her argument, Power cites with approval *The New Republic*'s Anna Husarska's grossly inaccurate historical analogy: "I guess if President Clinton had been around during the 1943 uprising in the Warsaw ghetto, he would also have called it 'those folks out there killing each other.' How would he describe the brief armed rebellion in the Treblinka concentration camp?" Once Milosevic becomes Hitler, all other states must play the role of a helpless Poland or Czechoslovakia, even if, like Croatia, they had once been avid Nazi allies themselves.

The West's widespread decision to heap all the blame for Yugoslavia's troubles on one man had the unfortunate consequence of absolving the other of his crimes. "Croatia," writes the international lawyer Adam M. Smith, "emerged from the Yugoslav wars as the only 'winner' in the contest, with its president Franjo Tudjman the only leader during the Dayton negotiations able to consolidate the territorial gains he had amassed during the conflict (and during the commission of awful crimes)." Although a number of Croats were eventually put on trial before the ICTY, Tudjman never was—one more serious stain on the ICTY's reputation as an impartial agency of justice. No individual in the former Yugoslavia wound up engaging in more political evil while paying so low a price for his crimes than Tudjman. That a political leader as reprehensible as he was could escape so much blame is tragic.

The final major theater for ethnic cleansing to emerge in the former Yugoslavia was in Kosovo, the province that served as bookends for the wars in this region. It was here that Milosevic first discovered the powerful attractions of ethnic nationalism in a 1989 speech in Kosovo Field, the site of the 1389 battle against the Ottomans that Serbs recall to this day as the inspiration for their quest for statehood. It was also in Kosovo that the seventh and last state was created out of the former Yugoslavia when its independence was declared in 2008. Historically and geographically linked to Serbia, Kosovo was not Serbian: 90 percent of its population was ethnically Albanian. When a minority ethnic group tries to impose its will on a much larger one, the case for blaming only one side for the resulting violence seems self-evident. In Kosovo there was plenty of reason to do so. Power calls the removal of more than a million Albanian Kosovars from their homes by Serbian military forces "the largest, boldest single act of ethnic cleansing of the decade, and it occurred *while* the United States and its allies were intervening to prevent further atrocity." In Kosovo, as in Croatia and Bosnia before them, Serbian troops showed no mercy, engaging in all the rape, pillage, and murder that made them so notorious.

One aspect of the Kosovo conflict, however, would be different from the others that preceded it. This time the West intervened with force in the form of the bombing campaign led by NATO. Numerous blunders accompanied the campaign: innocent civilians were killed, convoys carrying refugees were attacked, at one point a missile was launched against the Bulgarian capital of Sofia, and, worst of all, Milosevic took advantage of the bombing to step up the pace of the ethnic cleansing in which he was so much involved. Still, the war proved, at least militarily speaking, to be a success. In June 1999, under pressure from the bombing and understanding that his major ally, Russia, had begun to cooperate with the West, Milosevic agreed to withdraw his troops and allow for the presence of a NATO peacekeeping force in the province. A fragile peace followed, frequently interrupted by outbreaks of violence between Kosovar Albanians and Serbs. Kosovo's independence was contingent on future ratification. Even after it was declared, the province remained under what was essentially a European Union protectorate. But a corner had been turned, and although no one can know when and whether a fully independent state of Kosovo will emerge, the war in Kosovo finally brought an end to the ethnic cleansing that had so plagued this region of the world for so long.

If military intervention in Kosovo represented something new, however, the rhetoric of good and evil accompanying it was both tiresome and dangerous. Fed up with Milosevic, and perhaps feeling guilty for their failure to intervene earlier, Western leaders finally got the message activists had been sending for over a decade and joined in the campaign to equate the Serbs with the Nazis. Bill Clinton offers one such example. Power excoriates Clinton for his failure to take the killing in the former Yugoslavia seriously when it was confined to Bosnia and Croatia, but as soon as the killing spread to Kosovo, Clinton discovered the attractions of the appeasement analogy. "What if someone had listened to Winston Churchill and stood up to Adolf Hitler earlier?" he asked rather plaintively from the Oval Office. "How many people's lives might have been saved? And how many American lives might have been saved?" Power was not satisfied. In her view, Clinton should have followed up his words with deeds and committed ground troops to the region. Still, after Kosovo, no one could continue to argue that Western leaders were reluctant to call genocide by name. If anything, they seem to have been gripped by a need to call upon the Holocaust whenever contemplating military action anywhere around the world.

Intervention in Kosovo, authorized by Clinton and strongly supported by the British prime minister, Tony Blair, on the same grounds of confronting evil, became liberalism's war, a campaign designed, once and for all, to get human rights right. This time not only did we know what was happening, we would use our knowledge to ensure a better life for the innocent victims of Serbian aggression. In going to war in Kosovo, the West would only incidentally be fighting Milosevic, or so its advocates maintained. The real aim was to take a firm stand against radical evil. Only this tight connection between military deployment and liberal political goals can explain why so many Democrats in the United States would eventually find themselves in the somewhat odd position of supporting a military figure, General Wesley Clark, who had commanded the NATO forces, for president in 2004.

The problem was that such a framing of the casus belli as a liberal campaign against radical evil had never made much sense in the former Yugoslavia. Milosevic, for all his murderous instincts, possessed less than absolute power within his own country and never had any intention of expanding Greater Serbia outside the borders of the former Yugoslav federation. By the time Clinton and Blair stumbled upon their version of the Munich analogy, the comparison had become even more removed from reality. In 1999, Milosevic resembled a character from *A Burnt-Out Case* more than one from *Heart of Darkness*. Losing popularity within Serbia as quickly as he was losing wars abroad, Milosevic would be voted out of power shortly after the war in Kosovo came to an end. His evil, like all political evil, had deadly consequences. But it was also limited by the political conditions that shaped his rule, a reality studiously ignored by the moralistic rhetoric deployed by so many Western leaders and thinkers.

Not only was Milosevic at this point no longer all that evil, the Kosovo Albanians were not exactly moral paragons. It is true that their leader, Ibrahim Rugova, a former student of the distinguished French intellectual Roland Barthes, adopted nonviolent resistance against the Serbs and was often pronounced the Gandhi of the Balkans. But his policy, developed for strategic rather than idealistic reasons, was, as the historian Tim Judah writes, "based on the hard fact that war, at this stage, would simply mean that the Albanians would lose and risk being ethnically cleansed." Rugova, in any case, was mostly a figurehead. It was a terrorist organization, the Kosovo Liberation Army (KLA), that organized popular resistance to Serbian attacks. Blending Marxist-Leninist rhetoric with quasi-fascist nationalistic appeals, the KLA not only attacked Serbs but in classic terrorist style went after fellow Kosovar Albanians it viewed as collaborators. Nor was the KLA opposed to violent retaliation. Like the ethnic groups that came under Serbian fire in the other provinces of the former Yugoslavia, the Kosovar Albanians responded to ethnic cleansing against them with some of their own, eventually forcing more than two hundred thousand Serbs out of their territory. The inclinations of the KLA toward violence not only confused the moral picture but created a strategic dilemma for the West. The KLA, as Secretary of State Madeleine Albright, whose interest in the area was shaped by her own Eastern European background, later wrote, was not given to "Jeffersonian thinking." "I wanted to stop Milosevic from marauding through Kosovo," she continued, "but I didn't want that determination exploited by the KLA for purposes we opposed."

Albright had good reasons for her concern. By portraying the conflict in Kosovo as a struggle between good and evil, Western leaders found themselves working against their declared objectives. It was bad enough that they wound up supporting a group occupying a prominent place on the U.S. list of foreign terrorist organizations. (Even though the KLA was removed from that list before the September 11 attacks, the fact that the United States had a long history of allying itself with terrorists whose goals it once found acceptable would prove a major embarrassment when George W. Bush declared his global war on terror.) Nor did it help the case for moral clarity that Kosovo's prime minister, Hashim Thaci, during his days as a resistance fighter, ran a Mafia-like organization that engaged in the black-market trading of kidneys from the corpses of those it killed. By supporting the KLA—or, for that matter, any of the ethnic groups that responded to Serbian attacks with violence of their own—the West, as the Bulgarian-French intellectual Tzvetan Todorov concludes, "ended up falling in with the very same policy of ethnic cleansing by supporting those who were fighting exclusively for the 'right to self-determination' and by favoring the creation of a multitude of 'ethnically pure' mini-states. Of course, the West used very different methods. It did not deport people or terrorize them; it just sent its diplomats to set up embassies in the new capitals and shipped in humanitarian aid." When all is said and done, the fact that seven states emerged where there once had been only one conveyed the indisputable message that violence to further the cause of nationhood, even when designed to drive another ethnic group from one place to another, can be effective. The war against totalitarianism ultimately produced a victory for democracy. The wars against ethnic cleansing, from Croatia to Kosovo, proved that ethnic cleansing works.

Each outbreak of ethnic cleansing contains lessons about what to avoid and what to encourage in the future. Israel's decision to clear out Arabs from areas of Palestine it was determined to incorporate within its new state ought to caution us against denouncing ethnic cleansing for the goals it seeks, since those goals are so widely shared. The carnage that ravaged the former Yugoslavia, alternatively, ought to remind us that however much ethnic cleansing ventures into the territory of political evil, it is, and always will remain, something quite different from the Nazi extermination of the Jews. Nothing is more important in responding to the form of political evil known as ethnic cleansing than avoiding the temptation to compare it to the worst evils of all time. And nothing, if the determined campaign to assign so much of the blame for Yugoslavia's troubles to one man is any indication, is harder to resist.

STATES OVER NATIONS

ONE CONSEQUENCE OF the spread of democracy in recent years has been the creation of new societies. In 1945, when the United Nations came into being, it had 51 members. Today it has 192. (There are 3 independent states in the world that are not U.N. members: Kosovo, the Vatican, and Taiwan.) Two periods are responsible for the largest share of this growth: 1960–62, when 28 new members were admitted to the U.N. as decolonization came to the Third World, and 1991–93, when the breakup of the Soviet bloc resulted in 26 additional ones. A significant proportion of these new societies were created along predominantly ethnic lines. "This making and breaking of nations," wrote the late Tony Judt of the second of these periods, "was comparable in scale to the impact of the Versailles treaties that followed World War One—and in certain respects more dramatic." The lesson in both cases was clear.

When people wish to express their identity and have the means to do so politically, the international community is unlikely to stand in their way.

As powerful a force as self-determination has become, what kind of political unit will exercise a right to autonomy is still open to question. Although the term "nation-state" is frequently used to describe such units, nations and states are not the same thing. A nation, so long as it feels a strong sense of common consciousness rooted in its ethnic identity, need not be independent; Serbia in this sense was a nation even when, as a province of the former Yugoslavia, it lacked independent statehood. States, by contrast, are frequently carved out of ethnic enclaves but can just as frequently combine many different groups into one unified political whole; France, for example, which prides itself on its Frenchness, was in the recent past composed of people likely to identify themselves first as Bretons or Alsatians. Nationhood appeals to the emotions associated with blood and belonging. States are legal entities that seek a monopoly on the use of violence within their borders. Because nation-states combine the fervor of the one with the matter-of-fact formality of the other, they are best viewed as constant works in progress rather than as permanent creations. In recent years such major nation-states as Germany and the Soviet Union dramatically changed their form in response to new political conditions.

Generally speaking, existing states tend not to be in favor of the creation of new ones. Statesmen above all else prize stability; an existing division of power is one to which they have made some accommodation, whereas any redistribution of power creates unknowns that might well diminish their influence. When Yugoslavia first began to break apart in 1991, most European leaders reacted with typical caution, warning against the premature recognition of the newly independent entities. Yugoslavia had been a communist state under the leadership of Marshal Tito, and while communism contained its own share of evils and Tito was an unappealing strongman, his regime did manage to avoid ethnic cleansing. Recognizing that one or another form of multiethnic statehood might have produced less violence than the creation of a series of new ethnically defined nations, a number of prominent statesmen, including U.N. secretary-general Javier Pérez de Cuéllar, former U.S. secretary of state Cyrus Vance, and Britain's Lord Carrington, secretary-general of NATO, tried their best to preserve some form of multiethnic statehood. Carrington's plan, for example, would have bound together the newly independent countries in a primarily economic union. The possibility that international recognition of new nations could lead to violence was very much on the minds of these statesmen. Considerations of realpolitik led them to the conclusion that the preservation of existing states is always less destabilizing than the creation of new ones, especially if those new ones are organized along ethnic lines.

The moment Serbia began its campaign of violence against the newly independent states, however, the tide, ridden especially well by the German foreign minister, Hans-Dietrich Genscher, turned in favor of their recognition. At the time, it seemed to make sense to recognize the first of them, Slovenia, not only because of the small number of Serbs living there but also because its people were viewed as easily absorbable into a Western political culture emphasizing capitalist economics and democratic politics. Nor was Slovenia's stability the only reason to believe that recognition might proceed peacefully. Yugoslavia was widely believed to be on a path to disintegration in any case. The European Union, furthermore, attached conditions to its recognition: any state accepted as legitimate by it had to pledge that it would not engage in violence against ethnic minorities within its borders. Western European leaders, finally, were moved by humanitarian concerns in their policies toward recognition. Because Yugoslavia had been a communist state, those seeking to break away from it were viewed as fighting on behalf of the freedoms for which the West stood. In Germany, in particular, recognition of the new states was not only anticommunist but antifascist: Germans were anxious to support ethnic minorities as atonement for the sin of Nazism under which at least two such minorities, the Jews and the Gypsies, had met their horrible fate. Western governments, wanting to do right by peoples viewed as victims of Serbian aggression, clearly thought the gamble of recognition worth taking.

Alas for the prospects for peace in the region, however, Western governments, by extending diplomatic recognition to each new nation, found themselves in the awkward position of providing legitimacy to ethnic cleansers, who appreciated, even if Western leaders did not, the free hand that recognition offered them. When in July 1991 the U.S. ambassador to Yugoslavia, Warren Zimmerman, met with Croatia's Tudjman, he told him that he should never count on any U.S. military support. "I don't believe you," Tudjman replied. "I know more about your government than you do and you're going to support us." Tudjman proved to be correct, though he never did receive military support. The West, by allowing an independent Croatia to come into existence, had little leverage left to stop the process by which each new state was transformed into an ethnic nation through violence. The fear that precipitate recognition of breakaway nations could ignite what German chancellor Helmut Kohl had called a "powder keg" in the region proved well grounded. Wilsonian principles produced ugly consequences.

It is too late to do anything about Yugoslavia: the question of whether history would have been different had recognition of the new states been delayed is not one we can answer. Nonetheless, the experience with Yugoslavia is relevant to other potential cases of ethnic cleansing in the world today. When faced with possible ethnic conflict, the world community ought to do its best to refrain from identifying one side of the conflict as guilty and the other as innocent and rushing to protect the latter against the former. An illustration of how this can be done is furnished by the 2008 efforts by the former Soviet republic of Georgia to gain control over two breakaway provinces and the response by Russia to stop them.

Because the Soviet Union had been an empire linking together into one state a sizable number of different ethnic groups, its breakup, occurring almost simultaneously with the collapse of Yugoslavia, encouraged Western leaders to grant diplomatic recognition to the newly created states that had once been Soviet republics. One such republic was Georgia, which was recognized by the United States in December 1991, eight months after it had declared its independence. Georgia, however, much like the Soviet Union itself, contained its own variety of ethnic groups, including Armenians, Azeris, Greeks, and Russians. More significant, it also exercised control over the semiautonomous republics of Abkhazia and South Ossetia. Upon Georgia's independence, both provinces attempted to secede from it, and Russia, furious at Georgia's decision to set out on its own, encouraged them in their efforts. Georgia, in turn, provoked by what it viewed as Russian interference with its autonomy, responded with a military invasion of the two republics, although without much success. Wars in the Caucasus frequently lead to ethnic cleansing, and such was the case here. All sides to the conflict engaged in it, but Georgia, the loser, experienced the most, especially in the more highly populated Abkhazia; some two hundred thousand ethnic Georgians fled the province during the war. Although the violence in the Caucasus was extensive, these wars have been aptly described as "forgotten." Neither the violence itself nor the unstable cease-fire that brought it to an end attracted much attention in the West.

The situation changed dramatically in 2008, when, citing fears of additional ethnic cleansing, the new Georgian president, Mikheil Saakashvili, attempted once again to regain control of both provinces through force. This time the main conflict took place in South Ossetia, but as was the case during the earlier war, Georgia failed to achieve its military objectives. Russia, which includes within its borders the region known as North Ossetia, became actively engaged in the fighting and swept Georgian forces out of the South Ossetian capital of Tskhinvali. International pressure brought the war to a quick end, leaving European Union monitors to enforce a new cease-fire but also allowing Russian troops to remain behind and thereby reinforcing their control over the two disputed areas. Even if ethnic cleansing was by and large avoided this time around, the war demonstrated the lingering potential for violence in Europe whenever new experiments in map drawing are undertaken.

Despite the fact that the Caucasian events of 2008 involved less ethnic cleansing than those of 1991–92, they nonetheless received far more attention in the West. The simple reason was that they took place during an American presidential campaign. Saakashvili spoke near-perfect English, hated Russia, and made his pro-Western sympathies obvious. Not surprisingly, he became an appealing figure among those as suspicious of Vladimir Putin's Russia as they once had been of the Soviet Union. John McCain, the Republican presidential candidate in 2008, urged on by neoconservative advisers, some with close ties to Georgia, took up Saakashvili's cause by endorsing Georgian membership in NATO, leaving his Democratic opponent, Barack Obama, anxious not to appear too weak, to join the call. If the American presidential campaign was any indication, the stage was set to transform the South Ossetian war into the familiar script of a struggle between good and evil, with Saakashvili playing the role of oppressed victim and Putin the new Hitlerian aggressor, even if this time, in direct contrast to the events in Kosovo, the United States found itself resisting rather than accommodating secessionist demands.

Russia, as it happened, demonstrated its willingness to play its part in the dramatization of the crisis as well. Although the Russians had cooperated with the West in bringing ethnic cleansing to an end in Kosovo, Putin and other hard-liners, as if to reassert their historic affinity with Serbia, decided to play a trick on the West. "Moscow," as the diplomat and scholar Ronald Asmus writes, "wanted its response [in Georgia] to be as painful to Washington as recognition of Kosovo was to Moscow." Learning their own lesson from the Balkan situation, the Russians extended diplomatic recognition to South Ossetia and Abkhazia, implicitly asking the rest of the world community to join it. The desire to escalate events in the region out of their local context was as intense in Moscow as it was in Washington.

The most striking feature of the aftermath of the Georgia–South Ossetian war is that none of these efforts to portray the conflict in black-and-white terms wound up gaining any traction. After the war ended, an investigation by the European Union led by the Swiss diplomat Heidi Tagliavini confirmed what many experts in the region already knew: Georgia had begun the war in violation of international law, thereby making it all but impossible to cast Saakashvili as an innocent victim. Once it came to power, the Obama administration made clear that it would be decidedly cool toward Saakashvili, and he in turn had no choice but to put any lingering plans for a Greater Georgia on indefinite hold. While all this was happening, Russia's efforts to sponsor diplomatic recognition of the breakaway provinces came to naught, gaining the support only of such outliers as Nicaragua and Venezuela. Meanwhile, the very same Tagliavini report that pronounced Georgia's invasion illegal made a similar judgment with respect to Russia's attempts to assert that Abkhazia and South Ossetia were independent states. In the Caucasus the international community did what it was unable to do in the Yugoslav conflict: it refused to find unambiguous heroes and villains. Georgia consequently became the European powder keg that never exploded.

If ethnic cleansing breaks out somewhere else in the future, one question is likely to dominate the discussion: Will the rest of the world follow the Yugoslav script and rush to welcome ethnically defined new nations, or will it follow the Georgian script and work to defuse ethnic tensions? Whatever the answer, it is unlikely to be demonstrated in Europe, where multiethnic powder kegs are now relatively sparse. As

Tony Judt pointed out, the rush to nationhood that took place in the last two decades of the twentieth century represented the end of the many empires that once dominated Europe. With no empires left, few if any new nations can be created. It follows that future outbreaks of ethnic cleansing are likely to take place in the Third World rather than in Europe or North America. "The greatest threat," as the sociologist Michael Mann puts it, "is the spread into the South of the ideal of the nation-state, where this confuses the *demos* and the *ethnos*, the mass electorate and the ethnic group." If he is correct, there is at least one thing the West can do to help prevent the quest for statehood in the Third World from experiencing the worst aspects of nationhood: it can think in new ways about the promotion of democracy.

When new nations seek independence in the contemporary world, they frequently do so in the name of the people. Much of this is bogus from the start; new nations are far more likely to be authoritarian than democratic in nature. Still, making the world safe for democracy, the quintessential Wilsonian ideal, is one of those rare Washington programs that can muster bipartisan support. George W. Bush cited it as a reason for U.S. involvement in Iraq, just as liberals view it as a way to promote human rights and confront oppressive governments. Both viewpoints have considerable justification, for democracy does offer larger numbers of people a better way of life than authoritarianism. But democracy promotion can also become a dangerous venture, encouraging political fanaticism and support for terrorism, as in Gaza, or increasing sectarian violence, as took place in Iraq. Democracy in the context of ethnic tension is especially problematic. As the Yale law professor Amy Chua points out, rapid transitions to democracy and capitalism fuel ethnic hatreds by rewarding ethnic minorities while embittering ethnic majorities. Democracy, Mann reminds us, is far more likely to be the cause of ethnic cleansing than its cure.

When promoting democracy, Western powers therefore need to remember that ethnic democracy is not the only kind there is. Western societies themselves contain significant examples of nonethnic democracies. Ethnic tensions are notoriously difficult to manage, and some Western societies—one thinks immediately of Belgium—experience considerable problems doing so. But ethnic conflicts are not hopeless: Switzerland contains a number of ethnic and linguistic groups sharing a common country, and for all the talk of breakup a few decades ago, Canada remains unified. Nor does the United States define itself ethnically. American national unity has historically been understood in terms of commitments to basic ideals rather than to ethnically formed ties of blood, although a recent rise in immigrant bashing suggests that such commitments are weakening. Democracy in America, moreover, includes in its very Constitution such deliberative mechanisms as checks and balances designed to quell the kinds of passions so frequently associated with ethnic hatreds. There is, in short, a significant difference between democratic nations and democratic states. With levels of immigration throughout the liberal democratic world so high, few if any democracies are rooted in common national characteristics so much as they have become homes to many peoples trying to find ways to live together politically.

No new member states have been added to the United Nations since 2006, which suggests that however much ethnic cleansing we will be witnessing in the next half century, it is likely to be less than in the previous fifty years. Still, given the continued redrawing of maps in parts of the world that were once Western colonies, as well as the powerful appeals of ethnic identity everywhere, there will be more than enough ethnic cleansing to arouse the world's conscience and to promote campaigns to stop it. No fixed formulas exist for doing so. In one part of the world, for example in Sudan's south, secession and the international recognition of a new state, a process already begun, may be the best option. In other societies, such as Rwanda, ethnically based political independence is impossible given the close proximity in which Hutus and Tutsis live. Bullets always are used when ethnic cleansing takes place. Unfortunately, there exists no magic bullet that can prevent it. People who hate each other, and have access to weapons, are not easily persuaded to live in peace.

Despite the absence of easy solutions, there is nonetheless much to be learned from the examples of ethnic cleansing that dominated the headlines during the twentieth century. Aristotle once told us that we ought to pay attention to how political systems fall apart. The degenerate form that ethnic nationalism takes is chauvinistic populism. The negative future for multiethnic states is separatism, if not civil war. It may not be possible in all cases to avoid either result. Still, the violence associated with ethnic cleansing can be limited when the advantages of statehood come to seem more attractive than the benefits of nationhood. By encouraging states that make efforts to include different ethnic groups, rather than just assuming that every new nation deserves its own form of statehood, the West will be in a better position to respond to ethnic violence when it threatens again.

AN ISRAELI NATION OR AN ISRAELI STATE?

THE SAME QUESTION posed by the violence in Yugoslavia and Georgia can be asked of the violence in the Middle East today: Are multiethnic states preferable to ethnically defined nations? Invariably, discussions of the future of the conflict between Israel and Palestine include two possibilities: a one-state or a two-state solution. The former would result in the creation of one large political unit containing significant numbers of both Jews and Arabs. The other would produce two distinct political identities, one primarily Jewish, the other primarily Arab. If the lesson taught from other outbreaks in the twentieth century is the encouragement of multiethnic states, we ought to conclude that the best outcome for the Middle East would lie along the lines of a one-state solution.

For many who debate this issue, the creation of one state in the region would encourage rather than suppress ethnic conflict. If the single state contained a majority of Arabs, the expulsion of Jews would be only a matter of time. If the majority were Jewish, the ethnic cleansing necessary to create that fact on the ground would be horrendous. This has not stopped advocates of a one-state solution from making their case. But given the demographic realities of the region, in particular high Arab birthrates plus the prospect of Palestinians in the diaspora returning home, one-state solutions have generally been associated with the Arab side. It stands to reason that you would favor one state if you will be the dominant group after it is created.

One-state solutions are therefore viewed by many of Israel's supporters as equivalent to the destruction of Israel, at least in its present form: either Jews would become a minority in their own country or they would have no choice but to use authoritarian methods to retain their state's Jewish character. Such a state would either be a democracy and not Jewish or Jewish and not a democracy. Israel, those holding to this perspective maintain, should never have to face such a Hobson's choice. Even if a multiethnic state may be the best antidote to ethnic cleansing in theory, in the Middle East it is a solution that must be avoided.

It is no longer clear that it can be. A two-state solution in the region is not completely out of the question and could come into being if Palestinians in the West Bank, applying Zionist history to their own cause, were to declare the existence of a state and seek international recognition for it. But the other, and once more realistic, path to a two-state solution, one negotiated in good faith by both parties, becomes increasingly unlikely with every passing year. Israeli settlements leave less and less land on which the Palestinians could build a state, and it is difficult to imagine either an Israeli leader paying the political costs associated with the dismantling of those settlements or an American leader willing to force the issue. Although a rapprochement is beginning to take place, Palestinians remain divided between moderates in the West Bank and militants in Gaza, undermining the prospect that a future Palestinian state will be sufficiently unified to survive. Formally speaking, a peace process still exists premised upon a two-state solution. But it is also clearly an exhausted one, unable to overcome Israeli intransigence and Palestinian suspicion.

Under conditions such as these, thinkers and activists from across the political spectrum are beginning to give one-state solutions another look. Tony Judt, for example, who had so carefully studied the Balkan violence, wrote a highly controversial essay in *The New York Review of Books* arguing that states based on ethnic nationalism were in danger of becoming anachronistic. Given the passions aroused by the fact that Israel was created in the aftermath of the Holocaust, Judt was denounced as a self-hating Jew for even suggesting the possibility of a binational state of Israel. It is true that his use of the word "anachronism" was incendiary; people who have struggled so hard and lost so many lives to build a state do not generally like to be told that their efforts have been in vain. But Judt's larger point was valid. Yugoslavia taught him that states in general, and liberal democratic ones in particular, are better off when they can manage ethnic tensions rather than reflect them.

Interestingly enough, Judt is not alone in his belief. Although a one-state solution for this area is associated with the pro-Palestinian left, it has also in recent years been endorsed by prominent right-wing Israelis, including former defense minister Moshe Arens and Uri Elitzur, former chairman of the Yesha Council of Settlements. Incorporating the West Bank into Israel, Arens points out, would greatly increase the percentage of Arab citizens within Israel, from roughly 20 percent to 30 percent. But, he also writes, Israel already contains other minori-

ties such as Christians and Druze and therefore has had some experience dealing with non-Jews. "Would a 30 percent Muslim minority
in Israel create a challenge that would be impossible for Israeli society
to meet?" he asks. "That is a question that Israeli politicians, and all
Israelis—Jews and Arabs alike—need to ponder." The fact that someone of Arens's stature and political views is willing to ponder it is an
important development. Clearly conservatives who are expressing support for a one-state solution want to ensure that the resulting state is a
Jewish one; Arabs would not become full citizens of such a state until
sometime in the future, if ever. But their recognition of the reality of
multiethnic societies suggests, in its own way, an appreciation of Judt's
point: liberal democracies can survive and even flourish with multiple
ethnic identities.

When it comes to peace in the Middle East, so many hopes have been
dashed for so many years that optimism is another term for foolishness.
But it is worth noting that the efforts made by right-wing governments
in Israel to encourage settlement activity, as damaging as they have
been to the prospects of a two-state solution, put back on the table the
theoretically preferable one-state alternative. Theory is a long way from
practice, especially in the Middle East, and no one should be deluded
into believing that the creation of a multiethnic state in the region will
somehow bring the violence to an end. At its worst, in fact, one state,
instead of resulting in perpetual war between Israelis and Palestinians,
would lead to endless civil war over who would retain power within
it. Peace will not come to the Middle East until both sides want it; no
political arrangement can substitute for such a mutual desire. Still, if the
lessons of Yugoslavia and Georgia teach anything, it is that ethnic tensions are better confined within one political entity than spread among
many. The creation of one state in the region might indeed result in the
destruction of Israel as a specifically Jewish political entity—or, then
again, it might not. But were the two sides to the conflict ever to want
to live in peace with each other, a remote prospect at the present time to
be sure, Israelis, Jewish and Arab alike, might achieve greater security as
joint citizens pursuing a joint venture.

There is one more lesson from previous instances of ethnic conflict that needs to be applied to the Middle East, and that is the necessity of honest brokerage. In Yugoslavia, the West, determined to assign
the bulk of the blame to one side, never acted as an honest interme-

diary between all parties involved in the conflict. In Georgia, despite deep-seated suspicion between the United States and the Soviet Union, as well as the long shadow of cold war politics within the United States, impartiality was on much greater display. All political evil may be local. But some forms of political evil, especially ethnic cleansing that spins out of control and threatens wider war, will nonetheless require international intervention. Avoiding the one-sidedness on display in Yugoslavia in favor of the greater even-handedness witnessed in Georgia will be essential if that intervention is to work effectively.

Honest brokerage in the Middle East will not be easy to come by. Chastened by one failure after another to bring peace to the region, European states are reluctant to become more involved until the parties directly involved assume more of the burden themselves. Although furious debates have broken out in the United States over whether there exists an all-powerful Israel lobby, no one can question that recent American presidents have been either too supportive of Israel or too reluctant to confront its leaders to wring the concessions necessary to curtail the power of the settlers or to take Palestinian concerns more seriously. (It is an open question whether this will change with Obama.) A certain calm has settled over the Israel-Palestine conflict in recent years. But that cannot be expected to last, especially as the domestic tenor of both U.S. and Israeli politics shifts to the right on the one side and Palestinian anger toward the settlers and toward Israeli control over Gaza increases on the other. The questions of statehood and the forms they will take in the Middle East have been delayed rather than answered.

If honest brokerage is so essential to control ethnic conflict, why do we not witness it more often? This can be explained primarily by the widespread tendency within the West, and especially within the United States, to view foreign policy decisions in Manichaean terms. Once local struggles are treated as deadly contests between good and evil, honest brokerage is rendered impossible: one does not negotiate with Satan but renounces him. This is yet another reason why black-and-white thinking must be avoided when it comes to ethnic tensions. Ethnic hostilities are difficult enough to resolve without making them stand-ins for larger morality plays. As hard as it may be to resist treating one side as more evil than another, maintaining credibility on both sides is essential to preventing political evil from further spreading its wings. American leaders must begin to realize that not all terrorists abhor politics and that not all democracies have clean hands. Honest broker-age is important not only because it can be effective diplomatically but because it induces a more nuanced understanding of how politics in the world actually works.

Pessimism with respect to the Arab-Israeli conflict may be war-ranted, but carried to extremes, it becomes dangerous. As difficult as it might have been to imagine such a scenario during the height of the Yugoslav crisis, relative peace has been restored to the Balkans. Both Serbia and Croatia, understanding the benefits of the region's recent economic growth, have proved themselves anxious to become more integrated with Europe and to put the past behind them in order to do so. They even manage to stage soccer matches between them that do not result in unusual levels of violence. It is therefore not impos-sible to imagine that at some point similar desires to join the world and enjoy the benefits of prosperity could result in peace between Israelis and Palestinians, especially given the fact that both groups have histori-cally valued education, promoted commerce, and learned to live with each other in the respective diasporas. Ethnic hatreds are as powerful as any hatreds can be. It is anyone's guess, however, whether they are more powerful than the love of profit. The more Israel reaps the benefits of its incredibly innovative high-tech sector, and the more the Palestinians discover their own niche in the global economy, the sooner the possi-bility that ethnic nationalism will be viewed as anachronistic by those once nationalistic themselves.

As reassuring as it may be that the fires of ethnic cleansing can-not burn indefinitely, it is still best if they are never ignited in the first place. Violent cleansing will always be tempting to any ethnic group determined to transform itself into an independent nation, especially when land is in dispute between it and another ethnic group bent on the same objective. Yet condemning such politically evil means without either acknowledging the widespread appeal of nationhood or engag-ing in diplomacy to limit the potential violence associated with it has not proved a particularly effective way of stopping this form of political evil. The examples of Israel, the former Yugoslavia, and Georgia teach us that we must recognize the evil of ethnic cleansing without succumbing to language of good and evil. For better or worse, there are reasons why ethnic cleansing takes place, and we have little choice but to take those reasons into account when responding to it.

CHAPTER EIGHT

The Politics of Counterevil

OUR DEBT TO POLITICAL EVIL

LIBERAL DEMOCRACIES came into being in opposition to political evil. What made them liberal was that their founding documents granted individuals not only freedom of thought and faith but bodily protection against arbitrary political authority; King George III may not have been much of a tyrant compared to Saddam Hussein or Omar al-Bashir, but his minions in the colonies were nasty enough to have generated the need for constitutional protection against cruel and unusual punishment. What made such societies democratic was the fact that periodic elections and representative government were designed to prevent the emergence of leaders whose power to inflict harm was unlimited; power checked was power less likely to be abused.

For all the horrors associated with political evil, its appearance in the past few decades contains one potential benefit: it serves to remind those who enjoy the blessings of liberal democracy of how fortunate they are to live in societies that respect human dignity and suspect uncontrolled state authority. The fact that terrorists, convinced that liberal democratic societies are decadent and unholy, single them out for their attacks ought to reaffirm the powerful moral and practical advantages that open societies offer. The obsessive grandeur characteristic of so many genocidal leaders can teach the continued importance of constitutional checks and balances. News that ethnic cleansers are rounding up innocent people and sending them off to camps should make clear why it is so important to have an effective bill of rights. A period such as our own that has witnessed more than its fair share of political evil ought to be one in which liberal democracies find new sources of resilience.

Yet in dealing with political evil, all too many Western leaders have from time to time opted to flirt with evil themselves. They have relied upon torture to coerce confessions. They have denied suspects, including those whose innocence is beyond doubt, the most basic of legal rights. They have launched wars of aggression that have produced disproportionate damage among noncombatants. They have authorized other regimes to carry out their dirty work in secret. They have engaged in collective punishment, inflicting suffering on the innocent many to teach lessons to the guilty few. Their actions, it is important to emphasize, generally have not resulted in anywhere near the number of deaths associated with those they are fighting against. But far from decreasing the amount of political evil in the world, their decisions not only add to its total but inevitably corrupt liberal democracy's time-honored commitments to personal dignity and respect for law. Liberal democratic citizens must assume some responsibility for limiting the damage carried out by those who speak and act on their behalf.

There are no easy ways to respond to political evil when one's own side engages in it. An unusual but highly publicized approach includes efforts to rely on foreign courts to bring the relevant decision makers to justice. Another involves attempts by domestic, usually nonpartisan, investigative bodies to discover exactly what happened and why. The underlying idea of both is to ascertain accountability. If those who engage in evil, even in defense of widely admired political values, are left unpunished or at the very least unashamed, the argument runs, a green light will be given to those in the future to repeat similar actions.

Here I will argue that efforts along these lines, however well intentioned, run the same risk associated with the ways we respond to other forms of evil in the modern world: they downplay the political reasons why such methods were relied upon in the first place. Counterevil—which I earlier defined as the determination to inflict uncalled-for suffering on those presumed or known to have inflicted the same upon you—is not an administratively inevitable response to the shock induced by horrific acts, an unfortunately necessary policy fashioned by disinterested lawyers and carried out by patriotic leaders, or a judgment call designed to ensure the safety of the country under attack. Its employment, rather, is nearly always undertaken either to promote the fortunes of one political party at the expense of another or to prove the superiority of one ideological outlook over its rivals. Leaders engage in evil to fight evil because they want to and because they can. Those who oppose them all too frequently lack the desire, the votes, the money, or the confidence to put obstacles in their way. Political in nature, counterevil must be confronted politically. Doing so will never be easy, not, at least, when people live in so much fear of terrorists and the damage they are capable of inflicting. It nonetheless remains the case that counterevil will not be brought under control until liberal democracies have a full and open debate about the true nature of political evil—and then elect leaders who need not fear a political backlash if they insist that their societies ought to live up to their ideals no matter how serious the challenges facing them.

BRINGING LIGHT TO THE DARK SIDE

"FEELINGS WERE VERY RAW," was how Bradford Berenson, who worked in the Bush White House as associate counsel, described the atmosphere after the September 11 attacks. "There were thousands of bereaved American families. Everyone was expecting additional attacks. The only planes in the air were military. At a moment like that, there's an intense focus on responsibility and accountability on the person of the President. It's a responsibility to protect the nation. It's visceral. You feel the President owes all of his power to preventing another attack."

Berenson's recollections accurately convey how those in positions of authority confronted the uncertainties of America's sudden introduction to political evil on so grand a scale. They also leave the impression that the way these officials responded was inevitable. National emergencies unify people, who in turn demand forceful leadership, or so their argument goes, and for that reason President Bush in the aftermath of the terrorist attack acted like any president would have. It is true that he assumed special powers in his own office, but so did Harry Truman when he seized the steel industry during the Korean imbroglio. Nor was Bush's reliance on tough measures to punish the terrorists and to deter future attacks all that unusual: Abraham Lincoln's suspension of habeas corpus in 1862 during the Civil War served as precedent. So long as Americans are threatened by political evil, any responsible leader, we are told, will have to take stern measures to protect them.

As persuasive as such reasoning may have appeared immediately after the September 11 attacks, in retrospect nothing was inevitable about the decisions of the Bush administration to advocate highly dubious assertions about the unlimited powers granted to the president by the U.S. Constitution, which were then used to implement harsh interrogation methods banned by both domestic and international law.

If anything, the politics surrounding their decisions suggest the exact opposite of inevitability. In order to put such policies into place, Vice President Dick Cheney; his counsel and eventual chief of staff, David Addington; and his key ally Secretary of Defense Donald Rumsfeld had to run roughshod over those figures, including some in the very highest reaches of their own administration, who, recognizing the unprecedented nature of their plans, had opposed them from the start. The move toward counterevil undertaken by the Bush administration was as politically tenacious as it was politically contingent: Cheney, Addington, and Rumsfeld simply outmaneuvered and out-argued their opponents to get their way. Without their single-mindedness, the torture regimes at Guantánamo and Abu Ghraib could never have come into being in the way they did.

The policies of the Bush administration that led the United States into the territory of counterevil were approved by lawyers, especially Jay Bybee, who had served as assistant attorney general for the Office of Legal Counsel in the U.S. Department of Justice, and John Yoo, the deputy assistant attorney general. There was a practical reason for this; if the OLC determines that an action is legal, those who carry it out cannot later be prosecuted for having broken the law. But just because lawyers played such an important role in the aftermath of September 11 does not mean that what emerged placed the law above politics. On the contrary, key officials in the Bush administration decided what they wanted to do and then selected those lawyers willing to provide whatever justification they required. Law can act as a check upon politics only if political leaders express a willingness to be checked. Because men such as Cheney, Addington, and Rumsfeld detested the very idea of being held accountable in any way, the Bush White House became a place in which politics triumphed over everything else.

No single individual was more responsible for the implementation of the Bush administration's program of supreme executive authority and reliance on torture than Cheney. As practiced by him, the politics of counterevil contained three essential components. The first was its explicit partisanship. When a Nigerian Islamist tried and failed to blow up an airplane on Christmas Day in 2009, Cheney issued a statement charging President Obama with "trying to pretend we are not at war." In words widely viewed as a break from a long-established tradition of former leaders extending to current ones the benefit of the doubt, Cheney went on to say this of the president: "He seems to think if he gives terrorists the rights of Americans, lets them lawyer up and reads them their Miranda rights, we won't be at war." In speaking in such tones, Cheney was acknowledging just how little respect he had for the foreign policy bipartisanship that had guided previous leaders. Far more than Bush, whose retirement from the presidency was accompanied by a distinct if awkward grace, Cheney, along with his daughter Liz, had become one of the most intensely partisan Republicans in the country, using every avenue open to him to insist that a Democratic preference for legality could not be trusted to keep the country safe (even though Republicans, when they had been in office, also "lawyered up" the terrorist suspects they had successfully tried and convicted). Politics for Cheney did not stop at the water's edge but demanded continuous plunges into swirls of controversy.

Cheney's partisanship had little to do with patronage or electoral success. It instead grew out of the second component of his approach to politics: a strongly held theory of how government ought to work. Cheney had served as chief of staff to former president Gerald Ford, who had assumed office in the wake of Richard Nixon's resignation from the presidency as a result of the Watergate scandal. Determined to prevent future presidents from covering up their engagement in criminal activity the way Nixon had, Congress passed a series of reforms designed to bring more transparency to the executive office. Cheney believed that all such efforts were seriously misguided. When the Reagan administration broke the law by engaging in a deal to provide arms to Iran to help fund the contras in Nicaragua, Cheney, then a congressman, praised the instigator of the plan, Oliver North, and insisted that a president need not be bound by congressional laws when carrying out foreign policy actions he deems in the national interest. Long before he became vice president, Cheney was touting the unlimited powers possessed by the president.

Cheney did not advocate the importance of presidential authority for its own sake. Instead, his partisan attacks on Democrats and his views on executive authority blended into a third aspect of his political outlook: a deeply held set of convictions about the very nature of evil. Like other members of the Bush administration, Cheney, despite warnings from Clinton administration officials such as National Security Advisor Samuel Berger and terrorism expert Richard Clarke that al-Qaeda would become the nation's primary enemy, was taken aback by the September 11 attacks. But the moment they occurred, he took the lead in proposing a theory designed to explain them. Terrorists, Cheney was convinced, had targeted the United States because they perceived it to be weak. As he put the matter in one of the many television interviews he granted in the aftermath of the attack, Bill Clinton's failure to respond more aggressively during the 1990s had "encouraged people like Osama bin Laden . . . to launch repeated strikes against the United States, and our people overseas and here at home, with the view that he could, in fact, do so with impunity." The post-2001 political world, in Cheney's view, closely resembled the one that had existed during the Iran-contra affair. He had concluded from the earlier experience that congressional Democrats were not responsible fellow Americans with whom one debated but political opponents whose misguided faith in civil liberties, insistence on congressional oversight of the executive, and squeamishness toward firm methods would weaken the country and thereby give all the wrong signals to the enemy. He was going to use his close relationship with George W. Bush to keep them from meddling in the decisions he was planning to make in the upcoming war on terror.

The fact that the Bush administration's decision to fight evil with evil was politically motivated helps explain one of its most puzzling aspects. Soon after September 11, Cheney gave the most famous of his interviews on *Meet the Press*. Once he had informed host Tim Russert that he could not provide any details about the administration's plans, he went on to say, "We'll have to work sort of the dark side, if you will. . . . We've got to spend time in the shadows in the intelligence world. A lot of what needs to be done here will have to be done quietly, without any discussion." Cheney's comments quickly became the stuff of legend; they provided *The New Yorker*'s Jane Mayer, who wrote the best book on the administration's resort to torture, with her title. The view that Cheney had become the Darth Vader of American politics stemmed from this kind of obsession with secrecy. Cheney, unlike most politicians, seemed to hate the limelight. The dark side was not only a place to which he would go but one in which he seemed to belong.

The irony of the Russert interview, however, should not be lost. Here was a sitting vice president appearing on the most widely watched television interview show in the country not only to discuss what he insisted was undiscussable but also to proclaim openly his intention to keep what he was doing out of sight. Those in law enforcement who engage in torture and never let the world know remain in the realm of law enforcement, in corrupt fashion to be sure, but nonetheless in ways designed to get at the truth of who might have committed a crime. Whether or not the confessions they coerce are accurate—in most cases those obtained under torture are not—what goes on between them and their victims is confined to the two of them. Cheney's preference for torture, by contrast, was only marginally a matter of law enforcement. For Cheney's worldview to make sense, he *had* to bring light to the dark side: if torture takes place in secret, it serves no political purpose. Not only did Cheney want potential terrorists to realize what might be in store for them, he also wanted civil libertarians and Democrats to appreciate how far he would go in challenging their basic political assumptions. *Meet the Press* is the place where politicians announce their plans. Cheney spoke of going over to the dark side in the same way other politicians talk about which primaries they plan to enter.

Cheney's conversation with Russert helped establish a precedent upon which a number of Bush administration figures relied. In September 2002, Cofer Black, the most aggressive CIA official pushing for harsh interrogation methods, bragged to key members of Congress about his brutality: "All you need to know," he told them, "is that there was a 'before 9/11' and there was an 'after 9/11.' After 9/11, the gloves came off." For all its talk about the need for tight security, the Bush administration wanted word of what it was doing to get widespread attention. Even the president got involved. "The United States does not torture," Bush said in a September 2006 statement announcing the creation of military commissions. At the same time, he also made public the fact that the CIA was using "an alternative set of procedures" to obtain information from individuals trained to resist interrogation. "In these cases, it has been necessary to move these individuals to an environment where they can be held secretly, questioned by experts, and—when appropriate—prosecuted for terrorist acts." These were not the words of a politician trying to pull the wool over the public's eyes. The president wanted the public to know, even while being told the opposite, that torture was taking place and that he was proud to be associated with it.

Bush administration figures believed that because they were more willing than Democrats to cross over into the dark side, their policies would be more effective in controlling terror. In reality, political considerations inevitably trumped security necessities on their watch. Strong partisans and committed ideologues have one thing in common: they know what they know and seal themselves off against any evidence that might question their basic presuppositions. Effective national security policies, by contrast, require flexibility and work best when shaped by experience. It is now widely agreed that the Bush administration's policies toward terror—from its decision to invade Iraq on false grounds to its reliance on repressive regimes to carry out torture against detainees—fueled the conditions of rage and helplessness that attract people to terror to begin with. Yet no understanding that their policies were backfiring could enter their "fantasyland," the term one dissenting lawyer used in describing to Mayer the hall of mirrors Cheney and his like-minded colleagues had built around themselves. As dogged as the vice president was in asserting that only firmness would impress the al-Qaeda terrorists and induce them to stop their attacks, "there's no evidence to support Cheney's view," as Steven Simon, a terrorist expert who had worked in the Clinton White House, concluded. "I don't know where Cheney gets the idea from, but it's not from the documentary evidence, at any rate. It may just be sheer displacement on his part; in other words, that's how he would have done things and that's how he conducts politics, so there's an element of projection there, probably."

It is common among students of international relations to divide foreign policy decision makers into realists and idealists. The former hold that states ought to do whatever makes them stronger irrespective of whether their policies promote moral or ethical ends. The latter insist that states, and especially liberal democratic ones, ought to promote their way of life by encouraging other states to adopt similar values. When it came to the politics of counterevil, this way of thinking became unusually scrambled. The Cheney-Addington-Rumsfeld worldview, at least in theory, insisted on toughness, a quality long associated with the realist tradition. Its inclination toward secrecy came right out of a pre–liberal democratic era when leaders were free to do pretty much anything they wanted. Its conception of presidential authority owed much to the divine right of kings. It associated morality, let alone diplomacy and its necessary cynicism, with softness. To further its goals, it was willing to make alliances with corrupt and cruel regimes that would do nasty things in return for money and protection. Nothing would be more offensive to these men than to call them idealistic.

At the same time, the Bush administration's resort to the politics of counterevil, while hardly idealistic, was also noticeably unrealistic. Its certainty that its methods would produce solid intelligence was based on little more than faith in the unseen. There always existed a surprising naïveté about how much it could bend the world to its will. It never understood, as any realist would have known instinctively, that those it was fighting, however ruthless their tactics and messianic their goals, were also in their own way realists, engaged in strategic action to get what they wanted. Most surprising of all, key figures in the Bush administration seemed incapable of grasping the fact that their enemies were trying to evoke a forceful response from them in order to confirm the image they were propagating about Western violence and that al-Qaeda would have been upset if the Bush administration had chosen *not* to be so militant. Recent history should have taught them as much. When no strong response from the United States came after al-Qaeda's attack on the USS *Cole* during the Clinton administration, bin Laden, as Lawrence Wright points out in his book *The Looming Tower,* was "angry and disappointed" because he had not seduced the United States into repeating the Soviet mistake of trying to control Afghanistan. The men in the Bush White House, unlike genuine realists, scoffed at such history. It therefore made sense that Brent Scowcroft, national security advisor to President George H. W. Bush, and Lawrence Wilkerson, chief of staff to Secretary of State Colin Powell, opposed the plans of Cheney and his colleagues so vigorously. These more old-fashioned practitioners of realpolitik were fully aware that the political outlook associated with reliance on unchecked executive authority and torture would produce results harmful to American national interests.

Americans like to believe that they are governed by laws rather than by men. Precisely because they violate liberal democratic tenets, policies promoting counterevil are fashioned by men rather than by laws. The whole panoply of Bush administration techniques that stood in such sharp contrast to the principles upon which liberal democracies are built—unchecked presidential powers, denial of habeas corpus, rendition to other countries, waterboarding, the dogs and sexual humiliation of Abu Ghraib—came into being because specific people chose them to pursue specific political objectives. September 11 did indeed, as Berenson's recollections remind us, send shock waves through the American political system. But what would happen in the wake of those shocks was an open question. The fact that Cheney and those like him had preconceived ideas about how the world ought to work helped shape how it actually did.

Despite the excesses of the Bush administration, counterevil remains the exception in American political life. Clearly any administration, whatever its ideology, would have responded forcefully to the September 11 attacks and would likely have sought expanded executive powers. (As we shall see below, the Obama administration defended and in some cases expanded many of the most controversial claims of executive authority proposed during the Bush years, even winning Dick Cheney's approval along the way.) But it is impossible to imagine any other administration creating a secret office for torture located in the office of the vice president and given carte blanche to do whatever it wanted by sloppily argued legal memoranda produced by lawyers selected solely for their fidelity to extremely conservative principles. One must make a distinction between presidents who violate the civil liberties of Americans (or even presidents who break the law) and those who countenance torture and confine innocent people for life. The United States has had more than its share of imperial presidents. It has had very few leaders who ventured so far into the territory of political evil as Cheney, Addington, Rumsfeld, and the lawyers who abetted them.

As if to demonstrate just how radical were the views of Cheney and his allies, they could not survive even into the second Bush term. Over time more principled Republican conservatives such as Attorney General John Ashcroft and administration attorneys Jack Goldsmith and James Comey began to question and even to quash the more notorious go-ahead memos. Bush, as if finally discovering that he was president after all, distanced himself from his vice president. Rumsfeld, at long last, resigned in disgrace. Key military officials began to realize the dangers that would face U.S. troops if the floodgates of torture were opened to others. At least some Democrats tired of being constantly browbeaten on national security issues. As these developments unfolded, advocates of a politics of counterevil lost much of their influence and the American reliance on torture came to an end, at least for the time being. One of the reasons Cheney was so aggressively partisan out of office, it is not unreasonable to speculate, is that he did not finally prevail when in office.

There exist compelling moral reasons to protest forcefully when liberal democracies engage in torture: evil is evil and it corrupts the people and the societies that sponsor it. Because counterevil is political, however, it must also be opposed on political grounds. Designed to demonstrate toughness, a reliance on torture reveals just how weak its practitioners believe liberal democracies to be. Surely such societies ought to show greater self-confidence than this. When terror leads to torture that then leads to more terror, someone has to end the cycle—and it won't be the terrorists. As rocky as the path may sometimes seem, liberal democracy has a way of returning to its roots: because those who torture in its name need to bring light to the dark side, that very light eventually exposes them for what they are. The key question is how well the lessons of their failure have been learned. If they have not been learned well, the temptation to engage in a counterevil will still be alluring if ever the United States should once again come face-to-face with political evil as it did on September 11, 2001.

IN SEARCH OF ZERO CASUALTIES

IN ELECTIONS HELD in January 2006, the terrorist organization Hamas defeated its rival Fatah to gain control over the Gaza Strip. Once in power, it began to intensify its terrorist attacks against those Israeli cities and towns it could reach with its Qassam rockets. The death and destruction caused by those attacks easily qualify as major political evils; in the town of Sderot alone, perfectly innocent Israelis lost their lives while walking to their cars (Oshri Oz and Shirel Friedman), crossing the street (Fatima Slutsker), or working in a factory (Yaakov Yaakobav). Fed up with such loss of life, Israel, in December 2008, responded with Operation Cast Lead, a military offensive designed to protect its citizens against such heinous acts. The campaign began with a week of intensive air strikes against major military targets in Gaza. There followed two weeks of furious ground combat, after which a cease-fire was declared and Israel began to withdraw its troops.

Because Gaza is one of the most densely populated places on earth, Israel's military offensive resulted in widespread suffering, including extensive damage to property as well as an unusually high number of civilian casualties. In response, the United Nations created a fact-finding mission, chaired by the South African jurist Richard Goldstone, to investigate what took place there. With no formal input into its work from Israel, which boycotted the entire U.N. investigation, the Goldstone report opted to pull no punches. Israel, it charged, had engaged in "a deliberately disproportionate attack designed to punish, humiliate and terrorize a civilian population, radically diminish its local economic capacity both to work and to provide for itself, and to force upon it an ever increasing sense of dependency and vulnerability." Although Goldstone and his colleagues never used the term "evil" to describe what Israel had done, and even though they reported on human rights abuses carried out by the Palestinians as well, their harsh tone left little doubt that, in their view, Israel had crossed an unacceptable moral boundary when it engaged in Operation Cast Lead. Israel's actions, in the eyes of the report's signers, violated the Geneva Conventions, amounted to war crimes, and were in breach of international law.

Not surprisingly, the Goldstone report was widely denounced within Israel and among its supporters around the world. The historian Michael Oren, Israel's ambassador to the United States, wrote that it "goes further than [Iranian president Mahmoud] Ahmadinejad and the Holocaust deniers by stripping the Jews not only of the ability and the need but of the right to defend themselves." In an interview with Israel's Army Radio, Alan Dershowitz called Goldstone a traitor to the Jewish people, and after comparing his report to the notorious anti-Semitic screed *The Protocols of the Elders of Zion,* he characterized it as "a defamation written by an evil, evil man." Less hyperbolically (and in my view more persuasively), the prominent liberal Israeli philosopher Moshe Halbertal found Israel's actions in Gaza "morally problematic and strategically counterproductive" but nonetheless condemned the Goldstone report's charge of deliberate Israeli action as "false and slanderous" and concluded that the report was too one-sided to be taken seriously. Goldstone had touched a nerve, and the Israeli reaction proved it was a deep one. The tide of world opinion, once generally sympathetic to Israel and its plight, was clearly shifting. The Goldstone report, if left unrefuted, would continue that trend.

That trend did not, in fact, continue. On April 1, 2011, Goldstone published an op-ed in the *Washington Post* repudiating one of his major accusations. Furnished with information from the Israeli authorities that he had initially lacked, Goldstone now concluded that Palestinian civilians in Gaza "were not intentionally targeted as a matter of policy." "Had I known then what I know now," he wrote, "the Goldstone report would have been a different document."

After this bombshell appeared, the debate over the Goldstone report became even more a debate over Goldstone. To those who had long admired his career, Goldstone's reconsideration added to their esteem; unlike so many public figures, he possessed the courage to acknowledge when he was wrong. Others believed that Goldstone, unable to stand being effectively shunned by so much of the Jewish community, simply caved. There were also the unforgiving: because the man had proven himself so biased and naïve, the entire report should be dismissed out of hand. Israel was now vindicated, this last group of critics argued. No one could deny that many Gazans died during Operation Cast Lead and that some of them were civilians. But these were tragedies, not crimes. Israel's enemies, especially Hamas, therefore retain any monopoly on evil. As in the medieval era, Jews were being charged with blood libel, held to be singularly responsible for crimes they never committed. The fact that Goldstone, a Jew, had added to those charges made his retraction welcome but did not correct the damage he had done.

The argument over Goldstone's motives, however impassioned, is also something of a distraction. The important question is not why the major author of the report changed his mind but whether the actions of the two parties in Gaza had ventured into the territory of political evil. In both the report itself and in his subsequent rethinking, Goldstone left no doubt that, because it relied so heavily on terror, Hamas did. As for Israel's conduct, the Goldstone report covered many more topics than the one on which he wrote about in the *Washington Post*. In particular, the report spoke of two aspects of Israeli conduct during Operation Cast Lead that were morally problematic: one involved collective punishment; the other concerned the always controversial question of proportionality.

One of the charges to which Goldstone and his colleagues paid particular attention concerned the blockade that Israel had imposed on the area before, during, and after Operation Cast Lead. Because food, clothing, and building materials were prevented from entering Gaza, the report pointed out, Palestinians suffered the consequences of homelessness and extremely crowded conditions: 79 percent of its residents lived below the official poverty line, and 70 percent lived in deep poverty. Starvation was avoided, just barely, and then only because of the work of humanitarian organizations. Hospitals found it difficult if not impossible to obtain necessary medical equipment. On the question of the blockade, the report's verdict was unambiguous: "The Mission concludes that the conditions resulting from deliberate actions of the Israeli forces and the declared policies of the Government with regard to the Gaza Strip before, during and after the military operation cumulatively indicate the intention to inflict collective punishment on the people of the Gaza Strip. The mission, therefore, finds a violation of the provisions of Article 33 of the Fourth Geneva Convention." Collective punishment is not a charge to throw about lightly. It brings to mind such wanton destruction as General Sherman's burning of the South during the Civil War or the Amritsar massacre carried out by troops under the command of a British brigadier general in India in 1919.

Goldstone's critics responded by arguing that the blockade was a necessary step to bring terror to an end. They also insisted that in a situation such as the one in Gaza, where terrorists thrive when the local population does not oppose them, Israel was justified in making life difficult for all Gazans, whether terrorists or not. There is surely some merit in these arguments: terrorists unquestionably use civilians to protect themselves. But this does not mean that Israel should somehow be absolved of blame for its actions in Gaza. The stringency of the blockade, especially the banning of concrete that would have allowed for the rebuilding of the Gazan infrastructure, along with the arbitrariness that did not permit Gazans to know from day to day which food and medical supplies they could obtain, were undoubtedly designed to impose suffering on civilians, women and children most definitely included, in the hopes that this would cause their leaders to cease their attacks. "The limitation on the transfer of goods is a central pillar in the means at the disposal of the State of Israel in the armed conflict between it and Hamas," read an official Israeli document that came to light in the wake of a 2010 lawsuit brought by Gisha, an Israeli human rights organization dedicated to protecting Palestinian freedom of movement. Other documents produced as a result of the suit showed that Israel had made calculations about minimal caloric intake necessary for survival and had procedures in place for monitoring the shortages produced by the blockade. To the international community, the suffering experienced by ordinary Gazans during the blockade was an outrage. To Israel, it was a by-product of a well-established policy.

Israel contributed to the widespread conviction that it paid insufficient respect to the lives of noncombatants when in May 2010 its commandos boarded the *Mavi Marmara,* part of a flotilla of Turkish ships protesting the Gaza blockade, and killed nine people, one of whom was an American citizen. In the wake of the furor over that incident, Israel eventually agreed to ease its blockade of Gaza. That decision was long overdue. Blockades rarely achieve their strategic objectives; in the case of Gaza, they strengthened the claims of the most militant factions within Hamas. Because their direct target is ordinary people, some of whom may even be opponents of the regime under attack, they are also deeply troubling from a moral point of view. On this issue, the Goldstone report, which is indeed one-sided and unsympathetic to the legitimate security concerns of ordinary Israeli citizens, got it right: collective punishment did take place and Israel was responsible for it.

In addition to focusing on the blockade, Goldstone and his colleagues faulted Israel for relying upon military tactics that produced a disproportionate number of Palestinian deaths. As will inevitably be the case when such controversial actions take place, the number of Palestinians killed during the operation is in dispute, as is the percentage of them who were innocent civilians rather than terrorists or their sympathizers. Still, the estimates associated with the Israeli human rights organization B'Tselem have been widely accepted. Characterizing the gap in casualties between the two sides as "unprecedented," B'Tselem claimed that 1,385 Palestinians lost their lives during the three-week period, more than half of whom were noncombatants and 318 of whom were under the age of eighteen. Israel, by contrast, lost 13—6 soldiers, 3 civilians, and 4 due to friendly fire. Such a level of disproportionality, like the blockade, raised serious moral questions about Israeli military tactics. As it happens, Israel has a history of asking its most prominent philosophers to ponder the ethical implications of the IDF's actions. The way these thinkers dealt with the issue of disproportionality helps shed light on the issue.

Michael Gross, who chairs the department of international relations at the University of Haifa, points out that over the past century or so states began to adhere to humanitarian conventions regulating what was permissible in war and what was not. "Humanitarianism," he writes, "prohibits torture, summary execution, and weapons that cause unnecessary suffering, while protecting noncombatants from direct attack, pillage, reprisals, indiscriminate destruction of property, and kidnapping." By this definition, Israel's actions in Gaza unquestionably failed the humanitarian test, for the fact that noncombatants experienced widespread suffering during Israel's offensive is acknowledged even by the Goldstone report's fiercest critics. But there is more to the debate than this. It may be true, critics of the Goldstone report contend, that casualty imbalances during conventional wars raise serious ethical concerns about the tactics that bring them about. Operation Cast Lead, however, took place during conditions of unconventional, or, as it is sometimes called, asymmetrical, warfare, defined as a conflict in which the two sides have radically different means available to them to carry on their fight. The moral question raised by Operation Cast Lead was therefore whether tactics that would clearly be unjust during conditions of conventional war can nonetheless be considered morally acceptable during an asymmetrical one.

Halbertal's response to the Goldstone report illustrates some of the forms this shift in the moral equation can take when wars are asymmetrical. "What was mainly a clash between states and armies," he explains, "has turned into a clash between a state and paramilitary terror organizations." Asymmetrical war, he further notes, "is defined by an attempt on the part of those groups to erase two basic features of war: the front and the uniform." Halbertal is aware that terrible things happened during Operation Cast Lead. The mere fact that large numbers of innocent people died during the campaign does not, however, end the conversation. When terrorists use civilians as shields, attacks that produce civilian deaths may be morally justifiable. Nothing can be taken for granted during asymmetrical war.

A similar insistence on the distinctiveness of asymmetrical war is at the heart of the defense of Operation Cast Lead propounded by Asa Kasher, a well-known philosopher who helped develop the code of ethics that guides the Israel Defense Forces. Kasher is primarily concerned with just war theory, the efforts made by philosophers and theologians since Augustine to define how wars can be fought on moral grounds. One of the best-known aspects of just war theory concerns the principle of proportionality. This principle, Kasher points out, does not hold that the deaths incurred on both sides be roughly equal; the fact that far more

Palestinians were killed than Israelis in Gaza does not itself make the war unjust. Proportionality, rather, suggests that the means employed be proportionate to the ends sought. Under conditions of conventional war, the end sought is victory. In asymmetrical war, by contrast, victory, if by that is meant the elimination of a terrorist threat, is all but impossible. The crucial issue is therefore whether the means employed in Operation Cast Lead were proportionate to the realizable objective of offering Israeli citizens greater protection against terror attacks. There is no doubt in Kasher's mind that they were. Like any other state, Israel, he believes, has a compelling moral duty to protect its own people. Since no state can allow indiscriminate rocket attacks to be launched against its own cities and towns, Operation Cast Lead was in his view just.

Asymmetrical wars, as we saw earlier with respect to terrorism, are indeed different from conventional ones. Yet the analysis by Halbertal and Kasher about what makes them distinctive leaves much to be desired. A war becomes asymmetrical when one side makes up for its relative lack of military might by relying on tactics such as terrorism or the use of civilian shields that are unquestionably evil. But it does not follow that asymmetrical wars leave the more powerful side no choice but to match the evil of the less powerful one. When critics of the Goldstone report invoke the concept of asymmetrical war in their defense of Operation Cast Lead, they write as if the logic of such a war is so predetermined that the targeted state has its hands tied by the tactics of its enemies. *They* are the ones who choose asymmetrical war, runs the argument, not us, and once our enemies decide to not wear uniforms or to hide their weapons in private houses, we have little choice but to use seemingly disproportionate force to stop them. The terrorists have all the power to decide what kind of war is going to be fought, and Israel, in their view, only reacts.

The problem with this line of argument is that choices are always present when states go to war. To argue otherwise is to treat asymmetrical wars as having the same aura of inevitability as defenders of the Bush administration understood their response to the September 11 attacks to have. Israel, in fact, made a conscious policy decision when it launched Operation Cast Lead, and it proved to be a significant one. The innovative aspect of that decision was *not* that Israel deliberately set out to kill as many innocent Palestinians as it could; on that point Goldstone was correct to retract the charge made in his report. Nor was Israel breaking any new ground by inflicting more punishment on its enemies than it experienced in return. Disproportionality had for some time been a characteristic of Israeli military efforts. Long before the Gaza operation took place, Israel had been relying upon tactics that caused more damage among its enemies than it in turn received. Operation Defense Shield, for example, the 2002 response to the second intifada, witnessed the killing of some five hundred Palestinians, compared to twenty-nine Israeli troops. The 2006 Lebanese war, moreover, saw so much destruction of civilian infrastructure that a new name, the Dahiya doctrine, was coined to describe it. (The name refers to a suburb of Beirut that was particularly hard hit.) Cast Lead, in this sense, although it produced a casualty ratio even more favorable to Israel than either Defense Shield or Lebanon, did not change much of anything. Both the killing of civilians and the disproportionate numbers were in line with previous approaches to asymmetrical wars.

The truly distinctive aspect of Operation Cast Lead involved not how many were killed in Gaza but the change in military policy that led to their deaths. Although the details are inevitably murky, during Operation Cast Lead commanders on the ground appeared to have adopted an unprecedented policy of keeping the number of IDF casualties as close to zero as possible. "Not one hair will fall off a soldier of mine, and I am not willing to allow a soldier of mine to risk himself by hesitating," one Israeli soldier, in a recording played on Israeli television, quoted his officer as having said. "If you are not sure—shoot." Although it may seem obvious that commanders want to protect those who fight under their command to the greatest possible extent, the truth is that risk is always inherent in war. To try to reduce risk to zero is therefore to choose to fight war with unusually brutal means. In his critique of the Goldstone report, Halbertal suggests as much. "Some units," he writes, "took risks in the Gaza in order to avoid the collateral killing of civilians, while some units accepted the policy of no risk to soldiers. This does not amount to a war crime, but it is a wrong policy." Halbertal is right to suggest that zero tolerance for casualties is a policy matter. But substantial grounds exist for concluding that it is an immoral policy and not just a wrong one.

One Israeli writer who understands the moral importance of a zero-casualty policy is Gross. Israel's actions in Gaza, he pointed out, should have prompted two moral debates, not one. "The first, which

received enormous publicity, centered on the question of proportionality and the limits of acceptable civilian casualties in a zero-tolerance
ground war. The second but less well-publicized debate addressed the
underlying ethical question of a zero-tolerance ground war, namely,
Is it permissible for a modern army to strive to protect its soldiers at
any cost?" The problems that follow from not addressing the second of
these debates are on full display in Kasher's defense of Operation Cast
Lead. Much like Cheney and Addington in the United States, Kasher
argued that asymmetrical wars allow for exceptionally harsh responses.
In doing so, he invoked the principle of double effect associated with
the medieval Catholic theologian Saint Thomas Aquinas. "According to
this principle," he explained, "when we are seeking a goal that is morally
justified in and of itself, then it is also morally justified to achieve it even
if this may lead to undesirable consequences—on the condition that
the undesirable consequences are unavoidable and unintentional, and
that an effort was made to minimize their negative effects." Kasher did
not discuss specific incidents alleged to have taken place during Operation Cast Lead because his examples were posed as hypotheticals. But
he did write that "civilian casualties—though an undesirable, painful,
and troubling reality—are an acceptable outcome of a military action *if
they cannot be avoided*" (emphasis added).

The trouble with this line of reasoning ought to be obvious: killing
civilians could have been avoided by not adopting a zero-casualty policy in the first place. Once Israel decided on such a policy, a significant
number of Palestinian civilians had to be killed not just to defend Israel
against terrorist attacks but to do so in one particular way. No one will
ever know how many "surplus" Palestinian deaths were caused by the
attempt to reduce Israeli casualties to zero. But no one can doubt that
many deaths occurred that might not have as a result of it. Once this
fact is acknowledged, Kasher's defense of the justice of Israel's actions
on the grounds that the civilian deaths they produced were unavoidable
falls apart. Passionate defenders of Israel, it goes without saying, would
consider the saving of even one Israeli life as a good enough reason to
kill as many Palestinians as necessary. But Israel's own military code, as
Halbertal notes, includes the expectation that "soldiers assume some
risk to their own lives in order to avoid causing the deaths of civilians."

We may not know for some time the exact origin of the zero-casualty
policy. But there is evidence that it was developed within the ranks

of the IDF. According to the British newspaper *The Independent,* one (unnamed) high-ranking IDF officer suggested that the IDF's previously restrictive rules about avoiding civilian casualties were intentionally suspended during Operation Cast Lead. If so, Israel's reliance on deliberately cruel methods is quite different from the decision of the United States to engage in such practices as torture and extraordinary rendition, for in Israel there did not exist a zealous group of elected and appointed public officials like those around Cheney determined to force military officers to adopt policies many of them resisted. If we view a political decision as one made entirely by politicians, Israel's zero-casualty policy was not political in that sense. There is no smoking gun pointing to Prime Minister Ehud Olmert, Foreign Minister Tzipi Livni, or Defense Minister Ehud Barak instructing military commanders to reduce the risks facing Israeli troops to zero in order to increase their electoral fortunes.

Still, there can be no denying that zero-casualty objectives served political as well as military goals. Israeli public opinion has turned increasingly hawkish in recent years, and the harsh policies toward Palestinians adopted by all recent governments remain very popular. Yagil Levy, an Israeli political scientist, argues that political and social changes in Israeli society, especially the growing number of less educated troops whose motivation for military service is more materialistic than self-sacrificial, lie behind the increasing reliance on a zero-casualty policy. There also exist ideological reasons for this change in emphasis: a zero-casualty policy fits the current mood of resignation toward the slim prospects for peace, exhaustion from years of terror, and a determination to teach the Palestinians a lesson that characterizes the current Israeli leadership irrespective of party. Politically, Operation Cast Lead was launched while Israel was in the midst of an election campaign—one right-wing critic, Caroline Glick, called it Operation Cast Ballots—and all the leading players were quite conscious of the challenge from Benjamin Netanyahu that would eventually displace them from office. Not only that, but the United States, Israel's closest ally, held its own presidential election a month before Cast Lead began. This suggested to many observers that the offensive was designed to take place before the incoming Obama administration assumed office, thereby presenting it with a fait accompli. For all these reasons, it is safe to assume that even if the key figures in the Israeli war cabinet may not have explicitly said yes to the idea of zero casualties, neither were they ever going to say no. The political calculations associated with counterevil can vary from one country to another. In the United States they were explicit and made public. In Israel they were more indirect and covert. Yet in both cases military actions resulting in the death and suffering of innocents were at least in part attributable to the desire of politicians to legitimate their worldview and retain their political popularity.

Those who argue that Israel must take strong military action to defend itself against terror are correct. But while self-defense is a just objective, the decisions reached during Operation Cast Lead, as well as those that led to the blockade, cannot pass the well-defined tests of morality that have for some time characterized Western ways of conducting wars, even asymmetrical ones. Both the blockade and the zero-casualty policy caused extensive harm to innocent civilians. Both were implemented from afar, putting few Israelis at risk while causing enormous damage on the other side. For that reason, both were politically popular among a domestic electorate fed up with the frustrations of the peace process and seeking revenge. One can therefore conclude that Israel's actions in Gaza, like policies associated with Dick Cheney in the United States, do rise to the level of counterevil. To say this is not to charge that Israel's leaders belong in that special circle of hell reserved for al-Qaeda murderers or Bosnian Serb ethnic cleansers, let alone that they are turning their country into a fascist or totalitarian state. But the decisions they made were awful enough. Liberal democracies ought to be held to a higher moral standard than are terrorists and tyrants. In the events surrounding Operation Cast Lead, Israel did not meet that standard. Richard Goldstone's change of position does not alter that reality.

THE PINOCHET PRECEDENT

ON OCTOBER 10, 1998, Baltasar Garzón, a criminal court judge in Spain, issued a warrant for the arrest of General Augusto Pinochet for the torture he had inflicted on Spanish citizens while serving as president of Chile during the 1970s. Pinochet's crimes were extensive; he had been indicted on over three hundred charges by Chilean courts for everything from organizing death squads and assassinating his rivals to tax evasion and passport fraud. Despite his notorious reputation as a practitioner of political evil, however, Pinochet had benefited from principles of state sovereignty that had dominated Western thinking for centuries. A Chilean, those principles held, should be judged by Chilean courts. Since Pinochet had lived for years in exile, this effectively meant that no court could judge him.

Garzón's decision to indict Pinochet became so noteworthy because it represented one of the most serious efforts in recent years to establish an alternative to the principle of state sovereignty. Certain kinds of crimes are so repugnant and so violate human rights, according to this line of thought, that they ought to be adjudicated in any court in the world. Garzón's decision fit this approach perfectly. It also proved effective in its own way. As a result of his ruling, Pinochet was arrested in London, where he had gone for medical treatment. A long and complex debate ensued over whether the British were obligated to offer him immunity or whether he could be sent to Spain for trial. Ultimately, questions about Pinochet's health led the British home secretary, Jack Straw, to decide against extradition to Spain. In 2000, Pinochet returned to Chile. He died there six years later without ever having been tried for, let alone convicted of, his crimes while in office. Still, the fact that a judge in one country could issue a ruling that led to criminal charges, house arrest, and negative publicity in another was considered by many of the general's opponents, such as the prominent Chilean author and human rights activist Ariel Dorfman, a victory for principles of international justice.

All those who engaged in the politics of counterevil during the Bush years were American citizens whose actions had been approved in advance by the White House Office of Legal Counsel. The chances of bringing any of them before a U.S. court are therefore nil. Given that reality, individuals and organizations determined to hold those responsible for counterevil in the United States accountable for their acts concluded that their best chance was to rely on the Pinochet precedent. The leading player from the American side in this regard was the Center for Constitutional Rights, located in New York. Its claims were based on the principle of universal justice. This principle held that since no effort had been made within the American criminal justice system to climb the chain of command for what happened at Guantánamo and Abu Ghraib, as if the evil there were solely the product of impressionable enlisted soldiers, criminal charges in other countries could legitimately be filed against the higher-ups. The CCR at first selected Germany and France as the places to lodge their complaints and focused their efforts on one Bush administration official in particular: Donald Rumsfeld. In both countries, however, the courts ruled against the complaints and concluded that only in American courts could such actions be brought.

Spain proved to be a different matter. There a case against six Bush administration officials—former attorney general Alberto Gonzales, former Pentagon general counsel William Haynes, former undersecretary of defense Douglas Feith, as well as Addington, Bybee, and Yoo—was assigned to the same Judge Garzón who had indicted Pinochet. All these officials were charged with culpability for the employment of torture in Guantánamo, where two of the detainees had been Spanish citizens and others had sought extradition to Spain. In January 2010, Garzón ruled that the case could proceed. Whether it will is open to question. Shortly after his decision, Garzón found himself under investigation for another decision he had made regarding the Franco era that could result in his suspension from the bench. Spanish politics can be byzantine, and Garzón, although a judge, is not above the political fray.

Bush administration officials were not the only ones to have been subjected to international justice. In December 2009, a British court issued an arrest warrant for former Israeli foreign minister Tzipi Livni, one of the officials responsible for Operation Cast Lead, only to withdraw it when she canceled her visit to the United Kingdom. Six months later Livni, along with other high-ranking Israeli officials, was named in an indictment filed in Belgium, a country that has a universal jurisdiction law making it possible for judges to try cases originating elsewhere in the world. As these examples suggest, Israel, like the United States, has lost considerable moral standing as a result of policies that many in the world believe to constitute war crimes. To the activists who view such leaders as war criminals, national borders should not stand in the way of their prosecution.

While actions such as these may seem to their advocates to be a necessary measure to hold leaders accountable, the principle of universal justice upon which they are based is unlikely to produce any meaningful legal victories. Garzón's decision in the Pinochet case did constitute a step in the direction foreshadowed by such a principle. Pinochet's case, however, differs from those of the American and Israeli officials in one key respect: they used evil methods to respond to political evil, while Pinochet was directly involved in political evil without provocation. This does not detract from the fact that those who practice the politics of counterevil cause significant suffering to innocent others. But in the case of both the United States and Israel, they also operated within the parameters of a liberal democratic political system and could offer debatable, although not widely persuasive, reasons for their actions. Pinochet, by contrast, was a ruthless dictator willing and able to use his control over the state apparatus to torture and kill whoever stood in his way. If a figure as disgraceful as Pinochet managed to find a way to escape criminal conviction under the rules of universal justice, it is difficult to imagine successful convictions against subordinate officials in the Bush administration or members of the Israeli war cabinet.

There are additional reasons that efforts to use foreign courts to judge practitioners of counterevil are so likely to come to naught. Israel and especially the United States, for all the moral authority they have lost in recent years, still possess considerable economic and political leverage. Countries that take human rights seriously, especially those in Western Europe, also tend to be allies of both countries and hence unwilling to alienate them. Even in those cases where judges may consider legal action against key decision makers, in addition, they have little power to punish. It is not even clear that international indictments cause any special moral shame to those singled out. Livni may have canceled her trip to the United Kingdom in reaction to the ruling against her, but her reputation in the West remains untouched: compared to Netanyahu, she and her party seem models of moderation. As if that were not enough to expose the limits of such indictments, British leaders have been trying to change the law to make them more difficult to issue in the future. Attempting to replicate the Pinochet precedent produces more failures than successes.

Those failures have disappointed advocates of universal justice. But there is no reason to conclude that all the news on this front is bad. Despite its idealistic appeal, the notion of universal justice is full of dangerous traps. For one thing, it confuses the realms of law and politics in ways strikingly similar to the dynamics of how counterevil came into existence in the first place. Just as Yoo and Bybee tried to put a legal cover on what were essentially political acts, judges such as

Garzón transformed their political opposition to the Bush administration into legal venues. Liberal democracies separate law and politics for a reason; all sides to political controversies, whatever their ideological disposition, are served by the existence of referees widely regarded as fair. Judges who cross the line into political controversies replicate the ideological and partisan motives of those they accuse. Having rendered themselves unable to judge political evil when it is undertaken by those whose causes they support, any decisions they make are likely to be considered illegitimate, and not only by those put in the dock. Politicians who abuse their authority are not that different from judges who misuse their neutrality.

Universal justice, furthermore, undercuts the very principles of accountability it seeks. Liberal democracies have their own means of holding leaders accountable. They are called elections. When that responsibility is taken out of the hands of voters and lodged in foreign courtrooms, democratic citizens are relieved of their obligation to ensure that their own leaders live up to the ideals for which their societies stand. In this unexpected way, universal justice resembles the process of globalization that worries so many on the political left. Just as foreign firms can make decisions causing plant closings in the home country that force workers to lose their jobs, the holdings of foreign courts can make it more difficult for the political institutions in the home country to work effectively. It is true that in the case of both Israel and the United States citizens have not shown any strong desire to hold their leaders accountable for the counterevil in which they engaged; elections, as we shall see shortly, have their flaws as accountability instruments. But transferring accountability abroad guarantees that elections will never be able to function as they should.

In the United States a debate has long taken place over whether it is proper for unelected judges to make what are in effect political decisions. Conservatives believe the U.S. Supreme Court did so when it ruled in favor of a woman's right to choose in *Roe v. Wade* (1973). Liberals think the same thing about the decision of the Roberts court to extend freedom of speech to corporations in *Citizens United v. Federal Election Commission* (2010). However one thinks about this issue—there are times, such as the 1954 *Brown v. Board of Education* decision advancing civil rights, when courts must act on matters of political substance, and in the current U.S. political atmosphere the rights of immigrants are likely to be better protected by courts than by fear-driven legislators—the problems of democratic unaccountability that arise when domestic courts make policy decisions are doubled when foreign courts do so. It is one thing when political decisions are made without the consent of the citizens involved. It is another when they are made by foreign judges without the consent of any of their citizens either. All things considered, the citizens of any particular country must be assigned the primary responsibility for judging their own leaders. The potential for abuse is simply too great when judges wander across national borders in search of universal justice to serve as an effective correction to counterevil.

We live in a globalized world in which international opinion can and does matter. People in one country have every right to pass judgment over what people in other countries do. Leaders should not refrain from criticizing other leaders when they believe their actions harmful to peace or in violation of agreed-upon international standards. Despite all this, justice is not served by the likes of publicity seekers such as Baltasar Gárzon. Augusto Pinochet was a unique case. Other ways will have to be found than reliance on foreign judges if those who commit evil in the face of evil are to be held accountable for their actions. No matter how globalized the world becomes, citizens of any particular country must be the ones primarily responsible for holding the actions of their leaders up to scrutiny.

INCOMPLETE INVESTIGATIONS

To HOLD LEADERS accountable for their actions we must rely on domestic political institutions. Elections, as we have seen, offer in theory the best method of doing so. But especially in wartime conditions, elections are not always up to the task. Citizens typically want to show a unified face to their enemies. Negative advertising, anonymous political contributions, and outright lying, all of them on prominent display during recent American election campaigns, hardly establish the preconditions for serious discussions of ethical and moral conduct. No matter how much citizens may disagree with any particular war, they are reluctant to change leaders in the middle of one; even George W. Bush was reelected in 2004 despite considerable opposition to the war in Iraq.

There exists an important alternative that has frequently been relied upon to provide the accountability elections have difficulty establishing. After wars are over, legal and administrative investigations can offer generally fact-based and nonpartisan examinations into whether policymakers relied upon unjust, illegal, or immoral tactics in the decisions they made. Israel, for example, has an elaborate system for investigating possible abuses by IDF forces. In the aftermath of Operation Cast Lead, it carried out an extensive investigation that, while not intended as a response to the charges contained in the Goldstone report, nonetheless examined a number of the incidents the report had brought to light. A similar process of investigation exists in the United States. In the wake of revelations of the extent to which Cheney and his colleagues in the Bush administration had violated the Geneva Conventions and other domestic and international laws prohibiting torture, the Office of Professional Responsibility of the U.S. Department of Justice carried out an investigation of the role its lawyers had played in giving them the green light. Liberal democracies attach enormous importance to proper procedures. They cannot allow clear violations of those procedures to occur without looking into what happened and why.

From time to time investigations such as these can be surprisingly informative. The Winograd Commission in Israel, established in 2006 to investigate the debacle of the Second Lebanon War, was unsparing in putting the blame on Israeli politicians. In Britain, the Iraq Inquiry, chaired by Sir John Chilcot and brought into being by Prime Minister Gordon Brown in July 2009, conducted a public investigation into how the country came to involve itself in the Iraq War. Its task was never to chastise officials; if anything, it gave former prime minister Tony Blair a chance to repeat his justification for joining in the American war effort in the first place. It also appeared to be disproportionately composed of members unlikely to be critical of Britain's decision to go to war and for that reason has been subject to major political criticism. Still, for all its flaws, and whatever it eventually concludes in its report due late in 2011, it did enable the British to have an open debate over the war, and Blair's role within it, lacking at the time the momentous decision was made. No investigation can ever undo the damage done by political leaders when they become too zealous in the determination to fight against evil. But in both of these cases, efforts were made to repair at least some of it.

From the perspective of holding wayward leaders accountable in the United States, the OPR investigation of the conduct of Jay Bybee and John Yoo began on a similarly positive note. Bybee's name had been attached to the most infamous of the Bush administration memos on torture, "Re: Standards of Conduct for Interrogation under 18 U.S.C. §§ 2340–2340A." Dated August 1, 2002, the Bybee memo, as it came to be called, defined torture in such a way that almost anything short of imminent death was acceptable. Bybee did not write the memo; Yoo did. Nonetheless, the OPR held that "Bybee's signature had the effect of authorizing a program of CIA interrogation that many would argue violated the torture statute, the War Crimes Act, the Geneva Convention, and the Convention Against Torture." Although the OPR did not charge Bybee with professional misconduct, it did conclude that "he acted in reckless disregard of his obligation to provide thorough, objective, and candid legal advice."

The actual author of the Bybee memo came in for much harsher criticism. Yoo undoubtedly committed professional misconduct, the OPR report held. Even while acknowledging that the period immediately after September 11 was a time of "great stress, danger, and fear," the investigation concluded that Yoo "knowingly provided incomplete and one-sided advice" by refusing to take cognizance of the uncertainties in the law, ignoring information provided to him that contradicted the interpretations of the law he offered, and overstating the extent to which legal scholars had supported his positions. Nor was the OPR in any doubt of his motives for all this: "Yoo put his desire to accommodate his client above his obligation to provide thorough, objective, and candid legal advice." This is stunningly frank language, highly unusual for reports of this kind. Had the OPR's report held, Yoo would have faced the prospect of disbarment for his conduct.

The OPR report, alas, did not hold. The Department of Justice's procedures call for a review of the findings of the OPR by the associate deputy attorney general. The official who held that position in early 2010, David Margolis, determined that "OPR failed to identify a known, unambiguous obligation" against which the conduct of Bybee and Yoo could be judged. Margolis felt that both attorneys had "exercised poor judgment by overstating the certainty of their conclusions and underexposing countervailing arguments." Nonetheless, the investigation into their conduct, he went on to say, was less than perfect. The OPR developed various drafts of its conclusion, and the fact that standards varied among them suggested the lack of unambiguous guidelines. In addition, it was unable to prove that Bybee and Yoo had written or signed the memos with the conscious and deliberate aim of misleading their clients. Margolis's decision to let the two lawyers off the hook brought the matter to a close. The reputations of both attorneys were sullied by the investigation into their conduct, but neither of them was punished. Bybee remains on the federal bench, and Yoo is still a tenured law professor at the University of California, Berkeley.

For those who believe in holding leaders accountable for their actions, this was a depressing outcome. Here was an investigation limited to lawyers examining the actions of other lawyers. The scope of the inquiry was not fully revealed until both the OPR report and the Margolis memo were posted online. There was never any question of either Bybee or Yoo being charged with a crime. Had either man been slapped on the wrist under conditions such as these, partisan uproar might have been kept to a minimum and basic standards of justice upheld. Yet it still proved impossible to pin the responsibility for torture on specific individuals or to demand that they pay a price. We may never know why Margolis opted not to let the original OPR charges stand. Most likely, he wanted to protect the reputation of the Department of Justice, with which he had long been associated. In this he seems to have succeeded, for his memo unleashed no significant protests and was by and large greeted with indifference. When it comes to the actions carried out by Cheney, Addington, and their allies, there has been little truth and even less reconciliation. It is still possible to make a career out of counterevil in the United States and never be held accountable.

The Israeli investigation into possible abuses by IDF forces during Operation Cast Lead also produced disappointing results. At one level, the investigation was anything but a whitewash. In two reports issued in 2009 and 2010, the military advocate general of the IDF, Avichai Mandelblit, summarized his findings. Israel opened forty-seven investigations into actions that took place during Cast Lead, his reports pointed out. Some of those investigations did result in significant punishment of those responsible for unusually cruel conduct. As is so often the case when the military investigates itself, a good deal of blame, when blame was found, was placed on the actions of low-ranking soldiers. Still, higher-ups were also singled out; a brigadier general and a colonel, neither of whom was named, were disciplined "for approving the use of explosive shells in violation of the safety distances required in urban areas." Even more impressively for such an investigation, Mandelblit's July 2010 report acknowledged that Israel had indeed relied upon white phosphorus, an especially gruesome (if nonetheless legal) weapon, in its Gaza campaign, a charge that the state of Israel had routinely denied. For all its flaws, the Goldstone report did prompt Israel to take a serious look at what took place during Operation Cast Lead and for that reason performed a valuable service.

At the same time, however, it was also clear from the start that the Cast Lead investigation would not echo the more hard-hitting Winograd Commission. For one thing, it was not critical of the Israeli leadership and especially of the IDF's general strategy and tactics. Nor was the investigation an exemplar of introspective moral reasoning. Sounding very much like Kasher, one of the reports emphasized that "in complex combat situations, errors of judgment, even with tragic results, do not necessarily mean that violations of the Law of Armed Conflict have occurred." In general, the military advocate general's investigation remained limited because in cases of doubt it relied on the testimony of Israeli troops. If a soldier claimed that he perceived civilians in Gaza as a threat, his actions were deemed not to violate the IDF code of ethics. As honest as the IDF investigation into its own conduct was in some areas, it lacked the overall credibility to persuade those with an open mind that Israel's actions on the whole were morally justifiable.

In the final analysis, neither the investigation into the policies promoted by Bybee and Yoo nor those that examined Operation Cast Lead proved capable of cutting deep enough. Israelis, frightened by terrorism and supportive of a military that includes so many of their sons and daughters, are unlikely to accept allegations that question too strenuously the integrity of IDF actions. Despite earlier and successful investigations of Watergate and CIA abuses, American politics in recent years has been so partisan as to make all but impossible any serious examination of the abuses of liberal democratic norms that took place under the Bush administration. If the experience of these two countries is any indication, the abuses supervised by Cheney and Rumsfeld and those associated with Israel's conduct in Gaza were serious enough that they could not be ignored. But, evidently, they were not so serious that reprimands were issued capable of punishing those responsible for them.

Domestic investigations do overcome the major problem associated with foreign courts in holding officials accountable for their acts. Like political evil in general, counterevil is local, and where it happened is still the best place to examine why and how it happened. At the same time, such investigations are likely to be incomplete. As a result, there remains a huge gap between the way such actions as Operation Cast Lead or the torture regime established at Guantánamo are perceived in Israel and the United States and the horror they evoke in the rest of the world. If foreign courts are too removed from the political conditions that make counterevil possible, domestic investigations are too close. Especially when matters of national security are at stake, the urge to protect decision makers combines with the desire to return to business as usual as quickly as possible to keep such investigations within politically acceptable boundaries. The stains left behind by policies of counterevil, in short, are exceptionally difficult to remove. That is why liberal democracies risk so much of what is valuable about them when their officials descend into that territory.

THE OBAMA DISAPPOINTMENT

DURING HIS 2008 election campaign, and then by his conduct in his first few months as president, Barack Obama signaled that he would take his country's war on terror in a new, and more hopeful, direction. In a major speech in Cairo shortly after assuming office, he distanced himself as far as possible from the concept of Islamofascism, repudiating in the process the worldview of Dick Cheney. He continued to talk about closing the prison at Guantánamo Bay. His attorney general, Eric Holder, announced plans to put terrorists on trial in regular courts, right in the heart of Manhattan, in fact, where the deadliest terror attacks took place. All in all, as I said earlier, Obama seemed intent on calming the fervid political atmosphere that September 11 had produced in some quarters of the United States, thereby allowing not only a more thoughtful response to terrorism but one more in keeping with America's liberal democratic values.

It therefore came as a shock to many of Obama's supporters that the new president, announcing that his focus would be on the future and not on the past, opposed any efforts to hold Bush administration officials responsible for their attraction to political evil. That shock, however, was minor compared to the dismay induced by Obama's decisions to continue, and even strengthen, many aspects of the theory of executive power relied upon by his predecessor. Like Bush, Obama issued signing statements indicating which parts of laws passed by Congress he will disregard. He allowed the Bush administration's wiretapping to continue unabated. The prison at Guantánamo Bay remained in use. Extraordinary rendition was still allowed. The civilian trials promised by Holder did not take place. On the contrary, despite successful prosecutions of terrorists in previous years, Holder's Justice Department asked federal courts *not* to hear cases involving alleged torture on the grounds that state secrets would be revealed. In the most shocking decision of all, the Justice Department went so far as to claim that a lawsuit seeking to prevent the United States from assassinating a Muslim cleric who is also an American citizen should be thrown out, thereby allowing America's intelligence agencies to go forward with any assassination plots they might have been hatching. All of this fell short of the literal establishment of a torture regime coordinated from the office of the vice president. But it remained chilling enough.

If there is anything to learn from the Obama disappointment, it is that the political conditions that allowed the United States to venture into the territory of counterevil will prove enormously difficult to change. The politics of counterevil, I suggested previously, contains three elements: partisanship, a theory of governance, and a particular understanding of the nature of evil. Each will have to be confronted before an American president can find himself in a position to resist those who tell him that his country has no choice but to go over to the dark side in its struggle against its enemies.

The partisanship associated with the politics of counterevil presents an especially thorny challenge. Obama's actions in this regard carry on a by now decades-old tradition in which Democrats seek to protect themselves against Republican charges of weakness by pretending to be Republicans themselves. As long as that remains the case, changing parties will only partially change policies. To his credit, the Republican tradition Obama carried forward was the conservative one of the second Bush administration and not the bloody, torture-prone one associated with Cheney and Rumsfeld. At the same time, Obama opted not to use the power of persuasion to challenge a deeply ingrained worldview that instinctively looks for military solutions to political problems. In so doing, he left in place the bloated bureaucracies, inclinations toward secrecy, and failures to take responsibility for mistakes so characteristic of postwar national security policymaking.

All this might be understandable if such caution actually did give Democratic presidents some political space to protect themselves against Republican attacks. But so hyperpartisan has public life in the United States become that the closer a Democratic president moves toward Republican national security policies, the greater the intensity of the Republican criticism he receives. No sooner had Obama carried out his plan to kill bin Laden, for example, than Republicans close to Bush and Cheney began to claim that harsh interrogation methods were responsible. Under conditions such as these, one can understand why Obama, who took on so many other challenges, opted to keep so many Bush policies in place. At the same time, his approach, or lack of one, will only make it that much more difficult for a future Democratic president to shift American foreign policy in a more effective direction. Excessive partisanship and wise decisions rarely go together. For the foreseeable future, the United States will be witnessing an abundance of the former. That means it will also possess a scarcity of the latter. All it will take is a single terrorist attack during Obama's remaining time in office for conservative Republicans to turn their already over-the-top attacks on the president into a full-scale vendetta against the alleged weakness of the Democratic Party.

Replacing the Cheney-Addington theory of governance will also be required if the United States is to come to terms with its experience of counterevil. To a small but significant degree, this has already taken place; the attempt by Yoo to supply a constitutional grounding for extreme views on executive authority has so little credibility that almost no one takes it seriously. Cheney and his allies literally tried to foist a whole new constitutional understanding of American government on the nation. In this, they failed. The idea of an imperial presidency, as Arthur Schlesinger Jr. once called the consolidation of power in the executive branch, is here to stay. But it never has to be quite as Caesar-like as it was in the Bush years. Thanks in large part to Cheney's extremism, the idea that the United States is a country of laws and not of men has regained at least part of its salience.

All of this, however, simply reinforces the Obama disappointment. Despite the move back from extreme claims of presidential prerogatives, there still exists a tendency on the part of Americans to believe that matters of national security begin and end with the executive branch. To say this is not to imply that Congress would do a better job in responding to global threats; the parochialism of that institution is notorious. But the framers of the U.S. Constitution insisted on checks and balances because of their fear of monarchical forms of authority. That a president as intelligent as Barack Obama either forgot this or was persuaded that checks and balances had somehow become obsolete is a sad commentary on the nature of contemporary American political life. Obama and Biden are not Bush and Cheney. If Woodward's account of White House decision making is correct, Obama, for all his efforts to protect the unilateral powers of the executive, cultivates dissenting opinions and is moved by actual evidence. But centralization of power in the executive branch has nonetheless become far too extensive for the country's own good. Obama's White House is an improvement on the one that preceded it, but it is still too protective of its powers to use those powers with appropriate restraint.

The final component of the politics of counterevil that needs to be changed is the ideological understanding of the nature of evil itself. Counterevil happens because radical evil is presumed to exist. If the evil we face is deemed to be thoroughly without scruple, global in ambition, and resistant to diplomatic engagement, our leaders inform us, we have no choice but to use every means at our command to combat it. But although enthusiasts for harsh methods claim that they are forced by the malevolence of their enemies to escalate their toughness, the reverse is more accurate. Men such as Cheney ratcheted up the stakes in defining what they were fighting and then found themselves trapped by their own rhetoric. Political evil is always a choice, and counterevil is no exception. Its practitioners take the first step down the road to torture and extraordinary rendition the moment they subscribe to a worldview in which the political evil around them is treated as the worst evil there ever was. Finding radical evil everywhere, they become radical in reaction. It is because they view the world as a dark place that they find themselves occupying the dark side.

Of all the dynamics of counterevil that need to be changed, this one offers the most hope. One cannot find evil lurking everywhere in the world unless it is attached to a presumed target, and since the end of the cold war, Islam has replaced communism as the source of all evil for those inclined to Manichaean ways of thinking. During the early years of the Obama administration, efforts were certainly made to inflame American fears by picturing Islam, in all of its forms, as inherently given to violence and the evil associated with it. A controversy over a plan to build an Islamic community center in an area of Lower Manhattan close to the World Trade Center, for example, gave politicians such as Newt Gingrich and Sarah Palin the opportunity to confuse Islam with radical Islamism. Other incidents around the country, including talk about burning the Qur'an in Florida or the vandalizing of a mosque in Tennessee, added to the sense that the United States was entering a period of extensive Muslim witch-hunting. With all the talk of Muslims within the United States hatching new terror plots in every mosque they built, it seemed that the United States was about to return to those moments of shame in its history when it created camps for loyal Japanese Americans or tried to deport Mexican Americans from Arizona. These are not exactly the right kinds of conditions for having thoughtful discussions about the best ways to think about the nature of evil.

Should another Islamic-inspired terror attack against the United States take place in the future, it is not difficult to imagine fears of Islam assuming the same importance in American life that the fear of communism once did. For now, however, anti-Muslim hysteria has not spun out of control. In response to the controversy over the Islamic community center in Lower Manhattan, New York City's mayor, Michael Bloomberg, made a widely praised speech reminding Americans of their liberal democratic heritage. Experts who actually know something about Islam, including very conservative ones such as Reuel Marc Gerecht, a former CIA Middle East intelligence analyst, have poked holes in the rants and raves of the most irresponsible anti-Muslim extremists. Other experts, many with ties to the military, have pointed out how anti-Muslim rhetoric would only help those Islamic radicals who have already been preaching that the United States has a long history of bigotry and intolerance. Even though Obama was urged to send troops as turmoil broke out in one Middle Eastern country after another in early 2011, his eventual responses stood in sharp contrast to the way the Bush administration had chosen to fight in Iraq. The Obama administration took a measured course in Egypt, resisting those who urged support for the regime of Hosni Mubarak on realist grounds, as well as those who viewed the popular uprisings there as equivalent to the revolutions against communism in 1989 and after. A more complicated picture presented itself in Libya, where Muammar Gaddafi, a genuinely politically evil leader, had reigned for decades. Here Western intervention did take place in what was essentially a civil war—and, at least with respect to the United States, without the authorization of Congress. Still, some lessons from the Bush administration were learned, as Obama resisted its unilateralism and reliance on shock tactics. (Only time will tell whether the West will once again be dragged into a situation from which it cannot easily extricate itself.) Signs such as these suggest at least the possibility that Americans are not quite as susceptible to black-and-white thinking about evil as they were in the past.

From the perspective of ensuring liberal democracies against a return to counterevil, one can only hope that Muslim bashing and aggressive intervention are behind us. I have been arguing throughout this book that we should treat terrorism, ethnic cleansing, and genocide as examples of political evil rather than as evil in general. One of the benefits of doing so is that it will lessen the temptation to respond to any of them with evil means. Toning down the rhetoric of evil will dampen the enthusiasm for it, while recognizing that one's enemies have strategic aims will guard against overreaction. That evil exists in the world is a truism that cannot be denied. That the existence of evil somehow forces us to ape our enemies is an empirical proposition, and one whose falsity has been demonstrated time and again. If the rise of political evil in our time does not cause us to reflect on the great accomplishment that liberal democracy represents, and if it does not also serve to remind us to do everything in our power to preserve and protect what makes it liberal as well as what makes it democratic, a tremendous opportunity will be lost. We cannot let political evil win. It must be fought whenever it appears. But it has to be fought on our terms if we are to defeat it.

CONCLUSION

Getting Serious (Once Again) About Political Evil

THE QUESTION OF NATIONAL SERIOUSNESS

BORN IN VIRGINIA in 1970 to Palestinian American parents from the West Bank, Nidal Malik Hasan joined the army after high school and attended Virginia Tech and then the Uniformed Services University of the Health Sciences in Maryland, where he earned his medical degree. It was not his work as a psychiatrist that brought Hasan to public attention, however. On November 5, 2009, as he was about to be shipped overseas, Hasan began shooting everyone in sight at the Soldier Readiness Processing Center of Fort Hood, an army base 150 miles south of Dallas. When he had finished, thirteen people lay dead and thirty more were wounded. Hasan survived the attack to face numerous charges of premeditated and attempted murder. As of this writing, no trial date for him has been set.

Like some other examples of highly publicized violence that have taken place in the United States in recent years—the 2009 killing of thirteen at an immigration center in Binghamton, New York; the 2010 crash of a small plane piloted by an antitax protester into an Austin, Texas, office building; or, depending upon what more we learn about the shooter, the Arizona attack on Congresswoman Gabrielle Giffords and those surrounding her in 2011—the Hasan incident can be viewed as the work of either a disturbed murderer or a determined zealot. Seen one way, Hasan is not that different from the Columbine killers or the Beltway snipers. Driven insane for reasons having more to do with his troubled personality than any particular cause, he took advantage of the widespread availability of guns to call attention to his unhappy life. There exists, however, a contrary narrative. Hasan, from this point of view, symbolizes an association between Islam and violence. It is therefore best to view him as the equivalent of those who brought down the World Trade Center, a Muslim radicalized by U.S. foreign policy who killed out of a twisted understanding of what his faith required him to do. Some mass killings are neither entirely personal nor entirely political, and the one carried out by Hasan seems to be among them.

As happens whenever there is an incident like this, the Fort Hood shooting immediately prompted a national debate about its meaning. Although the *New York Times* op-ed columnist David Brooks shared the conviction that Hasan's actions were tied up with his attraction to radical Islam, he directed his reflections toward us rather than toward him. Worried about appearing politically incorrect or engaging in religious bigotry, Americans, Brooks wrote, were far too attracted to psychological explanations for Hasan's conduct. Excusing away cold-blooded and cause-motivated murder by invoking therapeutic categories, he argued, is precisely the wrong way to understand what he and his acts represent. Hasan chose his fate as he chose his faith. Once we appreciate that he was engaged in a religiously inspired crusade, psychologizing Hasan's motives, as Brooks put it, "denied, before the evidence was in, the possibility of evil. It sought to reduce a heinous act to social maladjustment. It wasn't the reaction of a morally or politically serious nation."

The question implied by Brooks's conclusion—what makes a nation serious?—is a fascinating one. For many who share his position on the more conservative end of the political spectrum, the answer is clear. Americans, they remind us, were once a deeply religious people impressed with the awesomeness of God. At some point in the recent past—the 1960s are usually cited—they began to worship themselves more than their creator. In the process, psychology and its emphasis on the self substituted for theology and its insistence upon the divine as a way of making sense out of a bewildering world. Having rejected strict forms of religion in favor of a moral relativism uncomfortable with the language of sin and salvation, Americans, this way of thinking continues, now find themselves unprepared for those so ruthlessly committed to creating a utopia in heaven that they would stop at nothing to achieve their ends on earth. We should certainly regard these fanatics as evil. But no one can doubt that they are also serious. Those on our side, by contrast, as Brooks described upper-middle-class Americans in his book *Bobos in Paradise*, want to lead a life "of many options, but maybe not a life of do-or-die commitments, and maybe not a life that ever offers access to the profoundest truths, deepest emotions, or highest aspirations." We are not a serious nation because we lack serious people. Evil exists. We have simply lost the capacity to recognize it.

There is a good deal of truth in the way Brooks characterized the attitudes of the American upper-middle class, and I say this not only because he relied on some of my own sociological work documenting the pervasive nonjudgmentalism that influences how Americans think. Still, the moral relativism about which he and I have been concerned cannot be quite as dominant as we both have maintained. Six months after Brooks published his reflections on the Bobos in our midst, after all, Americans elected George W. Bush as their president. Not long after that, Bush responded to the September 11 attacks by invoking the concept of evil as if it were a mantra. If the widespread applause Bush received for his speeches is any indication, Americans, anything but therapeutic in their understanding of the demands of national security, seek to punish those who threaten them far more than they wish to empathize with them. Even the Christians among them, much like Bush himself, all too often seem unaware of Jesus's role as a peacemaker and prefer an all-out war against evil that owes little to the actual teachings central to their faith's leading theologians. As much as Americans adhere to considerations of political correctness in the ways they characterize their friends and neighbors, they get downright nasty when they talk about their enemies. The problem is not that Americans are reluctant to speak in the language of good and evil. It is instead that they do so in not very helpful ways.

Along with Brooks (and even a few other conservatives), I believe that there is much truth in the idea that the experience of the 1960s did not prepare us well for the outbreak of political evil that followed in subsequent decades. The tumult of the Age of Aquarius should have taught us that human beings, far from being free spirits standing to benefit from the loosening constraints of faith and family, really do have a dark side. Under the right conditions, some of them will unleash every horror at their command upon others. Is there anyone who lived through the 1960s and 1970s who can ever forget Charles Manson or the Reverend Jim Jones? The years in which they carried out their gruesome acts were in their own way a blissful age of innocence, producing exactly the kind of misguided idealism ill equipped to stare evil down. Given what we know now, we would all have been better off reading Arthur Koestler's *Darkness at Noon* than Charles Reich's *The Greening of America*. Any nation fascinated by *Hair* or *Jesus Christ Superstar* is not one to be taken seriously.

I therefore took it as good news that as the twentieth century came to its awful conclusion, an impressive number of Western thinkers did in fact turn back to Koestler, the Hungarian-born former communist who so insightfully explored the totalitarian temptation, as well as to such impressive intellectuals as George Orwell, Ignazio Silone, Raymond Aron, Czeslaw Milosz, Simone Weil, Lionel Trilling, and Leszek Kolakowski, all of whom, whether religious or not, knew that Satan still walked among us. Confronting the string of horrors that began in Cambodia and culminated on September 11, those writing under the guidance of Koestler and his soul mates became the ones most sensitive to the political evils of our day. The same era that saw the publication of *The Black Book of Communism,* the 1997 accumulation of totalitarian horrors edited by the French historian Stéphane Courtois, also witnessed the publication of *The Black Book of Bosnia,* a 1996 compilation of articles from the circle writing for *The New Republic* documenting the monstrous deeds carried out in the Balkans. No one could read either black book and maintain that the writers who contributed to them failed to recognize the seriousness of the problem of evil. On the contrary, genocide in Africa and ethnic cleansing in the Balkans served as a powerful reminder that the dream of a better world holds out such a compelling attraction that some will become determined to kill everyone who stands in the way of its realization. The best place to turn for an analysis of political evil was to the books and articles they wrote because more idealistic liberals were too preoccupied with emphasizing the good times around the corner to pay attention to the horrors around the bend.

Or so, at least, it seemed. Unfortunately for the question of national seriousness, if the 1960s failed to offer sufficiently firm guidance for dealing with political evil, so too, we now know, did the 1990s. We have for the past two or more decades witnessed enough cases of political evil to teach us that the age of moral clarity that followed the age of moral relativism has had problems of it own. We should have learned from the all too frequent failures of our responses to genocide and ethnic cleansing not to look back to the dark days of Nazi and Soviet aggression but to focus on causes local and contextual. It also should have been apparent that if it is correct to avoid the kind of grand, sweeping thinking that seductively leads to utopia, it is also essential to avoid being tempted by grand, sweeping ideas about sin and its temptations. Little was gained when the moral thinness bequeathed to us from the 1960s gave birth to the unvarnished Manichaeism that emerged in the 1990s. Political evil resists the strictures of orthodoxy as much as the blandishments of liberation. It does not occur because we are too permissive, and it is not controlled when we become too strict. Koestler and those who thought like him, brilliant critics of one era, turned out to be unreliable guides for another.

If anything, yesterday's seriousness has become today's shallowness. Because so many thinkers of our time continue to find the specter of totalitarianism in every outbreak of political violence in the contemporary world, the tough-minded awareness and deep appreciation of the darker side of human nature so prominent in the decade or two before the 1960s and 1970s has turned rigid, sectarian, and at times downright pathetic in the decades after. It is not just that those who once exposed tyranny on the left have become indifferent to, if not apologists for, reactionary regimes on the right: no ideology has a monopoly on double standards. The calcification of political thought runs much deeper than that. Political leaders whose speechifying insists that Americans are an exceptional people blessed by God to advance the cause of liberty rushed to copy the ugliest methods of the totalitarian states that once were their enemies. Thinkers who ask the West to appreciate the need for limits taught by the Judeo-Christian religions transformed themselves into advocates for endless war against the world's only other major monotheistic faith. Genocide inflation is much preferable to Holocaust denial, but neither gets recent history correct. Ethnic cleansing was brought to an end by allowing it to run its course. Promoters of democracy and statehood for one people in the Middle East found all kinds of reasons to deny the same benefits to another people in the same region. Those who once called for moral clarity became deeply implicated in moral confusion. The guidance they offer is more than wrong. When followed to its conclusions, as it was during the Bush years, it is downright dangerous.

The most striking example of our current national shallowness is neoconservatism, and its most symptomatic adherent is the former editor of *Commentary,* Norman Podhoretz. One of the first writers in the wake of the 1960s to argue that the West faced a mortal struggle against communism, Podhoretz wound up endorsing the political aspirations of that unabashed intellectual lightweight Sarah Palin. Such frivolity makes him a walking self-parody. Still, his journey is revealing. No surviving 1960s radical, no matter how woolly-headed, could ever be so open to caricature as this frivolous right-wing seeker, just as no McGovern-type national candidate of the Democratic Party in those mixed-up times can match in sheer vapidity the ones competing for public attention, or even the presidential nomination, in the increasingly extremist Republican Party today. In the first decades of the twenty-first century, the culture of narcissism once located on the left has found its home among those who believe that Americans are a good people simply because their politicians say they are. A party and movement with such a superficial view of goodness can never even begin to understand badness. Its leading public figures know how to utter the word "evil," but they have no idea of its intellectual genealogy. They are as ignorant of history as they are thoughtless in the lessons to be learned from it.

The situation on the liberal side of the political spectrum is better, but not by that much. When the violence in the former Yugoslavia and Rwanda exploded, there emerged among liberal intellectuals a new concern about the necessity for the West to intervene abroad in order to protect human rights. That consensus now stands in disarray. It took no time at all for born-again hawks to back the wrong war, as they did in Iraq, while their newfound sympathy for humanitarian intervention, as some of their leading advocates quickly came to realize, all too often was received by those for whom it was intended as outside meddling. If Podhoretz illustrates the moral emptiness on the born-again right, the French *nouvelle philosophe* Bernard-Henri Lévy perfectly captures the descent into narcissism on the hawkish left. It is not just that Lévy proved himself indifferent to the suffering of ordinary people when he rushed to the defense of his friend Dominique Strauss-Kahn, former head of the International Monetary Fund, without even considering that the woman Kahn was charged with attackig might be telling the truth. It is more that he has become what the American social critic Russell Jacoby, following Hans Magnus Enzensberger, calls a "tourist of the revolution," traveling the globe, usually in the company of other celebrities, in search of evil to denounce. It takes more than one discredited thinker to sink an intellectual movement. But when such a movement is already in decline, as the liberal hawks are, one such thinker can become a symbol of its decadence.

Where political evil is concerned, America—indeed, the West in general—needs to become serious once more. Political evil, as I have been maintaining throughout this book, is dualistic in nature: it relies on transcendental appeals nearly always associated with religious faith to pursue carefully chosen strategic goals in the world of power and policy. Getting serious about political evil means responding to both of the faces it shows us. We must never lose sight of the fact that political evil violates the central tenets of the West's leading faiths as well as its most profound political philosophies. But we must also observe carefully the concrete conditions on the ground where it takes place, or is about to take place, if we are to limit its reach and control its consequences.

Responding effectively to political evil's dual nature means overcoming the long-standing hostility between religious thinkers and those of a more secular bent. No one can take the problem of evil seriously without recognizing the contributions made by the world's religions to evil's persistence and power. It is not a question of converting to this or that faith, or even of believing in God. It *is* a question of drawing insight from prophets and believers who knew something about human imperfection. Evil is a problem for all, but especially for those who sing the praises of a beneficent God. If God is not and cannot be responsible for the evil we see everywhere around us, someone or something else must be. The search for that elusive cause is what gives theological reflection on the nature of evil its depth. Until very recent times, to be preoccupied with the problem of evil was to be obsessed with precisely where God's plans for us went awry.

At the same time, political evil forces us into the secular terrain of nation-states and their drive for prestige and security. It thereby asks us to confront the insights of thinkers and policymakers without a theological bone in their body. Machiavelli is as important to understanding evil as Augustine or Luther. He may not have had much to say about the problem of theodicy, but he does have much to teach us about why power attracts, why nation-states pursue it, and what responses are required when the conflicts spurred by human greed spin out of control. Religion, in short, can help us understand why evil exists. Politics helps explain why it persists. Combining the two in appropriate ways offers the best method of avoiding the twin traps of bland indifference and overweening self-confidence that have bedeviled us so much in a world marked by terror, genocide, and ethnic cleansing.

THE ADVANTAGES OF SECULAR CALVINISM

WITHIN THE CHRISTIAN tradition at least, nearly all theological reflection on the problem of evil begins with Augustine. Reluctant to allow the possibility that a good God could nonetheless have created evil in the world, Augustine argued in his *Confessions* that evil possessed no real substance. Yet, as we saw earlier, he returned later in life to a darker, more pessimistic understanding of the temptations of evil. One can read Augustine and come away with either a Manichaean appreciation of Satan's power over us or a sense of God's overwhelming love for the human beings he created. There is an Augustine of hope as well as an Augustine of dread. However doomed we may be in this world, we can always look forward to the bliss of the next one.

Nothing like the same ambivalence characterized the thought of John Calvin, the sixteenth-century reformer who, along with Martin Luther, contributed so much to the Protestant Reformation. Persuaded that human beings lack the will to overcome their inherently depraved state, Calvin saw our sinful nature everywhere he looked. After agreeing with Augustine in his *Institutes of the Christian Religion* (1536) that infants bring "their condemnation with them from their mother's womb" and as a result possess a nature that is "a seed-bed of sin, and therefore cannot but be odious and abominable to God," Calvin went on to argue that "just as a lighted furnace sends forth sparks and flames, or a fountain without ceasing pours out water . . . those who have defined original sin as the want of the original righteousness which we ought to have had, though they substantially comprehend the whole case, do not significantly enough express its power and energy. For our nature is not only utterly devoid of goodness, but so prolific in all kinds of evil, that it can never be idle." Codified in the various creedal statements in the years following Calvin's death, Calvinism, whether in Europe or in the New World version known as Puritanism, developed a well-defined theological system emphasizing not only the evil that human beings have inherited through Adam and Eve's original sin but the unquestioned authority of God to decide, on whatever basis he chooses, who among us shall be saved and who shall not.

Calvinism is the kind of religion commentators today have in mind when they suggest that we need to become serious about the problem of evil. They have substantial reason to do so. Calvinism helped form the ideas of brilliant writers such as Jonathan Edwards and Nathaniel Hawthorne. Its contributions to the rise of capitalism were immortalized by Max Weber. Its insistence on biblical literalism promoted the spread of literacy. Committed to a covenantal understanding of scripture, Calvinism gave the modern world the ideas of constitutionalism and limited government. To be sure, Calvinism was accompanied by its share of intolerance and repression. But without it, the emergence of the Enlightenment that followed in its wake becomes difficult to imagine. This is not because Calvinism offered a ringing defense of freedom; its outlook on the world was far too gloomy for that. Calvinism, rather, presented the world with a challenge many Christians found impossible to resist. Precisely because not everyone could be saved, the question of salvation and what was required to achieve it became a matter of impressive examination. Calvinism is an introspective religion, forcing those who adhere to its tenets to explore how they have gotten right with God and how they have not. Of all the Protestant sects, it is among the most intellectually demanding. Calvinism pays so much attention to the problem of evil because it pays so much attention to everything in God's realm.

Whatever Calvinism's contribution to Enlightenment thought and practice, all too many strict religious believers today are likely to view themselves as critics of the Enlightenment's legacy, especially its belief in human reason and its preference for individual autonomy. The ideas of the Chinese-born, British-educated, and American-residing evangelical essayist and lecturer Os Guinness are representative. For Guinness, as he explains in his book *Unspeakable,* the modern world has not abolished evil but increased its capacity for damage. It is not only that modernity invents new and far more efficient mechanisms for bringing about mass death. It is also that the freedom modernity promises transforms itself, in the absence of a recognition of God's authority, into "the unbridled passion to transgress, the drive to destroy traditions, flout standards, and defy conventions." There is a reason we fail to understand the evil carried out by people such as Osama bin Laden and Slobodan Milosevic: they recognized no restraints, and we are reluctant to acknowledge them as well. "Thus, radical idea by radical idea, violent film by violent film, explicit song by explicit song, brutal video game by brutal video game, edgy cable show by edgy cable show, and shameless scandal by shameless scandal," Guinness concludes, "the momentum grows and the binding forces concentrate." When the world loses its conscience, as Dostoyevsky's Grand Inquisitor so famously pointed out, anything goes and evil is one of the results.

Guinness, who attends an Anglican church in Virginia, does not claim that his faith is the only one capable of coming to terms with the problem of evil: any religion is acceptable. But, he insists, it must be *a* religion. Secularism will not do, and for two reasons. One is that sources of thought that downplay or ignore the presence of divine authority lack the history of deep reflection on the problem of evil that religious traditions have provided their followers. The other is that secularism itself is one of the great forces for evil in the modern world. "More than one hundred million human beings were killed by secularist regimes and ideologies in the last century," Guinness writes, citing the examples of Nazi Germany and Cambodia. Such results can be attributed to the ideas that guide them. Atheistic philosophies "are just as 'totalitarian' as the three 'religions of the Book.' What secularists believe is so total, or all-encompassing, that it excludes what the religious believer believes." So long as we are tempted by the sin of pride—so long, that is, as we believe that humans shape their own world and develop the rules to govern it—we not only will fail to deal with evil but will make our own contribution to its spread.

If one really believes that faith in God constitutes the first step in coming to terms with evil, nonbelief easily becomes complicity with it. Yet the fact remains that thinkers lacking faith of any sort not only have explored the same questions that worry Guinness but have done so in ways strikingly similar to those of the most conservative forms of religion, Calvinistic ones included. As odd as it may sound, given Calvin's insistence on God's unquestioned authority over us, there is such a thing as secular Calvinism. It includes those who find the Puritans endlessly fascinating, such as Andrew Delbanco, and also brings within its reach those, such as the late historian and social critic Christopher Lasch, who believe that human beings consume too much, waste too much, exploit nature too much, or in other ways fail to understand how their arrogant self-pride runs roughshod over limits built into the human condition. There is no reason to restrict the idea of inherent human depravity to those who believe in God. The jeremiad, the Puritan lament for our increasingly fallen state, attracts writers and thinkers from every faith tradition as well as those who do not believe. One of Calvinism's contributions to the modern world is an understanding of human nature that is available to all and not just to those who adhere to the teachings of the man who provided it.

I would never describe myself as a secular Calvinist, and certainly not in a Laschian sense; I am too committed to ideas of both social progress and personal growth for that. But when it comes to the problem of evil, Calvinism and other deeply religious traditions serve the important purpose of reminding us of evil's seductive power. This is not to argue that the world finds itself menaced by tyrants, terrorists, and torturers because Adam and Eve disobeyed God in the Garden of Eden. Reflections on their disobedience nonetheless offer a crucial insight into temptation that anyone who thinks seriously about politics must acknowledge. Power is, among other things, a temptation. Some individuals will fall so totally under its appeal that laws, conscience, religious duties, or moral teachings will never stand in the way of their getting what they want. They are, in a perverse kind of way, the opposite of Calvin's elect, individuals who stand out as different from the rest not because God has arbitrarily granted his grace to them but because they exemplify in stunning fashion the utter depravity Calvinists wrongly attribute to everyone.

Understood in this way, secular Calvinism's great advantage is its ability to remind us to keep a watchful eye upon any political leader whose pretensions toward grandeur may lead him or her down the path to political evil. This is a truth brought home to Americans from one of the great secular Calvinists in their history, the political theorist, Constitution writer, and president James Madison. Educated at what was then a Princeton University steeped in the Calvinist tradition, Madison created a system of checks and balances explicitly applying the insights of his Presbyterian style of religion to the new democracy he was founding. None of us are angels, or so Madison would point out in the *Federalist Papers*. Since there was no way to expect ambitious politicians ever to control their own lust for power, the only realistic method was to have them checked by the equally sinful ambitions of others. Madison took Calvinist brooding and turned it into a semioptimistic theory of governance. The great accomplishment of the political system he designed was that it would not reform a corrupt human nature so much as bring it under control and even use it to the advantage of all.

This Madisonian warning against those who become so impressed with their own importance that they no longer consider themselves subject to the rules of either God or man is as necessary today as it was in the age of monarchy. For one thing, no Madisonian ever would have signed off on the proposition that the American president is free to detain whomever he wants or to disobey any law he chooses. John Yoo and others in the Bush-Cheney administration who took such a position developed a policy at odds with the U.S. Constitution; even more important, at least for people who take faith seriously, they also asked their countrymen to trust their political leaders in ways strongly antithetical to how the Puritans and their followers understood human nature. The reliance on counterevil during the years that Yoo was advising the president makes one long for that *more* religious America in which creeds were understood to have real applicability to the world human beings actually live in and where sin was always a brimming, and seductive, presence. Anyone who appreciates limits cannot accept unlimited torture and extraordinary rendition. A preference for the methods of counterevil is as much a sign of our overweening pride as it is a crime against humanity. It is based on the notion that human beings possess unlimited power to obtain what they want, even if doing so treats others as unworthy of God's, or anyone else's, compassion. One does not have to subscribe to the doctrine of original sin to understand why this is so wrong. The torture regime established during the Bush years not only violated the humanism of liberal Christianity but stood worlds apart from the dark theology of conservative Christianity as well.

The same kind of secular Calvinism can also help us fashion more appropriate responses to the political evil manifested by terrorists and tyrants around the world. Calvinism, in subscribing to the proposition that God created the world, reminds us that there will always be something imperfect about human beings who live in a world created by a force larger than themselves. This appreciation of our inherent weakness, and its corresponding warning never to commit the sin of imagining oneself to possess all the power at God's disposal, are routinely ignored by those who argue that one should refuse all engagement with terrorists, or that radical Islam inherited its totalitarian nature from

Nazi Germany, or that all forms of ethnic cleansing are genocidal in intent, or that evil means can be justified in an endless war against evil. Underlying all these flawed attempts to respond to political evil is the conviction that human beings can know with certainty which side is always the good one and which one the bad. Those who have imbibed the insights of Calvinism, in either its religious or its secular forms, recognize the problems that follow—arrogance, blindness, and contempt, among others—when we think of ourselves as capable of making judgments on so grand a scale. Humility, a Christian virtue, is available to anyone, religious or not. It can be a good thing—it can even become an effective thing—when applied to the conduct of nation-states. Powerful nation-states that do not use their power with restraint waste the advantages their power gives them. Powerful states that recognize that even the greatest nations in the world need always to be aware of their own imperfections will keep their power that much longer.

We live, for better or worse, in a time in which we are not quite as beholden to claims of faith as were our ancestors. In matters of politics, this is primarily for the better. Secularism has bequeathed to us ideas about rights, pluralism, recognition, and freedom without which modern life, and all its many possibilities, could not exist. It is precisely because the world of modern politics has become so thoroughly indebted to a secular understanding of human purpose, in fact, that we can safely turn to religion for ways of thinking that can help us wrestle with the paradoxes of political evil. Calvinism tamed is Calvinism useful. The strictest of religious believers will not be happy with the secular ends to which their faith traditions can be put. But if the advantages of relying on secular Calvinism include a place in which political evil is brought more under control, the payoffs will be too considerable to ignore. The United States routinely descends into Manichaean thinking not because it is so religious a society but because it so often fails to understand what the religions that shaped it actually taught. Secularism is hardly the cause of so much evil in the world, as Os Guinness wrongheadedly maintains. Indeed, those who insist that human beings are autonomous agents capable of determining their own lives, precisely because they do not put their fate in the hands of an authority beyond their reach, are in the best position to single out those among them who commit crimes against humanity and create institutions powerful enough to hold them accountable.

THE NECESSITY OF A MORALISTIC REALISM

ONE LIKELY CONSEQUENCE of the overblown rhetoric about launching a war against evil associated with the Bush administration will be a new respect for the realist traditions in foreign-policy making. Taking their cue from Machiavelli, realists deliberately downplay the notion that statesmen should act out of considerations of ethics or morality. Nation-states ought to do what is in their own best interest, the realist tradition insists. Far from striving to abolish evil from the world, leaders must be willing to form alliances with the most unsavory of characters if doing so will give them a strategic advantage. From a realist's perspective, neoconservatives and liberal hawks are equally guilty of dangerous utopianism. Not only should the United States never have invaded Iraq with the intention of implanting democracy there, this view dictates, it should be cautious about intervening to stop genocide and ethnic cleansing and suspicious of any forms of international justice that compromise the sovereignty of nation-states.

Realism has its attractions. It does nation-states no good to pursue unrealistic goals they are incapable of achieving, among them bringing democracy to parts of the world inexperienced in its intricacies or promising an end to evil as if just the right combination of dollars and guns can somehow stop bad leaders from carrying out hateful acts. But as far as combating political evil is concerned, realism, at least in the form adopted by Jeane Kirkpatrick, and especially Henry Kissinger, faces a singular handicap: it so lacks a sense of compassion that political evil rarely if ever appears on its radar screen. When everything is reduced to the question of whether it serves the interest of a particular nation-state, nothing can be held sacred. Having no particular regard for the well-being of ordinary people, and holding the rights they claim to life, property, and protection from cruelty irrelevant, realists at best cooperate with evil and at worst engage in considerable amounts of it themselves. We saw naked realism at work in the U.S. support for the Pinochet regime in Chile, and we see it now in the willingness of American leaders, blinded by the potential of vast markets for American products, to overlook China's disregard for human rights. That kind of realism is properly shunned. One must stare political evil down rather than look the other way.

The sheer ubiquity of political evil in our times, then, should lead to a rejection of the more stringent versions of realist ways of thinking. Foreign-policy making *must* have a moral dimension. Liberal democracies cannot survive long if they take as their standards of conduct in foreign policy those used by the highly illiberal states with which on occasion they have to deal. As political systems, liberal democracies are aspirational. They come into being to make the world a better place, and they fail to serve their history and ideals if they give up on that objective. The urge to improve upon the human condition prominent in so many religious traditions *is* an appropriate goal for political leaders to pursue as they confront tyrants and terrorists. We are put on this earth not just to live on it but to make it a more purposeful and better place for all people to live.

At the same time, it is worth emphasizing that not all foreign policy realists have been quite as cynical as Kissinger and his epigones. The security analysts Anatol Lieven and John Hulsman are correct to point out that a number of important thinkers associated with the realist tradition, especially Reinhold Niebuhr, George F. Kennan, and Hans Morgenthau, were, unlike Kissinger, motivated by strong ethical convictions. Niebuhr, of course, was a theologian working broadly within the Augustinian tradition. For all his support for a strong foreign policy meant to respond to Soviet aggression, he was well aware of the dangers to nation-states posed by excessive arrogance. A devout Christian, Niebuhr was not the kind of thinker to excuse away the failings of his own country by blaming its enemies for all the problems that existed in the world. His great lesson to us is that one can be a realist without becoming a cynic.

Neither Kennan, the diplomat and writer who did more than any other single figure to fashion America's foreign policy stance during the cold war, nor Morgenthau, the German émigré and University of Chicago political theorist, was a religious believer. But like theologians, they did think seriously about the problem of evil. Along Niebuhrian lines, both concluded that there are no simple formulas available to guide policymakers in balancing realistic and ethical objectives. As realists, these men knew that sometimes their own side might have to engage in lesser evils, actions that might violate their own moral principles. As moralists, by contrast, however much they were opposed to utopian schemes designed to change the world, they were supportive of more modest efforts to improve it in the hopes of achieving a decent peace between nation-states. Aware that states might be tempted to swing radically back and forth between a Wilsonian idealism and a determined Manichaeism, these thinkers held that the primary approach to the problem of political evil was to avoid unrealistic attempts to eliminate it if the failure to do so would inevitably cause it to spread.

Lieven and Hulsman argue that it was precisely such a middle-of-the-road ethical realism that was responsible for the great successes of U.S. foreign policy during the cold war. Because of its mature understanding of the problem of evil, the United States was tempted neither in a pacifist direction that would have refused any confrontation with the Soviet Union nor with an overly bellicose effort to fight an unwinnable nuclear war against it. Instead, the United States acted with patience, and the eventual result was a collapse of the Soviet bloc primarily from within. Among its other virtues, they show, ethical realism can work. The cold war ended not only with peace but with a new respect for the benefits of democratic forms of governance.

There are similar lessons to be learned with respect to the political evils that bedevil us today. When we see genocide, or even something like it, our immediate reaction, the one that derives from our religious heritage, may be, like the efforts of the heroic Nazi resister Dietrich Bonhoeffer, to do everything in our power to stop it. It is not difficult to understand why such an imperative may move us: Bonhoeffer was a singularly courageous man and the evil he confronted was especially vicious. Realism is out of place when evil is so radical. The Lutheran injunction—here I stand and can do no other—is rightly the stuff of legend.

The problem is that there are times when there are other things we can do. When it prevents us from considering them, moralizing can cost lives rather than save them. We can never forget that foreign-policy making is always about politics and that politics demands flexibility toward options. When it comes to political evil, refusing to tolerate it and insisting upon shunning it are not the best guides for action, especially if they stiffen the spine of those engaged in mass killing and make it more difficult for us to find diplomatic and economic levers that in the long run will be more effective. Moral perfectionism can easily turn itself into moral smugness, as if berating those who fail to live up to our standards will somehow get them to change. When it comes to political evil, being correct is not enough.

Even if Western leaders wanted to return to the amoral foreign policy of the Kissinger years, it is doubtful that they could and it is certain that they should not. Unlike all other states throughout human history, today's nation-states exist in the aftermath of totalitarianism. Because they do, try as they like—say, for example, as the leaders of Iran are currently doing—they can never assume that the rest of the world will be indifferent to the human rights violations they impose on their own people. I have been critical of the claims to moral superiority of activists against political evil, but there is no doubting that the cause motivating them is a cause we all ought to share. Coming to the defense of victims of political evil is the right *and* the realistic thing to do. It has taken Western leaders considerable time to learn that global stability and respect for individual dignity are not antithetical but complementary. Social mobility, entrepreneurial potential, and individual freedom, all of them among the great benefits offered by open societies, create a more lasting peace than tyranny and oppression. We cannot let dictators have their way. We just have to find better ways of stopping them than threatening them with wars we cannot win and do not have the taste to conduct.

This is a truth more readily apparent in Europe than in the United States. European leaders, viewed by American neoconservative writers as unserious and indifferent to evil, are in fact serious about the problem of political evil in different, and more thoughtful, ways. They know, as American leaders seemingly do not, the horrors of war. In the years since 1945, they have created among themselves one of the most remarkable and durable forms of peace in human history. It is true that, with respect to political evil, even that which takes place in their own region of the world, they are reluctant to call in the troops. But the work their leading public figures do in promoting humanitarian ideals, upholding international standards of justice, and securing peace is exemplary. There is less Sturm und Drang in the European approach to dealing with political evil than in the calls so frequently heard in the United States for military action. But the "soft" kinds of intervention Europeans promote, based more on integrating recalcitrant states into existing diplomatic and economic frameworks than on launching invasions against them, look better and better in light of America's problems in Iraq and Afghanistan.

Will both Israel and the United States learn from this European success and turn more toward a combination of realistic and moral approaches to foreign-policy making? One can only hope they will. There is no reason to assume that the political evils associated with terrorism, genocide, and ethnic cleansing will disappear. But there is at least reason to hope that even societies so habituated to reliance on military means to guarantee their security can learn to put into practice a more nuanced appreciation of the benefits of democracy and freedom as they face the problem of how to respond to political evil. Venus has her attractions when Mars fails to deliver. The sooner bluster and arrogance are retired as methods of dealing with political evil, the sooner the world can bring this scourge under greater control.

SERIOUS ONCE AGAIN

WE COME BACK, then, to the question of what makes a nation serious. Whenever an act of political evil dominates the headlines, we are frequently warned that we do not treat the problem of evil with the depth it deserves. Responding to the September 11 attacks, for example, the American political ethicist Jean Bethke Elshtain pursued this line of thought in her reflections on terrorism. Those with generous instincts toward the world and influenced by Western humanistic ideals, she argued, "have banished the word *evil* from their vocabularies. Evil refers to something so unreasonable, after all! Therefore, it cannot really exist." Elshtain singles out naïve religious leaders and left-wing academics as the focus of her sarcasm. They are, she points out, reminiscent of those Niebuhr called the children of light, individuals so certain that human beings are good that they cannot imagine those who are bad. Although, like David Brooks, hesitant to rely on therapeutic language, Elshtain finds that one Freudian term is appropriate here. These are individuals who are in denial about the depravity always lurking in the human heart.

Elshtain's views are hardly idiosyncratic. She speaks, indeed, for all those who believe that the path to a more serious nation lies along the lines of naming evil when we see it and confronting it when required. We should, from this point of view, take evildoers at their word. The aftermath of their acts is not the time for apologies and explanations. Elshtain summarizes this entire way of thinking when she concludes that "only when we stop the spread of evil can good flourish and mani-fest itself." When it comes to the problem of evil, there really are two sides, and we must be determined to be on the right one. Seriousness is therefore equivalent to firmness. We know that Satan will use every wily means at his disposal to weaken our resolve. We must be tough-minded in response, not only through our willingness to rely on military force but also in our determination not to be swayed from judgment and justice.

This way of thinking about the problem of evil will no longer do. However much those who share this perspective understand and appreciate Niebuhr's warnings about the children of light, they have insufficiently absorbed his strictures about the children of darkness. The latter possess the world-weariness that naïve idealists lack. But they are not without problems of their own. "Evil," Niebuhr wrote in this context, "is always the assertion of some self-interest without regard to the whole, whether the whole be conceived as the immediate community, or the total community of mankind, or the total order of the world." The children of darkness suffer from the sin of pride, and in politics pride leads to blind patriotism, a defense of what one's own country does without regard for its effects on others. It may not have been the appropriate political response for Americans to engage in extensive self-criticism in the aftermath of September 11. But liberal democracies will never avoid the temptations of evil if they refuse to engage in self-criticism out of the mistaken conviction that the problem of evil, when all is said and done, is simply a matter of naming and confronting it. Niebuhr called his book *The Children of Light and the Children of Darkness* not to advocate the struggle between the two but to warn against the dangers of both.

It *is* time to think in tough-minded ways about political evil. The hard part, the part that makes it tough, is that we have to stop relying on the lessons we thought we learned from the evil of the times of totalitarianism. During those dreadful years in which Adolf Hitler ruled Nazi Germany and Joseph Stalin led the Soviet Union, moral outrage in the rest of the world was all too muted. Hitler had his defenders, especially on the far right, and many of his opponents were defeatists uncertain that there was much that could be done to stop him. Too many leftists, adept at the art of double standards, either turned their eyes away from Stalin's abuses or found what now seem cringing and cowardly excuses for his crimes. It is a credit to the intellectual level of political discourse in Western Europe and the United States in the postwar years that the apologetics and double standards so evident during the 1930s and 1940s went into remission. We saw evil at work and we learned from our experience. We would neither turn our backs nor duck our heads. What we witnessed we were determined never again to excuse away.

Having grasped the full horror of what we tried to ignore during the era of the dictators, however, we then, as if to compensate for our earlier neglect, became too easily persuaded that the evil of totalitarianism was about to make its reappearance in every conflict in which significant numbers of people were being killed. "Never again" was transformed into "everywhere and always." Isolationism and pacifism were replaced by an uncritical acceptance of militarism. Once we may have neglected evil, but now we became obsessed by it. In both cases, the one thing we needed most in dealing with the problem of political evil—perspective—was the one thing we lacked.

It is time to get the balance right. Political evil, much as Hannah Arendt foresaw, is indeed one of the fundamental intellectual questions of our time. In seeking to respond to it, we must not rush to war or throw up our hands in hopeless resignation. The former not only tempts us to engage in evil ourselves but demands that we confront evil on the very playing field evildoers prefer. The latter allows evil to continue and gives the bloodthirsty what they crave. Neither overreaction nor underreaction allows us to do what the reality of political evil demands, which is to examine the mistakes we have made in responding to terrorism, ethnic cleansing, and genocide—and then to learn from them. Political evil will never disappear. That is all the more reason for getting our response to it right the next time around. Being serious about the problem of political evil demands no less.

ACKNOWLEDGMENTS

As always when I find myself writing, I am indebted to my colleagues at the Boisi Center, who not only provide the right atmosphere but are amazingly supportive and cooperative. Susan Richard, Erik Owens, Suzanne Hevelone, and Brenna McMahon deserve special praise. Three undergraduates, Matt McCluney, Kara McBride, and Emily McCormick, helped with the footnotes and the text.

My agent, Andrew Stuart, was enthusiastic about this project from the start and could not have represented me better. Jonathan Segal, my editor, read a fifty-page proposal for an entire book and made me realize that it properly should be only one section of a chapter; he understood the larger and more ambitious book I wanted to write before I did. John Wilson of *Books and Culture* was the first to suggest that I write about evil. Among my intellectual colleagues, I owe a special debt to Damon Linker. Damon was an invaluable guide on my previous book, and on this one his enthusiasm gave me the burst of energy necessary to its completion. In this book I take issue with the views of some of my friends and colleagues at *The New Republic*. This in no way diminishes the respect I have for them or the many debts I owe them.

May I take a moment to say something about Tony Judt? We could not be described as friends; I had dinner with him just once. But not only did his monumental scholarship on Europe shape my thinking, the bravery and eloquence he showed while fighting his fatal disease left me awestruck. I also admire what he wrote about Israel and the Middle East. I do not agree with all of it, although I do agree with most of it. The important point to stress, however, is his intellectual honesty. His desire to get things right was an inspiration to me.

Finally, I was able to finish this book in no small part because of the friendship shown to me by those I was privileged to meet over the past few years at the WRC. I want to use this opportunity to thank Richard Bates, Sue Harrison, Bill Marcus, Michael St. Clair, Ken Bell, Winslow Burhoe, Alex Joseph, Pam Hartzband, and, most especially, Collin Wild. I do not know what I would have done without them.

NOTES

INTRODUCTION
THE FUNDAMENTAL QUESTION OF THE TWENTY-FIRST CENTURY

3 "the problem of evil": Hannah Arendt, "Nightmare and Flight," in *Essays in Understanding, 1930–1954,* ed. Jerome Kohn (New York: Harcourt, Brace, 1994), 134.

4 fascination with the problem of evil: Susan Neiman, *Evil in Modern Thought: An Alternative History of Philosophy* (Princeton, N.J.: Princeton University Press, 2002).

6 Al-Qaeda spent five years planning: Bruce Hoffman, *Inside Terrorism,* rev. ed. (New York: Columbia University Press, 2006), 249.

15 witness frequent clashes of civilizations: The obvious reference here is to Samuel P. Huntington, *The Clash of Civilizations and the Remaking of World Order* (New York: Simon and Schuster, 1996).

CHAPTER ONE   THE DISTINCTIVENESS OF POLITICAL EVIL

21 scholars were declaring: Daniel Bell, *The End of Ideology: On the Exhaustion of Political Ideas in the Fifties* (Glencoe, Ill.: Free Press, 1962); David Martin, *A General Theory of Secularization* (New York: Harper, 1978); Talcott Parsons, *The System of Modern Societies* (Englewood Cliffs, N.J.: Prentice Hall, 1971); Francis Fukuyama, *The End of History and the Last Man* (New York: Free Press, 1992).

21 cosmic war and future jihad: Reza Aslan, *How to Win a Cosmic War: God, Globalization, and the End of the War on Terror* (New York: Random House, 2009); Walid Phares, *Future Jihad: Terrorist Strategies Against America* (New York: Palgrave Macmillan, 2005).

21 One of the best-known books: Andrew Delbanco, *The Death of Satan: How Americans Have Lost the Sense of Evil* (New York: Farrar, Straus and Giroux, 1995).

21 "I myself feel": Interview with Andrew Delbanco, http://www.pbs.org/wgbh/pages /frontline/shows/faith/interviews/delbanco.html.

22 many conflicting and imperfect definitions: For a thorough discussion of the definitional issues surrounding terrorism, see Tamar Meisels, *The Trouble with Terror: Liberty, Security, and the Response to Terrorism* (Cambridge: Cambridge University Press, 2008), 7–29.

22 Israel's own "axis of evil": Gideon Alon, "IDF: 'Axis of Evil' Seeks to Prevent Calm in Territories," *Haaretz,* February 2, 2005, http://www.haaretz.com/hasen/pages/ShArt .jhtml?itemNo=534968&contrassID=1&subContrassID=5&sbSubContrassID=0& listSrc=Y.

22 the perpetrator transforms himself: The definitive study is by Robert A. Pape, *Dying to Win: The Strategic Logic of Suicide Terrorism* (New York: Random House, 2006).

23 "in the strict sense": Michael Walzer, *Just and Unjust Wars: A Moral Argument with Historical Illustrations,* 4th ed. (New York: Basic Books, 2006), 198.

23 "The intention of ethnic cleansing": Norman M. Naimark, *Fires of Hatred: Ethnic Cleansing in Twentieth-Century Europe* (Cambridge, Mass.: Harvard University Press, 2001), 3.

23 as the UCLA sociologist Michael Mann: Michael Mann, *The Dark Side of Democracy: Explaining Ethnic Cleansing* (Cambridge: Cambridge University Press, 2005).

24 Our age and century: Samantha Power, *"A Problem from Hell": America and the Age of Genocide* (New York: Basic Books, 2002); and Eric D. Weitz, *A Century of Genocide: Utopias of Race and Nation* (Princeton, N.J.: Princeton University Press, 2003).

24 "for the first time, Stalin had decided": Anne Applebaum, *Gulag: A History* (New York: Anchor Books, 2003), 429.

24 Stalin's overall treatment: Norman M. Naimark, *Stalin's Genocides* (Princeton, N.J.: Princeton University Press, 2010).

25 "murderous if not genocidal": Ibid., 63.

25 With the opening: Timothy Snyder, "Hitler v. Stalin: Who Was Worse?," http://www .nybooks.com/blogs/nyrblog/2011/jan/27/hitler-vs-stalin-who-was-worse/.

25 his administration adopted: For an overview, see Laura K. Donohue, *The Cost of Counterterrorism: Power, Politics, and Liberty* (Cambridge: Cambridge University Press, 2008).

28 Philosophers use the term "category error": Gilbert Ryle, *The Concept of Mind* (New York: Barnes and Noble, 1949).

28 "I want to tear a throat": Cited in Dave Cullen, *Columbine* (New York: Twelve, 2009), 294.

29 quickly came to the conclusion: Daniel Pipes, "The Beltway Snipers' Motives," August 19, 2003, http://www.danielpipes.org/blog/2003/08/the-beltway-snipers-motives .html.

30 "You had a hundred billion chances": See http://www.msnbc.msn.com/id/32082922/ ns/us_news-crime_and_courts/.

30 as Samuel Taylor Coleridge said of Iago: R. A. Foakes, ed., *Coleridge's Criticism of Shakespeare* (Detroit: Wayne State University Press, 1989), 113.

31 most widely read and discussed: Hannah Arendt, *Eichmann in Jerusalem: A Report on the Banality of Evil* (New York: Viking, 1963).

32 Even before he chose a life of: Simon Sebag Montefiore, *Young Stalin* (New York: Knopf, 2007).

33 "he helped phrase the charges": Robert Gellately, *Lenin, Stalin, and Hitler: The Age of Social Catastrophe* (New York: Knopf, 2007), 270.

33 "The levels of hero-worship": Ian Kershaw, *Hitler, 1889–1936: Hubris* (New York: Norton, 1998), 484.

33 "The success of the two cults": Richard Overy, *The Dictators: Hitler's Germany, Stalin's Russia* (New York: Norton, 2004), 119.

34 all the seagulls: Tzvetan Todorov, *Hope and Memory: Lessons from the Twentieth Century,* trans. David Bellos (Princeton, N.J.: Princeton University Press, 2003), 115.

35 "Here, there are neither political": Hannah Arendt, *The Origins of Totalitarianism* (Cleveland: Meridian Books, 1958), 443.

35 as the historian Michael Burleigh: Michael Burleigh, *Sacred Causes: The Clash of Religion and Politics, from the Great War to the War on Terror* (New York: Harper, 2008).

36 "There is only one thing": Arendt, *The Origins of Totalitarianism,* 459.

36 it is common to describe the last years: For just one typical example, see Joachim Fest, *Hitler* (Boston: Houghton Mifflin, 2002), 724–50.

36 there would have been no twilight: For an account of the Nazis' ambivalence toward this opera, see Stephen McClatchie, "Götterdämmerung, Führerdämmerung," *Opera Quarterly* 23 (August 2008): 187.

36 Defenders of Arendt have: See, for example, Richard J. Bernstein, *Radical Evil: A Philosophical Interrogation* (Cambridge: Polity Press, 2002), 205–24.

36 "it is indeed my opinion now": " 'Eichmann in Jerusalem': An Exchange of Letters Between Gershom Scholem and Hannah Arendt," in Hannah Arendt, *The Jew as*

Pariah: Jewish Identity and Politics in the Modern Age, ed. Ron H. Feldman (New York: Grove, 1978), 251, cited in Bernstein, *Radical Evil,* 218.

37 In his search for the origins: Ron Rosenbaum, *Explaining Hitler: The Search for the Origins of His Evil* (New York: Random House, 1998).

39 prominent examples of political evil: Mark Juergensmeyer, *Terror in the Mind of God: The Global Rise of Religious Violence,* 3rd ed. (Berkeley: University of California Press, 2003), 14.

40 Despite cries of alarm: See, for example, David Frum and Richard Perle, *An End to Evil: How to Win the War on Terror* (New York: Random House, 2003), 147–58.

40 "the main reason for the retreat": Olivier Roy, *Globalized Islam: The Search for a New Ummah* (New York: Columbia University Press, 2004), 61. See also Gilles Kepel, *The War for Muslim Minds: Islam and the West* (Cambridge, Mass.: Harvard University Press, 2004).

41 it participates actively in: Augustus Richard Norton, *Hezbollah: A Short History* (Princeton, N.J.: Princeton University Press, 2007), 45–46.

41 can be interpreted as offering: Matthew Levitt, *Hamas: Politics, Charity, and Terrorism in the Service of Jihad* (New Haven, Conn.: Yale University Press, 2006).

42 "there will be for the foreseeable future": Walter Laqueur, *The New Terrorism: Fanaticism and the Arms of Mass Destruction* (New York: Oxford University Press, 1999), 281.

43 one of the world's leading students of Islam: Michael A. Sells, *The Bridge Betrayed: Religion and Genocide in Bosnia* (Berkeley: University of California Press, 1996).

43 "is a clear case of ideological fanaticism": Meir Litvak, "Religious and Nationalist Fanaticism: The Case of Hamas," in *Fanaticism and Conflict in the Modern Age,* eds. Matthew Hughes and Gaynor Johnson (London: Frank Cass, 2005), 156.

43 "Terrorists, like other people": Pape, *Dying to Win,* 62.

45 "were nationalistic but hardly Hitlerian": Naimark, *Fires of Hatred,* 152.

45 "the camps of Bosnia": Power, *"A Problem from Hell,"* 269.

46 "rape and other forms of sexual violence": See http://www.un.org/News/Press/docs /2008/sc9364.doc.htm.

46 "improbable tales of camp love": Applebaum, *Gulag,* 315.

CHAPTER TWO WIDESPREAD EVIL WITHIN

48 "it always wasn't real": *A Unit to Accompany the Film "Darfur Now" and the Book "Not on Our Watch"* (Boston: Facing History and Ourselves, 2008).

48 "we need to look hard": Jonathan Glover, *Humanity: A Moral History of the Twentieth Century* (New Haven, Conn.: Yale University Press, 2001), 7.

48 "ordinary people are capable": James Waller, *Becoming Evil: How Ordinary People Commit Genocide and Mass Killing* (New York: Oxford University Press, 2002), 102.

49 "loaded": The citations in this and the next two paragraphs are from Saint Augustine, *Confessions,* trans. R. S. Pine-Coffin (London: Penguin, 1961), 47–50, 136–37.

51 "So convinced were they that evil": Peter Brown, *Augustine of Hippo* (Berkeley: University of California Press, 1969), 47.

52 "arises in the will of rational creatures": G. R. Evans, *Augustine on Evil* (Cambridge: Cambridge University Press, 1982), 104.

52 "Evil action is a kind of action": Charles T. Mathewes, *Evil and the Augustinian Tradition* (Cambridge: Cambridge University Press, 2001), 78.

52 This was the question raised by: B. R. Rees, *Pelagius: A Reluctant Heretic* (Woodbridge, Suffolk: Boydell Press, 1988).

53 "Adam's sin so flawed": Evans, *Augustine on Evil,* 122.

53 "What is reprehensible": Augustine, *City of God,* ed. Vernon J. Bourke (Garden City, N.Y.: Doubleday, 1958), 47.

54 "Vice in the soul": Cited in Mathewes, *Evil*, 79.

55 "As long as the will": The citations are from Augustine, *City of God*, 52, 54, 62, 113, 112.

57 to devote her dissertation to Augustine: Hannah Arendt, *Love and Saint Augustine*, ed. Joanna Vecchiarelli Scott and Judith Chelius Stark (Chicago: University of Chicago Press, 1996).

57 Arendt's friend and later colleague: Hans Jonas, *Augustin und das paulinische Freiheitsproblem: Eine philosophische Studie zum pelagianischen Streit* (Göttingen: Vandenhoeck and Ruprecht, 1965); Hans Jonas, *The Gnostic Religion: The Message of the Alien God and the Beginnings of Christianity* (Boston: Beacon Press, 1958).

57 posthumously published magnum opus: Hannah Arendt, *Willing* (New York: Harcourt Brace Jovanovich, 1978).

58 which she defined not only as: Hannah Arendt, *The Human Condition* (Chicago: University of Chicago Press, 1958).

58 the drudgery of labor: Ibid., 145.

58 "Eichmann was not Iago": Hannah Arendt, *Eichmann in Jerusalem: A Report on the Banality of Evil* (New York: Penguin, 1977), 287.

58 "The trouble with Eichmann": Ibid., 276.

59 "portrayal of Eichmann": Richard J. Bernstein, *Radical Evil: A Philosophical Interrogation* (Cambridge: Polity Press, 2002), 220.

59 "a new type of criminal": The citations are from Arendt, *Eichmann in Jerusalem*, 276, 33, 146, 125, 117, 286.

62 "Eichmann": David Grumett, "Arendt, Augustine, and Evil," *The Heythrop Journal* 41 (April 2000): 160.

62 "Self-Hating Jewess Writes": Cited in Peter Novick, *The Holocaust in American Life* (Boston: Houghton Mifflin, 1999), 134.

62 "In place of the monstrous Nazi": Norman Podhoretz, "Hannah Arendt on Eichmann," *Commentary* (September 1963): 201–8, cited in Elisabeth Young-Bruehl, *Hannah Arendt: For Love of the World* (New Haven, Conn.: Yale University Press, 1982), 347.

63 Gershom Scholem called her: Richard J. Bernstein, *Hannah Arendt and the Jewish Question* (Cambridge, Mass.: MIT Press, 1996), 160.

63 Hans Jonas refused to speak: Young-Bruehl, *Hannah Arendt*, 351.

63 Arendt can never be entirely satisfying: Eugene McCarraher, "The Incoherence of Hannah Arendt," *Books and Culture* 12 (March/April 2006): 32–37.

63 "Arendt, correctly in my view": Waller, *Becoming Evil*, 102.

64 "a bland and colorless": Cited in Marianna Torgovnick, *The War Complex: World War II in Our Time* (Chicago: University of Chicago Press, 2005), 65.

64 one of the critics who called Arendt: Michael Ezra, "The Eichmann Polemics: Hannah Arendt and Her Critics," http://dissentmagazine.org/democratiya/article_pdfs/d9Ezra.pdf.

64 the best of which were collected: Harry Golden, *Only in America* (Cleveland: World Publishing, 1958).

64 white-cloaked authority figures: The original publication is Stanley Milgram, "Behavioral Study of Obedience," *Journal of Abnormal and Social Psychology* 67 (October 1963): 371–78.

64 "human nature, or—more specifically": Stanley Milgram, *Obedience to Authority: An Experimental View* (New York: Harper Perennial, 1975), 189.

64 Nor do many get to be played by: Thomas Blass, *The Man Who Shocked the World: The Life and Legacy of Stanley Milgram* (New York: Basic Books, 2004), 261–62.

65 "it's certainly possible": Blass, *Man*, 63.

65 "A commonly offered explanation": The citations in this paragraph are from Milgram, *Obedience to Authority*, 5–6.

65 "agentic shift": Ibid., 132–34.

66 generated more controversies: The citations are from Dianna Baumrind, "Some Thoughts on the Ethics of Research: After Reading Milgram's 'Behavioral Study of Obedience,'" *American Psychologist* 19 (June 1964): 421–23, 85, 48, 55.

67 other psychologists concluded: M. T. Orne and C. H. Holland, "On the Ecological Validity of Laboratory Deceptions," *International Journal of Psychiatry* 6 (1968): 282–93.

67 the desire of people to be: Don Mixon, "Instead of Deception," *Journal for the Theory of Social Behavior* 22 (October 1972): 145–77.

67 the subject was Brevard Childs: As told to me by Nicholas Wolterstorff, an emeritus professor of theology at Yale.

67 "If this were Russia": The citations are from Milgram, *Obedience to Authority,* 48, 84, 178.

69 "It is fitting": Blass, *Man,* 269–70.

69 Pennsylvania State University has developed: See http://www.reuters.com/article/pressRelease/idUS192618+23-Mar-2009+PRN20090323 and http://stanley.milgram.media.psu.edu/moreInfo_40149DVD.html.

69 Psychologists have replicated: Jerry Burger, "Replicating Milgram: Would People Still Obey Today?," *American Psychologist* 64 (January 2009): 1–11.

69 "should be part of the basic training": Adam Cohen, "Four Decades After Milgram, We're Still Willing to Inflict Pain," *The New York Times,* December 28, 2008.

70 "Phil's our vice president": Blass, *Man,* 9.

70 would be discussed in one of: Malcolm Gladwell, *The Tipping Point: How Little Things Can Make a Big Difference* (Boston: Little, Brown, 2000), 152–55.

70 place student subjects into the roles: C. Haney, W. C. Banks, and P. G. Zimbardo, "A Study of Prisoners and Guards in a Simulated Prison," *Naval Research Review* 30 (1973): 4–17.

70 "The line between Good and Evil": The citations are from Philip Zimbardo, *The Lucifer Effect: Understanding How Good People Turn Evil* (New York: Random House, 2007), 195, 288, 6.

72 "were from the lower orders": The citations are from Christopher R. Browning, *Ordinary Men: Reserve Police Battalion 101 and the Final Solution in Poland* (New York: HarperCollins, 1992), 48, 168, 173–74, 185.

74 "because of a set of beliefs": The citations are from Daniel Jonah Goldhagen, *Hitler's Willing Executioners: Ordinary Germans and the Holocaust* (New York: Knopf, 1996), 389, 379, 383.

74 "intense, at times even harsh": "The 'Willing Executioners'/'Ordinary Men' Debate: Selections from the Symposium, April 8, 1996," http://www.ushmm.org/research/center/publications/occasional/1996–01/paper.pdf.

75 "Germans": The citations in this paragraph are from Goldhagen, *Hitler's Willing Executioners,* 381, 378, 386.

76 "If only it were all so simple!": Cited in Glover, *Humanity,* 401–2.

76 "whether young or not": Primo Levi, *The Drowned and the Saved,* trans. Raymond Rosenthal (New York: Vintage International, 1989), 37–38.

77 "Though there were sadistic individuals": Jan T. Gross, *Neighbors: The Destruction of the Jewish Community in Jedwabne, Poland* (Princeton, N.J.: Princeton University Press, 2001), 133.

77 lay in the very heart: Timothy Snyder, *Bloodlands: Europe Between Hitler and Stalin* (New York: Basic Books, 2010).

78 "monitored progress and made sure": Gross, *Neighbors,* 59.

79 "There is good evidence": Daniel Chirot and Clark McCauley, *Why Not Kill Them All? The Logic and Prevention of Mass Political Murder* (Princeton, N.J.: Princeton University Press, 2006), 53.

79 "I do not know": Levi, *Drowned*, 48–49.

80 committing extraordinary acts of altruism: See Samuel P. Oliner and Pearl M. Oliner, *The Altruistic Personality: Rescuers of Jews in Nazi Europe* (New York: Free Press, 1988); and Samuel P. Oliner, *Do Unto Others: Extraordinary Acts of Ordinary People* (Boulder, Colo.: Westview, 2003).

CHAPTER THREE   UNRELENTING EVIL WITHOUT

82 "I have often spoken to you": See http://www.nytimes.com/2009/01/15/us/politics/15bush-text.html?_r=1&pagewanted=2.

82 "This suggests": Peter Singer, *The President of Good and Evil: The Ethics of George W. Bush* (New York: Dutton, 2004), 2, 225.

83 "Endure persecutions and temptations": "Excerpt from the Kephalia: The Three Blows Struck at the Enemy on Account of the Light," http://www.gnosis.org/library/manis.htm.

83 "was not only ignorant": The citations in this paragraph are from Saint Augustine, *Confessions*, trans. R. S. Pine-Coffin (London: Penguin, 1961), 96, 135.

84 brought back to life: Elaine Pagels, *The Gnostic Gospels: A New Account of the Origins of Christianity* (New York: Random House, 1979).

84 a spirit capable of gathering up: The best account is Michel Tardieu, *Manichaeism,* trans. M. B. DeBevoise (Urbana: University of Illinois Press, 2009).

85 "was a religion of pessimism": The citations are from Steven Runciman, *The Medieval Manichee: A Study of the Christian Dualist Heresy* (Cambridge: Cambridge University Press, 1955), 179, 176.

85 "the evolution of God": Robert Wright, *The Evolution of God* (New York: Little, Brown, 2009).

87 "one of the most difficult": Dennis J. Ireland, "A History of Recent Interpretation of the Parable of the Unjust Steward," *Westminster Theological Journal* 51 (1989): 293.

87 "moral cynics": The citations in this paragraph are from Reinhold Niebuhr, *The Children of Light and the Children of Darkness: A Vindication of Democracy and a Critique of Its Traditional Defense* (New York: Scribner's, 1944), 10, 40–41.

88 "too intent to assert the integrity": The citations are from Reinhold Niebuhr, *The Nature and Destiny of Man: A Christian Interpretation,* vol. 1, *Human Nature* (New York: Scribner's, 1941), 260, 262, 55.

89 "is the greatest": Charles T. Mathewes, *Evil and the Augustinian Tradition* (Cambridge: Cambridge University Press, 2001), 108.

89 "Humility was strength": Richard Wightman Fox, *Reinhold Niebuhr: A Biography* (San Francisco: Harper and Row, 1987), 232.

89 "she goes not abroad": See http://www.presidentialrhetoric.com/historicspeeches/adams_jq/foreignpolicy.html.

90 "It may be": James Burnham, *The Struggle for the World* (New York: John Day, 1947), 248.

90 thanks to the biographical efforts: Sam Tanenhaus, *Whittaker Chambers: A Biography* (New York: Random House, 1997); Michael Kimmage, *The Conservative Turn: Lionel Trilling, Whittaker Chambers, and the Lessons of Anti-Communism* (Cambridge, Mass.: Harvard University Press, 2009).

90 "utterly and crudely dualistic": Abbott Gleason, *Totalitarianism: The Inner History of the Cold War* (New York: Oxford University Press, 1995), 86.

90 "I see in Communism the focus": Whittaker Chambers, *Witness* (New York: Random House, 1952), 8.

91 What the historian Richard Hofstadter: Richard Hofstadter, *The Paranoid Style in American Politics, and Other Essays* (New York: Knopf, 1965).

91 "There is a moral or natural law": The citations are from John Foster Dulles, "A Policy of Boldness," *Life,* May 19, 1952, cited in J. Peter Scoblic, *U.S. vs. Them: How a Half Century of Conservatism Has Undermined America's Security* (New York: Viking, 2008), 31, 32.

92 In 1958, the conservative activist Phyllis Schlafly: Donald T. Critchlow, *Phyllis Schlafly and Grassroots Conservatism: A Woman's Crusade* (Princeton, N.J.: Princeton University Press, 2006), 80.

92 "We are at war with an evil": The citations in this paragraph and the next were originally cited in Scoblic, *U.S. vs. Them,* 41, 35.

92 Another who thought along similar lines: George F. Kennan, "The Sources of Soviet Conduct," *Foreign Affairs* 15 (July 1947): 566–82.

93 Just like Augustine: I am indebted for this point to Eugene McCarraher, "The Incoherence of Hannah Arendt," *Books and Culture* 12 (March/April 2006): 32–37.

93 "the totalitarian idea": Gleason, *Totalitarianism,* 74.

94 "No one, least of all": Hannah Arendt, *The Origins of Totalitarianism* (Cleveland: Meridian Books, 1958), 488–89.

94 "One possibility should be excluded": Carl J. Friedrich and Zbigniew Brzezinski, *Totalitarian Dictatorship and Autocracy,* 2nd ed. (Cambridge, Mass.: Harvard University Press, 1965), 375.

96 "the earlier totalitarian model": David D. Roberts, *The Totalitarian Experiment in Twentieth-Century Europe: Understanding the Poverty of Great Politics* (New York: Routledge, 2006), 413. For an example of the point Roberts is making, see Michael Geyer and Sheila Fitzpatrick, eds., *Beyond Totalitarianism: Stalinism and Nazism Compared* (Cambridge: Cambridge University Press, 2009).

96 "near hysterical insistence": Jacob Heilbrunn, *They Knew They Were Right: The Rise of the Neocons* (New York: Doubleday, 2008), 47–48.

97 "historical reluctance to see": See http://www.nationalcenter.org/ReaganEvilEmpire 1983.html.

98 "Time drives everything": Machiavelli, *The Prince,* Philip Smith, ed. (Mineola, N.Y.: Dover, 1992), 6.

99 "During their six decades in power": The citations are from Jeane J. Kirkpatrick, *Dictatorships and Double Standards: Rationalism and Reason in Politics* (New York: Simon and Schuster, 1982), 122–23, 32.

101 "Throughout my career": The citations are from Jeane J. Kirkpatrick, *Making War to Keep Peace* (New York: HarperCollins, 2007), 272, 300.

102 "epitomizes—no less than": The citations in this paragraph and the next are from Lawrence F. Kaplan and William Kristol, *The War over Iraq: Saddam's Tyranny and America's Mission* (San Francisco: Encounter Books, 2003), 3, 106, 105. The "virtually genocidal" quote appears on p. 10.

103 "Liberals": See http://www.nationalreview.com/interrogatory/interrogatory022403.asp.

104 "marked by this calculated": Samir al-Khalil [Kanan Makiya], *Republic of Fear: The Politics of Modern Iraq* (Berkeley: University of California Press, 1989), 119.

104 "Piety spread": Paul Berman, *Terror and Liberalism* (New York: Norton, 2003), 110.

105 "technologically, the weaknesses": The citations in this paragraph are from Burnham, *Struggle,* 118, 142.

106 "disastrous for the United States": The citations in this paragraph are from Kenneth M. Pollack, *The Threatening Storm: The Case for Invading Iraq* (New York: Random House, 2002), 37, 254.

107 "Hitler, when he took power": Cited in Samantha Power, *"A Problem from Hell": America and the Age of Genocide* (New York: Basic Books, 2002), 203.

109 "It was a matter of common sense": Peter Brown, *Augustine of Hippo* (Berkeley: University of California Press, 1969), 148.

CHAPTER FOUR THE MISUSES OF APPEASEMENT

113 "When greedy Mr. Hitler": Rick Perlstein, *Nixonland: The Rise of a President and the Fracturing of America* (New York: Scribner, 2008), 123.

113 "The fight against terror": See http://blogs.wsj.com/washwire/2008/05/15/bush-charges-appeasement-in-knesset-speech/.

116 "The First World War made Hitler": Ian Kershaw, *Hitler: A Biography* (New York: Norton, 2008), 47.

116 "towards systematic, total exploitation": Alan Kramer, *Dynamic of Destruction: Culture and Mass Killing in the First World War* (New York: Oxford University Press, 2007), 68.

117 "The most spectacular": Omer Bartov, *Murder in Our Midst: The Holocaust, Industrial Killing, and Representation* (New York: Oxford University Press, 1996), 4.

117 "The First World War brought communism": The citations are from Martin Malia, *The Soviet Tragedy: A History of Socialism in Russia, 1917–1991* (New York: Simon and Schuster, 1995), 273, 88–89.

118 Snyder estimates that as many as twenty-one million people: Timothy Snyder, *Bloodlands: Europe Between Hitler and Stalin* (New York: Basic Books, 2010), 383–84.

118 the costs were too high: Nicholson Baker, *Human Smoke: The Beginnings of World War II, the End of Civilization* (New York: Simon and Schuster, 2008).

118 "In the first half of the century": James J. Sheehan, *Where Have All the Soldiers Gone? The Transformation of Modern Europe* (Boston: Houghton Mifflin, 2008), 221.

118 To the American neoconservative writer: Robert Kagan, *Paradise and Power: America and Europe in the New World Order* (New York: Knopf, 2003).

119 as many political sociologists do: The best known is Seymour Martin Lipset, *Political Man: The Social Bases of Politics* (Garden City, N.Y.: Doubleday, 1960).

119 hyperinflation undermined bourgeois ideas: Bernd Widdig, *Culture and Inflation in Weimar Germany* (Berkeley: University of California Press, 2001), 24–25.

119 "People just didn't understand": Cited in Adam Smith [George J. W. Goodman], *Paper Money* (New York: Summit Books, 1981), 60.

119 "As Germany plunged deeper": Richard J. Evans, *The Coming of the Third Reich* (New York: Penguin Press, 2004), 246.

120 "The Great Slump": Volker R. Berghahn, *Europe in the Era of Two World Wars: From Militarism to Genocide and Civil Society, 1900–1950* (Princeton, N.J.: Princeton University Press, 2006), 69, 80.

121 the most serious case of deflation: For background, see Akio Mikuni and R. Taggart Murphy, *Japan's Policy Trap: Dollars, Deflation, and the Crisis of Japanese Finance* (Washington, D.C.: Brookings Institution Press, 2003).

122 "the obviously political types of reaction": Harold James, *The End of Globalization: Lessons from the Great Depression* (Cambridge, Mass.: Harvard University Press, 2001), 223.

122 "The Bolshevik Revolution": David D. Roberts, *The Totalitarian Experiment in Twentieth-Century Europe: Understanding the Poverty of Great Politics* (New York: Routledge, 2006), 21.

124 "Under conditions that elsewhere": Andrew J. Nathan, "Authoritarian Resilience," *Journal of Democracy* 14 (January 2003): 16.

126 "In my generation": Harry S. Truman, *Memoirs*, vol. 2, *Years of Trial and Hope* (Garden City, N.Y.: Doubleday, 1956), 351.

126 "needed no lessons": Joseph M. Siracusa, "The Munich Analogy," http://www.americanforeignrelations.com/E-N/The-Munich-Analogy.html.

126 "I feel there is a greater threat": Cited in Yuen Foong Khong, *Analogies at War: Korea, Munich, Dien Bien Phu, and the Vietnam Decisions of 1965* (Princeton, N.J.: Princeton University Press, 1992), 3.

127 "I wasn't any Chamberlain": All the quotes in this paragraph are cited in Jeffrey Record, "Perils of Reasoning by Historical Analogy: Munich, Vietnam, and American Use of Force Since 1945" (Occasional Paper No. 4, Center for Strategy and Technology, Air War College, March 1998), 9–10.

127 "Look, I know you don't agree": Cited in Khong, *Analogies at War,* 182.

129 "The differences between Hitler's Germany": Record, "Perils," 23.

131 "The Bosnian catastrophe that began": The citations in this paragraph are from Alan Steinweis, "The Auschwitz Analogy: Holocaust Memory and Debates over Intervention in Bosnia and Kosovo in the 1990s," *Holocaust and Genocide Studies* 19 (Fall 2005): 277, 279.

131 "veritable Neville Chamberlain": The citations in this paragraph were originally cited in Samantha Power, *"A Problem from Hell": America and the Age of Genocide* (New York: Basic Books, 2002), 278, 433.

132 "the British and French": "Stop Serbia Now," in *The Black Book of Bosnia: The Consequences of Appeasement,* ed. Nader Mousavizadeh (New York: Basic Books, 1996), 166.

132 "the worst humiliation": Power, *"A Problem from Hell,"* 433.

132 "secular-socialist machine": Newt Gingrich, *To Save America: Stopping Obama's Secular-Socialist Machine* (Washington, D.C.: Regnery, 2010), 4, 6.

134 "Terrorism is the new totalitarianism": See http://news.bbc.co.uk/2/hi/uk_news /politics/3507730.stm.

135 "The 20th century": Victor Davis Hanson, "The Wages of Appeasement," *The Wall Street Journal,* May 10, 2004.

136 Borrowing his title: Bruce Bawer, *While Europe Slept: How Radical Islam Is Destroying the West from Within* (New York: Broadway Books, 2006).

136 Bawer published another book: Bruce Bawer, *Surrender: Appeasing Islam, Sacrificing Freedom* (New York: Doubleday, 2009).

136 "Neville Chamberlain, en Español": Ramón Pérez-Maura, "Neville Chamberlain, en Español," *The Wall Street Journal,* March 20, 2004.

136 "Are Europeans prepared to grant": Robert Kagan, "Time to Save an Alliance," *The Washington Post,* March 16, 2004.

137 "a cruel and repressive racist regime": "U.S.: Ahmadinejad Speech Vile, but Doesn't Preclude Diplomacy," *Haaretz,* January 1, 2009, http://www.haaretz.com/news /u-s-ahmadinejad-speech-vile-but-doesn-t-preclude-diplomacy-1.267159.

137 speeches or interviews comparing Ahmadinejad: For citations in this paragraph see http://freerepublic.com/focus/f-bloggers/2234981/posts and Roger Boyes, "Israel: Iran Trying to Do 'What Adolf Hitler Did to Jewish People,'" *Times Online,* April 21, 2009, http://www.timesonline.co.uk/tol/news/world/europe/article6142841.ece.

137 "it is a peculiar American fascination": Ray Takeyh, "Ahmadinejad Is No Hitler," *Los Angeles Times,* November 19, 2006.

140 as former speaker of the Knesset: Avraham Burg, *The Holocaust Is Over; We Must Rise from Its Ashes* (New York: Palgrave Macmillan, 2008).

140 "as an online discussion": See http://en.wikipedia.org/wiki/Godwin%27s_law.

140 "It reminds me in some ways": Marin Cogan, "Bernie Sanders Compares Climate Skeptics to Nazi Deniers," *Politico,* February 23, 2010, http://www.politico.com/news /stories/0210/33371.html.

CHAPTER FIVE DEMOCRACY'S TERRORISM PROBLEM

145 One of that tradition's: Émile Durkheim and Marcel Mauss, *Primitive Classification,* trans. Rodney Needham (Chicago: University of Chicago Press, 1963).

146 Sociology contains a field: See the classic text, Harold Garfinkel, *Studies in Ethnomethodology* (Englewood Cliffs, N.J.: Prentice Hall, 1967).

146 the books that deal with them: In particular, I found helpful Gregory F. Treverton, *Intelligence for an Age of Terror* (Cambridge: Cambridge University Press, 2009).

146 "When I consider a terrorist atrocity": Louise Richardson, *What Terrorists Want: Understanding the Enemy, Containing the Threat* (New York: Random House, 2007), xii.

147 "the terrorists' goal has been": Yossi Klein Halevi, "Israel's Moral War," http://www .israelcc.org/NR/rdonlyres/2C167897–8831–401B-B8AD-E1024C3D8996/0/moral _war.pdf.

147 "how futile counterterrorist policies": Richardson, *What Terrorists Want*, xii.

147 "Terrorists": Jean Bethke Elshtain, *Just War Against Terror: The Burden of American Power in a Violent World* (New York: Basic Books, 2004), 19.

148 terrorists nearly always win: Alan M. Dershowitz, *Why Terrorism Works: Understanding the Threat, Responding to the Challenge* (New Haven, Conn.: Yale University Press, 2003).

148 invariably they attack democratic ones: See, on this point, Robert J. Art and Louise Richardson, *Democracy and Counterterrorism: Lessons from the Past* (Washington, D.C.: U.S. Institute of Peace Press, 2007); and Samy Cohen, ed., *Democracies at War Against Terrorism: A Comparative Perspective* (New York: Palgrave Macmillan, 2008).

150 "It is a certainty": Benjamin Netanyahu, *Fighting Terrorism: How Democracies Can Defeat Domestic and International Terrorists* (New York: Farrar, Straus and Giroux, 1995), 148. The other quotations in this paragraph are from p. 147 and p. 21.

150 a helpful distinction relevant to: Ami Pedahzur, *The Israeli Secret Services and the Struggle Against Terrorism* (New York: Columbia University Press, 2009), 1.

152 defeated one terrorist enemy: Zeev Maoz, *Defending the Holy Land: A Critical Analysis of Israel's Security and Foreign Policy* (Ann Arbor: University of Michigan Press, 2009), 217.

153 "It is doubtful whether Israel": Amos Harel and Avi Issacharoff, *34 Days: Israel, Hezbollah, and the War in Lebanon* (New York: Palgrave Macmillan, 2008), 87.

153 "The barrage of rockets": See http://www.cfr.org/publication/15385/winograd _commission_final_report.html.

153 terror attacks dropped by 90 percent: Pia Therese Jansen, "The Consequences of Israel's Counter Terrorism Policy" (Ph.D. thesis, University of St. Andrews, 2008), 59, http://www.docstoc.com/docs/3345185/Consequences-of-Israel-Counter-Terrorism -Policy.

154 decline dramatically from previous years: See http://www.shabak.gov.il/English /EnTerrorData/Reviews/Pages/terrorreport09.aspx.

154 In his critical analysis: Maoz, *Defending the Holy Land*, 499–543.

155 critics who do not believe: One of the best known is Tony Judt, "Israel: The Alternative," *The New York Review of Books*, October 23, 2003. For a similar kind of analysis, see Arno J. Mayer, *Plowshares into Swords: From Zionism to Israel* (London: Verso, 2008).

155 "those political institutions that hold": Dan Reiter and Allan C. Stam, *Democracies at War* (Princeton, N.J.: Princeton University Press, 2002), 193.

157 can quickly reduce the public taste: On this point, see Gil Merom, *How Democracies Lose Small Wars: State, Society, and the Failures of France in Algeria, Israel in Lebanon, and the United States in Vietnam* (Cambridge: Cambridge University Press, 2003).

158 "We *urgently* need": The citations in this paragraph are from National Commission on Terrorist Attacks, *The 9/11 Commission Report: Final Report of the National Commission on Terrorist Attacks Upon the United States* (New York: Norton, 2004), 201, 205.

159 "We have seen their kind before": All the excerpts from the president's speech are from "Transcript of President Bush's Address to a Joint Session of Congress on Thurs-

day Night, September 20, 2001," http://archives.cnn.com/2001/US/09/20/gen.bush
.transcript/.

162 "become more rare": Alexis de Tocqueville, *Democracy in America*, ed. Phillips Brad-
ley, vol. 2 (New York: Knopf, 1966), 281.

162 "The U.S. failure to secure": Ahmed Rashid, *Descent into Chaos: The United States
and the Failure of Nation Building in Pakistan, Afghanistan, and Central Asia* (New
York: Viking, 2008), xlii.

163 not by relying on the military: A. J. Rossmiller, "Stalemate," *The New Republic*, October 13, 2009, http://www.tnr.com/article/world/stalemate.

163 sending a message to your opponent: Joshua Alexander Geltzer, *U.S. Counter-Terrorism
Strategy and al-Qaeda: Signalling and the Terrorist World-View* (London: Routledge,
2010).

164 as Bob Woodward's book: Bob Woodward, *Obama's Wars* (New York: Simon and
Schuster, 2010).

165 "The only way to understand": Richard English, *Terrorism: How to Respond* (New
York: Oxford University Press, 2009), 55.

166 "has a highly centralized body": Walid Phares, *Future Jihad: Terrorist Strategies
Against America* (New York: Palgrave Macmillan, 2005), 131.

166 "the terrorism industry": John Mueller, *Overblown: How Politicians and the Terrorism Industry Inflate National Security Threats, and Why We Believe Them* (New York:
Free Press, 2006).

167 "Perhaps reflecting his training": The citations in this paragraph are from Jerrold M.
Post, *The Mind of the Terrorist: The Psychology of Terrorism from the IRA to Al-Qaeda*
(New York: Palgrave Macmillan, 2007), 202, 224.

167 "This flexibility and local initiative": Marc Sageman, *Understanding Terror Networks*
(Philadelphia: University of Pennsylvania Press, 2004), 165.

168 appear in every kind of stripe: Bruce Hoffman, *Inside Terrorism*, rev. ed. (New York:
Columbia University Press, 2006).

168 "derives from Islam": Daniel Pipes, "The Challenge of Islamism in Europe and the Middle East," http://www.danielpipes.org/2196/the-challenge-of-islamism-in-europe-the
-middle-east. See also Janet Tassel, "Militant About 'Islamism': Daniel Pipes Wages
'Hand-to-Hand Combat' with a 'Totalitarian Ideology,' " *Harvard Magazine*, January/
February 2005, 38–47.

168 the grand mufti of Jerusalem: David G. Dalin and John F. Rothmann, *Icon of Evil:
Hitler's Mufti and the Rise of Radical Islam* (New York: Random House, 2008). See
also Jeffrey Herf, *Nazi Propaganda for the Arab World* (New Haven, Conn.: Yale University Press, 2009).

168 "both movements are based on a cult": Christopher Hitchens, "Defending 'Islamofascism,' " http://www.slate.com/id/2176389/.

169 This was clearly the case: Fawaz A. Gerges, *The Far Enemy: Why Jihad Went Global*
(Cambridge: Cambridge University Press, 2005).

169 "how localized the insurgency was": Cited in Karen DeYoung, "U.S. Official Resigns
over Afghan War," *The Washington Post*, October 27, 2009.

170 an alternative strategy: Afghanistan Study Group, "A New Way Forward," http://www
.afghanistanstudygroup.org/.

170 "Terrorist campaigns end": The citations in this paragraph and the next are from
Audrey Kurth Cronin, *How Terrorism Ends: Understanding the Decline and Demise of
Terrorist Campaigns* (Princeton, N.J.: Princeton University Press, 2010), 206, 196.

171 "the most serious danger": English, *Terrorism*, 119.

172 as the prominent economist Amartya Sen: See http://www.thaindian.com/news
portal/business/indias-response-to-mumbai-attack-was-matured-amartya-sen
_100132223.html.

172 "our message must be this": Dershowitz, *Why Terrorism Works*, 24–25.

174 has lost considerable popularity: Peter Bergen and Paul Cruickshank, "The Unraveling," *The New Republic*, June 11, 2008.

CHAPTER SIX THE CASE AGAINST DRAMATIZING GENOCIDE

177 Although traceable to ancient times: This is a theme of Ben Kiernan's in his *Blood and Soil: A World History of Genocide and Extermination from Sparta to Darfur* (New Haven, Conn.: Yale University Press, 2007).

178 Daniel Jonah Goldhagen labels: Daniel Jonah Goldhagen, *Worse Than War: Genocide, Eliminationism, and the Ongoing Assault on Humanity* (New York: PublicAffairs, 2009), 496.

180 4 percent of the world's population: Ibid., 50.

180 "Our time has been an age": Ibid., 55–56.

181 the Columbia University political scientist: Mahmood Mamdani, "The Politics of Naming: Genocide, Civil War, Insurgency," *London Review of Books* 29 (March 2007): 5–8.

181 One of the best-known: Samantha Power, *"A Problem from Hell": America and the Age of Genocide* (New York: Basic Books, 2002).

182 "The genocide in Rwanda is the first": Linda Melvern, "The Past Is Prologue: Planning the 1994 Rwandan Genocide," in *After Genocide: Transitional Justice, Post-Conflict Reconstruction and Reconciliation in Rwanda and Beyond,* ed. Phil Clark and Zachary D. Kaufman (New York: Columbia University Press, 2009), 22. See also her book *Conspiracy to Murder: The Rwandan Genocide* (London: Verso, 2004).

182 "any of the following acts": See http://www.preventgenocide.org/law/convention/text.htm.

182 at the rate of 333⅓ deaths: Michael Barnett, *Eyewitness to a Genocide: The United Nations and Rwanda* (Ithaca, N.Y.: Cornell University Press, 2002), 1.

183 "between those opposed to": Lee Ann Fujii, *Killing Neighbors: Webs of Violence in Rwanda* (Ithaca, N.Y.: Cornell University Press, 2009), 56.

183 for in Rwanda the perpetrators: Mahmood Mamdani, *When Victims Become Killers: Colonialism, Nativism, and the Genocide in Rwanda* (Princeton, N.J.: Princeton University Press, 2001), 185.

184 "Please don't kill me": Power, *"A Problem from Hell,"* 334.

185 "could see only civil war": Barnett, *Eyewitness to a Genocide,* 157.

185 "bears some moral responsibility": This and the other quotation in this paragraph are from Barnett, *Eyewitness to a Genocide,* 174.

186 brought the human cost: Philip Gourevitch, *We Wish to Inform You That Tomorrow We Will Be Killed with Our Families: Stories from Rwanda* (New York: Farrar, Straus and Giroux, 1998).

187 "I don't know if it is genocide": Cited in Chris Herlinger and Paul Jeffrey, *Where Mercy Fails: Darfur's Struggle to Survive* (New York: Seabury Books, 2009), 17.

187 "Of course this is genocide": Quoted in Mahmood Mamdani, *Saviors and Survivors: Darfur, Politics, and the War on Terror* (New York: Pantheon, 2009), 64.

187 "Radical evil has become commonplace": Richard Just, "The Truth Will Not Set You Free," *The New Republic*, August 27, 2008, 41.

187 Along with the human rights activist: Don Cheadle and John Prendergast, *Not on Our Watch: The Mission to End Genocide in Darfur and Beyond* (New York: Hyperion, 2007), 205–6.

188 publicizing the atrocities: David Montgomery, "The Darkest Light: Outside the Holocaust Museum, the Genocide in Darfur Is Illuminated in a Nightly Photographic Exhibit," *The Washington Post*, November 21, 2006.

188 a video game: Alex de Waal, "The Humanitarian Carnival: A Celebrity Vogue," *World Affairs Journal* 171 (Fall 2008): 43–55.

188 black leather boot: Corporate Social Responsibility Newswire, http://www.csrwire .com/News/4580.html.

188 "We know what it means": Cited in David J. Silverman and Rachel Silverman, "After Experience of Holocaust, Jewish Groups Out Front on Darfur," http://www.ujc.org /page.aspx?id=110935.

188 "The Arabs arrived": The quotations in this paragraph are from Gérard Prunier, *Darfur: A 21st Century Genocide*, 3rd ed. (Ithaca, N.Y.: Cornell University Press, 2008), 100–101.

189 "have become an African Auschwitz": Eric Reeves, *A Long Day's Dying: Critical Moments in the Darfur Genocide* (Toronto: Key Publishing House, 2007), 85.

189 even the fact that Hitler: Eric Reeves, "On China and the 2008 Olympic Games: An Open Letter to Darfur Activists and Advocates," http://www.sudanreeves.org /Page-10.html. For a similar argument from one of America's most prominent columnists, see Nicholas D. Kristof, "China's Genocide Olympics," *The New York Times*, January 24, 2008.

190 "the Sudanese citizens racially perceive": Jok Madut Jok, *Sudan: Race, Religion, and Violence* (Oxford: Oneworld, 2007), 6.

191 violence was part of a process: Alex de Waal, "Who Are the Darfurians? Arab and African Identities, Violence, and External Engagement," *African Affairs* 104 (April 2005): 181–205.

191 "Darfur's is hardly the first case": M. W. Daly, *Darfur's Sorrow: A History of Destruction and Genocide* (Cambridge: Cambridge University Press, 2007), 13.

192 lived so close together: Scott Straus, *The Order of Genocide: Race, Power, and War in Rwanda* (Ithaca, N.Y.: Cornell University Press, 2006), 8.

192 as two economists from the World Bank: E. Elbadawi and N. Sambanis, "Why Are There So Many Civil Wars in Africa? Understanding and Preventing Violent Conflict," *Journal of African Economics* 9 (October 2000): 244–69.

192 universally Muslim in its religious affiliations: For background on the religious situation in the region, see Ahmed Kamal El-Din, "Islam and Islamism in Darfur," in *War in Darfur and the Search for Peace*, ed. Alex de Waal (Cambridge, Mass: Justice Africa, 2007), 92–112.

193 singled out Darfur as one of two cases: Daniel Pipes, "The Challenge of Islamism in Europe and the Middle East," http://www.danielpipes.org/2196/the-challenge -of-islamism-in-europe-the-middle-east.

194 according to an estimate: Debarati Guha-Sapir and Olivier Degomme, *Darfur: Counting the Deaths*, Center for Research on the Epidemiology of Disasters, University of Louvain, May 26, 2005.

194 "The practice of genocide": Prunier, *Darfur*, 105.

194 "acts with genocidal intent": *Report of the International Commission of Inquiry on Darfur to the United Nations Secretary-General*, January 25, 2005, http://www.un.org /news/dh/sudan/com_inq_darfur.pdf.

195 "getting out their wig boxes": John Bolton, *Surrender Is Not an Option: Defending America at the United Nations and Abroad* (New York: Simon and Schuster, 2007), 349.

195 took the radical step: "Bolton Bars Darfur Briefing," *International Herald Tribune*, October 12, 2005, http://www.iht.com/articles/2005/10/11/news/bolton.php.

195 "horrendous death toll": Fabrice Weissman, "Darfour, l'ONU impuissante," *Le Monde*, November 3, 2006. See also http://www.doctorswithoutborders.org /publications/article.cfm?id=1893.

195 he would not use the word: Steve Bloomfield, "Waiting for the Court," *Newsweek*, January 16, 2009, http://www.newsweek.com/id/180008.

197 "Does what happened in Darfur": See http://www.guernicamag.com/interviews/610 /crisis_darfur/ and Bernard-Henri Lévy, *Left in Dark Times: A Stand Against the New Barbarism,* trans. Benjamin Moser (New York: Random House, 2008).

198 "race-murder campaign": Christopher Hitchens, "Defending 'Islamofascism,' " http://www.slate.com/id/2176389/.

198 took out an ad: Sam Dealey, "An Atrocity That Needs No Exaggeration," *The New York Times,* August 12, 2007.

199 "This is genocide": This and the other quotation in this paragraph are from Reeves, *A Long Day's Dying,* 73, 91.

199 far more people have died: Mamdani, *Saviors and Survivors,* 20–21, 281.

199 Western liberals are frequently caught: Richard Just, "Evils and Excuses," *The New Republic,* September 9, 2009, 28.

200 "must respond to genocide": Power, *"A Problem from Hell,"* 514.

201 "The idea that foreign troops": Conor Foley, *The Thin Blue Line: How Humanitarianism Went to War* (New York: Verso, 2008), 10.

201 a political insurgency gone awry: Prunier, *Darfur,* 102–3, 154.

202 specifically used the term: Colin L. Powell, "The Crisis in Darfur," in *Genocide in Darfur: Investigating the Atrocities in the Sudan,* ed. Samuel Totten and Eric Markusen (New York: Routledge, 2006), 259–68.

202 "For too long the people of Darfur": See http://www.foxnews.com/story/0,2933 ,275994,00.html.

203 such a policy would have made it: David Rieff, "Good vs. Good," *Los Angeles Times,* June 24, 2007.

203 what they call complicity with evil: See, for example, Adam LeBor, *"Complicity with Evil": The United Nations in the Age of Modern Genocide* (New Haven, Conn.: Yale University Press, 2006).

203 one prominent international lawyer: Antonio Cassese, "Flawed International Justice for Sudan," http://www.project-syndicate.org/commentary/cassese4.

204 "as of today": This quotation and the next one in this paragraph are from Neil MacFarquhar, "As Darfur Fighting Diminishes, U.N. Officials Focus on the South of Sudan," *The New York Times,* August 27, 2009.

204 "to advance peace and security": Ginger Thompson, "Obama Drops Plan to Isolate Sudan Leaders," *The New York Times,* October 16, 2009.

204 opted to place Darfur: See http://blogs.ushmm.org/COC2/670/.

204 "it undermines international urgency": Cited in MacFarquhar, "Darfur."

205 "the level of interest": Julie Flint and Alex de Waal, *Darfur: A New History of a Long War* (London: Zed Books, 2008), 184.

207 the early post–World War II humanitarianism: See Mary Ann Glendon, *A World Made New: Eleanor Roosevelt and the Universal Declaration of Human Rights* (New York: Random House, 2001). For a fascinating history of humanitarian efforts, see Gary J. Bass, *Freedom's Battles: The Origins of Humanitarian Intervention* (New York: Knopf, 2008).

207 In its first fourteen years: Treatments of the court's problems can be found in Martin Ngoga, "The Institutionalization of Impunity: A Judicial Perspective on the Rwandan Genocide," in Clark and Kaufman, *After Genocide,* 311–32; and Adam M. Smith, *After Genocide: Bringing the Devil to Justice* (Amherst, N.Y.: Prometheus Books, 2009).

208 "outsourcing": Smith, *After Genocide,* 336.

208 56 percent Catholic and 26 percent Protestant: Phil Clark, "The Rules (and Politics) of Engagement: The Gaccaca Courts and Post-Genocide Justice, Healing, and Reconciliation in Rwanda," in Clark and Kaufman, *After Genocide,* 306.

209 "fundamental aspects of the *gacaca* proposals": Cited in Charles Mironko and Ephrem Rurangwa, "Rwanda," in *Constructing Justice and Security After War,* ed. Charles T. Call (Washington, D.C.: U.S. Institute of Peace Press, 2007), 208, which contains a good summary of all the criticisms of the *gacaca* system.

209 the results of an investigation: Howard W. French, "U.N. Congo Report Offers New View on Genocide," *The New York Times,* August 27, 2010.

209 despite the praise he has received: Stephen Kinzer, *A Thousand Hills: Rwanda's Rebirth and the Man Who Dreamed It* (New York: Wiley, 2008).

209 "What can you say": These quotations are from Jean Hatzfeld, *The Antelope's Strategy: Living in Rwanda After the Genocide,* trans. Linda Coverdale (New York: Farrar, Straus and Giroux, 2009), 78, 126.

210 "Supporting domestic rule of law": Smith, *After Genocide,* 345.

211 "How can we *choose*": Goldhagen, *Worse Than War,* 597.

CHAPTER SEVEN ETHNIC CLEANSING'S SEDUCTIVE ATTRACTIONS

212 is typically accompanied by rape: For a list of the practices associated with ethnic cleansing, see Drazen Petrovic, "Ethnic Cleansing: An Attempt at a Methodology," *European Journal of International Law* 5, no. 1 (1994): 345–46.

212 an influential number of thinkers: For examples of this way of thinking applied directly to the events in the former Yugoslavia, see Nader Mousavizadeh, ed., *The Black Book of Bosnia: The Consequences of Appeasement* (New York: Basic Books, 1996); and Thomas Cushman and Stjepan G. Mestrovic, eds., *This Time We Knew: Western Responses to Genocide in Bosnia* (New York: New York University Press, 1996).

216 developed what the Israeli historian: The citations in this paragraph and the next are from Benny Morris, *The Birth of the Palestinian Refugee Problem Revisited* (Cambridge: Cambridge University Press, 2004), 424–25.

217 "transfer": "Transfer" is often viewed as a euphemism for ethnic cleansing. See, for example, Rashid Khalidi, *The Iron Cage: The Story of the Palestinian Struggle for Statehood* (Boston: Beacon Press, 2006), 5.

217 "blueprint for ethnic cleansing": Ilan Pappé, *The Ethnic Cleansing of Palestine* (Oxford: Oneworld, 2006), 82.

218 a controversial historian: See, for example, Efraim Karsh, "Pure Pappé," *Middle East Quarterly* 13 (Winter 2006): 82–83; and Benny Morris, "Politics by Other Means," *The New Republic,* March 22, 2004, 25–30.

218 in favor of a preventive Israeli attack: Benny Morris, "Using Bombs to Stave Off War," *The New York Times,* July 18, 2008.

218 called for a ground invasion of Gaza: Benny Morris, "Israel Has No Choice but to Be Tough on Hamas—and Iran," *Times Online,* January 4, 2009, http://www.times online.co.uk/tol/news/world/middle_east/article5439608.ece.

218 "From the start, the operations": Morris, *Birth,* 425.

218 "So when the commanders of Operation Dani": Ari Shavit, "Survival of the Fittest," *Haaretz,* January 16, 2004, http://ethics.rabbinics.org/Interview%20with%20Benny %20Morris.pdf.

220 Behind every citizen: Alan Wolfe, *An Intellectual in Public* (Ann Arbor: University of Michigan Press, 2003), 10.

220 the Irish peace activist: See http://www.google.com/hostednews/afp/article/ALeq M5hdEkp3D-8KcTN-AQm4t7lk3MfsJw.

220 "are all different ways for implementing": See http://www.zcommunications.org/the -ethnic-cleansing-of-palestine-by-ilan-pappe-1. The magazine in question is *Znet.*

220 the events of 1948: Pappé, *Ethnic Cleansing*, 248–56.

221 "more Jewish town": Nathan Jeffay, "Israel's Mixed Cities on Edge After Riots," *The Jewish Daily Forward*, October 31, 2008, http://www.forward.com/articles/14435/.

224 "possibly the most thoroughly devastated town": Samuel Totten and Paul R. Bartrop, eds., *Dictionary of Genocide*, vol. 2 (Westport, Conn.: Greenwood Press, 2008), 463.

226 "For three-and-a-half years": Norman M. Naimark, *Fires of Hatred: Ethnic Cleansing in Twentieth-Century Europe* (Cambridge, Mass.: Harvard University Press, 2001), 159.

226 It was he who thanked God: Michael Mann, *The Dark Side of Democracy: Explaining Ethnic Cleansing* (Cambridge: Cambridge University Press, 2005), 378.

227 "a fundamentalist, Algerian, and wog": Naimark, *Fires of Hatred*, 171.

228 "contemptible and indefensible": Cushman and Mestrovic, *This Time We Knew*, 16.

228 "the repressive policies of the Serbian president": Samantha Power, *"A Problem from Hell": America and the Age of Genocide* (New York: Basic Books, 2002), 262.

228 "equivocation and relativism": Cushman and Mestrovic, *This Time We Knew*, 19, 21.

229 "I guess if President Clinton": Cited in Power, *"A Problem from Hell,"* 307.

229 "Croatia": Adam M. Smith, *After Genocide: Bringing the Devil to Justice* (Amherst, N.Y.: Prometheus Books, 2009), 282.

229 "the largest, boldest single act": The quotations are from Power, *"A Problem from Hell,"* 450, 449.

230 "What if someone had listened": Cited in Power, *"A Problem from Hell,"* 449.

232 "based on the hard fact that war": Tim Judah, *Kosovo: What Everyone Needs to Know* (New York: Oxford University Press, 2008), 71.

232 organized popular resistance to Serbian attacks: For background, see Henry H. Perritt Jr., *Kosovo Liberation Army: The Inside Story of an Insurgency* (Urbana: University of Illinois Press, 2008).

232 "I wanted to stop": Cited in Judah, *Kosovo*, 83.

232 ran a Mafia-like organization: Doreen Carvajal and Marlise Simons, "Report Names Kosovo Leader as Crime Boss," *The New York Times*, December 16, 2010.

232 "ended up falling in with": Tzvetan Todorov, *Hope and Memory: Lessons from the Twentieth Century*, trans. David Bellos (Princeton, N.J.: Princeton University Press, 2003), 248–49.

233 "This making and breaking of nations": Tony Judt, *Postwar: A History of Europe Since 1945* (New York: Penguin, 2005), 637.

234 Nationhood appeals to the emotions: Michael Ignatieff, *Blood and Belonging: Journeys into the New Nationalism* (New York: Farrar, Straus and Giroux, 1994).

236 "I don't believe you": The quotations in this paragraph were originally cited in Richard Caplan, *Europe and the Recognition of New States in Yugoslavia* (Cambridge: Cambridge University Press, 2005), 107.

237 these wars have been aptly described: Alexandros Petersen, "The 1992–93 Georgia-Abkhazia War: A Forgotten Conflict," *Caucasian Review of International Affairs* 2 (Autumn 2008): 9–21. For background on the ethnic cleansing involved, see UNHCR (United Nations Refugee Agency), "The Dynamics and Challenges of Ethnic Cleansing: The Georgia-Abkhazia Case," http://www.unhcr.org/refworld/country,,WRITENET,,GEO,4562d8cf2,3ae6a6c54,0.html.

237 the familiar script of a struggle: For one example, see Svante E. Cornell and S. Frederick Starr, eds., *The Guns of August 2008: Russia's War in Georgia* (Armonk, N.Y.: M. E. Sharpe, 2009).

238 "Moscow": Ronald D. Asmus, *A Little War That Shook the World: Georgia, Russia, and the Future of the West* (New York: Palgrave Macmillan, 2010), 193.

239 the rush to nationhood: Judt, *Postwar*, 638.

239 "The greatest threat": Mann, *Dark Side*, 509.

239 rapid transitions to democracy: Amy Chua, *World on Fire: How Exporting Free Market Democracy Breeds Ethnic Hatred and Global Instability* (New York: Doubleday, 2003).

241 have generally been associated with the Arab side: See, for example, Ali Abunimah, *One Country: A Bold Proposal to End the Israeli-Palestinian Impasse* (New York: Metropolitan Books, 2006); and Virginia Tilley, *The One-State Solution: A Breakthrough for Peace in the Israeli-Palestinian Deadlock* (Ann Arbor: University of Michigan Press, 2005).

242 a highly controversial essay: Tony Judt, "Israel: The Alternative," *The New York Review of Books,* September 25, 2003, http://www.nybooks.com/articles/archives/2003/oct/23/israel-the-alternative/?page=2.

242 Judt was denounced: For just one of many examples, see Steven Plaut, "Collaborators in the War Against the Jews: Tony Judt," *Front Page Magazine,* September 9, 2009, http://archive.frontpagemag.com/readArticle.aspx?ARTID=36238.

242 including former defense minister: Moshe Arens, "Is There Another Option?," *Haaretz,* February 6, 2010, http://www.haaretz.com/print-edition/opinion/is-there-another-option-1.293670.

242 former chairman of the Yesha Council of Settlements: See Noam Sheifaz, "Endgame," *Haaretz,* July 15, 2010, http://jewishpeacenews.blogspot.com/2010/08/endgame-rightist-visions-of-single.html.

244 Although furious debates have broken out: Those debates were provoked by John J. Mearsheimer and Stephen M. Walt, *The Israel Lobby and U.S. Foreign Policy* (New York: Farrar, Straus and Giroux, 2007).

245 understanding the benefits: See Christopher Cviic and Peter Sanfey, *In Search of the Balkan Recovery: The Political and Economic Reemergence of South-Eastern Europe* (New York: Columbia University Press, 2010).

245 The more Israel reaps the benefits: On this point, see Bernard Avishai, *The Hebrew Republic: How Secular Democracy and Global Enterprise Will Bring Israel Peace at Last* (Boston: Houghton Mifflin, 2008).

CHAPTER EIGHT THE POLITICS OF COUNTEREVIL

248 "Feelings were very raw": Cited in Jane Mayer, *The Dark Side: The Inside Story of How the War on Terror Turned into a War on American Ideals* (New York: Anchor Books, 2009), 49.

249 "trying to pretend we are not at war": Alexander Mooney, "Cheney, White House Spar over Terrorism," http://www.cnn.com/2009/POLITICS/12/30/cheney.obama.war/index.html.

251 "encouraged people like Osama bin Laden": Cited in Joshua Alexander Geltzer, *US Counter-Terrorism Strategy and Al-Qaeda: Signalling and the Terrorist World-View* (London: Routledge, 2010), 98.

251 "We'll have to work": The quotations are from Mayer, *The Dark Side,* 9–10, 43.

252 "The United States does not torture": See http://georgewbush-whitehouse.archives.gov/news/releases/2006/09/20060906–3.html.

253 "fantasyland": Mayer, *The Dark Side,* 177.

253 "there's no evidence to support Cheney's view": Geltzer, *US Counter-Terrorism,* 99.

254 "angry and disappointed": Lawrence Wright, *The Looming Tower: Al-Qaeda and the Road to 9/11* (New York: Vintage, 2007), 374.

256 When terror leads to torture: The links between these two phenomena are explored in Werner G. K. Stritzke and Stephan Lewandowsky, "The Terrorism-Torture Link: When Evil Begets Evil," in *Terrorism and Torture: An Interdisciplinary Perspective,* eds. Werner G. K. Stritzke et al. (Cambridge: Cambridge University Press, 2009), 1–17.

257 "a deliberately disproportionate attack": *Human Rights in Palestine and Other Occupied Arab Territories: Report of the United Nations Fact Finding Mission on the Gaza Conflict,* advanced edited version, September 15, 2009, 525.

257 "goes further than": Michael Oren, "Deep Denial: Why the Holocaust Still Matters," *The New Republic,* October 6, 2009, http://www.tnr.com/article/world/deep-denial.

257 "a defamation written by an evil, evil man": "Dershowitz: Goldstone Is a Traitor to the Jewish People," *Haaretz,* January 31, 2010, http://www.haaretz.com/hasen /spages/1146392.html.

257 "morally problematic and strategically counterproductive": Moshe Halbertal, "The Goldstone Illusion," *The New Republic,* November 6, 2009, 23.

257 Goldstone published an op-ed: Richard Goldstone, "Reconsidering the Goldstone Report on Israel and War Crimes," *The Washington Post,* April 1, 2011.

259 "The Mission concludes that the conditions": *Human Rights in Palestine,* 537. The starvation charge can be found on p. 259, and the poverty figures are from p. 338.

259 "The limitation on the transfer of goods": Tim Franks, "Details of Gaza Blockade Revealed in Court Case," http://news.bbc.co.uk/2/hi/8654337.stm.

260 "unprecedented": See http://www.btselem.org/english/Gaza_Strip/Castlead_Oper ation.asp.

260 1,385 Palestinians lost their lives: For the report of an investigation claiming that many of the Palestinian civilians who died in Gaza were actually combatants, see Avi Mor, Tal Pavel, Don Radlauuer, and Yeal Sharar, *Casualties in Operation Cast Lead: A Closer Look* (Herzlia, Israel: Interdisciplinary Center of the International Institute for Counter-Terrorism, 2009).

260 "Humanitarianism": Michael L. Gross, *Moral Dilemmas of Modern War: Torture, Assassination, and Blackmail in an Age of Asymmetric Conflict* (Cambridge: Cambridge University Press, 2010), 2.

261 "What was mainly a clash": Halbertal, "The Goldstone Illusion," 22.

261 concerned with just war theory: Asa Kasher, "Operation Cast Lead and the Ethics of Just War," *Azure* 37 (Summer 2009): 43–75.

263 "Not one hair will fall off": Cited in Public Committee Against Torture in Israel, *No Second Thoughts: The Changes in the Israeli Defense Forces' Combat Doctrine in Light of "Operation Cast Lead,"* http://www.stoptorture.org.il/files/no%20second%20 thoughts_ENG_WEB.pdf.

263 "Some units": Halbertal, "The Goldstone Illusion," 25.

263 "The first, which received enormous publicity": Gross, *Dilemmas,* 254.

264 "According to this principle": Kasher, "Just War," 61.

264 "soldiers assume some risk": Halbertal, "The Goldstone Illusion," 24.

265 one (unnamed) high-ranking IDF officer: Donald Macintyre, "Israeli Commander: 'We Rewrote the Rules of War for Gaza,' " *The Independent,* February 3, 2010, http:// www.independent.co.uk/news/world/middle-east/exclusive-israeli-comman%20 der-we-rewrote-the-rules-of-war-for-gaza-1887627.html.

265 political and social changes in Israeli society: See Yagil Levy, *Israel's Materialist Militarism* (Lanham, Md.: Lexington Books, 2007). For an application of his thesis to more recent events, see http://jewishpeacenews.blogspot.com/2009/04/yitzhak-laor-yagil -levy-on-soldiers.html.

265 one right-wing critic: Caroline Glick, "Pictures of Victory," *The Jerusalem Post,* January 19, 2009, http://www.carolineglick.com/e/2009/01/.

266 a warrant for the arrest: The best overview of the whole affair is Naomi Roht-Arriaza, *The Pinochet Effect: Transnational Justice in the Age of Human Rights* (Philadelphia: University of Pennsylvania Press, 2005).

267 a victory for principles of international justice: See http://news.bbc.co.uk/2/hi /466800.stm.

267 Its claims were based on the principle: For background, see Katherine Gallagher, "Universal Jurisdiction in Practice: Efforts to Hold Donald Rumsfeld and Other High-Level United States Officials Accountable for Torture," *Journal of International Criminal Justice* 7 (November 2009): 1087–116.

273 "Bybee's signature had the effect": U.S. Department of Justice, Office of Professional Responsibility, *Investigation into the Office of Legal Counsel's Memoranda Concerning Issues Relating to the Central Intelligence Agency's Use of "Enhanced Interrogation Techniques" on Suspected Terrorists*, July 29, 2009, 255.

273 "great stress, danger, and fear": The citations in this paragraph are from Ibid., 252–54.

273 "OPR failed to identify a known": Associate Deputy Attorney General, "Memorandum for the Attorney General," January 5, 2010, 27.

274 In two reports issued in 2009 and 2010: The State of Israel, "Gaza Operations Investigations: An Update," January 2010, http://www.mfa.gov.il/MFA/Terrorism-+Obstacle +to+Peace/Hamas+war+against+against+Israel/Gaza_Operation_Investigations _Update_Jan_2010.htm. The July 2010 update is available at www.mfa.gov.il/ . . . Israel/Gaza_Operation_Investigations_Second_Update_July_2010.htm.

275 "for approving the use of explosive shells": July 2010 update, 3.

275 "in complex combat situations": January 2010 update, 46.

277 Like Bush, Obama issued signing statements: The best guide to Obama's actions with respect to executive power are the articles in *The New York Times* written by Charlie Savage. See, for example, "U.S. Tries to Make It Easier to Wiretap the Internet," September 27, 2010; "Court Dismisses a Case Charging Torture by C.I.A.," September 10, 2010; "Detainees Barred from Access to U.S. Courts," May 21, 2010; "Detainees Will Still Be Held, but Not Tried, Official Says," January 22, 2010; "U.S. Debates Response to Targeted Killing Lawsuit," September 15, 2010.

278 The idea of an imperial presidency: Arthur M. Schlesinger Jr., *The Imperial Presidency* (Boston: Houghton Mifflin, 1989). On the Cheney years in particular, see Bruce P. Montgomery, *Richard B. Cheney and the Rise of the Imperial Vice Presidency* (Westport, Conn.: Praeger, 2009).

278 is here to stay: For an argument along these lines, see Garry Wills, *Bomb Power: The Modern Presidency and the National Security State* (New York: Penguin, 2010).

279 If Woodward's account: Bob Woodward, *Obama's Wars* (New York: Simon and Schuster, 2010).

280 by picturing Islam: A representative collection can be found in Jamie Glazov, *Showdown with Evil: Our Struggle Against Tyranny and Terror* (Toronto: Mantua Books, 2010).

280 Experts who actually know something: See http://www.theatlantic.com/interna tional/archive/2010/10/reuel-gerecht-on-pamela-gellers-foul-anti-muslim -ideology/64478/.

CONCLUSION GETTING SERIOUS (ONCE AGAIN) ABOUT POLITICAL EVIL

283 "denied, before the evidence was in": David Brooks, "The Rush to Therapy," *The New York Times*, November 9, 2009.

283 "of many options": David Brooks, *Bobos in Paradise: The New Upper Class and How They Got There* (New York: Simon and Schuster, 2000), 246.

285 The same era that saw the publication: Stéphane Courtois, ed., *The Black Book of Communism: Crimes, Terror, Repression*, trans. Jonathan Murphy and Mark Kramer (Cambridge, Mass.: Harvard University Press, 1999); Nader Mousavizadeh, ed., *The Black Book of Bosnia: The Consequences of Appeasement* (New York: Basic Books, 1996).

286 wound up endorsing the political aspirations: Norman Podhoretz, "In Defense of Sarah Palin," *The Wall Street Journal*, March 29, 2010. An example of Podhoretz's earlier work is *The Present Danger: "Do We Have the Will to Reverse the Decline of American Power?"* (New York: Simon and Schuster, 1980).

287 the culture of narcissism once located: Christopher Lasch, *The Culture of Narcissism: American Life in an Age of Diminishing Expectations* (New York: Norton, 1991).

287 as some of their leading advocates: David Rieff, *A Bed for the Night: Humanitarianism in Crisis* (New York: Simon and Schuster, 2003); Fiona Terry, *Condemned to Repeat? The Paradox of Humanitarian Action* (Ithaca, N.Y.: Cornell University Press, 2002).

287 rushed to the defense: "Bernard-Henri Lévy Defends Accused IMF Director," http://www.thedailybeast.com/blogs-and-stories/2011-05-16/bernard-henri-lvy-the -dominique-strauss-kahn-i-know.

287 "tourist of the revolution": Russell Jacoby, "Left Behind: The Exploits of BHL," *World Affairs Journal* 3 (Winter 2009): 21–30.

289 "their condemnation with them": John Calvin, *Institutes of the Christian Religion*, trans. Henry Beveridge (Grand Rapids, Mich.: Eerdmans, 1962), book 2, section 1.

290 Its contributions to the rise of capitalism: Max Weber, *The Protestant Ethic and the Spirit of Capitalism*, trans. Talcott Parsons (New York: Scribner, 1958).

290 gave the modern world the ideas: John Witte Jr., *The Reformation of Rights: Law, Religion, and Human Rights in Early Modern Calvinism* (Cambridge: Cambridge University Press, 1987).

290 "the unbridled passion to transgress": The quotations are from Os Guinness, *Unspeakable: Facing Up to Evil in an Age of Genocide and Terror* (San Francisco: HarperSanFrancisco, 2005), 103–4, 41–42.

291 those who find the Puritans endlessly fascinating: Andrew Delbanco, *The Puritan Ordeal* (Cambridge, Mass.: Harvard University Press, 1989).

291 the late historian and social critic Christopher Lasch: Lasch's debt to secular Calvinism is emphasized by his recent biographer: Eric Miller, *Hope in a Scattering Time: A Life of Christopher Lasch* (Grand Rapids, Mich.: Eerdmans, 2010). For other examples of this way of thinking, see Juliet B. Schor, *The Overspent American: Upscaling, Downshifting, and the New Consumer* (New York: Basic Books, 1998); Wendell Berry, *Home Economics: Fourteen Essays* (San Francisco: North Point, 1987); and Bill McKibben, *The Bill McKibben Reader: Pieces from an Active Life* (New York: Holt, 2008).

292 Reflections on their disobedience: For two such recent examples, see Terry Eagleton, *On Evil* (New Haven, Conn.: Yale University Press, 2010); and Alan Jacobs, *Original Sin: A Cultural History* (New York: HarperOne, 2008).

296 thinkers associated with the realist tradition: Anatol Lieven and John Hulsman, *Ethical Realism: A Vision for America's Role in the World* (New York: Vintage, 2006).

298 viewed by American neoconservative writers: Robert Kagan, *Paradise and Power: America and Europe in the New World Order* (New York: Knopf, 2003).

298 they have created among themselves: James J. Sheehan, *Where Have All the Soldiers Gone? The Transformation of Modern Europe* (Boston: Houghton Mifflin, 2008).

298 But the "soft" kinds of intervention: For an evaluation, see Fotios Moustakis and Tracey German, *Securing Europe: Western Interventions Towards a New Security Community* (New York: Palgrave Macmillan, 2009).

299 "have banished the word *evil*": The quotations are from Jean Bethke Elshtain, *Just War Against Terror: The Burden of American Power in a Violent World* (New York: Basic Books, 2004), 1.

300 "Evil": Reinhold Niebuhr, *The Children of Light and the Children of Darkness: A Vindication of Democracy and a Critique of Its Traditional Defense* (New York: Scribner's, 1944), 9.

INDEX

Abkhazia, 236–7, 238

Abu Ghraib, 25, 157, 249, 254, 267–8

Abu Sayyaf, 41

Acheson, Dean, 92

Acts of Faith (Caputo), 205

Adam, 52, 53, 109, 289, 292

Adams, Gerry, 41

Adams, John Quincy, 89–90, 111

Addington, David, 249, 253, 255, 264, 268, 274, 278

Afghanistan, 254; Obama administration's approach to, 162–5, 169–70; Taliban regime in, 9, 159, 161, 163, 164, 165, 166, 167, 169–70; U.S. military actions against al-Qaeda bases in, 159, 163

AfPak (Afghanistan-Pakistan border), 162

Africa, 13–14, 15, 23. *See also* Darfur killings; Rwandan genocide

aggregation, rhetoric of, 161–2, 163, 165, 173. *See also* disaggregation

Agwai, Martin Luther, 204

Ahmadinejad, Mahmoud, 137–8, 257

Air Force, U.S., 26

Albanian Kosovars, 45, 133, 229, 230, 231–2. *See also* Kosovo

Albright, Madeleine, 232

Algeria, 40, 193

Allon, Yigal, 216, 217

Allport, Gordon, 68

al-Qaeda, 6, 22, 148, 174; appeasement analogy and, 135–6; Bush's war against, 159–62; Clinton administration's intelligence on, 158; exploiting vulnerabilities in, 171; goals of, 41–2; Obama administration's strategies against, 162–5; organizational capacities of, 166–8; USS *Cole* attacked by, 254. *See also* September 11 attacks

al-Qaeda in Iraq, 42

Amin, Idi, 23, 99–100

Amnesty International, 209

anarchism, 23

anti-Semitism, 96, 139; of Nazis, 37, 61–2, 74, 75, 168 (*see also* Holocaust); of Palestinians, 168

appeasement analogy, 113–41; Ahmadinejad's Iran and, 137–8, 139; appeasement of Hitler in Munich and, 113–14, 115, 125, 127, 128, 131, 135, 136; Balkans violence and, 130, 131–4, 230; cynical uses of, 139–40; global warming and, 140–1; Iraq War and, 135–6, 139; Korea and, 125–6, 127, 128; moral reasoning and, 130–4; Powell and Weinberger doctrines and, 129–30; problematic assumptions in, 114–15; terrorism and, 134–6, 150; unlikely reappearance of totalitarianism and, 114, 115–25; Vietnam and, 126–30

Applebaum, Anne, 24, 46

Arab-Israeli war of 1948, 216, 220

Arafat, Yasser, 41, 152

Arendt, Hannah, 3, 4, 35–6, 44, 57–64, 68, 187, 301; Augustine's impact on, 57–61, 63, 75; on banality of evil, 31, 36, 58–9, 60, 62, 63, 93; Christian scholars' embrace of, 63; Eichmann trial and, 31, 58–64, 70, 93; Milgram's obedience research and, 65; on totalitarianism, 35–6, 60, 93, 94, 104, 115

Arens, Moshe, 242–3

Aristotle, 3, 240

Armenian genocide, 24, 179–80, 184

Ashcroft, John, 255

Asmus, Ronald, 238

asymmetrical warfare, 261–3, 264

Augustine, Saint, 3, 35, 49–57, 88, 289; Arendt's thinking indebted to, 57–61, 63, 75; evil in political world placed in background by, 56–7, 60; evil psychologized by, 54, 59; evil viewed as default position by, 53–4, 80, 111; free will as viewed by, 52, 56–7, 88, 89, 109; Józefów massacre and, 74–5; Manichaeism and, 50–1, 55, 83, 84, 85, 108, 109; Milgram's obedience research and, 65, 68; Niebuhr and, 88–9; pear tree incident and, 49–50;

A NOTE ABOUT THE AUTHOR

Alan Wolfe is a professor of political science and the director of the Boisi Center for Religion and American Public Life at Boston College. In the spring of 2011, he was the John Winant Visiting Professor of American Government at Oxford University. The author or editor of twenty-one books, he is a contributing editor of *The New Republic* and chairman of the Task Force on Religion and Democracy in the United States of the American Political Science Association.

A NOTE ON THE TYPE

This book was set in Minion, a typeface produced by the Adobe Corporation specifically for the Macintosh personal computer, and released in 1990. Designed by Robert Slimbach, Minion combines the classic characteristics of old-style faces with the full complement of weights required for modern typesetting.

Composed by North Market Street Graphics, Lancaster, Pennsylvania
Printed and bound by Berryville Graphics, Berryville, Virginia
Book design by Robert C. Olsson